高职高专电气自动化技术专业规划教材
GAOZHI GAOZHUAN DIANQI ZIDONGHUA JISHU ZHUANYE GUIHUA JIAOCAI

电气自动化专业英语

主　编　王　琳
副主编　夏　怡
编　写　徐志成　张金红
主　审　陈雪丽

中国电力出版社
http://jc.cepp.com.cn

内 容 提 要

本书为高职高专电气自动化技术专业规划教材。

全书分为5章，共计26课。第1章电工电子技术基础，主要介绍电路元器件、电路网络分析、二极管、运算放大器、逻辑电路等；第2章电机和电机控制，主要介绍直流电动机、交流异步电动机、电动机控制电路、脉宽调制理论、变频器等；第3章工业计算机控制技术，主要介绍PLC、单片机、现场总线等；第4章传感器，主要介绍温度传感器、霍尔传感器、光电传感器及红外线传感器等；第5章自动控制系统，主要介绍自动控制系统简介、传递函数、波德图、过程控制等。本书所有课文均精心选自国外相关网站和教材，具有专业性和实用性强、难度适宜等特点，有助于培养学生阅读电类英文资料的能力。

本书可作为高职高专电气自动化技术等相关专业的教材，也可供中等职业学校相关专业使用及专业英语爱好者学习参考。

图书在版编目（CIP）数据

电气自动化专业英语／王琳主编. —北京：中国电力出版社，2009.12（2018.8重印）

高职高专电气自动化技术专业规划教材

ISBN 978-7-5083-9340-7

Ⅰ.电… Ⅱ.王… Ⅲ.自动化技术－英语－高等学校：技术学校－教材 Ⅳ.H31

中国版本图书馆CIP数据核字（2009）第147063号

中国电力出版社出版、发行

（北京市东城区北京站西街19号 100005 http://jc.cepp.com.cn）

三河市百盛印装有限公司印刷

各地新华书店经售

*

2009年12月第一版 2018年8月北京第九次印刷

787毫米×1092毫米 16开本 17.25印张 416千字

定价**27.60**元

高职高专电气自动化技术专业规划教材

编　委　会

前 言

随着新技术革命的发展及经济全球化的到来，社会对专业人才的外语能力要求越来越高。理工科的学生除了应具有一定的听说读写能力外，还应掌握一定的本专业基本词汇，具有基本的阅读本专业外文资料和进行专业交流的能力。为了更好地培养学生的专业外语应用能力，编者编写了这本《电气自动化专业英语》。

本书由电工电子技术基础、电机和电机控制、工业计算机控制技术、传感器和自动控制系统五章组成，共计 26 课。电工电子技术基础主要介绍电路元器件、电路网络分析、二极管、运算放大器、逻辑电路等；电机和电机控制主要介绍直流电动机、交流异步电动机、电动机控制电路、脉宽调制理论、变频器等；工业计算机控制技术主要介绍 PLC、单片机、现场总线等；传感器主要介绍温度传感器、霍尔传感器、光电传感器及红外线传感器等；自动控制系统主要介绍自动控制系统简介、传递函数、波德图、过程控制等。

本书所有课文均精心选自国外相关网站和教材，具有专业性和实用性强的特点，难度适宜等特点，有助于培养学生阅读电类英文资料的能力。为了便于学生自学，所有课文都附有参考译文。

本书由王琳主编、夏怡副主编，其中王琳编写第一章，夏怡编写第二、三章，张金红编写第四章，徐志成编写第五章。本书承蒙南京师范大学陈雪丽教授审阅，提出了宝贵的修改意见，在此表示衷心感谢。

限于编者水平，书中难免存在疏漏和错误之处，敬请读者批评指正。

编　者

2009 年 6 月

Contents

Chapter 1

Electric and Electronic Technology Fundamentals

Unit 1 Electrical Elements and Network

The concept of electrical elements is used in the analysis of electrical networks. Any electrical network can be modeled by decomposing it down to multiple, interconnected electrical elements in a schematic diagram or circuit diagram[1]. Each electrical element affects the voltage in the network or current through the network in a particular way. By analyzing the way a network is affected by its individual elements, it is possible to estimate how a real network will behave on a macro scale.

Elements vs. components

There is a distinction between real, physical electrical or electronic components and the ideal electrical elements by which they are represented.

- Electrical elements do not exist physically, and are assumed to have ideal properties according to a lumped element model.
- Conversely, components do exist, have less than ideal properties, their values always have a degree of uncertainty, they always include some degree of nonlinearity and typically require a combination of multiple electrical elements to approximate their functions.

Circuit analysis using electric elements is useful for understanding many practical electrical networks using components.

The elements

The four fundamental circuit variables are current, I; voltage, U; charge, Q; and magnetic flux, Φ_m. Only 5 elements are required to represent any component or network by manipulating these four variables.

Two sources:

- Current source, measured in amperes —— produces a current in a conductor. Affects charge according to the relation $dQ = -Idt$.
- Voltage source, measured in volts —— produces a potential difference between two points. Affects magnetic flux according to the relation $d\Phi_m = Udt$.

Three passive elements:

- Resistance R, measured in ohms —— produces a voltage proportional to the current flowing through it. Relates voltage and current according to the relation $dU = RdI$.
- Capacitance C, measured in farads —— produces a current proportional to the rate of change of voltage across it. Relates charge and voltage according to the relation $dQ = CdU$.

- Inductance L, measured in henries —— produces a voltage proportional to the rate of change of current through it. Relates flux and current according to the relation $d\Phi_m = LdI$.

Examples

The following are examples of representation of components by way of electrical elements.

- On a first degree of approximation, a battery is represented by a voltage source. A more refined model also includes a resistance in series with the voltage source, to represent the battery's internal resistance (which results in the battery heating and the voltage dropping when in use). A current source in parallel may be added to represent its leakage (which discharges the battery over a long period of time).
- On a first degree of approximation, a resistor is represented by a resistance. A more refined model also includes a series inductance, to represent the effects of its lead inductance[2] (resistors constructed as a spiral have more significant inductance). A capacitance in parallel may be added to represent the capacitive effect of the proximity of the resistor leads to each other. A wire can be represented as a low-value resistor.
- Current sources are more often used when representing semiconductors. For example, on a first degree of approximation, a bipolar transistor may be represented by a variable current source that is controlled by the input voltage.

Electrical network

An electrical network is an interconnection of electrical elements such as resistors, inductors, capacitors, transmission lines, voltage sources, current sources, and switches.

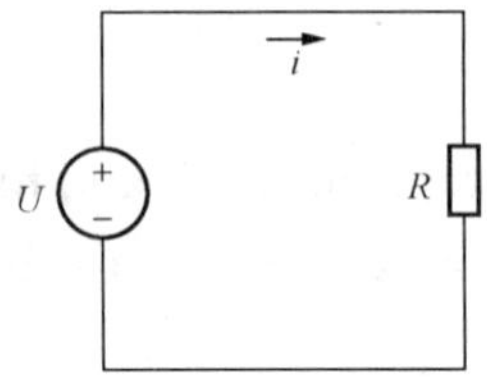

Fig.1.1 A simple electric circuit

An electrical circuit is a network that has a closed loop, giving a return path for the current (Fig.1.1). A network is a connection of two or more components, and may not necessarily be a circuit.

Electrical networks that consist only of sources (voltage or current), linear lumped elements (resistors, capacitors, inductors), and linear distributed elements (transmission lines) can be analyzed by algebraic and transform methods to determine DC response, AC response, and transient response.

A network that also contains active electronic components is known as an electronic circuit. Such networks are generally nonlinear and require more complex design and analysis tools.

Technical Words and Expressions

electronic	[ilek'trɔnik]	adj.	电子的
electrical	[i'lektrik(ə)l]	adj.	电的，有关电的

element	['elimənt]	n.	元件
network	['netwəːk]	n.	网络，网状物
model	['mɔdl]	n.&v.	样式，模型；作……的模型
decompose	[ˌdiːkəm'pəuz]	vt.	分解
multiple	['mʌltipl]	adj.	多样的，多重的
schematic	[ski'mætik]	adj.	示意性的
diagram	['daiəgræm]	n.	图样，图表，图像，示图
circuit	['səːkit]	n.	电路
schematic diagram			示意图
circuit diagram			电路图
macro	['mækrəu]	adj.	巨大的，大量使用的
component	[kəm'pəunənt]	n.	元件，组（部）件
lumped element model			集总元件模型
nonlinearity	[ˌnɔnlini'æriti]	n.	非线性
approximate	[ə'prɔksimeit]	adj. & v.	近似的，大约的；近似，接近
variable	['vɛəriəbl]	n.	变量
current	['kʌrənt]	n.	电流
voltage	['vəʊltidʒ]	n.	［电工］电压，伏特数
charge	[tʃɑːdʒ]	n.	电荷，充电
magnetic	[mæg'netik]	adj.	磁的，有磁性的，有吸引力的
flux	[flʌks]	n.	［物］流量，通量
current source			电流源
ampere	['æmpeə(r)]	n.	安培
conductor	[kən'dʌktə]	n.	［物］导体
voltage source			电压源
potential	[pə'tenʃ(ə)l]	adj. & n.	势的，位的；电位
potential difference			电位差
passive	['pæsiv]	adj.	无源的
resistance	[ri'zistəns]	n.	电阻，阻抗
ohm	[əum]	n.	［物］欧姆
proportional	[prə'pɔːʃənl]	adj.	（成）适当比例的，（与……）相称的（to）
capacitance	[kə'pæsitəns]	n.	容量，电容
farad	['færəd]	n.	［电］法拉（电容单位）
across	[ə'krɔs]	prep.	跨接
inductance	[in'dʌktəns]	n.	电感
henry	['henri]	n.	亨利（电感单位）
representation	[ˌreprizen'teiʃən]	n.	表示法
approximation	[əˌprɔksi'meiʃən]	n.	（数）近似值；近似法

battery	['bætəri]	n.	电池
series	['siəri:z]	n.	（电）串联（接）
parallel	['pærəlel]	n.	（电）并联
leakage	['li:kidʒ]	n.	漏，泄漏，渗漏
discharge	[dis'tʃɑ:dʒ]	v.	（电）放（电）
lead	[li:d]	n.	导线
spiral	['spaiərəl]	n.	螺线
capacitive	[kə'pæsitiv]	adj.	电容的
proximity	[prɔk'simiti]	n.	近似
semiconductor	['semikən'dʌktə]	n.	［物］半导体
bipolar	[bai'pəulə]	adj.	有两极的，双极的
transistor	[træn'zistə]	n.	［电子］晶体管
switch	[switʃ]	n.	开关
loop	[lu:p]	n.	回路
distributed	[dis'tribju:tid]	adj.	分布式的
algebraic	[ˌældʒi'breiik]	adj.	代数的
transform method			变换法
response	[ris'pɔns]	n.	响应
transient	['trænziənt]	adj.	瞬时的
active	['æktiv]	adj.	有源的

Notes

[1] Any electrical network can be modeled by decomposing it down to multiple, interconnected electrical elements in a schematic diagram or circuit diagram.

译文为：任何电网络都可通过分解为原理图或电路图中多个相互连接的电气元件，来建立模型。

此句中 any electrical network 译为任何电网络。

[2] A more refined model also includes a series inductance, to represent the effects of its lead inductance.

译文为：更精确的模型中含有串联电感，可用来表示电阻导线中的电感效应。

句中 to represent…为目的状语。

Exercises

Ⅰ. Mark the following statements with T (true) or F (false) according to the text.

1. Each electrical element affects the voltage in the network or current through the network in a particular way. (   )

2. There isn't a distinction between real, physical electrical or electronic components and the ideal electrical elements by which they are represented. (   )

3. Components do exist, have some ideal properties. (   )

4. Voltage source, measured in volts——produces a potential difference between two points. ( )

5. Current sources are more often used when representing conductors. ( )

Ⅱ. Complete the following sentences.

1. The concept of ______ is used in the analysis of ______.

2. Each electrical element affects the ______ in the network or ______ through the network in a particular way.

3. Resistance *R*, measured in ______ —— produces a voltage ______ the current flowing through it.

4. On a first degree of approximation, a bipolar transistor may be represented by a ______ that is controlled by the ______.

5. A network is a connection of ______ or ______ components, and may not necessarily be a ______.

Reading 1 Circuit Diagram

A circuit diagram (also known as an electrical diagram, wiring diagram, elementary diagram, or electronic schematic) is a simplified conventional pictorial representation of an electrical circuit. It shows the components of the circuit as simplified standard symbols, and the power and signal connections between the devices. Arrangement of the components interconnections on the diagram does not correspond to their physical locations in the finished device.

Unlike a block diagram or layout diagram, a circuit diagram shows the actual wire connections being used. The diagram does not show the physical arrangement of components. A drawing meant to depict what the physical arrangement of the wires and the components they connect is called "artwork" or "layout" or the "physical design".

Circuit diagrams are used for the design (circuit design), construction (such as PCB layout), and maintenance of electrical and electronic equipment.

Legends

On a circuit diagram, the symbols for components are labelled with a descriptor (or reference designator) matching that on the list of parts. For example, C1 is the first capacitor, L1 is the first inductor, Q1 is the first transistor, and R1 is the first resistor (note that it isn't written R1, L1,…). The letters that precede the numbers were chosen in the early days of the electrical industry, even before the vacuum tube (thermionic valve), so "Q" was the only one available for semiconductor devices in the mid-twentieth century. Often the value or type designation of the component is given on the diagram beside the part, but detailed specifications would go on the parts list.

Symbols (Fig.1.2)

Circuit diagram symbols have differed from country to country and have changed over time, but are now to a large extent internationally standardized. Simple components often had symbols intended to represent some feature of the physical construction of the device. For example, the symbol for a resistor shown here dates back to the days when that component was made from a long piece of wire wrapped in such a manner as to not produce inductance, which would have made it a coil. These wire-wound resistors are now used only in high-power applications, smaller resistors being cast from carbon composition (a mixture of carbon and filler) or fabricated as an insulating tube or chip coated with a metal film. The internationally standardized symbol for a resistor is therefore now simplified to an oblong, sometimes with the value in ohms written inside, instead of the zigzag symbol. A less common symbol is simply a series of peaks on one side of the line representing the conductor, rather than back-and-forth as shown here.

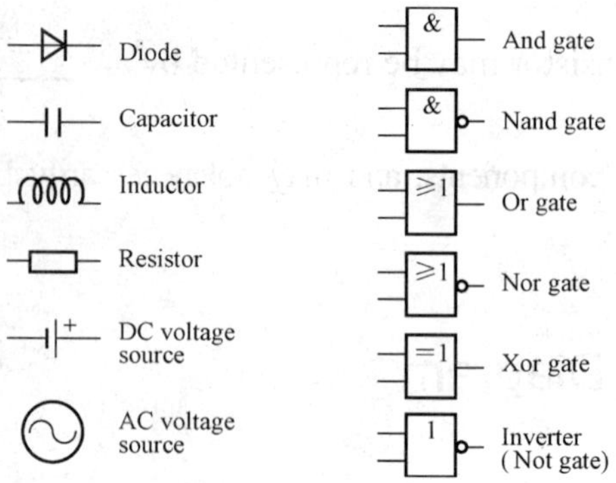

Fig.1.2 Circuit element symbols

Linkages

The linkages between leads were once simple crossings of lines; one wire insulated from and "jumping over" another was indicated by it making a little semicircle over the other line. With the arrival of computerized drafting, a connection of two intersecting wires was shown by a crossing with a dot or "blob", and a crossover of insulated wires by a simple crossing without a dot. However, there was a danger of confusing these two representations if the dot was drawn too small or omitted. Modern practice is to avoid using the "crossover with dot" symbol, and to draw the wires meeting at two points instead of one. It is also common to use a hybrid style, showing connections as a cross with a dot while insulated crossings use the semicircle. Several styles of schematic wire junctions are shown in Fig.1.3.

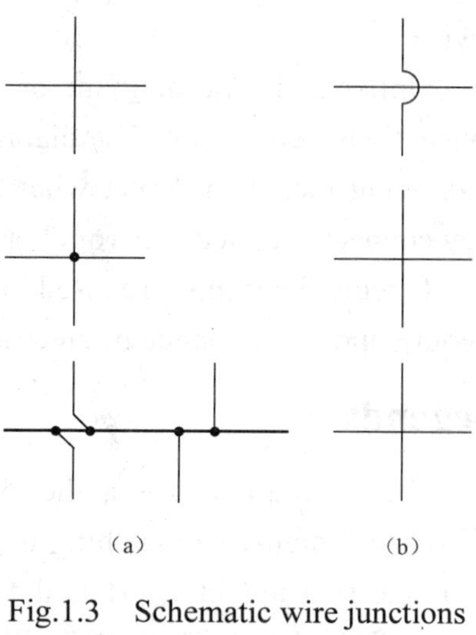

Fig.1.3 Schematic wire junctions

(a) connection; (b) no connection

Technical Words and Expressions

wiring diagram 接线图

elementary diagram		原理图
pictorial	adj.	图示的
power	n.	电源
arrangement	n.	排列，布局
layout diagram		布置图
depict	vt.	描述，描写
artwork		布线图
physical design		布图设计
construction	n.	建造
legend	n.	图例
descriptor	n.	描述符
vacuum tube		真空管
thermionic valve		热离子管，热阴极电子管
specification	n.	规格，说明书
wrap	v.	卷，缠绕
cast	v.	浇铸
carbon composition		碳组分
filler	n.	填充剂
fabricate	v.	制造
insulating tube		绝缘管
metal film		金属膜
oblong	n.	长方形
zigzag	n.	锯齿形
peak	n.	波峰
back-and-forth		来回地，往复地
linkage	n.	连接
crossing	n.	交叉，相交
draft	vt.	设计
blob	n.	圆点
crossover	n.	交叉
hybrid	adj.	混合的
semicircle	n.	半圆形
junction	n.	连接，接合，交叉点，汇合处

Comprehension

1. A circuit diagram is also known as an electrical diagram, ______.
   A. wiring diagram　　B. elementary diagram
   C. electronic schematic　　D. all

2. Unlike a block diagram or layout diagram, a circuit diagram shows the ______ wire connections being used.
   A. virtual　　B. actual　　C. approximate　　D. physical

3. According to the text, the distinction between a block diagram and a circuit diagram is that ______.

A. a block diagram can show the physical arrangement of components

B. a circuit diagram can show the physical arrangement of components

C. a circuit diagram shows the actual wire connections being used

D. a block diagram shows the actual wire connections being used

4. According to the text, which of the following description about circuit diagram is right? ______.

A. Arrangement of the components interconnections on the diagram does correspond to their physical locations in the finished device.

B. There is no distinction between a circuit diagram and a layout diagram.

C. A circuit diagram can show the physical arrangement of components.

D. Circuit diagrams are used for the design (circuit design), construction (such as PCB layout), and maintenance of electrical and electronic equipments.

5. The internationally standardized symbol for a resistor is therefore now simplified to ______, sometimes with the value in ohms written inside.

A. a semicircle　　B. an oblong

C. a triangle　　D. a circle

Unit 2　Network Analysis

A network, in the context of electronics, is a collection of interconnected components. Network analysis is the process of finding the voltages across, and the currents through, every component in the network. There are a number of different techniques for achieving this. However, for the most part, they assume that the components of the network are all linear. The methods described in this article are only applicable to linear network analysis except where explicitly stated.

Definitions

Component: A device with two or more terminals into which, or out of which, charge may flow.

Node: A point at which terminals of more than two components are joined. A conductor with a substantially zero resistance is considered to be a node for the purpose of analysis.

Branch: The component (s) joining two nodes.

Mesh: A group of branches within a network joined so as to form a complete loop.

Port: Two terminals where the current into one is identical to the current out of the other.

Equivalent circuits

A useful procedure in network analysis is to simplify the network by reducing the number of components. This can be done by replacing the actual components with other notional components that have the same effect. A particular technique might directly reduce the number of components, for instance by combining impedances in series. On the other hand it might merely change the form in to one in which the components can be reduced in a later operation. For instance, one might transform a voltage generator into a current generator using Norton's theorem in order to be able to later combine the internal resistance of the generator with a parallel impedance load.

A resistive circuit is a circuit containing only resistors, ideal current sources, and ideal voltage sources. If the sources are constant (DC) sources, the result is a DC circuit. The analysis of a circuit refers to the process of solving for the voltages and currents present in the circuit. The solution principles outlined here also apply to phasor analysis of AC circuits.

Two circuits (see circuit 1 and circuit 2 in Fig.1.4) are said to be equivalent with respect to a pair of terminals if the voltage across the terminals and current through the terminals for one network have the same relationship as the voltage and current at the terminals of the other network [1].

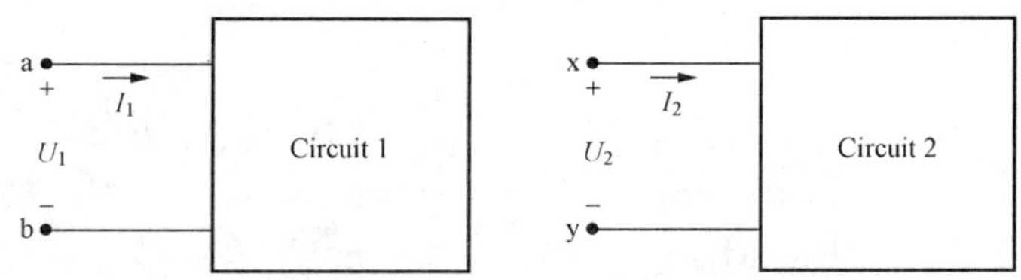

Fig.1.4 Circuit equivalence

If $U_2 = U_1$ implies $I_2 = I_1$ for all (real) values of U_1, then with respect to terminals ab and xy, circuit 1 and circuit 2 are equivalent.

The above is a sufficient definition for a one-port network. For more than one port, then it must be defined that the currents and voltages between all pairs of corresponding ports must bear the same relationship[2]. For instance, star and delta networks are effectively three port networks and hence require three simultaneous equations to fully specify their equivalence.

Impedances in series and in parallel

Any two terminal network of impedances can eventually be reduced to a single impedance by successive applications of impedances in series or impedances in parallel.

Impedances in series: $Z_{eq}=Z_1+Z_2+\cdots+Z_n$

Impedances in parallel: $\dfrac{1}{Z_{eq}}=\dfrac{1}{Z_1}+\dfrac{1}{Z_2}+\cdots+\dfrac{1}{Z_n}$

The above simplified for only two impedances in parallel: $Z_{eq}=\dfrac{Z_1Z_2}{Z_1+Z_2}$

Source transformation

A generator with an internal impedance (ie non-ideal generator) can be represented as either an ideal voltage generator or an ideal current generator plus the impedance. These two forms (Fig.1.5) are equivalent and the transformations are given below. If the two networks are equivalent with respect to terminals ab, then U and I must be identical for both networks. Thus,

$$U_S = RI_S \quad \text{or} \quad I_S = \frac{U_S}{R}$$

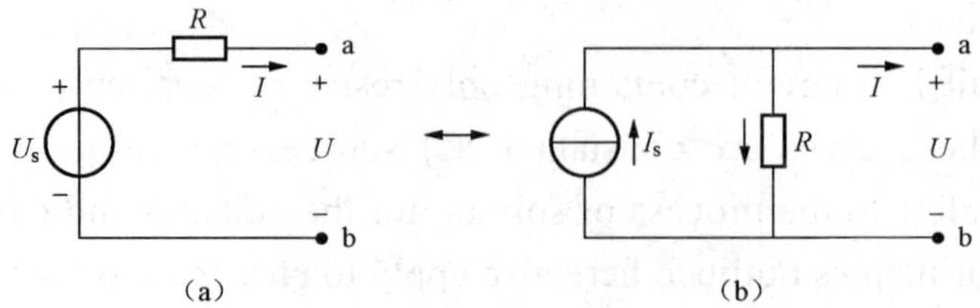

Fig.1.5 Source transformation

(a) Voltage source; (b) Current source

Technical Words and Expressions

in the context of			在……情况下
explicitly		adv.	明白地，明确地
terminal	['tə:minl]	n.	终端，接线端
node	[nəud]	n.	节点
substantially	[səb'stænʃ(ə)li]	adv.	实质上
branch	[brɑ:ntʃ]	n.	支路
mesh	[meʃ]	n.	网孔
port	[pɔ:t]	n.	端口
notional	['nəuʃənəl]	adj.	概念的，想象的
impedance	[im'pi:dəns]	n.	阻抗
in series		adv.	串联
generator	['dʒenəreitə]	n.	发电机，发生器
Norton's theorem			诺顿定理
load	[ləud]	n.	负载
resistive	[ri'zistiv]	adj.	电阻的，电阻性的
DC		n.	直流电
AC		n.	交流电
outline	['əutlain]	v.	概述，略述
phasor	['feizə]	n.	相量
equivalent	[i'kwivələnt]	adj.	等效的
one-port network			一端口网络
simultaneous	[ˌsiməl'teinjəs]	adj.	同时的，同时发生的
successive	[sək'sesiv]	adj.	连续的

in parallel			并联
transformation	[ˌtrænsfəˈmeiʃən]	n.	变换

Notes

[1] Two circuits (see circuit 1 and circuit 2 in Fig.1.4) are said to be equivalent with respect to a pair of terminals if the voltage across the terminals and current through the terminals for one network have the same relationship as the voltage and current at the terminals of the other network.

译文为：如果一个网络的端电压和流过端点间的电流之间的关系与另一个网络端点间的电压和电流关系相同，这两个端点间的电路（图 1.4 中的电路 1 和电路 2）等效。

此句由 if 引导条件状语从句；主句为被动语态，在翻译的时候，可译成主动。

[2] For more than one port, then it must be defined that the currents and voltages between all pairs of corresponding ports must bear the same relationship.

译文为：对于一端口以上的网络，应该定义所有相应的端口间具有相同的电流、电压关系。

此句中 it 为形式主语，真正的主语为 that 所引导的从句。

Exercises

Ⅰ. Mark the following statements with T (true) or F (false) according to the text.

1. A node is a point at which terminals of less than two components are joined. (　　)

2. A useful procedure in network analysis is to simplify the network by reducing the number of components. (　　)

3. The solution principles used for DC circuits can't apply to phasor analysis of AC circuits. (　　)

4. Any two terminal network of impedances can eventually be reduced to a single impedance by successive applications of impedances in series or impedances in parallel. (　　)

5. A generator with an internal impedance is an ideal generator. (　　)

Ⅱ. Complete the following sentences.

1. Network analysis is the process of finding the ______ across, and the ______ through, every ______ in the network.

2. A useful procedure in network analysis is to ______ the network by reducing the ______ of components.

3. A resistive circuit is a circuit containing only ________, ideal ________, and ideal ______.

4. Star and delta networks are effectively ______ networks and hence require ______ simultaneous equations to fully specify their ______.

5. A generator with an ______ (ie. non-ideal generator) can be represented as either ______ or ______ plus the impedance.

Reading 2 Kirchhoff's Circuit Laws

Kirchhoff's circuit laws are two equalities that deal with the conservation of charge and energy in electrical circuits, and were first described in 1845 by Gustav Kirchhoff. Widely used in electrical engineering, they are also called Kirchhoff's rules or simply Kirchhoff's laws (see also Kirchhoff's laws for other meanings of that term).

Both circuit rules can be directly derived from Maxwell's equations, but Kirchhoff preceded Maxwell and instead generalized work by Georg Ohm.

Kirchhoff's Current Law (KCL)

This law is also called Kirchhoff's first law, Kirchhoff's point rule, Kirchhoff's junction rule (or nodal rule), and Kirchhoff's first rule.

The principle of conservation of electric charge implies that:

At any point in an electrical circuit that does not represent a capacitor plate, the sum of currents flowing towards that point is equal to the sum of currents flowing away from that point.

Adopting the convention that every current flowing towards the point is positive and that every current flowing away is negative (or the other way around), this principle can be stated as:

$$\sum_{k=1}^{n} I_k = 0$$

n is the total number of currents flowing towards or away from the point. This formula is also valid for complex currents:

$$\sum_{k=1}^{n} \tilde{I}_k = 0$$

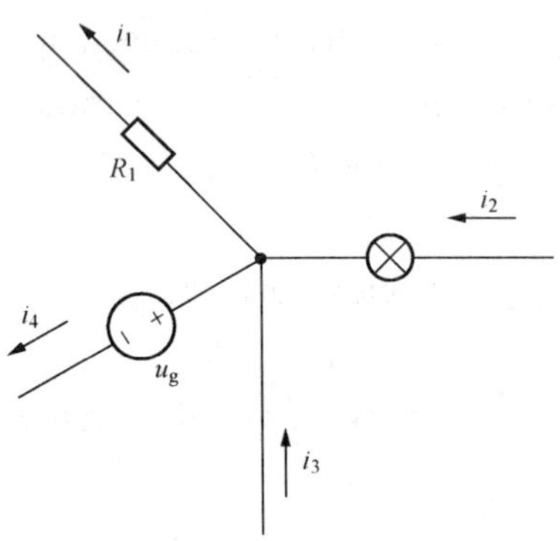

Fig.1.6 A diagram of Kirchhoff's Current Law

Applying Kirchhoff's Current Law to the diagram shown below (Fig.1.6), the current entering any junction is equal to the current leaving that junction: $i_1 + i_4 = i_2 + i_3$.

Changing charge density

Physically speaking, the restriction regarding the "capacitor plate" means that Kirchhoff's current law is only valid if the charge density remains constant in the point that it is applied to. This is normally not a problem because of the strength of electrostatic forces: the charge buildup would cause repulsive forces to disperse the charges.

However, a charge build-up can occur in a capacitor, where the charge is typically spread over wide parallel plates, with a physical break in the circuit that prevents the positive and negative charge accumulations over the two plates from coming together and cancelling. In this case, the sum of the currents flowing into one plate of the capacitor is not zero, but rather is equal to the rate of charge accumulation. However, if the displacement current dD/dt is included, Kirchhoff's current law once again holds. (This is really only required if one wants to apply the current law to a point on a capacitor plate. In circuit analyses, however, the capacitor as a whole is typically treated as a unit, in which case the ordinary current law holds since exactly the current that enters the capacitor on the one side leaves it on the other side.)

Kirchhoff's Voltage Law (KVL)

This law is also called Kirchhoff's second law, Kirchhoff's loop (or mesh) rule, and Kirchhoff's second rule.

The directed sum of the electrical potential differences around any closed circuit must be zero.

Similarly to KCL, it can be stated as:

$$\sum_{k=1}^{n} U_k = 0$$

Here, n is the total number of voltages measured. The voltages may also be complex:

$$\sum_{k=1}^{n} \widetilde{U}_k = 0$$

Direction of the voltages

This law often leads to confusion due to sign errors.

Typically, in a schematic diagram, one has to choose whether to define a voltage measured clockwise or counter-clockwise as positive. It is a question of convenience, but once decided, all voltages must be treated this way.

The confusion comes from the direction of the voltage at voltage sources and capacitors.

Considering the schematic diagram (Fig.1.7), we may decide to measure all voltages clockwise, that is, from a to b, from b to c, from c to d and from d to a. The sum of all the voltages around the loop is equal to zero. $u_1+u_2+u_3+u_4=0$.

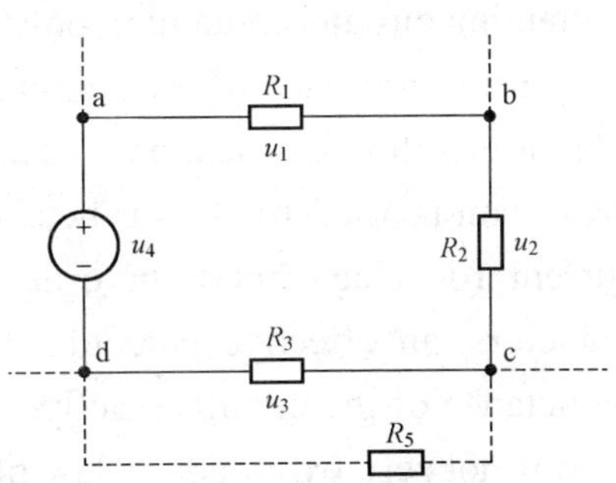

Fig.1.7 A diagram depicting Kirchhoff's Voltage Law

At the resistors, the voltage will be positive, because we measure from "plus to minus". But when we measure from d to a, we will measure a negative voltage, because we measure from "minus to plus". We have to do this because otherwise, we would be measuring counter-clockwise if we measured the other way around.

If our voltage source is a capacitor, we will also notice that we must consider the charge negative, which is due to: $Q = CU$.

There is the rule of thumb that one must just "reverse supply voltages" in order to make the calculation match KVL. There is, however, the risk that this may lead to additional confusion in more complex circuits, in which it is not clear what the supply voltage exactly is.

It is actually not a contradiction that we measure from "minus to plus"; inside a voltage source, this is the direction in which the current flows. If a magnetic field induces a voltage into an inductor, making it a voltage source (which is the principle of an electrical generator), this should be obvious. Even in a battery, the circuit is closed because of Ions flowing and representing charge carriers.

Inside capacitors, there is no flow of charge carriers. The KVL is valid anyway, but we have to consider the electric field inside the capacitor in order to see this.

Electric field and electric potential

Kirchhoff's voltage law as stated above is equivalent to the statement that a single-valued electric potential can be assigned to each point in the circuit (in the same way that any conservative vector field can be represented as the gradient of a scalar potential).

This could be viewed as a consequence of the principle of conservation of energy. Otherwise, it would be possible to build a perpetual motion machine that passed a current in a circle around the circuit.

Considering that electric potential is defined as a line integral over an electric field, Kirchhoff's voltage law can be expressed equivalently as

$$\oint_C E\mathrm{d}l = 0$$

which states that the line integral of the electric field around closed loop C is zero.

In order to return to the more special form, this integral can be "cut in pieces" in order to get the voltage at specific components.

This is a simplification of Faraday's law of induction for the special case where there is no fluctuating magnetic field linking the closed loop. Therefore, it practically suffices for explaining circuits containing only resistors and capacitors.

In the presence of a changing magnetic field the electric field is not conservative and it cannot therefore define a pure scalar potential —— the line integral of the electric field around the circuit is not zero. This is because energy is being transferred from the magnetic field to the current (or vice versa). In order to "fix" Kirchhoff's voltage law for circuits containing inductors, an effective potential drop, or electromotive force (emf), is associated with each inductance of the circuit, exactly equal to the amount by which the line integral of the electric field is not zero by Faraday's law of induction.

Technical Words and Expressions

equality	n.	等式
conservation	n.	守恒
energy	n.	能量
derive	vt.	起源于，出自

generalize	vt.	归纳，概括，推广
capacitor plate		电容器极板
be equal to		等于
positive	adj.	正的
negative	adj.	负的
formula	n.	公式
complex	adj	[数] 复数的
density	n.	[物] 浓度，密度
restriction	n.	限制，约束
electrostatic force		静电力
repulsive	adj.	推斥的，排斥的
disperse	v.	（使）分散，（使）散开
build-up	n.	增强，增长；上升
accumulation	n.	积聚
cancel	vt.	取消
displacement current		位移电流
confusion	n.	混乱，混淆
clockwise	adj. & adv.	顺时针方向的；顺时针方向地
counter-clockwise	adj. & adv.	逆时针方向的；逆时针方向地
convenience	n.	便利，方便
thumb	n.	拇指
contradiction	n.	矛盾
ion	n.	离子
charge carrier		电荷载体，载荷子
vector field		矢（向）量场
gradient	n.	梯度，倾斜度，坡度
scalar potential		标量势
consequence	n.	结果
perpetual motion machine		永动机
line integral		线积分
suffice	vi.	足够，有能力
electromotive force (emf)		电动势

Comprehension

1. Kirchhoff's circuit laws are two equalities that deal with the conservation of ______ in electrical circuits.

A. current and voltage B. current and energy

C. charge and energy D. charge and voltage

2. Applying Kirchhoff's Current Law to the diagram shown in Fig.1.6, the relation of the

four currents can be written as ______.

A. $i_1 + i_2 = i_3 + i_4$ B. $i_1 + i_4 = i_2 + i_3$

C. $i_1 + i_3 = i_2 + i_4$ D. $i_1 = i_2 + i_3 + i_4$

3. Kirchhoff's voltage law can be summarized as follows: ______.

A. around any closed loop in a circuit, the sum of all changes in potential (emfs and potential drops across resistors and other circuit elements) must equal zero

B. around any closed loop in a circuit, the sum of all changes in potential (emfs and potential drops across resistors and other circuit elements) mustn't equal zero

C. at each instant of time, the algebraic sum of the voltage rise is more than the algebraic sum of the voltage drops, both being taken in the same direction around the closed loop

D. at each instant of time, the algebraic sum of the voltage rise is less than the algebraic sum of the voltage drops, both being taken in the same direction around the closed loop

4. Kirchhoff's voltage law can be applied only to ______.

A. nodes B. junctions C. branches D. closed loops

5. At the resistors, the voltage will be ______, because we measure from "plus to minus".

A. positive B. negative C. zero D. uncertain

Unit 3 Diodes

In electronics, a diode is a two-terminal device. Diodes have two active electrodes between which the signal of interest may flow, and most are used for their unidirectional electric current property. The varicap diode is used as an electrically adjustable capacitor.

The directionality of current flow most diodes exhibit is sometimes generically called the rectifying property. The most common function of a diode is to allow an electric current to pass in one direction (called the forward biased condition) and to block the current in the opposite direction (the reverse biased condition). Thus, the diode can be thought of as an electronic version of a check valve.

Real diodes do not display such a perfect on-off directionality but have a more complex non-linear electrical characteristic, which depends on the particular type of diode technology. Diodes also have many other functions in which they are not designed to operate in this on-off manner.

Early diodes included "cat's whisker" crystals and vacuum tube devices. Today the most common diodes are made from semiconductor materials such as silicon or germanium.

Semiconductor diodes

Most modern diodes are based on semiconductor p-n junctions. In a p-n diode, conventional current can flow from the p-type side (the anode) to the n-type side (the cathode), but cannot flow in the opposite direction. Another type of semiconductor diode, the Schottky diode, is formed from the contact between a metal and a semiconductor rather than by a p-n junction.

Current–voltage characteristic

A semiconductor diode's current-voltage characteristic, or *I–U* curve, is related to the transport of carriers through the so-called depletion layer or depletion region that exists at the p-n junction between differing semiconductors [1]. When a p-n junction is first created, conduction band (mobile) electrons from the N-doped region diffuse into the P-doped region where there is a large population of holes (places for electrons in which no electron is present) with which the electrons "recombine". When a mobile electron recombines with a hole, both hole and electron vanish, leaving behind an immobile positively charged donor on the N-side and negatively charged acceptor on the P-side. The region around the p-n junction becomes depleted of charge carriers and thus behaves as an insulator.

However, the depletion width cannot grow without limit. For each electron-hole pair that recombines, a positively-charged dopant ion is left behind in the N-doped region, and a negatively charged dopant ion is left behind in the P-doped region. As recombination proceeds and more ions are created, an increasing electric field develops through the depletion zone which acts to slow and then finally stop recombination. At this point, there is a "built-in" potential across the depletion zone.

If an external voltage is placed across the diode with the same polarity as the built-in potential, the depletion zone continues to act as an insulator, preventing any significant electric current flow. This is the reverse bias phenomenon. However, if the polarity of the external voltage opposes the built-in potential, recombination can once again proceed, resulting in substantial electric current through the p-n junction. For silicon diodes, the built-in potential is approximately 0.6 V. Thus, if an external current is passed through the diode, about 0.6 V will be developed across the diode such that the P-doped region is positive with respect to the N-doped region and the diode is said to be "turned on" as it has a forward bias.

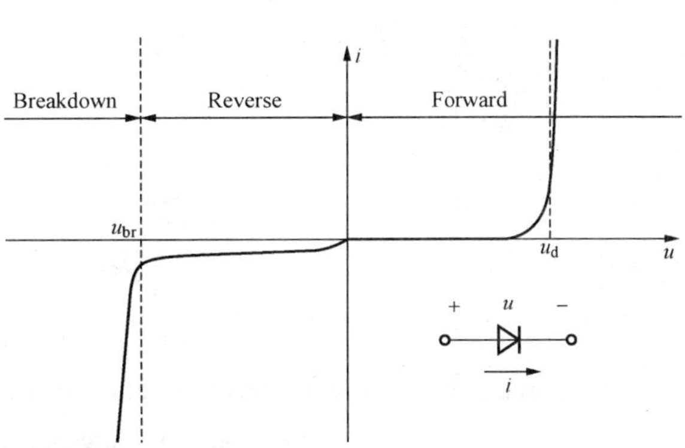

Fig.1.8 *I–U* characteristics of a p-n junction diode

A diode's *I–U* characteristic can be approximated by four regions of operation (Fig.1.8).

At very large reverse bias, beyond the peak inverse voltage or PIV, a process called reverse breakdown occurs which causes a large increase in current that usually damages the device permanently. The avalanche diode is deliberately designed for use in the avalanche region. In the zener diode, the concept of PIV is not applicable. A zener diode contains a heavily doped p-n junction allowing electrons to tunnel from the valence band of the p-type material to the conduction band of the n-type material, such that the reverse voltage is "clamped" to a known value (called the zener voltage), and avalanche does not occur. Both devices, however, do have a limit to the maximum current and power in the clamped reverse voltage region.

The second region, at reverse biases more positive than the PIV, has only a very small reverse saturation current. In the reverse bias region for a normal p-n rectifier diode, the current through the device is very low (in the μA range).

The third region is forward but small bias, where only a small forward current is conducted.

As the potential difference is increased above an arbitrarily defined "cut-in voltage" or "on-voltage" or "diode forward voltage drop (U_d)", the diode current becomes appreciable (the level of current considered "appreciable" and the value of cut-in voltage depends on the application), and the diode presents a very low resistance.

The current-voltage curve is exponential. In a normal silicon diode at rated currents, the arbitrary "cut-in" voltage is defined as 0.6 to 0.7 volts. The value is different for other diode types —— Schottky diodes can be as low as 0.2 V and red light-emitting diodes (LEDs) can be 1.4 V or more and blue LEDs can be up to 4.0 V.

At higher currents the forward voltage drop of the diode increases. A drop of 1 to 1.5 V is typical at full rated current for power diodes.

Types of semiconductor diode

There are several types of junction diodes (Fig.1.9), which either emphasize a different physical aspect of a diode often by geometric scaling, doping level, choosing the right electrodes, are just an application of a diode in a special circuit, or are really different devices like the Gunn, laser diode and the MOSFET.

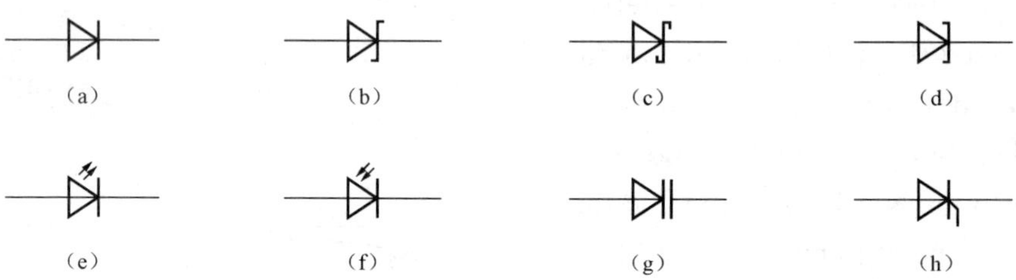

Fig.1.9 Some diode symbols

(a) Diode; (b) Zener diode; (c) Schottky diode; (d) Tunnel diode; (e) Light-emitting diode; (f) Photodiode; (g) Varicap; (h) Silicon controlled rectifier

Normal (p-n) diodes, which operate as described above, are usually made of doped silicon or, more rarely, germanium. Before the development of modern silicon power rectifier diodes, cuprous and later selenium was used; its low efficiency gave it a much higher forward voltage drop (typically 1.4～1.7 V per "cell", with multiple cells stacked to increase the peak inverse voltage rating in high voltage rectifiers), and required a large heat sink (often an extension of the diode's metal substrate), much larger than a silicon diode of the same current ratings would require. The vast majority of all diodes are the p-n diodes found in CMOS integrated circuits, which include two diodes per pin and many other internal diodes.

Applications

Radio demodulation

The first use for the diode was the demodulation of amplitude modulated (AM) radio broadcasts. The history of this discovery is treated in depth in the radio article. In summary, an AM signal consists of alternating positive and negative peaks of voltage, whose amplitude or "envelope" is proportional to the original audio signal. The diode (originally a crystal diode) rectifies the AM radio frequency signal, leaving an audio signal which is the original audio signal. The audio is extracted using a simple filter and fed into an audio amplifier or transducer, which generates sound waves.

Power conversion

Rectifiers are constructed from diodes, where they are used to convert alternating current (AC) electricity into direct current (DC). Automotive alternators are a common example, where the diode, which rectifies the AC into DC, provides better performance than the commutator of earlier dynamo [2]. Similarly, diodes are also used in Cockcroft-Walton voltage multipliers to convert AC into higher DC voltages.

Over-voltage protection

Diodes are frequently used to conduct damaging high voltages away from sensitive electronic devices. They are usually reverse-biased (non-conducting) under normal circumstances. When the voltage rises above the normal range, the diodes become forward-biased (conducting). For example, diodes are used in (stepper motor and H-bridge) motor controller and relay circuits to de-energize coils rapidly without the damaging voltage spikes that would otherwise occur[3]. (Any diode used in such an application is called a flyback diode.) Many integrated circuits also incorporate diodes on the connection pins to prevent external voltages from damaging their sensitive transistors. Specialized diodes are used to protect from over-voltages at higher power (see Diode types above).

Technical Words and Expressions

diode	[ˈdaiəud]	n.	二极管
electrode	[iˈlektrəud]	n.	电极
unidirectional	[ˌjuː nɪdiˈrekʃənəl]	adj.	单向的，单向性的
varicap	[ˌværiˈkæp]	n.	变容二极管
varicap diode			变容二极管
directionality	[diˌrekʃənˈnæliti]	n.	方向性
rectify	[ˈrektifai]	vt.	［电子学］把……整流
forward biased			正偏的

reverse biased			反偏的
check valve			单向阀
cat's whisker			触须
silicon	['silikən]	n.	［化］硅，硅元素
germanium	[dʒəː'meiniəm]	n.	锗
p-n junction			p-n 结
conventional	[kən'venʃənl]	adj.	惯例的，常规的
Schottky diode			肖特基二极管
current-voltage characteristic			伏安特性
depletion	[di'pliːʃən]	n.	耗散
doped	[dəupt]	adj.	掺杂质的
N-doped region			N 型掺杂区
hole	[həul]	n.	［物理学］空穴
electron	[i'lektrɔn]	n.	电子
immobile	[i'məubail]	adj.	静止的
donor	['dəunə]	n.	供体
acceptor	[əkˋseptə(r)]	n.	受体
deplete	[di'pliːt]	vt.	耗尽
dopant	['dəupənt]	n.	搀杂物，搀杂剂
substantial	[səb'stænʃəl]	adj.	实质的，真实的
breakdown	['breikdaun]	n.	［电学］击穿
avalanche	['ævəˌlɑːnʃ]	n.	雪崩
avalanche diode			雪崩二极管
deliberately			故意地
Zener diode			稳压二极管
tunnel	['tʌnl]	n.	隧道，地道
valence band			价电子带
tunnel diode			隧道二极管
clamp	[klæmp]	vt.	箝位
saturation	[ˌsætʃə'reiʃən]	n.	饱和（状态）
cut-in voltage			开启电压；阈值电压
appreciable	[ə'priːʃiəbl]	adj.	可感知的
exponential	[ˌekspəu'nenʃəl]	adj.	指数的，幂数的
light-emitting diode (LED)			发光二极管
geometric scaling			几何尺寸
Gunn		adj.	［电子］耿氏效应的，基于耿氏效应的
cuprous oxide			氧化亚铜

selenium	[si'li:niəm]	n.	[化] 硒
heat sink			散热片，散热装置
extension	[iks'tenʃən]	n.	扩大；伸展
substrate	['sʌbstreit]	n.	衬底；基片；基体
integrated circuit			集成电路
pin	[pin]	n.	引脚，管脚
anode	['ænəud]	n.	[电] 阳极，正极
cathode	['kæθəud]	n.	阴极
demodulation	['di:ˌmɔdju:'leiʃən]	n.	[讯] 解调，检波
amplitude modulated (AM) radio broadcast			调幅无线广播
envelope	['enviləup]	n.	包迹 [线]，包络（线，面）
rectifier	['rektifaiə]	n.	整流器
audio	['ɔ:diəu]	adj.	音频的
frequency	['fri:kwənsɪ]	n.	频率
extract	[iks'trækt]	vt.	推断出，引出
filter	['filtə]	n.	滤波器
automotive alternator		n.	机动车交流发电机
commutator	['kɔmjuteitə]	n.	换向器，转接器
dynamo	['dainəməu]	n.	发电机
Cockcroft-Walton voltage multiplier			科克罗夫-瓦耳电压倍增器
stepper motor			步进电机
H-bridge			H 桥电路
relay	['ri:lei]	n.	继电器
de-energize			去激励
spike	[spaik]	n.	[无] 尖峰信号，测试信号
flyback diode			回扫二极管

Notes

[1] A semiconductor diode's current-voltage characteristic, or *I–U* curve, is related to the transport of carriers through the so-called depletion layer or depletion region that exists at the p-n junction between differing semiconductors.

译文为：半导体二极管的电流-电压特性，即 *I–U* 曲线，与载流子流过的耗散层或耗散区有关，耗散层或耗散区位于不同类型半导体间形成的 p–n 结上。

句中 that 引导定语从句修饰 depletion layer 和 depletion region。

[2] Automotive alternators are a common example, where the diode, which rectifies the AC into DC, provides better performance than the commutator of earlier dynamo.

译文为：机动车交流发电机是一个常用的例子，其中二极管把交流变为直流，比早期的发电机换向器提供更好的性能。

句中 where 引导非限制性定语从句，从句的谓语为 provides。

[3] For example, diodes are used in (stepper motor and H-bridge) motor controller and relay circuits to de-energize coils rapidly without the damaging voltage spikes that would otherwise occur.

译文为：例如，二极管用在（步进电动机和 H 桥电路）电动机控制器和继电器电路中对线圈快速地去激励时，不会产生可能出现的具有危害性的电压尖峰。

句中 to 引导目的状语。

Exercises

Ⅰ. Mark the following statements with T (true) or F (false) according to the text.

1. Diodes are used for their bidirectional electric current property. (　　)

2. Today the most common diodes are made from semiconductor materials such as silicon or germanium. (　　)

3. In a p-n diode, conventional current can flow from the n-type side (the cathode) to the p-type side (the anode). (　　)

4. Rectifiers are constructed from diodes, where they are used to convert alternating current (AC) electricity into direct current (DC). (　　)

5. Many integrated circuits also incorporate diodes on the connection pins to prevent external voltages from damaging their sensitive transistors. (　　)

Ⅱ. Complete the following sentences.

1. Most modern diodes are based on semiconductor ______. In a p-n diode, conventional current can flow from the ______ side (the anode) to the ______ side (the cathode), but cannot flow in the ______ direction.

2. If an external voltage is placed across the diode with the same polarity as the ______ potential, the depletion zone continues to act as an ______, preventing any significant electric current flow.

3. In a normal silicon diode at rated currents, the arbitrary "cut-in" voltage is defined as ______ to ______ Volts.

4. The audio is extracted using a simple ______ and fed into an ______ or transducer, which generates sound waves.

5. ______ diodes are used to protect from ______ at higher power.

Reading 3　Transistors

In electronics, a transistor is a semiconductor device commonly used to amplify or switch electronic signals. A transistor is made of a solid piece of a semiconductor material, with at least three terminals for connection to an external circuit. A voltage or current applied to one pair of the transistor's terminals changes the current flowing through another pair of terminals. Because the controlled (output) power can be much larger than the controlling (input) power, the transistor provides amplification of a signal. The transistor is the fundamental building block of modern electronic devices, and is used in radio, telephone, computer and other electronic systems. Some transistors are packaged individually but most are found in integrated circuits.

Types (Fig.1.10)

Transistors are categorized by:

- Semiconductor material : germanium, silicon, gallium arsenide, silicon carbide, etc.
- Structure: BJT, JFET, IGFET (MOSFET), IGBT, "other types".
- Polarity: NPN, PNP (BJTs); N-channel, P-channel (FETs).
- Maximum power rating: low, medium, high.
- Maximum operating frequency: low, medium, high, radio frequency (RF), microwave. (The maximum effective frequency of a transistor is denoted by the term f_T, an abbreviation for "frequency of transition". The frequency of transition is the frequency at which the transistor yields unity gain.)
- Application: switch, general purpose, audio, high voltage, super-beta, matched pair.
- Physical packaging: through hole metal, through hole plastic, surface mount, ball grid array, power modules.
- Amplification factor h_{fe} (transistor beta).

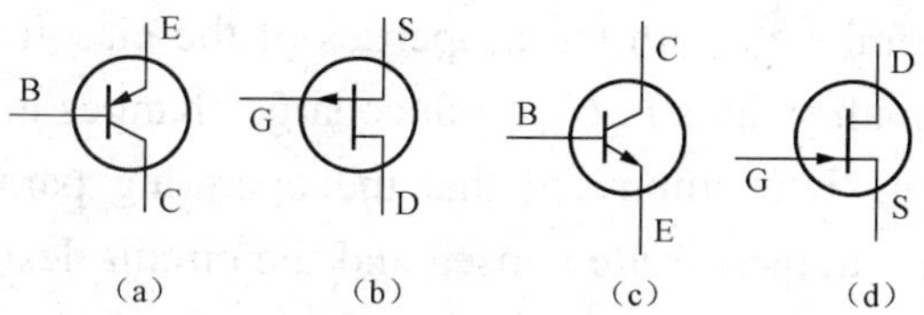

Fig.1.10 BJT and JFET symbols

(a) PNP; (b) P-channel; (c) NPN; (d) N-channel

Thus, a particular transistor may be described as: silicon, surface mount, BJT, NPN, low power, high frequency switch.

Usage

In the early days of transistor circuit design, the bipolar junction transistor, or BJT, was the most commonly used transistor. Even after MOSFETs became available, the BJT remained the transistor of choice for digital and analog circuits because of their ease of manufacture and speed. However, desirable properties of MOSFETs, such as their utility in low-power devices, have made them the ubiquitous choice for use in digital circuits and a very common choice for use in analog circuits.

Transistor as a switch

Transistors are commonly used as electronic switches, for both high power applications including switched-mode power supplies and low power applications such as logic gates.

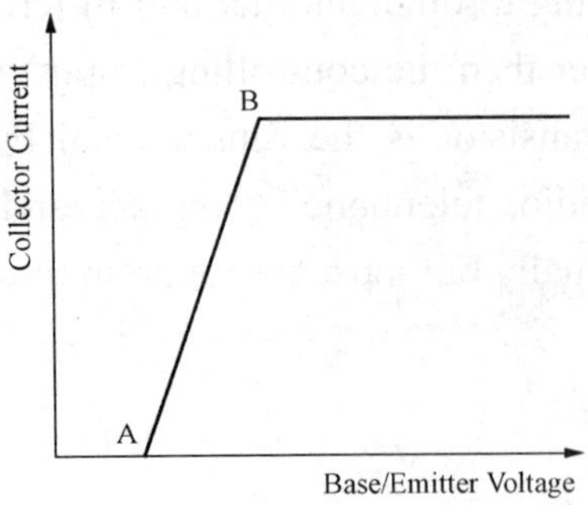

Fig.1.11 Operation graph of a transistor

It can be seen from the graph (Fig.1.11) that once the base voltage reaches a certain level, shown at B, no more current will exist and the output will be held at a fixed voltage. The transistor is then said to be saturated. Hence, values of input voltage can be chosen such that the output is either completely off, or completely on. The transistor is acting as a switch, and this type of operation is common in digital circuits where only "on" and "off" values are relevant.

Transistor as an amplifier

The below common emitter amplifier (Fig.1.12) is designed so that a small change in voltage in (U_{in}) changes the small current through the base of the transistor and the transistor's current amplification combined with the properties of the circuit mean that small swings in U_{in} produce large changes in U_{out}.

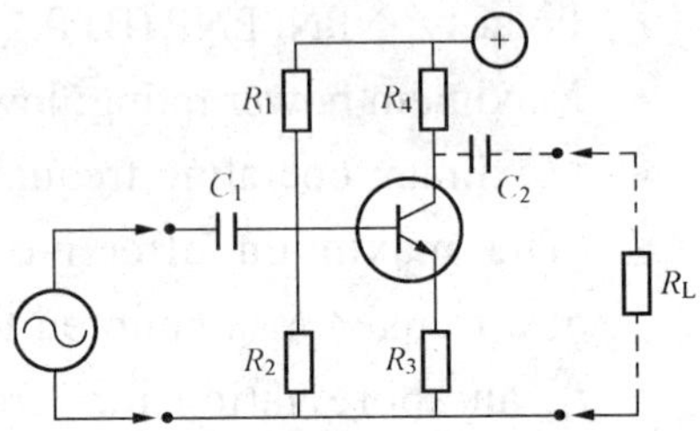

Fig.1.12 Common emitter amplifier

It is important that the operating parameters of the transistor are chosen and the circuit designed such that as far as possible the transistor operates within a linear portion of the graph, otherwise the output signal will suffer distortion.

Various configurations of single transistor amplifier are possible, with some providing current gain, some voltage gain, and some both.

From mobile phones to televisions, vast numbers of products include amplifiers for sound reproduction, radio transmission, and signal processing. The first discrete transistor audio amplifiers barely supplied a few hundred milliwatts, but power and audio fidelity gradually increased as better transistors became available and amplifier architecture evolved.

Modern transistor audio amplifiers of up to a few hundred watts are common and relatively inexpensive. Transistors have replaced valves (electron tubes) in instrument amplifiers.

Some musical instrument amplifier manufacturers mix transistors and vacuum tubes in the same circuit, as some believe tubes have a distinctive sound.

Packaging

Transistors come in many different packages (chip carriers) (Fig.1.13). The two main categories are through-hole (or leaded), and surface-mount, also known as surface mount device (SMD). The ball grid array (BGA) is the latest surface mount package (currently only for large transistor arrays). It has solder "balls" on the underside in place of leads. Because they are smaller and have shorter interconnections, SMDs have better high frequency characteristics but lower power rating.

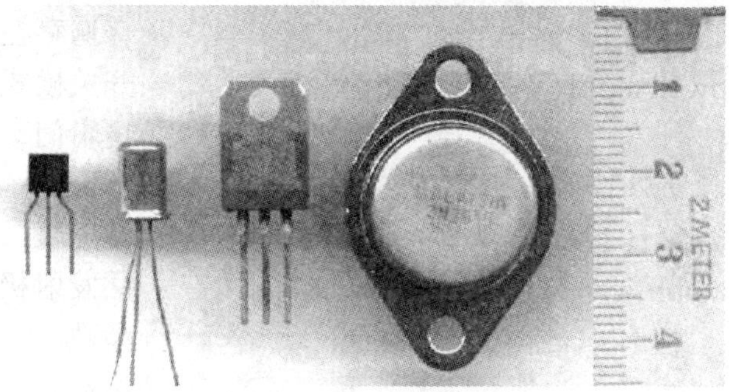

Fig.1.13 Transistor photo

Transistor packages are made of glass, metal, ceramic or plastic. The package often dictates the power rating and frequency characteristics. Power transistors have large packages that can be clamped to heat sinks for enhanced cooling. Additionally, most power transistors have the collector or drain physically connected to the metal can/metal plate. At the other extreme, some surface-mount microwave transistors are as small as grains of sand.

Often a given transistor type is available in different packages. Transistor packages are mainly standardized, but the assignment of a transistor's functions to the terminals is not: different transistor types can assign different functions to the package's terminals. Even for the same transistor type the terminal assignment can vary (normally indicated by a suffix letter to the part number, i.e. BC212L and BC212K).

Technical Words and Expressions

solid	adj.	固体（态）的
amplification	n.	放大
package	n. & vt.	晶体管外壳；封装
categorize	v.	加以类别，分类
gallium arsenide		砷化镓
carbide	n.	[化] 碳化物
polarity	n.	极性
channel	n.	沟道
maximum power rating		最大额定功率
radio frequency		高频
abbreviation	n.	缩写，缩写词
matched pair		配对
through hole		通孔，穿孔
surface mount		表面安装
ball grid array		球栅阵列（封装）
power module		电源模块
bipolar	adj.	双极的

ubiquitous	adj.	普遍存在的
switched-mode power supply		开关模式电源
logic gate		逻辑门
base	n.	基极
emitter	n.	发射极
common emitter amplifier		共发射极放大器
parameter	n.	参数
gain	n.	增益
mobile phone		移动电话
discrete	adj.	不连续的，离散的
barely	adv.	仅仅，刚刚，几乎不能
milliwatt		毫瓦
fidelity	n.	保真度
evolve	v.	（使）发展，（使）进展
musical	adj.	音乐的，悦耳的
chip carrier		晶片载体，芯片载体
dictate	v.	规定
ceramic	adj.	陶器的
collector	n.	集电极
drain	n.	漏极
grain	n.	晶粒
assignment	n.	排布
suffix	n.	后缀，下标

Comprehension

1. Transistors are commonly used as electronic ______, for both high power applications including switched-mode power supplies and low power applications such as logic gates.

A. heaters B. transformers

C. amplifiers D. switches

2. This arrangement where the emitter (E) is in the controlling circuit (base current) and in the controlled circuit (collector current) is called ______.

A. common collector mode B. common base mode

C. common emitter mode D. all above

3. Which of the following statements is not true about functional model of transistor? ______

A. The base-emitter junction behaves like a diode.

B. The small base current I_B controls the large collector current I_C.

C. The collector current I_C is controlled by the base current I_B.

D. A base current I_B flows only when the voltage U_{BE} across the base-emitter junction is less than 0.7V.

4. When a transistor works as an amplifier, its larger collector current I_C is ______ the base current I_B.

A. more than B. less than

C. proportional to D. equal to

5. The transistor should operate within a ______ portion of the graph, otherwise the output signal will suffer distortion.

A. nonlinear B. linear

C. cut-off D. saturation

Unit 4 Operational Amplifier

An operational amplifier, often called an op-amp, is a DC-coupled high-gain electronic voltage amplifier with differential inputs and, usually, a single output. Typically the output of the op-amp is controlled either by negative feedback, which largely determines the magnitude of its output voltage gain, or by positive feedback, which facilitates regenerative gain and oscillation[1]. High input impedance at the input terminals and low output impedance are important typical characteristics.

Op-amps are among the most widely used electronic devices today, being used in a vast array of consumer, industrial, and scientific devices. Many standard IC op-amps cost only a few cents in moderate production volume; however some integrated or hybrid operational amplifiers with special performance specifications may cost over $100 US in small quantities.

Modern designs are electronically more rugged than earlier implementations and some can sustain direct short-circuits on their outputs without damage.

Circuit notation

The circuit symbol for an op-amp is shown in Fig.1.14 where:

- U_+: non-inverting input;
- U_-: inverting input;
- U_{out}: output;
- U_{S+}: positive power supply;
- U_{S-}: negative power supply.

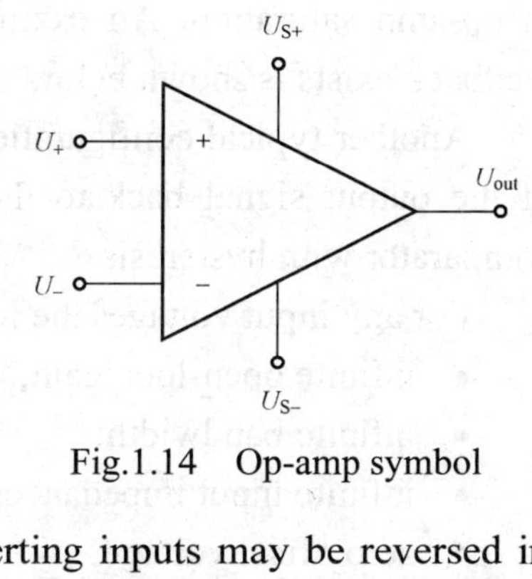

Fig.1.14 Op-amp symbol

The power supply pins (U_{S+} and U_{S-}) can be labeled in different ways. Despite different labeling, the function remains the same. Often these pins are left out of the diagram for clarity, and the power configuration is described or assumed from the circuit. The positions of the inverting and non-inverting inputs may be reversed in diagrams where appropriate; the power supply pins are not commonly reversed. For Example IC741 is an operational amplifier. It is used for doing arithmetic operations on analog computers, instrumentation and other control systems. Operational amplifier is in the class of linear ICs. Linear have a peculiarity that they can take continuous voltage signals like their analog counterparts. These are highly used today because of their high reliability and low cost. They are mainly used as voltage amplifiers. The basic operational amplifier works similar to the following sequence:

input stage→intermediate stage→level shifter→output stage.

Input stage consists of high input impedance it amplifies the difference between the given input signals. The intermediate stage consists of cascaded amplifiers to amplify the signals from the input. Due to high amplification the DC level of the signals goes up. So in order to bring them down to the rated value, level shifter or level translator is used. The output stage consists of class AB/ class B power amplifier in order to amplify the power of the output signal.

Operation of ideal op-amps

The amplifier's differential inputs consist of an inverting input and a non-inverting input, and ideally the op-amp amplifies only the difference in voltage between the two. This is called the "differential input voltage". In its most common use, the op-amp's output voltage is controlled by feeding a fraction of the output signal back to the inverting input. This is known as negative feedback. If that fraction is zero, i.e., there is no negative feedback, the amplifier is said to be running "open loop" and its output is the differential input voltage multiplied by the total gain of the amplifier, as shown by the following equation:

$$U_{out}=(U_{+}-U_{-})G$$

where U_{+} is the voltage at the non-inverting terminal, U_{-} is the voltage at the inverting terminal and G is the total open-loop gain of the amplifier.

Because the magnitude of the open-loop gain is typically very large and not well controlled by the manufacturing process, op-amps are not usually used without negative feedback. Unless the differential input voltage is extremely small, open-loop operation results in op-amp saturation. An example of how the output voltage is calculated when negative feedback exists is shown below in basic non-inverting amplifier circuit.

Another typical configuration of op-amps is the positive feedback, which takes a fraction of the output signal back to the non-inverting input. An important application of it is the comparator with hysteresis.

For any input voltages the ideal op-amp has:

- infinite open-loop gain;
- infinite bandwidth;
- infinite input impedances (resulting in zero input currents);
- zero offset voltage;
- infinite slew rate;
- zero output impedance, and zero noise.

Applications

Use in electronics system design

The use of op-amps as circuit blocks is much easier and clearer than specifying all their individual circuit elements (transistors, resistors, etc.), whether the amplifiers used are integrated or discrete. In the first approximation op-amps can be used as if they were ideal differential gain blocks; at a later stage limits can be placed on the acceptable range of parameters for each op-amp.

Circuit design follows the same lines for all electronic circuits. A specification is drawn up governing what the circuit is required to do, with allowable limits. For example, the gain may be required to be 100 times, with a tolerance of 5% but drift of less than 1% in a specified temperature range; the input impedance not less than 1 megohm; etc.

A basic circuit is designed, often with the help of circuit modeling (on a computer). Specific commercially available op-amps and other components are then chosen that meet the design criteria within the specified tolerances at acceptable cost. If not all criteria can be met, the specification may need to be modified.

Basic non-inverting amplifier circuit

The general op-amp has two inputs and one output. The output voltage is a multiple of the difference between the two inputs:

$$U_{out}= G(U_{+}-U_{-})$$

G is the open-loop gain of the op-amp. The inputs are assumed to have very high impedance; negligible current will flow into or out of the inputs. Op-amp outputs have very low source impedance.

If the output is connected to the inverting input (Fig.1.15), after being scaled by a voltage divider $K=R_1/(R_1+R_2)$, then:

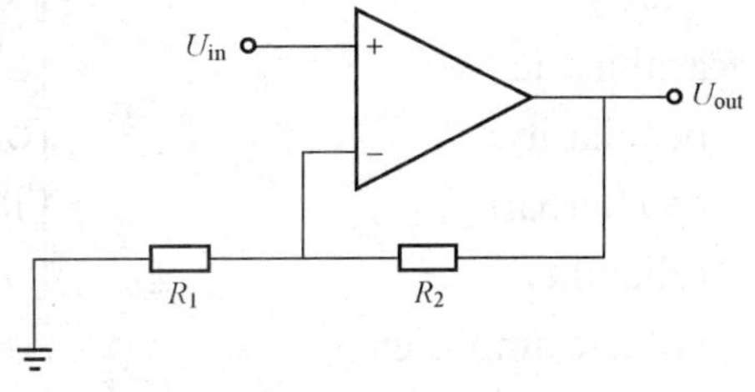

Fig.1.15 Non-inverting amplifier circuit

$$U_{+} = U_{in}$$

$$U_{-} = K\, U_{out}$$

$$U_{out} = G\,(U_{in}-K\, U_{out})$$

Solving for U_{out}/U_{in}, we see that the result is a linear amplifier with gain:

$$U_{out}/U_{in} = G/(1+G\,K)$$

If G is very large, U_{out}/U_{in} comes close to $1/K$, which equals $1+ (R_2/R_1)$.

This negative feedback connection is the most typical use of an op-amp, but many different configurations are possible, making it one of the most versatile of all electronic building blocks [2].

When connected in a negative feedback configuration, the op-amp will try to make U_{out} whatever voltage is necessary to make the input voltages as nearly equal as possible. This, and the high input impedance, are sometimes called the two "golden rules" of op-amp design (for circuits that use negative feedback):

1. No current will flow into the inputs.
2. The input voltages will be nearly equal.

Most single, dual and quad op-amps available have a standardized pin-out which permits one type to be substituted for another without wiring changes. A specific op-amp may be chosen for its open-loop gain, bandwidth, noise performance, input impedance, power consumption, or a compromise between any of these factors.

Technical Words and Expressions

operational amplifier			运算放大器
DC-coupled			直接耦合
differential	[ˌdifəˈrenʃəl]	adj.	差动的
feedback	[ˈfiːdbæk]	n.	反馈
magnitude	[ˈmægnitjuːd]	n.	大小
regenerative	[riˈdʒenərətiv]	adj.	再生的
oscillation	[ˌɔsiˈleiʃən]	n.	振荡
array	[əˈrei]	n.	大批；阵列
volume	[ˈvɔljuːm]	n.	量，大量，音量
rugged	[ˈrʌgid]	adj.	坚固的
short-circuit		n.	短路
non-inverting input			同相输入
inverting input			反相输入
clarity	[ˈklæriti]	n.	清楚，透明
arithmetic	[əˈriθmətik]	n.	算术，算法
peculiarity	[piˌkjuːliˈæriti]	n.	特性
counterpart	[ˈkauntəpɑːt]	n.	对应物
reliability	[riˌlaiəˈbiliti]	n.	可靠性
voltage amplifier			电压放大器
cascade	[kæsˈkeid]	n.	级联
level shifter			电平转换器
level translator			电平转换
comparator	[ˈkɔmpəreitə]	n.	比较器
hysteresis	[ˌhistəˈriːsis]	n.	迟滞
offset	[ˈɔːfset]	n.	失调
slew rate			延迟率
tolerance	[ˈtɔlərəns]	n.	误差
drift	[drift]	n.	漂移
versatile	[ˈvəːsətail]	adj.	通用的，万能的
quad	[kwɔd]	n.	4 路
open-loop gain			开环增益

consumption	[kən'sʌmpʃən]	n.	消耗
compromise	['kɔmprəmaiz]	n.	折中

Notes

[1] Typically the output of the op-amp is controlled either by negative feedback, which largely determines the magnitude of its output voltage gain, or by positive feedback, which facilitates regenerative gain and oscillation.

译文为：运放的输出端受负反馈或正反馈控制，负反馈在很大程度上决定输出电压增益的大小，正反馈可以促进再生增益和产生振荡。

which 引导非限制性定语从句。

[2] This negative feedback connection is the most typical use of an op-amp, but many different configurations are possible, making it one of the most versatile of all electronic building blocks.

译文为：负反馈连接是运放的最典型应用，但是可能有很多种不同的结构，使得其成为最通用的电子模块之一。

句中 making it one of the most versatile of all electronic building blocks 作句子的补语。

Exercises

Ⅰ. Mark the following statements with T (true) or F (false) according to the text.

1. Low input impedance at the input terminals and high output impedance are important typical Characteristics of operational amplifier . (　　)

2. Operational amplifier is in the class of nonlinear ICs. (　　)

3. The amplifier's differential inputs consist of an inverting input and a non-inverting input, and ideally the op-amp amplifies only the difference in voltage between the two. (　　)

4. In the first approximation op-amps can be used as if they were ideal differential gain blocks. (　　)

5. The general op-amp has one input and two outputs. (　　)

Ⅱ. Complete the following sentences.

1. An operational amplifier, often called an op-amp , is a ______ high-gain electronic voltage amplifier with ______ inputs and, usually, a single output.

2. Input stage consists of high ______ it amplifies the ______ between the given input signals.

3. In its most common use, the op-amp's ______ voltage is controlled by feeding a fraction of the output signal back to the ______ input.

4. Unless the differential input voltage is extremely ______, ______ operation results in op-amp saturation .

5. A specific op-amp may be chosen for its ______, bandwidth, noise performance, ______, power consumption, or a compromise between any of these factors.

Reading 4 The Basics of Integrated Circuits

Integrated circuits (ICs) are, much as their name would suggest, small circuits integrated into a plastic "chip". They provide a handy source of rich functionality in a tiny package. The ICs used in BEAM bots are really fairly simple —— often just consisting of multiple copies of a simple 2- or 3-element circuit, in a small, handy, package. This means that they are simple, easy to learn "circuit blocks", rather than very complex "black boxes".

Think of them as just a natural progression from circuits built from discrete components.

ICs come in a variety of packages (2 are predominant for our uses), and are based on a number of different core technologies (also known as logic families, we'll again be concerned with just 2).

Logic Families

For the purposes of BEAM bots, we'll just be concerned with two logic families (IC implementation approaches) (Table 1.1); note that both have multiple numbering schemes for their "members".

Table 1.1 Two Logic Families

TTL——Transistor/Transistor Logic	TTL chips require a fairly narrow range of supply voltage——5 volts, +/−0.5V. For TTL circuits, a logic "1" is usually defined as a signal of about 2.4 V, while logic "0" is about 0.5 V above ground; any signal between those values is undefined. Also, note that all unused inputs should be tied to ground. Bipolar TTL logic comes in many flavors (usually numbered in the"74××" format, occasionally in "54××" format) including 74LS/ALS types. These all require 1000s of times more power than TTL-compatible CMOS logic (like the 74HCT type, see below). Note that the 74HCT* ICs have the same logic thresholds as other TTL chips, allowing them used in a mixed circuits of TTL and HCT logic. While we won't use TTL logic in BEAM projects (as a general rule, it's too power-hungry), for completeness, here are some TTL "subfamilies": 74L××—— low-power TTL (1/10 the speed, 1/10 the power of "regular" TTL) 74H××—— high-speed TTL (twice as fast, twice as much power) 74S××—— Schottky TTL (for high-frequency uses) 74LS××—— combination of low-power & Schottky, same speed as regular TTL, but at 1/5 the power consumption
CMOS ——Complimentary Metal Oxide Silicon	CMOS ICs use much less power than TTL, plus they are fairly forgiving of "slop" in input voltage —— they're happy with anything between 3 (some, like 1381s, go lower) and 12 volts. CMOS, though, is much more susceptible to damage from static electricity (so get that grounding strap out!).

续表

CMOS ——Complimentary Metal Oxide Silicon	CMOS comes in two flavors, with corresponding numbering schemes: "CD40××" metal gate CMOS, and "74C××" silicon gate CMOS (note that this second subfamily borrows its numbering scheme from TTL ICs). Metal gate CMOS (CD40××) has a rated working voltage of 3～15 V, but can be used down to 2V. Silicon gate CMOS (74C××) logic has a working voltage range of 2～6 V, but can be used to less than 1V. For microwatt power applications you want to use the lowest possible voltage

Numbering systems and IC "sub-families"

Something I've learned to put up with is the mess that is IC numbering systems. One of the more common numbering systems used for CMOS ICs (most often used in BEAM bots) is borrowed from TTL —— that of 74xxxnnn —— here, "xxx" is AC, ACT, HC, or HCT (subfamily); and "nnn" is the specific chip ID.

So, basically, any given chip will come in a whole mess of variations (one per subfamily); if it's any consolation, we only need to be concerned with 4. For any given chip, you'll need to consider the plusses and minuses of two comparisons —— AC vs HC subfamilies, and AC/HC vs ACT/HCT (essentially, CMOS vs. TTL input levels).

AC vs HC

AC/ACT stands for Advanced CMOS Logic (ACL for short). HC/HCT stands for high-speed CMOS Logic (HCL).

The AC and ACT subfamilies are faster than the HC and HCT subfamilies, and draw some more power in some circuits. All chips in the AC* subfamily have lower output resistance than HC* and can sink and source 24 mA at logic levels and up 70 mA (typ) per gate for motor loads. As a result AC* gates can handle more than twice the current of HC* gates (50～70 mA vs. 24 mA). Note, though, that while most HC* chips have a 25 mA limit, the HC* driver chips such as the 74HC240 and the 74HC245 (i.e., buffers) can handle 35 mA per device, and a maximum of 75 mA per chip.

The AC & ACT families also draw about twice as much current as the HC & HCT chips (but we speaking here of microamps, so it's usually not a huge deal).

It is occasionally possible to find (high quality) motors that you can drive directly from an HC chip. For intermittent operation, such as you get with a quadcore, you could drive very efficient (i.e., very low-current) motors directly. You would definitely need a capacitor (say 0.47 μF) across each motor to keep the noise under control.

CMOS vs. TTL inputs

The main difference between AC-and HC-chips vs. ACT- and HCT-chips is that AC/HC chips work with CMOS-level inputs, while ACT/HCT chips work from TTL-level inputs and outputs. AC/HC chips allow a relatively-wide supply-voltage range (2～6 V), and works with

CMOS levels on input and output (i.e., doesn't like inputs or outputs to be ill-defined, prefers close to 0V for low and V_{dd} for high). ACT/HCT works only with a supply voltage of 5V ± 10%, and works with TTL levels on input and output (a valid input is close to 0V for low, and 2.4～5.0 V for high).

Technical Words and Expressions

progression	n.	进行，前进，进步，发展
BEAM bot		主要方式
flavor	n.	特色
slop	n.	不合格
susceptible	adj.	易受影响的
static electricity		静电
numbering scheme		编码方案
subfamily	n.	子系列
consolation	n.	（被）安慰
intermittent	adj.	间歇的，断断续续的
definitely	adv.	明确地

Comprehension

1. For TTL circuits, a logic "1" is usually defined as a signal of about ______, while logic "0" is about ______ above ground.

A. 3.6V, 1V　　B. 5V, 0.7V

C. 2.4V, 0.5V　　D. 12V, 1V

2. Note that the 74HCT* ICs have ______ logic thresholds ______ other TTL chips, allowing them used in a mixed circuits of TTL and HCT logic.

A. the same…as　B. more…than　C. less…than

3. The AC and ACT subfamilies are ______ than the HC and HCT subfamilies, and draw some ______ power in some circuits.

A. faster, less　　B. slower, more

C. faster, more　　D. slower, less

4. You would definitely need a ______ across each motor to keep the noise under control.

A. resistor　　B. capacitor

C. diode　　D. transistor

5. The main difference between AC- and HC-chips vs. ACT- and HCT-chips is that AC/HC chips work with ______ inputs, while ACT/HCT chips work from ______ inputs and outputs.

A. CMOS-level, TTL-level　　B. CMOS-level, CMOS-level

C. TTL-level, TTL-level　　D. TTL-level, CMOS-level

Unit 5 Digital Logic Gates

Introduction to logic gates

Digital logic gates, which are also known as combinational logic gates or simply "logic gates", are digital ICs whose output at any time is determined by the states of its inputs at that time. Since logic gates are digital ICs, their input and output signals can only be in one of two possible digital states, i.e., logic "0" or logic "1". Thus, the logic state in which the output of a logic gate will be put in depends on the logic states of each of its individual inputs.

The primary application of logic gates is to implement "logic" in the flow of digital signals in a digital circuit. Logic in its ordinary sense is defined as a branch of philosophy that deals with what is true and false, based on what other things are true and false. This essentially is the function of logic gates in digital circuits——to determine which outputs will be true or false, given a set of inputs that can either be true (logic "1") or false (logic "0").

The response output (usually denoted by Q) of a logic gate to any combination of inputs may be tabulated into what is known as a truth table. A truth table shows each possible combination of inputs to a logic gate and the combination's corresponding output. Table 1.2, which describes the various types of logic gates, provides a truth table for each of them as well.

Table 1.2 Logic Gates and their Properties

<table>
<tr><th>Gate</th><th>Description</th><th>Truth Table</th></tr>
<tr><td>AND Gate</td><td>The AND gate is a logic gate that gives an output of "1" only when all of its inputs are "1". Thus, its output is "0" whenever at least one of its inputs is "0". Mathematically, $Q = A \cdot B$</td><td><table><tr><th>A</th><th>B</th><th>Output Q</th></tr><tr><td>0</td><td>0</td><td>0</td></tr><tr><td>0</td><td>1</td><td>0</td></tr><tr><td>1</td><td>0</td><td>0</td></tr><tr><td>1</td><td>1</td><td>1</td></tr></table></td></tr>
<tr><td>OR Gate</td><td>The OR gate is a logic gate that gives an output of "0" only when all of its inputs are "0". Thus, its output is "1" whenever at least one of its inputs is "1". Mathematically, $Q = A + B$</td><td><table><tr><th>A</th><th>B</th><th>Output Q</th></tr><tr><td>0</td><td>0</td><td>0</td></tr><tr><td>0</td><td>1</td><td>1</td></tr><tr><td>1</td><td>0</td><td>1</td></tr><tr><td>1</td><td>1</td><td>1</td></tr></table></td></tr>
<tr><td>NOT Gate</td><td>The NOT gate is a logic gate that gives an output that is opposite the state of its input. Mathematically, $Q = \overline{A}$</td><td><table><tr><th>A</th><th>Output Q</th></tr><tr><td>0</td><td>1</td></tr><tr><td>1</td><td>0</td></tr></table></td></tr>
<tr><td>NAND Gate</td><td>The NAND gate is an AND gate with a NOT gate at its end. Thus, for the same combination of inputs, the output of a NAND gate will be opposite that of an AND gate. Mathematically, $Q = \overline{A \cdot B}$</td><td><table><tr><th>A</th><th>B</th><th>Output Q</th></tr><tr><td>0</td><td>0</td><td>1</td></tr><tr><td>0</td><td>1</td><td>1</td></tr><tr><td>1</td><td>0</td><td>1</td></tr><tr><td>1</td><td>1</td><td>0</td></tr></table></td></tr>
</table>

续表

Gate	Description	Truth Table
NOR Gate	The NOR gate is an OR gate with a NOT gate at its end. Thus, for the same combination of inputs, the output of a NOR gate will be opposite that of an OR gate. Mathematically, $Q=\overline{A+B}$	A B Output Q 0 0 1 0 1 0 1 0 0 1 1 0
EXOR Gate	The EXOR gate (for "EXclusive OR" gate) is a logic gate that gives an output of "1" when only one of its inputs is "1"	A B Output Q 0 0 0 0 1 1 1 0 1 1 1 0

Interestingly, the operation of logic gates in relation to one another may be represented and analyzed using a branch of mathematics called Boolean Algebra which, like the common algebra, deals with manipulation of expressions to solve or simplify equations[1]. Expressions used in Boolean Algebra are called, well, Boolean expressions.

Kinds of logic gates

There are several kinds of logic gates, each one of which performs a specific function. These are the: ① AND gate; ② OR gate; ③ NOT gate; ④ NAND gate; ⑤ NOR gate; and ⑥ EXOR gate. Table 1.2 above presents these and their characteristics.

Logic gates may be thought of as a combination of switches. For instance, the AND gate, whose output can only be "1" if all its inputs are "1", may be represented by switches connected in series, with each switch representing an input. All the switches need to be activated and conducting (equivalent to all the inputs of the AND gate being at logic "1"), for current to flow through the circuit load (equivalent to the output of the AND gate being at logic "1").

An OR gate, on the other hand, may be represented by switches connected in parallel, since only one of these parallel switches need to turn on in order to energize the circuit load.

In Boolean Algebra, the AND operation is represented by multiplication, since the only way that the result of multiplication of a combination of 1's and 0's will be equal to "1" if all its inputs are equal to "1". A single "0" among the multipliers will result in a product that's equal to "0". The Boolean expression for "A AND B" is similar to the expression commonly used for multiplication, i.e., $A \cdot B$.

The OR operation, on the other hand, is represented by addition in Booelean Algebra. This is because the only way to make the result of the addition operation equal to "0" is to make all the inputs equal to "0", which basically describes an "OR" operation. The Boolean expression for "A OR B" is therefore A+B.

The NOT operation is usually denoted by a line above the symbol or expression that is being negated: $\overline{A}=\text{NOT}(A)$. The NAND operation is simply an AND operation followed by a NOT operation. The NOR operation is simply an OR operation followed by a NOT operation. The symbols used for logic gates in electronic circuit diagrams are shown in Fig.1.16.

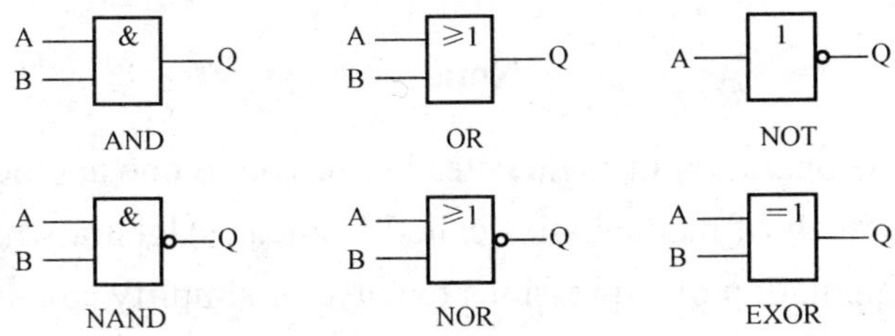

Fig.1.16 Logic gate symbols

One of the most useful theorems used in Boolean Algebra is De Morgan's Theorem, which states how an AND operation can be converted into an OR operation, as long as a NOT operation is available[2]. De Morgan's Theorem is usually expressed in two equations as follows:

$$\overline{A \bullet B} = \overline{A} + \overline{B}$$

and

$$\overline{A + B} = \overline{A} \bullet \overline{B}$$

De Morgan's Theorem has a practical implication in digital electronics —— a designer may eliminate the need to add more ICs to the design unnecessarily, simply by substituting gates with the equivalent combination of other gates whenever possible. Since NAND and NOR gates can be used as NOT gates, de Morgan's Theorem basically implies that any Boolean operation may be simulated with nothing but NAND or NOR gates. This is why NAND and NOR gates are also called universal gates.

Technical Words and Expressions

philosophy [fi'lɔsəfi] n. 哲学
tabulate ['tæbjuleit] vt. 把……制成表格
truth table 真值表
AND [ænd] n. 与（计算机逻辑运算的一种，或称逻辑乘法）
OR [ɔː,ə] n. 或（逻辑运算的一种）
NOT [nɔt] n. 非（逻辑运算的一种）
NAND [nænd] n. 与非
NOR [nɔː] n. 或非
Boolean Algebra 布尔代数
manipulation [məˌnipju'leiʃən] n. 操作；控制；处理；计算，运算
activate ['æktiveit] vt. 开（起）动，触发
multiplication [ˌmʌltipli'keiʃən] n. 乘法
multiplier ['mʌltiplaiə] n. 乘数
negate [ni'geit] vt. 求反，非
implication [ˌimpli'keiʃən] n. 含意，暗示

Notes

[1] Interestingly, the operation of logic gates in relation to one another may be represented and analyzed using a branch of mathematics called Boolean Algebra which, like the common algebra, deals with manipulation of expressions to solve or simplify equations.

译文为：有趣的是，逻辑门与另一个逻辑门之间的运算可以表示出来，并可使用数学的分支——布尔代数来分析。布尔代数，像普通代数一样，可以对要求的表达式进行运算或对等式进行简化。

句中 using a branch of mathematics called Boolean Algebra 作状语，which 引导限制性定语从句，修饰 Boolean Algebra。

[2] One of the most useful theorems used in Boolean Algebra is De Morgan's Theorem, which states how an AND operation can be converted into an OR operation, as long as a NOT operation is available.

译文为：布尔代数中最有用的定理之一为摩根定理，该定理表达了运用非运算，如何将与运算转化为或运算。

句中 as long as 引导条件状语从句。

Exercises

Ⅰ. Mark the following statements with T (true) or F (false) according to the text.

1. The primary application of logic gates is to implement "logic" in the flow of digital signals in a digital circuit. (   )

2. A truth table shows some important combinations of inputs to a logic gate and the combination's corresponding output. (   )

3. An AND gate, on the other hand, may be represented by switches connected in parallel. (   )

4. The OR operation, on the other hand, is represented by multiplication in Booelean Algebra. (   )

5. One of the most useful theorems used in Boolean Algebra is De Morgan's Theorem, which states how an AND operation can be converted into an OR operation, as long as a NOT operation is available. (   )

Ⅱ. Complete the following sentences.

1. The response output (usually denoted by Q) of a logic gate to any combination of inputs may be tabulated into what is known as ______.

2. Expressions used in Boolean Algebra are called, well, ______.

3. Logic gates may be thought of as a combination of ______.

4. The NOR operation is simply an OR operation followed by a ______ operation.

5. A designer may eliminate the need to add more ICs to the design unnecessarily, simply by ______ gates with the ______ combination of other gates whenever possible.

Reading 5 Binary Numbers

Electronic circuits count in binary. This is the simplest possible counting system because it uses just two digits, 0 and 1, exactly like logic signals where 0 represents false and 1 represents true. The terms low and high are also used for 0 and 1 respectively as shown in Table 1.3.

Table 1.3 **Logic states**

Logic states	
True	False
1	0
High	Low
$+U_s$	0V
On	Off

Counting one, two, three, four, five in binary: 1, 10, 11, 100, 101.

Binary numbers rapidly become very long as the count increases and this makes them difficult for us to read at a glance. Fortunately it is rarely necessary to read more than 4 binary digits at a time in counting circuits.

In a binary number each digit represents a multiple of two (1, 2, 4, 8, 16 etc.), in the same way that each digit in decimal represents a multiple of ten (1, 10, 100, 1000 etc.).

For example 10110110 in binary equals 182 in decimal:

Digit value:	128	64	32	16	8	4	2	1
Binary number:	1	0	1	1	0	1	1	0
Decimal value:	128+0+32+16+0+4+2+0=182							

Bits, bytes and nibbles

Each binary digit is called a bit, so 10110110 is an 8-bit number.

A block of 8 bits is called a byte and it can hold a maximum number of 11111111 = 255 in decimal. Computers and PIC microcontrollers work with blocks of 8 bits. Two (or more) bytes make a word, for example PICs work with a 16-bit word (two bytes) which can hold a maximum number of 65535.

A block of 4 bits is called a nibble (half a byte!) and it can hold a maximum number of 1111 = 15 in decimal. Many counting circuits work with blocks of 4 bits because this number of bits is required to count up to 9 in decimal. (The maximum number with 3 bits is only 7).

Hexadecimal (base 16)

Hexadecimal (often just called "hex") is base 16 counting with 16 digits. It starts with the decimal digits 0～9, then continues with letters A (10), B (11), C (12), D (13), E (14) and F (15). Each hexadecimal digit is equivalent to 4 binary digits, making conversion between the two systems relatively easy. You may find hexadecimal used with PICs and computer systems but it is not generally used in simple counting circuits.

Example: 10110110 binary = B6 hexadecimal = 182 decimal.

Technical Words and Expressions

binary	adj. & n.	二进位的，二元的；二进制
counting system		计数系统
decimal	adj. & n.	十进位的；十进制
bit	n.	（二进制）位，比特
byte	n.	（二进制的）字节
nibble	n.	四位字节，半字节
block	n.	组
hexadecimal	adj. & n.	十六进制的；十六进制
conversion	n.	转变，变换

Comprehension

1. Electronic circuits count in ______.
   A. Hexadecimal B. octal C. decimal D. binary
2. 110110 in binary equals ______.
   A. 182 B. 128 C. 56 D. 54
3. In a binary number each digit represents a multiple of ______.
   A. two B. ten C. eight D. sixteen
4. Each binary digit is called a ______, a block of 8 ______ is called a ______, A block of 4 ______ is called a ______.
   A. Bit, bits, nibble, bits, byte B. Bit, byte, bit, bytes, nibble
   C .Bits, bit, byte, bits, nibble D. Bits, bits, byte, bits, nibble
5. ______ (often just called "hex") is base 16 counting with 16 digits.
   A. Hexadecimal B. Octal C. Decimal D. Binary

Unit 6 Flip-flop

In digital circuits, a flip-flop is a term referring to an electronic circuit (a bistable multivibrator) that has two stable states and thereby is capable of serving as one bit of memory. A flip-flop is usually controlled by one or two control signals and/or a gate or clock signal. The output often includes the complement as well as the normal output. As flip-flops are implemented electronically, they require power and ground connections.

Implementation

Flip-flops can be either simple (transparent) or clocked. Simple flip-flops can be built around a pair of cross-coupled inverting elements: vacuum tubes, bipolar transistors, field effect transistors, inverters, and inverting logic gates have all been used in practical circuits —— perhaps augmented by some gating mechanism (an enable/disable input). The more advanced clocked (or non-transparent) devices are specially designed for synchronous (time-discrete) systems; such devices therefore ignore its inputs except at the transition of a dedicated clock signal (known as clocking, pulsing, or strobing). This causes the flip-flop to either change or retain its output signal based upon the values of the input signals at the transition. Some flip-flops change output on the rising edge of the clock, others on the falling edge.

Clocked flip-flops are typically implemented as master-slave devices where two basic flip-flops (plus some additional logic) collaborate to make it insensitive to spikes and noise between the short clock transitions[1]; they nevertheless also often include asynchronous clear or set inputs which may be used to change the current output independent of the clock.

Flip-flops can be further divided into types that have found common applicability in both asynchronous and clocked sequential systems: the SR ("set-reset"), D ("data" or "delay"), T ("toggle"), and JK types are the common ones; all of which may be synthesized from (most) other types by a few logic gates. The behavior of a particular type can be described by what is termed the characteristic equation, which derives the "next" (i.e., after the next clock pulse) output, Qnext, in terms of the input signal (s) and/or the current output, Q.

Set-Reset flip-flops (SR flip-flops)

The fundamental latch is the simple SR flip-flop (Fig.1.17) , where S and R stand for set and reset respectively. It can be constructed from a pair of cross-coupled NOR logic gates. The stored bit is present on the output marked Q.

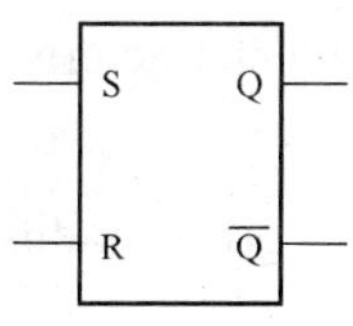

Fig.1.17 The symbol for an SR latch

Normally, in storage mode, the S and R inputs are both low, and feedback maintains the Q and $\overline{Q}$ outputs in a constant state, with $\overline{Q}$ the complement of Q[2]. If S (Set) is pulsed high while R is held low, then the Q output is forced high, and stays high even after S returns low; similarly, if R (Reset) is pulsed high while S is held low, then the Q output is forced low, and stays low even after R returns low (Table 1.4).

Table 1.4 SR Flip-Flop operation

Characteristic table			Excitation table				
S	R	Action	Q(t)	Q(t+1)	S	R	Action
0	0	Keep state	0	0	0	X	No change
0	1	Q = 0	0	1	1	0	Set
1	0	Q = 1	1	0	0	1	Reset
1	1	Unstable combination, see race condition	1	1	X	0	No change

("X"denotes a Don't care condition; meaning the signal is irrelevant.)

JK flip-flop

The JK flip-flop (Fig. 1.18) augments the behavior of the SR flip-flop (J=Set, K=Reset) by interpreting the S = R = 1 condition as a "flip" or toggle command. Specifically, the combination J = 1, K = 0 is a command to set the flip-flop; the combination J = 0, K = 1 is a command to reset the flip-flop; and the combination J = K = 1 is a command to toggle the flip-flop, i.e., change its output to the logical complement of its current value. Setting J = K = 0 does NOT result in a D flip-flop, but rather, will hold the current state. To synthesize a D flip-flop, simply set K equal to the complement of J. The JK flip-flop is therefore a universal flip-flop, because it can be configured to work as an SR flip-flop, a D flip-flop, or a T flip-flop. NOTE: The flip flop is positive edge triggered (Clock Pulse) as seen in the timing diagram (Fig.1.19).

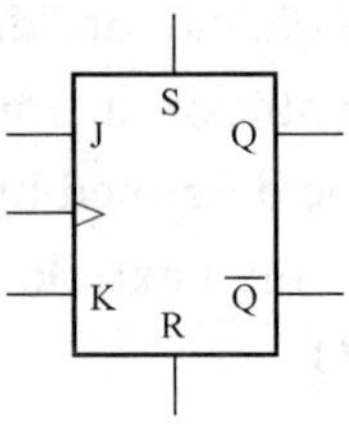

Fig.1.18 A circuit symbol for a JK flip-flop

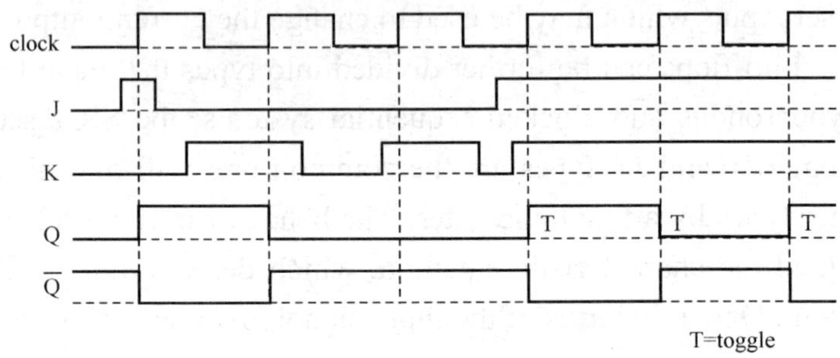

Fig.1.19 JK flip-flop timing diagram

The characteristic equation of the JK flip-flop is:

$$Q_{next}=J\overline{Q}+\overline{K}Q$$

and the corresponding truth table is Table 1.5.

Table 1.5 **JK Flip-Flop operation**

Characteristic table				Excitation table				
J	K	Q_{next}	Comment	Q	Q_{next}	J	K	Comment
0	0	Q_{prev}	hold state	0	0	0	X	No change
0	1	0	reset	0	1	1	X	Set
1	0	Q = 1	set	1	0	X	1	Reset
1	1	$\overline{Q_{prev}}$	toggle	1	1	X	0	No change

Uses

- A single flip-flop can be used to store one bit, or binary digit, of data. See preset.
- Any one of the flip-flop types can be used to build any of the others.
- Many logic synthesis tools will not use any other type than D flip-flop and D latch.
- Many FPGA devices contain only edge-triggered D flip-flops.
- The data contained in several flip-flops may represent the state of a sequencer, the value of a counter, an ASCII character in a computer's memory or any other piece of

information.

- One use is to build finite state machines from electronic logic. The flip-flops remember the machine's previous state, and digital logic uses that state to calculate the next state.

Flip-flop integrated circuits

Integrated circuit (ICs) exist that provide one or more flip-flops. For example, the 7473 Dual JK Master-Slave Flip-flop or the 74374, an octal D Flip-flop, in the 7400 series.

Technical Words and Expressions

flip-flop			触发器
bistable	[bai'steibl]	adj.	双稳（态）的
multivibrator	['mʌltivai'breitə]	n.	［无］多谐振荡器
complement	['kɔmplimənt]	n.	反码
cross-coupled			交叉耦合的
augment	[ɔː g'ment]	v.	增加，增大
gating mechanism			门控机制
enable	[i'neibl]	n.	使能
disable	[dis'eibl]	n.	禁止
rising edge			上升沿
falling edge			下降沿
clear	[kliə]	adj.	清零
set	[set]	n. & v.	置位
reset	['riːset]	v.	复位
toggle	['tɔgl]	n.	转换
synthesize	['sinθisaiz]	v.	综合，合成
latch	[lætʃ]	n.	锁存器
flip	[flip]	n.	翻转
command	[kə'mɑːnd]	n.	指令
trigger	['trigə]	vt.	触发
character	['kæriktə]	n.	字符
sequencer	['siːkwənsə]	n.	程序装置
finite state machine			有限状态机
master-slave flip-flop			主从触发器
octal	['ɔktl]	adj.	八进制的

Notes

[1] Clocked flip-flops are typically implemented as master-slave devices where two basic flip-flops (plus some additional logic) collaborate to make it insensitive to spikes and noise

between the short clock transitions.

译文为：钟控型触发器一般为主一从触发器，主从触发器由两个基本触发器组成，使得触发器对短时钟跃变期间所出现的尖峰和噪声不敏感。

where 引导定语从句，to make…在句中作目的状语。

[2] Normally, in storage mode, the S and R inputs are both low, and feedback maintains the Q and $\overline{Q}$ outputs in a constant state, with $\overline{Q}$ the complement of Q.

译文为：通常在存储模式，S 和 R 输入端都为低电平，反馈维持 Q 和 $\overline{Q}$ 输出恒定，$\overline{Q}$ 为 Q 的反码。

该句为并列句，在句中 with $\overline{Q}$ the complement of Q 作句子的状语。

Exercises

Ⅰ. Mark the following statements with T (true) or F (false) according to the text.

1. In digital circuits, a flip-flop is a term referring to an electronic circuit (a bistable multivibrator) that has only one stable states and thereby is capable of serving as one bit of memory. ( )

2. Clocked flip-flops are typically implemented as master-slave devices where two basic flip-flops (plus some additional logic) collaborate to make it insensitive to spikes and noise between the short clock transitions. ( )

3. The fundamental latch is the simple SR flip-flop, where S and R all stand for set. ( )

4. The JK flip-flop augments the behavior of the SR flip-flop (J=Set, K=Reset) by interpreting the S = R = 1 condition as a "flip" or toggle command. Specifically. ( )

5. To synthesize a D flip-flop, simply set K equal to the complement of J. ( )

Ⅱ. Complete the following sentences.

1. Some flip-flops change output on the rising edge of the clock, others on the ______ edge.

2. Similarly, if R (Reset) is pulsed high while S is held low, then the Q output is forced ______, and stays ______ even after R returns low.

3. To synthesize a D flip-flop, simply set K equal to the ______ of J.

4. The flip flop is ______ edge triggered (Clock Pulse) as seen in the timing diagram shown in Fig.1.19.

5. Many logic synthesis tools will not use any other type than ______ and ______.

Reading 6 Digital Counters

A digital counter, or simply counter, is a semiconductor device that is used for counting the number of times that a digital event has occurred. The counter's output is indexed by one LSB every time the counter is clocked.

A simple implementation of a 4-bit counter is shown in Fig.1.20, which consists of 4 stages of cascaded J-K flip-flops. This is a binary counter, since the output is in binary system format, i.e., only two digits are used to represent the count, i.e., "1" and "0". With only 4 bits, it can only count up to "1111", or decimal number 15.

As one can see from Fig.1.20, the J and K inputs of all the flip-flops are tied to "1", so that they will toggle between states every time they are clocked. Also, the output of each flip-flop in the counter is used to clock the next flip-flop. As a result, the succeeding flip-flop toggles between "1" and "0" at only half the frequency as the flip-flop before it.

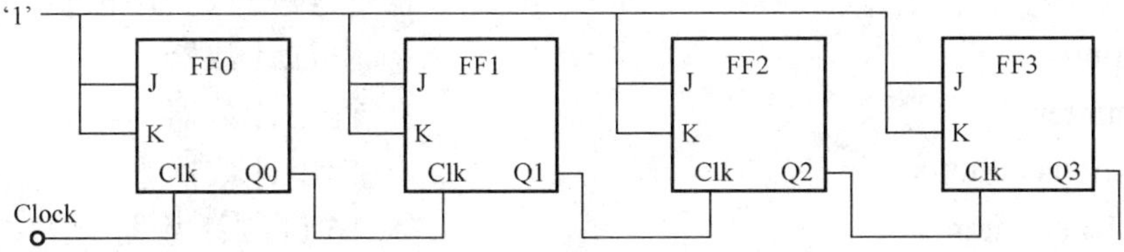

Fig.1.20 A simple ripple counter consisting of J-K flip-flops

Thus, in Fig.1.20's 4-bit example, the last flip-flop will only toggle after the first flip-flop has already toggled 8 times. This type of binary counter is known as a "serial", "ripple", or "asynchronous" counter. The name "asynchronous" comes from the fact that this counter's flip-flops are not being clocked at the same time.

A 4-bit counter, which has 16 unique states that it can count through, is also called a modulo-16 counter, or mod-16 counter. By definition, a modulo-k or base-k counter is one that returns to its initial state after k cycles of the input waveform. A counter that has N flip-flops is a modulo 2^N counter.

An asynchronous counter has a serious drawback —— its speed is limited by the cumulative propagation times of the cascaded flip-flops. A counter that has N flip-flops, each of which has a propagation time t, must therefore wait for a duration equal to $N \times t$ before it can undergo another transition clocking.

A better counter, therefore, is one whose flip-flops are clocked at the same time. Such a counter is known as a synchronous counter. A simple 4-bit synchronous counter is shown in Fig.1.21.

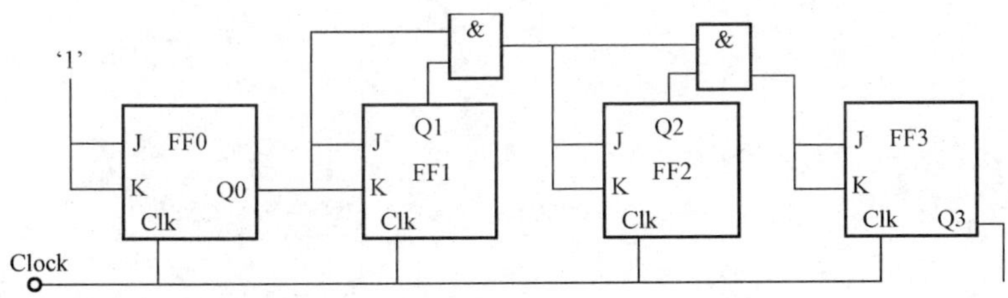

Fig.1.21 A simple synchronous counter consisting of J-K flip-flops and AND gates

Not all counters with N flip-flops are designed to go through all its 2^N possible states of count. In fact, digital counters can be used to output decimal numbers by using logic gates to force them to reset when the output becomes equal to decimal 10. Counters used in this manner are said to be in binary-coded decimal (BCD).

Technical Words and Expressions

counter	n.	计数器
implementation	n.	执行，履行；落实
stage	n.	[电子学] 级
digit	n.	阿拉伯数字，位数
serial counter		串行计数器
ripple counter		行波计数器
asynchronous counter		异步计数器
modulo-16 counter		16 进制计数器
drawback	n.	缺点，障碍
cumulative	adj.	累积的
propagation	n.	传播，传输
synchronous counter		同步计数器
binary-coded decimal	n.	二—十进制

Comprehension

1. With only 4 bits, a binary counter can only count up to "_______" in binary.

A. 1110　　B. 1111　　C. 1011　　D. 1001

2. The counter shown in Fig.1.21 is ______ counter.

A. serial　　B. ripple　　C. asynchronous　　D. synchronous

3. A better counter, therefore, is one whose flip-flops are clocked at the same time. Such a counter is known as a ______ counter.

A. serial　　B. ripple　　C. asynchronous　　D. synchronous

4. In fact, digital counters can be used to output decimal numbers by using logic gates to force them to reset when the output becomes equal to decimal ______.

A. 9　　B. 8　　C. 5　　D. 10

Chapter 2

Electrical Machines and Motor Control

Unit 7 Motor and DC Motor

Fundamentals of motors

An electric motor is a machine used to convert electrical energy to mechanical energy. Electric motors are extremely important to modern-day life, being used in many different places, e.g., vacuum cleaners, dishwashers, computer printers, fax machines, video cassette recorders, machine tools, printing presses, automobiles, subway systems, sewage treatment plants and water pumping stations.

The major physical principles behind the operation of an electric motor are known as Ampere's law and Faraday's law (Fig.2.1). The first states that an electrical conductor sitting in a magnetic field will experience a force if any current flowing through the conductor has a component at right angles to that field[1]. Reversal of either the current or the magnetic field will produce a force acting in the opposite direction. The second principle states that if a conductor is moved through a magnetic field, then any component of motion perpendicular to that field will generate a potential difference between the ends of the conductor.

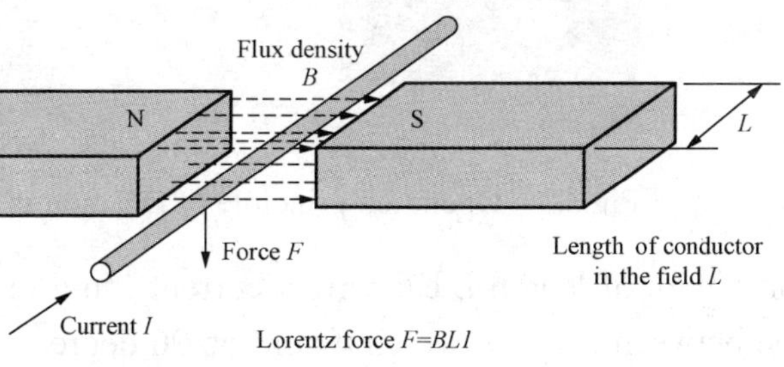

Fig.2.1 Ampere's law and Faraday's law

An electric motor consists of two essential elements. The first, a static component which consists of magnetic materials and electrical conductors to generate magnetic fields of a desired shape, is known as the stator[2]. The second, which also is made from magnetic and electrical conductors to generate shaped magnetic fields which interact with the fields generated by the stator, is known as the rotor. The rotor comprises the moving component of the motor, having a rotating shaft to connect to the machine being driven and some means of maintaining an electrical contact between the rotor and the motor housing (typically, carbon brushes pushed against slip rings)[3]. In operation, the electrical current supplied to the motor is used to generate magnetic fields in both the rotor and the stator. These fields push against each other with the result that the rotor experiences a torque and consequently rotates.

Electrical motors fall into two broad categories, depending on the type of electrical power applied-direct current (DC) and alternating current (AC) motors.

The first DC electrical motor was demonstrated by Michael Faraday in England in 1821. Since the only available electrical sources were DC, the first commercially available motors were of the DC type, becoming popular in the 1880s. These motors were used for both low power and high power applications, such as electric street railways. It was not until the 1890s, with the availability of AC electrical power that the AC motor was developed, primarily by the Westinghouse and General Electric corporations.

DC motor

A simple DC motor has a coil of wire that can rotate in a magnetic field. The current in the coil is supplied via two brushes that make moving contact with a split ring. The coil lies in a steady magnetic field. The forces in Fig.2.2 exerted on the current-carrying wires create a torque on the coil.

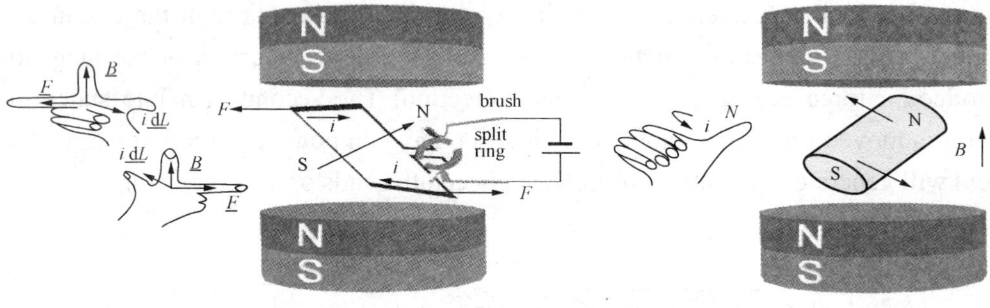

(a) (b)

Fig.2.2 Operation principle of DC motors

The force F on a wire of length L carrying a current i in a magnetic field B is iLB times the sine of the angle between B and i, which would be 90 degree，if the field were uniformly vertical[4]. The direction of F comes from the right hand rule, as shown in Fig. 2.2 (a). The two forces shown in Fig. 2.2 (a) are equal and opposite, but they are displaced vertically, so they exert a torque. (The forces on the other two sides of the coil act along the same line and so exert no torque.)

The coil can also be considered as a magnetic dipole, or a little electromagnet, as indicated by the arrow NS in Fig. 2.2 (b): curl the fingers of your right hand in the direction of the current, and your thumb is the North Pole. In the sketch at right, the electromagnet formed by the coil of the rotor is represented as a permanent magnet, and the same torque (North attracts South) is seen to be that acting to align the central magnet.

Note the effect of the brushes on the split ring. When the plane of the rotating coil reaches horizontal, the brushes will break contact (nothing is lost, because this is the point of zero torque anyway —— the forces act inwards). The angular momentum of the coil carries it past this break point and the current then flows in the opposite direction, which reverses the magnetic dipole. So, after passing the break point, the rotor continues to turn anticlockwise and starts to align in the opposite direction.

The torque generated over a cycle varies with the vertical separation of the two forces. It therefore depends on the sine of the angle between the axis of the coil and field. However, because of the split ring, it is always in the same sense. Fig.2.3 shows its variation in time.

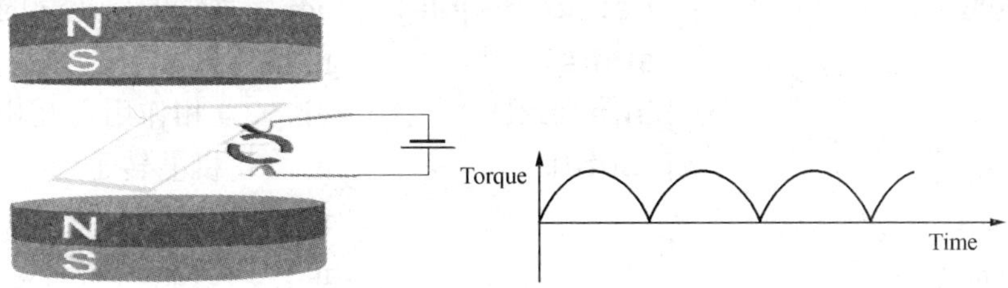

Fig.2.3 Torque variation of DC motor in time

Types of DC motor

DC motors are more common than we may think. A car may have as many as 20 DC motors to drive fans, seats, and windows. They come in three different types, classified according to the electrical circuit used. In the shunt motor, the armature and field windings are connected in parallel, and so the currents through each are relatively independent. The current through the field winding can be controlled with a field rheostat (variable resistor), thus allowing a wide variation in the motor speed. This type of motor is used for driving machine tools or fans, which require a wide range of speeds.

In the series motor, the field winding is connected in series with the armature winding, resulting in a very high starting torque since both the armature current and field strength run at their maximum. However, once the armature starts to rotate, the counter EMF reduces the current in the circuit, thus reducing the field strength. The series motor is used where a large starting torque is required, such as in automobile starter motors, cranes, and hoists.

The compound motor is a combination of the series and shunt motors, having parallel and series field windings. This type of motor has a high starting torque and the ability to vary the speed and is used in situations requiring both these properties such as punch presses, conveyors and elevators.

Technical Words and Expressions

motor	['məutə]	n.	发动机，电动机
convert	[kən'və:t]	vt.	使转变，转换……
vacuum cleaner		n.	真空吸尘器
dishwasher	['diʃwɔʃə(r)]	n.	洗碗机
machine tool		n.	机床

sewage treatment plant	[ˈsju(ː)idʒ]	n.	污水（处理）厂
water pumping station		n.	水泵站
printing press		n.	印刷机
automobile	[ˈɔːtəməubiːl]	n.	汽车，小汽车
Ampere's law /Faraday's law		n.	安培定律/法拉第定律
magnetic field		n.	磁场
perpendicular	[ˌpəːpənˈdikjulə]	adj.	垂直的，正交的
stator	[ˈsteitə]	n.	［机］定子
interact	[ˌintərˈækt]	vi.	互相作用，互相影响
rotor	[ˈrəutə]	n.	［机］转子
rotating shaft		n.	转轴
motor housing		n.	机壳
carbon brush		n.	炭刷
slip ring		n.	滑环
street railway		n.	（市内）电车道
General Electric corporations		n.	通用电气公司［美］
coil of wire		n.	线圈，线卷，线匝
exert	[igˈzəːt]	vt.	尽（力），施加（压力等）
torque	[tɔːk]	n.	扭矩，转矩
vertical	[ˈvəːtikəl]	adj.	垂直的，直立的
right hand rule		n.	右手定则
magnetic dipole		n.	磁偶极子
electromagnet	[ilektrəuˈmægnit]	n.	电磁体，电磁铁
permanent magnet		n.	［物］永久磁铁
horizontal	[ˌhɔriˈzɔntl]	adj.	地平线的，水平的
angular momentum		n.	角动量
shunt motor		n.	并励［并绕，分激］电动机
armature	[ˈɑːmətjuə]	n.	电枢，（电动机、发电机的）转子
field winding		n.	励磁绕组
field rheostat		n.	励磁变阻器
series motor		n.	串激［绕］电动机
starting torque		n.	启动力矩，启动转矩
armature current		n.	电枢电流
compound motor		n.	复励电机
punch press		n.	冲床

Notes

[1] The first states that an electrical conductor sitting in a magnetic field will experience a

force if any current flowing through the conductor has a component at right angles to that field.

译文为：安培定律指出：对于处在磁场中的带电导体，如果流过导体的电流的某一分量与磁场成直角，那么该导体将受到力的作用。

这是一个宾语从句：the first 指代 Ampere's law，为主语；state 在此取“陈述，规定，指出”的意思，为谓语；that 引导了宾语从句。其中 sitting in a magnetic field 和 flowing through the conductor 为现在分词作定语分别修饰 conductor 和 current。

[2] The first, a static component which consists of magnetic materials and electrical conductors to generate magnetic fields of a desired shape, is known as the stator.

译文为：第一部分被称为定子，是由导磁材料和导线组成的静止部件，用来产生所需形状的磁场的。

该句的主干是“The first（指代第一部分）is known as the stator”；中间部分“a static component”与“The first”并列，which 引导了一个定语从句。

[3] The rotor comprises the moving component of the motor, having a rotating shaft to connect to the machine being driven and some means of maintaining an electrical contact between the rotor and the motor housing (typically, carbon brushes pushed against slip rings).

译文为：转子为电动机中的运动部分，转子有一根转轴与被驱动机械相连，并有一些装置维持转子与电动机外壳间的电气接触（通常是炭刷与滑环的接触）。

“having a rotating shaft… and some means…”在句中作状语。

[4] The force F on a wire of length L carrying a current i in a magnetic field B is iLB times the sine of the angle between B and i, which would be 90 degree，if the field were uniformly vertical.

译文为：长为 L 且所带电流为 i 的导线在磁场强度为 B 的磁场中所受的力 F 等于 iLB 乘上 B 与 i 间夹角的正弦，如果磁场是均匀垂线，那么 B 与 i 夹角为 90 度。

主语为“The force F on a wire of length L carrying a current i in a magnetic field B”。从句“which would be 90 degree，if the field were uniformly vertical”为 the angle 的非限定性定语从句，该从句中又包含了一个 if 引导的条件状语从句。

Exercises

Ⅰ. Mark the following statements with T (true) or F (false) according to the text.

1. An electric motor is a machine used to convert mechanical energy to electrical energy. (　　)

2. Faraday's law states that an electrical conductor sitting in a magnetic field will experience a force if any current flowing through the conductor has a component at right angles to that field. (　)

3. The force F on a wire of length L carrying a current i in a magnetic field B is iLB. (　　)

4. The first DC electrical motor was demonstrated by Ampere in England in 1821. (　　)

5. In the series motor, the armature winding is connected in series with the field winding. (　　)

Ⅱ. Complete the following sentences.

1. The major physical principles behind the operation of an electric motor are known as ______ and ______.

2. An electric motor consists of two essential elements. The first, a static component which consists of magnetic materials and electrical conductors to generate ______ of a desired shape, is known as the ______. The second is known as the ______.

3. A simple DC motor has ______ that can rotate in a magnetic field. The current in the coil is supplied via two ______ that make moving contact with ______. The coil lies in a steady ______. The forces exerted on the current-carrying wires create a ______ on the coil.

4. When the plane of the ______ coil reaches horizontal, the brushes will ______ (nothing is lost, because this is the point of ______ anyway — the forces act inwards). The ______ of the coil carries it past this break point and the current then flows in the opposite direction, which reverses the ______.

5. In the ______, the armature and field windings are connected in ______, and so the currents through each are relatively independent.

Reading 7 Brushless DC Motors

Instead of having the magnets on the stationary casing and the windings on the rotor, we could put the magnets on the rotor and the windings on the stator. That way, we won't need brushes at all because the winding is stationary. However, now we need to find a way to switch the current through the windings at the right moment to ensure the torque on the rotor is always in the same direction. In a conventional motor, this happens automatically as the commutator acts as mechanical switch. With a brushless motor, we need some way to sense the position of the rotor, and then electronically switch the current so it's going the right way through the right winding.

Brushless motors are found in computer hard drives, CD and DVD players, and in anything else where efficiency and reliability are more important than price. As the cost of electronics continues to come down, perhaps one day all DC motors will be built this way.

Advantages: no brushes, simple, efficient, windings are attached to the casing, and easier to cool.

Disadvantages: requires complex drive electronics.

In fact, brushes are bad news. True, they're a clever way to ensure that, as the rotor turns, the current is automatically switched around the windings to ensure the motor keeps turning. However, everything else about them is bad: they are noisy, create friction, generate electrical interference (because of the sparking) and reduce efficiency (because there will always be a voltage drop across the brushes). Not only that, but they eventually wear out. With modern electronics, we can instead sense the position of the rotor (for example, with a Hall-effect device), then switch the current with, for example, a MOSFET transistor.

This is a fan (Fig.2.4) that spent most of its life inside a computer keeping the microprocessor cool. It runs off 12 volts DC and has a brushless motor, as it thoughtfully explains with large friendly letters on the label.

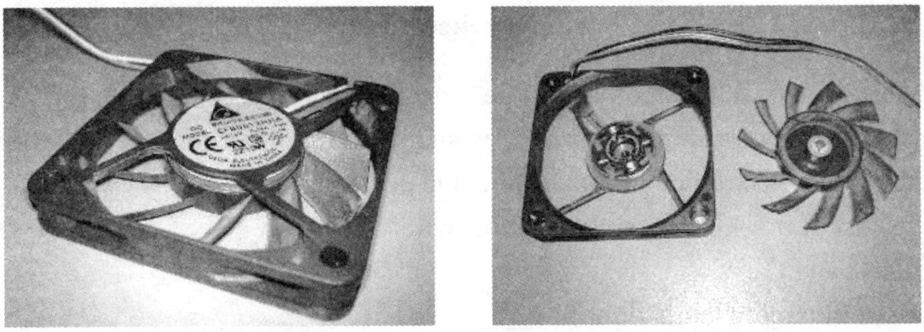

Fig.2.4 A fan with a brushless motor

As promised, the magnets are on the rotor (with fan blades attached) in a ring around the outside of the hub. By "feeling" them by using a small compass as a probe, we find that there are four poles, running N-S-N-S around the ring.

The "stator", in the centre, has four small coils with shaped pole pieces to create a strong magnetic field next to the rotor. Depending on which director the current flows through each coil, it will attract or repel a north pole. So, all we have to do is to keep switching the direction of current flow through the coils in synchronization with the rotation of the magnets, and we'll keep exerting a torque that keeps the fan turning.

Now we've peeled the label off and can see the electronics that does the switching. It consists of a single integrated circuit and a few small capacitors, so it's actually not all that complex! If we google the part number of the chip (LB1962M), we find it is a "*Fan motor single phase full-wave driver*", which I guess is reassuring.

But how does the motor know the exact moment that the magnet has passed one pole, and therefore that it's time to reverse the current flow? There are three techniques commonly used:

- Hall-effect sensors. This is a neat, non-contact way of knowing where the magnets are.
- Back EMF. This is even neater. We don't use sensors at all, but use the fact that the magnet moving past the coil will induce a voltage in it, and use this voltage to tell us where the magnet is.
- Don't bother. For the ultimate minimalist approach, just keep switching the coils in sequence and assume the rotor will keep up. For motors with a small load that is well defined (e.g., a fan), this works pretty well.

Technical Words and Expressions

brushless adj. 无刷的

friction n. 摩擦，摩擦力

synchronization n. 同步

reassuring	adj.	可靠的
Hall-effect sensor		霍耳传感器
back EMF		反电动势

Comprehension

1. Perhaps one day all DC motors will be brushless motors, because ______.
   A. brushless motors are more efficiency and reliability than conventional motors
   B. the cost of electronics continues to come down
   C. the cost of brushless motors comes down
   D. both A and C
2. which of the following is right? ______.
   A. Brushless motors are only found in computer hard drives, CD and DVD players
   B. With a brushless motor, we have to measure the position of the rotor
   C. With a brushless motor, the magnets are on the stationary casing and the windings are on the rotor
   D. Brushless motors always switch direction of the torque on the rotor
3. Brushes are bad news, because ______.
   A. they are noisy and create friction, generate electrical interference and increase efficiency
   B. they ensure the motor keeps turning
   C. one day they will be out of workout
   D. all above
4. LB1962M is ______.
   A. a "Fan motor there phase full-wave driver"
   B. a amplifier used in a fan motor
   C. a "Fan motor single phase full-wave driver"
   D. a power supply used in a fan motor
5. How does the brushless motor know that it's time to reverse the current flow? ______.
   A. Hall-effect sensors
   B. Back electromotive force
   C. Keep switching the coils in sequence and assume the rotor will keep up
   D. All above

Unit 8 Induction Motors

No modern home should be without one —— or maybe a dozen. You'll find an induction motor in the fan, fridge, vacuum cleaner, washing machine, dishwasher, clothes drier, and the little pump that circulates water in the fish tank to stop the water turning green and the fish going belly-up. Chances are there's also one in the air conditioner —— unless it's a particularly high-tech one[1].

Advantages: cheap, quiet, long lasting, creates no interference.

Disadvantages:

- wants to turn at constant speed (50Hz divided by half the number of poles);
- cannot turn faster than 1500r/m (4-pole motor);
- draws a massive starting current, or is inefficient, or both;
- kind of big and bulky for the power it develops.

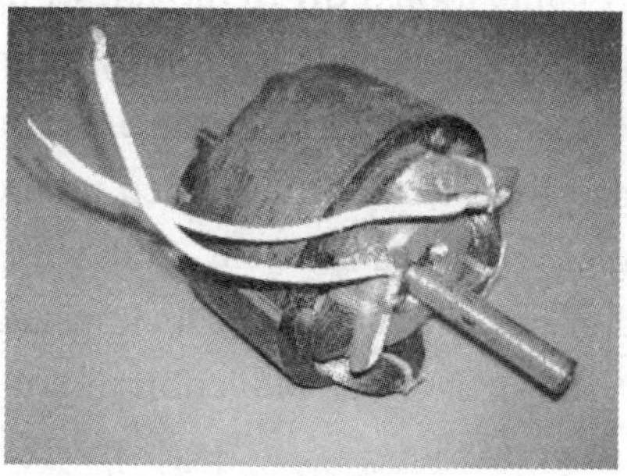

Fig.2.5 Signal phase induction motor

Induction motor in Fig.2.5 came out of a fan.

Actually, the bearings and end-caps of the motor have already been removed. We can pull the rotor out and Fig.2.6 (b) is what we're left with. There are four windings, and they are all simply in series.

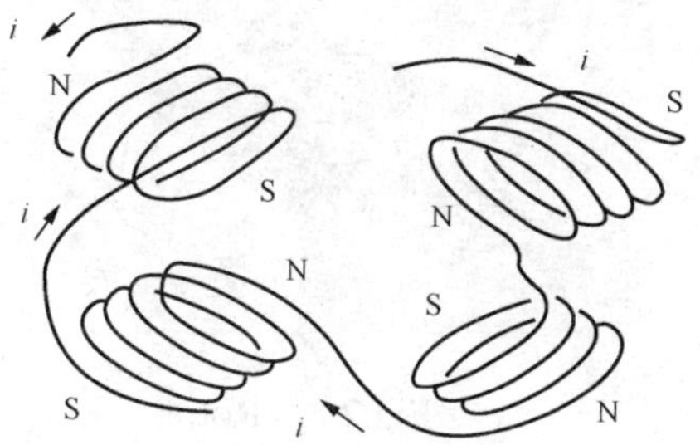

Fig.2.6 Signal phase induction motor without rotor

Well, not quite simply —— the current comes in the white wire, then the first winding [top right in Fig.2.6 (a)] is anticlockwise, the next one [bottom right in Fig.2.6 (a)] is clockwise, bottom left [in Fig.2.6 (a)] is anticlockwise again, top left is clockwise, then out the other white wire. So, imagine a positive half-cycle of the mains, with the current actually coming in that first wire. The first winding produces a north pole facing in; the second a south pole facing in; etc., like this: N-S-N-S.

Half a mains cycle later (10 ms) the current has reversed and so must the magnetic sense of the poles, which are now: S-N-S-N[2]. Now the magnetic field of stator have rotated 90 degrees. The rotor is an electrical conductor, and therefore tries to follow this field. To do so it has to rotate through 90 degrees. The rotor thus takes two full cycles of the mains (40 ms) to make a complete rotation, and so revolves at 1500 r/m. At least, it would if it could keep up with the rotating field. But it can't, quite, and in fact it's only because it's slipping behind that any torque is developed at all[3]. So, it rotates a bit slower than 1500 r/m (typically 1440 r/m) depending on how much torque it is being called upon to produce.

Note that the motor, as described so far, could rotate happily clockwise or anticlockwise. This kind of motor therefore needs some kind of internal cleverness to ensure it only turns in the right direction. This is achieved, in this motor, by the use of shaded poles.

Notice the winding at the top of Fig.2.7. See how there is a small additional pole (or set of iron laminations) off to the left of the main pole. It's excited by the same winding as the main pole, but is "shaded" from it by a thick copper band that wraps around the laminations and acts like a shorted electrical turn. The current induced in this band by the magnetic field generates a phase shift so that the shaded pole can generate a small component of magnetic field at right angles to the main field, and with the correct phase to ensure the fan turns the right way (otherwise the fan would suck instead of blowing)[4].

So in fact our induction motor is using induction already, and we haven't even got to the rotor yet!

Now we look at the rotor (Fig.2.8). This is a real disappointment —— it looks nothing like the "squirrel cage" in the text book! Where's the squirrel supposed to go, for starters?

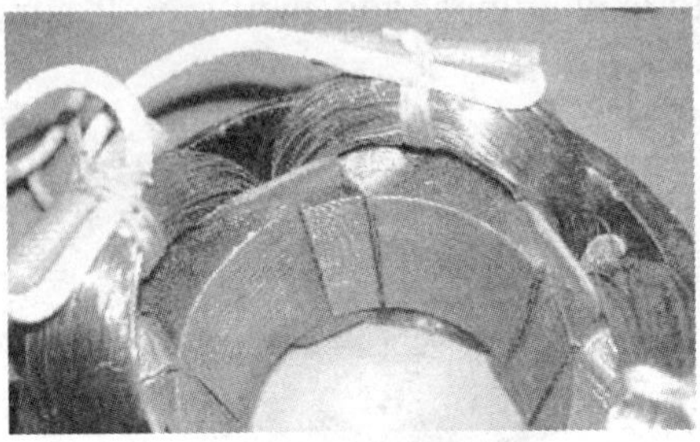

Fig.2.7 Shaded poles

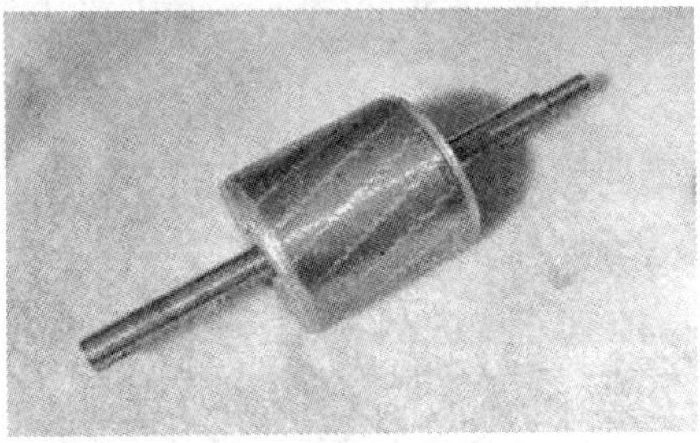

Fig.2.8 Rotor

What's happened here is that the rotor is actually made up of a stack of disc-shaped laminations of soft iron. That's right —— it's solid. This concentrates the magnetic field (generated by the windings) into the region where it will do the most good (the conducting bars of the rotor).

You can actually see the edges of the bars that run along the axis of the rotor, but they're at an angle of maybe 30 degrees to the shaft. What's going on here? Bad day at the factory? Chances are it's been designed that way to reduce cogging torque. If the bars ran parallel to the axis, the torque would rise and fall as each bar passed under the windings. By slanting the bars, the torque is kept more uniform as the rotor turns.

Now let's look at a different type of induction motor (Fig.2.9).

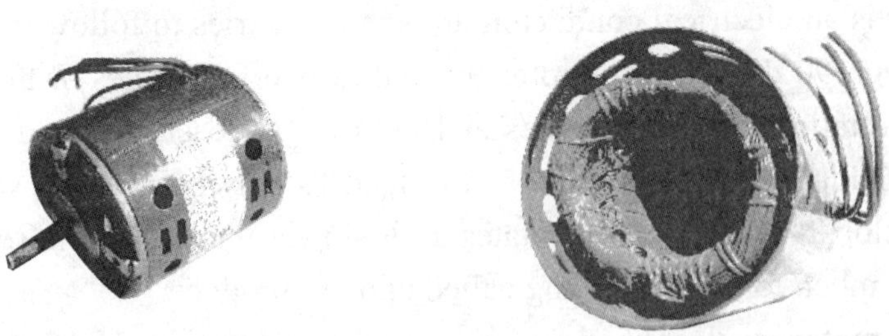

Fig.2.9 Induction motor came out of an astronomical telescope

This induction motor came out of an astronomical telescope. It was part of the photographic film transport, and needed to be able to turn both forwards and backwards. It therefore has two separate windings, and four wires coming out. One winding is fed directly from the mains (or "line" as our US colleagues call it); the other is fed through a capacitor that provides the necessary 90 degree phase shift. Swap the windings over, or reverse the connections to one of the windings, and the motor goes the other way.

No surprises when we take it apart, although note a very different winding pattern to the previous motor. It has more poles, and therefore turns slower.

Once again, the rotor is solid, and we can't see what's inside. The aluminium plate at the end of the rotor has been stamped and turned up into a series of small fins to make a crude cooling fan (Fig.2.10). (This wasn't necessary with our first motor —— it kept itself cool by the simple expedient of placing itself in the middle of, well, a fan.)

Fig.2.10 Rotor

Since astronomical telescopes no longer use film, we may as well cut the rotor in half and see if there's a squirrel in there.

No squirrel, but a magnificent set of aluminium conducting bars, just like in the text books. If you think of the rotor bars as forming (via the end rings) a single-turn secondary winding of a transformer, the primary of which (the windings on each pole) has some 50~100 turns, it is clear that the current through the rotor bars can be very high —— as much as 100 amps for a 240 watt motor. This explains the need for really chunky bars!

One disadvantage of the shaded pole motor is that the starting torque is rather low. This doesn't matter for something like a fan, where the load when stationary is almost zero. For other applications, like a washing machine, it would be a disaster. Such motors therefore use a capacitor to generate the required phase shift for the quadrature windings, as in this example.

Induction motors also come in other variations, but the two described above are the most common in domestic use.

For serious grunt, however, you need a three-phase induction motor. This takes advantage of the fact that commercial 3-phase power is delivered by three conductors, each of which carries a 50 Hz sine wave with 120 degrees of phase shift relative to the other two. A 3-phase motor simply places three windings at 120 degree intervals around the casing, and a rotating magnetic field is automatically produced. Three-phase induction motors are the "workhorse" of industry, with large units having ratings well in excess of a megawatt.

Technical Words and Expressions

induction motor		n.	感应电机
bearing	[ˈbɛəriŋ]	n.	轴承
end-cap		n.	弹簧盒盖，端盖
disassemble	[ˌdisəˈsembl]	vt.	解开，分解
r/m			转/分钟
internal	[inˈtəːnl]	n.	内在的，内部的
lamination	[ˌlæmiˈneiʃən]	n.	叠片结构
copper band			紫铜带/片
squirrel cage			鼠笼
a stack of			一堆
soft iron			软铁
concentrate	[ˈkɔnsentreit]	v.	集中，浓缩
cogging torque			齿槽效应转矩，磁阻转矩，齿滞
astronomical telescope			天文望远镜
photographic film transport			摄影胶片输片机构
main	[mein]	n.	（供电）干线
phase shift			相移
swap	[swɔp]	n.&v.	交换
aluminium plate			铝板，铝片
rotor bar			转子铜条，转子导条
secondary winding			二次绕组，次级绕组
shaded pole motor			罩极电动机
starting torque			启动转矩
quadrature winding			正交磁绕组，正交绕组，交磁绕组
three-phase induction motor			三相感应电动机
workhorse	[ˈwɜːkhɔːs]	n.	重负荷机器
megawatt	[ˈmegəwɔt]	n.	兆瓦特

Notes

[1] Chances are there's also one in the air conditioner —— unless it's a particularly high-tech one.

译文为：空调中可能也会有一个感应电机——除非它是特殊的高科技空调。

The chance is (that) .../The chances are (that) ...是固定搭配，表示“有可能……”。

[2] Half a mains cycle later (10 ms) the current has reversed and so must the magnetic sense of the poles, which are now: S-N-S-N.

译文为：半个电源周期（10ms）后电流反向，因此磁场的极向也反向，现在磁极方向为：

S-N-S-N。

"so must the magnetic sense of the poles"为倒装句型，一般以 so, nor, neither 开头，表示谓语所述的情况也适用于另一个人或一事物的肯定或否定句中，需要倒装，so 用于肯定句，表示"也一样""也这样"；nor, neither 用于否定句，表示"同样也不，也不这样"。该句正常语序为"the magnetic sense of the poles must have reversed"。

[3] But it can't, quite, and in fact it's only because it's slipping behind that any torque is developed at all.

译文为：但是转子和旋转磁场的转速不完全一致，事实上正是因为转子转速比旋转磁场低，才使得转矩产生。

"it can't, quite"是省略句式，完整的句子为"it can't keep up with the rotating field"。

[4] The current induced in this band by the magnetic field generates a phase shift so that the shaded pole can generate a small component of magnetic field at right angles to the main field, and with the correct phase to ensure the fan turns the right way (otherwise the fan would suck instead of blowing).

译文为：磁场在铜片中感应出电流，这个电流产生一个相位移，因此罩极能够给主磁场增加一个向右的小磁场分量，由于有正确的相位，可确保风扇按正确的方式旋转（否则风扇将吸风，而不是吹风了）。

并列连词 and 引导两个因果关系的从句。"and"前的句子结构：so that"因此，所以"，引导一个表示结果的状语从句，其主句结构为"[The current (induced in this band by the magnetic field 过去分词做定语)]（主语）+generates（谓语）+a phase shift（宾语）"。

Exercises

Ⅰ. Mark the following statements with T (true) or F (false) according to the text.

1. There are four windings in tow-phase induction motor , and they are all simply in parallel. (　　)

2. The rotor is an electrical conductor, and therefore tries to follow rotor magnetic field. (　　)

3. The rotor of induction motor is actually made up of a stack of disc-shaped laminations of soft iron. (　　)

4. One advantage of the shaded pole motor is that the starting torque is rather low. (　　)

5. For serious grunt, however, you need a three-phase induction motor. (　　)

Ⅱ. Complete the following sentences.

1. The disadvantages of induction motor: Wants to turn at ______ (50Hz divided by half the number of poles); Cannot turn faster than 1500r/m (4-pole motor); Draws a massive ______, or is ______, or both.

2. You can actually see the edges of the bars that run along the axis of the rotor, but they're at an angle of maybe 30 degrees to ______. It's been designed that way to reduce ______. If the ______ ran parallel to the axis, the torque would rise and fall as each bar passed under ______.

3. The rotor is ______, and we can't see that the ______ at the end of the rotor has been stamped and turned up into a series of small fins to make ______.

4. For other applications, like a washing machine, it use ______ to generate the required ______ for the ______.

5. A 3-phase motor simply places ______ at 120 degree intervals around the casing, and ______ is automatically produced.

Reading 8 Synchronous Machines: Generalities

The synchronous machine shown in Fig.2.11 is a particular type of rotating electrical machine having a rotation speed strictly connected to the frequency of the sinusoidal electrical quantities at the terminals.

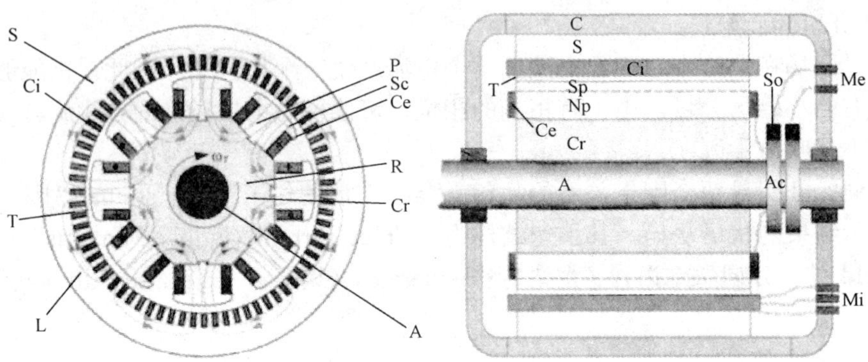

(a) (b)

Fig.2.11 Synchronous machine

(a) cross section; (b) longitudinal section

S—stator; P—salient pole; Ci—slots and armature conductors;

Sc—pole shoe; T—air gap;Ce—excitation conductors; L—induction vectorial lines;

R—rotor; A—shaft; Cr—rotor crown; C—frame; Ac—conducting rings; So—brushes;

Sp—pole shoe; Me—excitation terminals; Np—polar core; Mi—armature terminals

In the operation as a generator it is called alternator; when it operates as a motor it is called synchronous motor.

There are no fundamental differences between the two conditions and often the same machine can operate both as an alternator and as a motor. Even if the motor has important uses, in any case the fundamental application of the synchronous machine is as an alternator. As a matter of fact, nearly the whole of the electrical power used in the world is produced with alternators.

Usually the inductor is set in the rotor and the armature in the stator.

Rotor

The rotor can have salient poles, generally for a number of polar couples $p>3$, or it can be smooth (generally for $p<2$). In the first case the rotor includes a massive steel crown with polygonal section integral to the shaft. On it we have mounted the $2p$ polar cores in massive steel, and the pole shoes, that can be of massive steel or with bars, because their induction has time fluctuations. Around the polar cores the inductor or excitation conductors are wound, to form $2p$ coils identical between them.

The smooth rotor has been carried out in massive steel and it is equipped with longitudinal slots housing the inductor or excitation conductors; the slot distribution and the connections between the conductors are such to carry out two (or four) identical coils.

The coils of the consecutive poles are always connected in antiseries and the inductor winding resulting from it is supplied through creeping contacts made up of brushes and rings; the constant excitation current I_e is provided by a specific d.c. generator (exciter), that is often made up of a rotating generator, keyed on the same shaft of the synchronous machine.

Sometimes, in machines having not a very big power, the poles are magnetized by means of permanent magnets instead of excitation coils: in this case, being the excitation current not required, the machines are without rings and brushes and they are called brushless.

There are also synchronous machines (of small power) where the inductor is set in the stator, which is therefore equipped with salient poles, excited by coils or permanent magnets.

Stator

The stator, having the shape of a cylindrical crown, is carried out in bar iron, being the seat of periodically variable magnetic induction.

On its internal edge there are longitudinal slots of length L, evenly spaced, housing the armature conductors.

These are connected to carry out the armature windings that, connected among them, build up one or, more often, three armature windings, according to the fact that the machine is single phase or three-phase. The winding terminals are connected to the main terminals of the machine, and later they have to be connected to a mains in single phase or three-phase.

Inductor and armature conductors

The armature and inductor conductors are generally made of copper, isolated among them and as to the iron parts.

In the inductor (operating in d.c.) conductors of high section can be used; on the contrary in the armature (operating in a.c.), to reduce the skin effect, we apply to thinner elementary conductors, reciprocally isolated, that are transposed among them and parallel connected to the edges.

Similarly to the transformer ones, the rated values of a synchronous machine locate the levels of the main quantities with which we obtain the optimum operation of the machine.

The main rated values of the synchronous machine are listed:

P_n	Rated power [VA, W]
U_n	Armature rated voltage [V]
I_n	Armature rated current [A]
f_n	Rated frequency [Hz]
I_e	Excitation current [A]
U_e	Excitation voltage [V]
n_n	Rotation rated speed [r/m]
C_n	Rated couple at the shaft [Nm]

Armature rated voltage and current have the meaning of effective values.

In the case of alternators the rated power has the meaning of apparent delivered electrical power and it is expressed in VA; in the case of motors it has on the contrary a meaning of power returned to the shaft and it is expressed in W.

For single phase and three-phase alternators the following relationships are respectively valid:

$$P_n = U_n I_n \qquad P_n = \sqrt{3}\, U_n I_n$$

On the contrary for the synchronous motors we have:

$$P_n = C_n \frac{2\pi}{60} n_n$$

Technical Words and Expressions

rotating electrical machine		旋转电机
alternator	n.	交流发电机
synchronous motor		同步电动机
salient pole		凸极
air gap		气隙
pole shoe		极靴
polygonal	adj.	多角形的，多边形的
fluctuation	n.	波动，起伏
longitudinal slot		纵向槽
rated	adj.	额定的
excitation current		励磁电流

Comprehension

1. Which of the following is right? ______.

   A. Alternator is a kind of synchronous machine

   B. Alternator is a kind of rotating electrical machine

   C. Alternator is synchronous motor

   D. both A and B

2. Compared to synchronous motor, ______.

A. synchronous generator's fundamental is more complex

B. synchronous generator's construct is more complex

C. synchronous generator's applications are wider

D. all above

3. Which of the following states about rotor of synchronous machine is right? ______.

A. If the rotor is smooth, it includes a massive steel crown with polygonal section integral to the shaft

B. Rotor's excitation current I_e is provided by a specific a.c. generator

C. The inductor of synchronous machines can't be set in the stator

D. If the synchronous machines don't have a very big power, the rotor can be made of permanent magnets

4. Which of the following states about stator of synchronous machine is wrong? ______.

A. The stator looks like a cylindrical crown

B. The stator is located in a periodically variable magnetic filed

C. On its internal edge there are longitudinal slots of length, housing the armature conductors

D. Each winding's terminals are directly connected to the mains terminal

5. Which of the following states about synchronous generator is right? ______.

A. The inductor can use thinner section conductors

B. Armature rated voltage and current are effective values

C. The rated power has the a meaning of power returned to the shaft and it is expressed in VA

D. The armature uses high section elementary conductors to reduce the skin effect

Unit 9 Simple Motor Control Circuits

This article will discuss some simple AC motor control circuits.

1. Button lock circuit

The circuit shown in Fig.2.12 shows how to use relay contact to lock button position. When "START" button is pressed "M" relay activates and motor starts to rotate. At the same time one contact of relay "M" locks start button so that current continues to pass through relay "M". Stop button is used to cut the energy from relay "M", which will cut energy from motor.

2. Remote control circuit

The circuit shown in Fig.2.13 is used to control motor from different locations. All stop buttons are connected serially and start buttons connected parallel to each other. We can start and stop motor by using any start and stop buttons from any location.

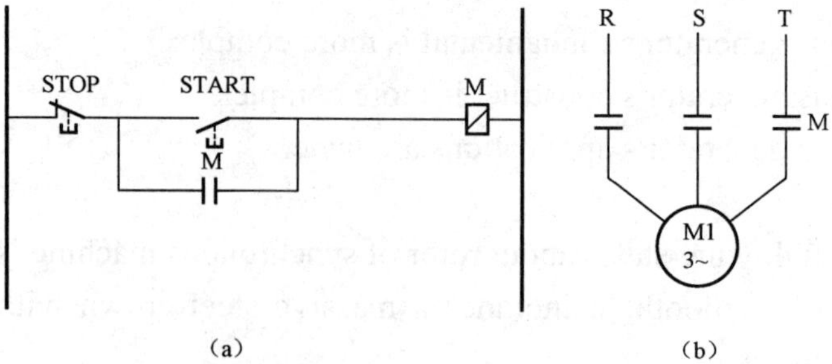

Fig.2.12 Button lock circuit

(a) Command Circuit; (b) Motor Circuit

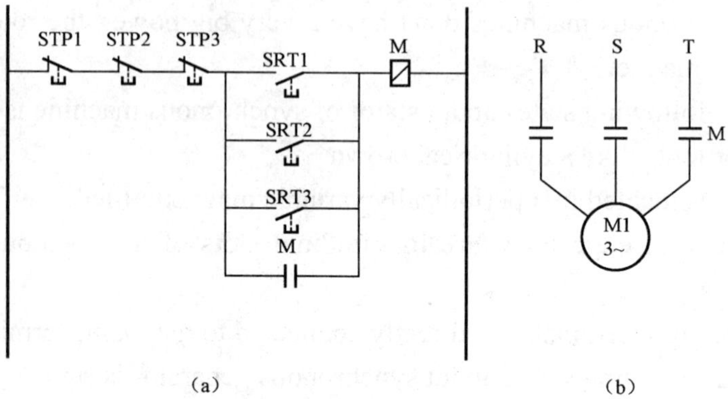

Fig.2.13 Remote control circuit

(a) Command Circuit; (b) Motor Circuit

3. Starter circuit for one phase Asynchronous Motor

The circuit shown in Fig.2.14 is used to start one phase asynchronous motor. By pressing start button "A" and "M" relays are activated and motor starts to rotate[1]. At the same time, timer "ZR" activates and starts to count. When timer finishes counting, relay "A" is cut off from energy by the contactor of time relay and motor continues to rotate without auxiliary winding[2].

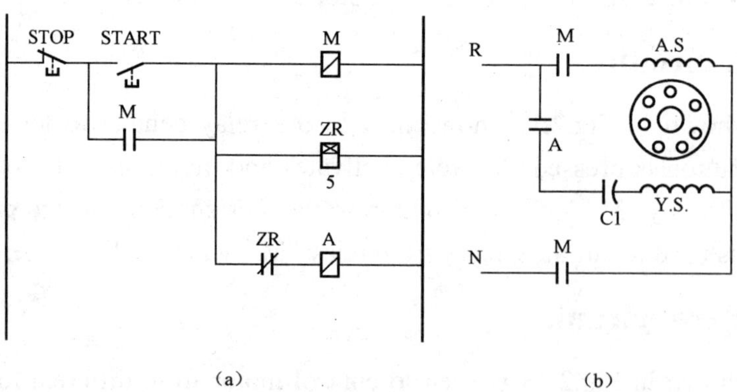

Fig.2.14 Starter circuit for one phase Asynchronous Motor

(a) Command Circuit; (b) Motor Circuit

4. Motor Starter circuit with single resistance

When the stator windings of an induction motor are connected directly to its 3-phase supply, a very large current (5~8 times full load current) flows initially. This surge current reduces as the motor accelerates up to its running speed. When very large motors are started direct-on-line they cause a disturbance of voltage (voltage dip) on the supply lines due to the large starting current surge[3]. This voltage disturbance may result in the malfunction of other electrical equipment connected to the supply. To limit the starting current some large induction motors are started at reduced voltage and then have the full supply voltage reconnected when they have run up to near rated speed[4].

The circuit shown in Fig.2.15 is used to start high power induction motors. When we click on start button "M" relay and "ZR" time relay are activated. Contactors of relay "M" connect motor to 3 phase power supply and auxiliary contact is used to keep relay in power. Motor voltage is reduced by resistances serially connected to motor. Time relay "ZR" starts to count down. When time relay finishes counting, relay "A" is activated by contactor of time relay. Contactors of relay "A" bypass resistances used in motor circuit and motor continues rotating with full supply voltage. Timer of time relay "ZR" must be arranged to count until motor gets to rated speed. Button Stop is used to cut power off from motor and all relays used in command circuit.

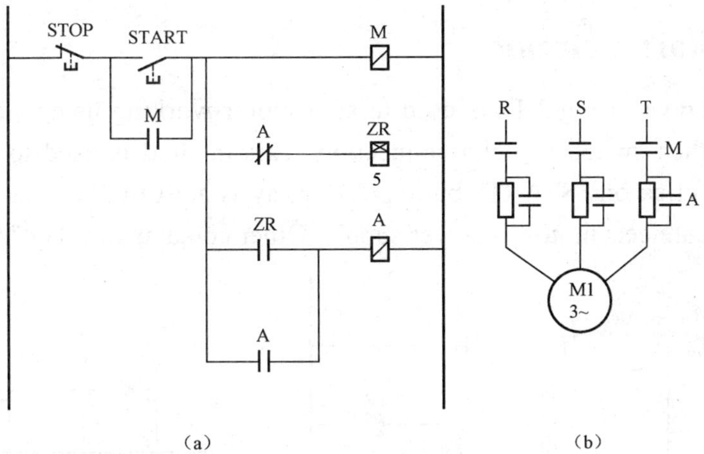

Fig.2.15 Motor Starter circuit with single resistance

(a) Command Circuit; (b) Motor Circuit

5. Motor starter circuit with double resistance

High power motors always need starter circuit for starting to work. In Fig.2.16, when we click on start button motor starts to work with low voltage because of usage of two resistances. First timer starts to count to specified time. When timer finishes counting relay "A" activates which is used to bypass first resistance in motor circuit and starts second timer.

When second timer finishes counting relay "B" activates and both resistances are bypassed in motor circuit.

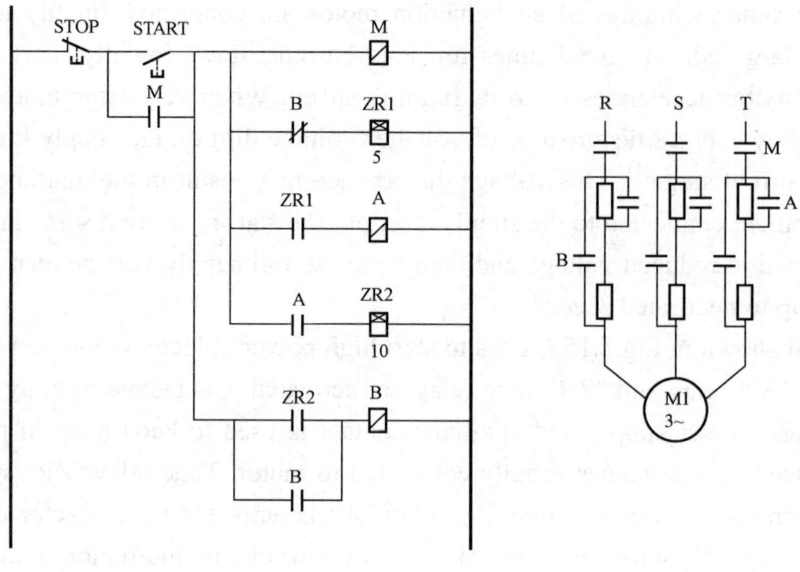

(a) (b)

Fig.2.16 Motor starter circuit with double resistance

(a) Command Circuit; (b) Motor Circuit

6. Star-Delta starter circuit

The circuit shown in Fig.2.17 is used to start motor working using star connection for some period and then switch to delta connection. This method is used to start high power motors. When we click on "START" button, "A" relay is activated and its contact activates relay "M", which connects motor to power supply. Other contacts of relay "A" connect motor

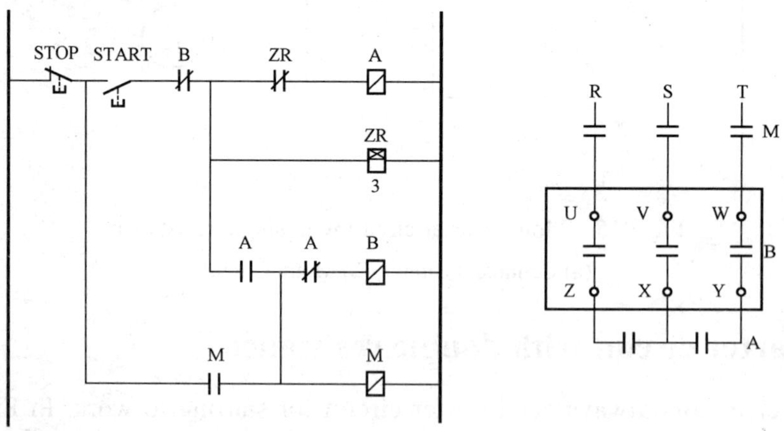

(a) (b)

Fig.2.17 Star-Delta starter circuit

(a) Command Circuit; (b) Motor Circuit

windings in star to connection. Motor starts rotate using low voltage. Time relay "ZR" is also activated by "START" button. When time relay finishes counting its normally closed contact activates and relay "A" is deactivated, which activates relay "B". Relay "B" converts motor connection type to delta. Auxiliary contact of relay "B" deactivates time relay "ZR". When we click on "STOP" button all relays are deactivated and motor circuit is cut off from power supply.

7. Changing rotation direction with protection lock

In Fig.2.18, we have two buttons to rotate motor in separate directions. "ILERI" button activates Relay "I" which rotates motor in forward direction and "GERI" button activates relay "G" which rotates motor in backward direction. At the same time button "ILERI" is used to cut energy from relay "G", in case it was activated, before activating relay "I". This is preventing from short circuit in motor circuit. Button "GERI" is also used in the same way. Button "STOP" is used to cut energy from both relays "I" and "G", which cuts energy from motor.

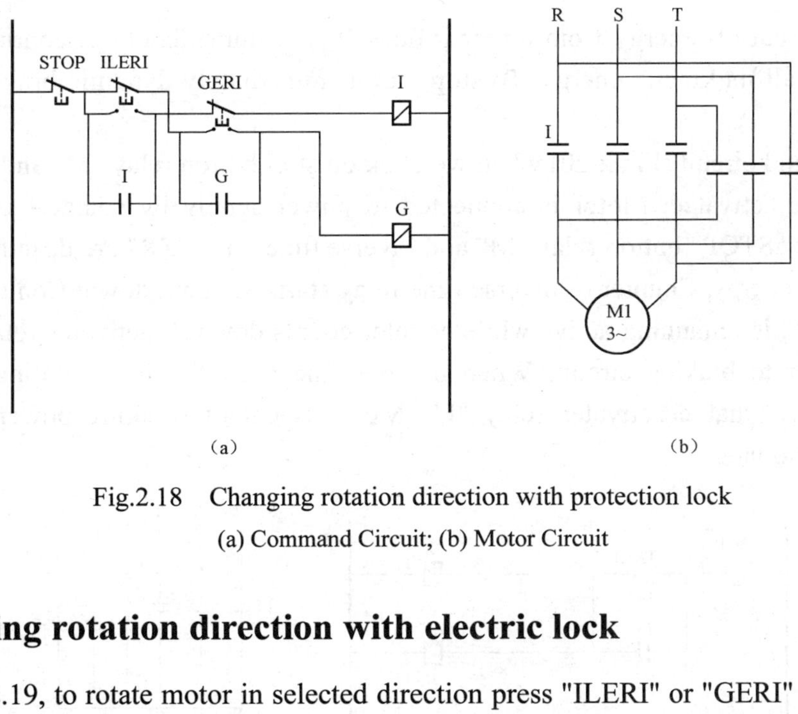

Fig.2.18 Changing rotation direction with protection lock

(a) Command Circuit; (b) Motor Circuit

8. Changing rotation direction with electric lock

In Fig.2.19, to rotate motor in selected direction press "ILERI" or "GERI" buttons. While motor is rotating in one direction it is electrically impossible to rotate it in another direction without stopping it[5]. If you try to change direction of rotation while it is rotating in one direction. Command circuit will not activate related relay because of security contact. For example we start to rotate motor in forward direction by pressing "ILERI" button. Relay "I" is activated and motor starts to rotate. Normally closed contact of relay "I" located before relay "G" will prevent activation of relay "G". Therefore we have to stop motor by clicking "STOP" button and deactivate active relay "I" in case to rotate motor in reverse direction.

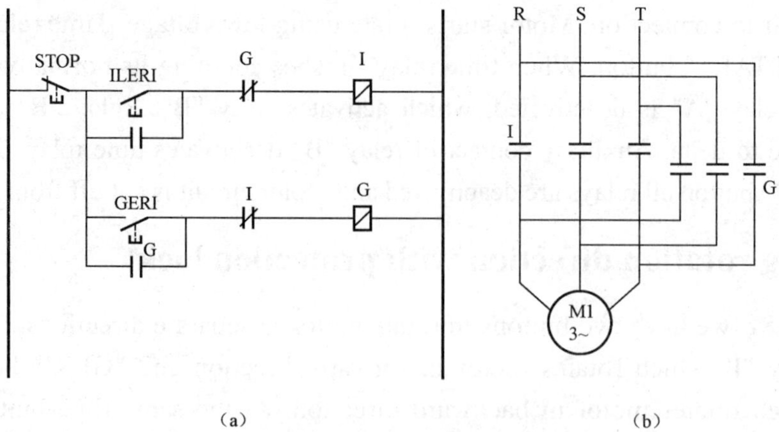

Fig.2.19 Changing rotation direction with electric lock
(a) Command Circuit; (b) Motor Circuit

9. Dynamic forced braking

When we cut off energy from motor it doesn't stop immediately. It continues rotating until it looses all its kinetic energy. To stop motor immediately dynamic braking circuit is used.

In command circuit (Fig.2.20) when we click on start button relay "M" and inverse time relay "ZR" are activated. Motor is connected to power supply by contacts of relay "M". When we click "STOP" button relay "M" and inverse time relay "ZR" are deactivated. Motor is cut off from energy. Counter of inverse time relay starts to count down. Contact of inverse time relay "ZR" is remaining active while counter counts down. It activates relay "F" which connects motor to braking circuit. When inverse time relay finishes counting, its contact became inactive, that deactivates relay "F". Motor is cut off braking power supply and remains fully stopped.

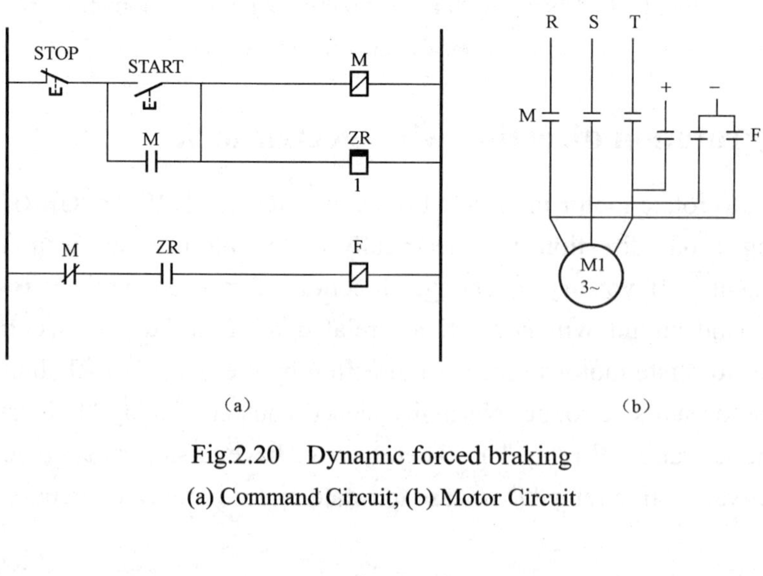

Fig.2.20 Dynamic forced braking
(a) Command Circuit; (b) Motor Circuit

10. Optional dynamic braking

The circuit shown in Fig.2.21 has optional dynamic braking button "FREN". Start motor rotation by pressing "START" button. To stop it we have two choices. First by pressing "FREN" button which will cut main power and apply braking circuit to motor for short period. Second by pressing "STOP" button which will just cut power from motor circuit.

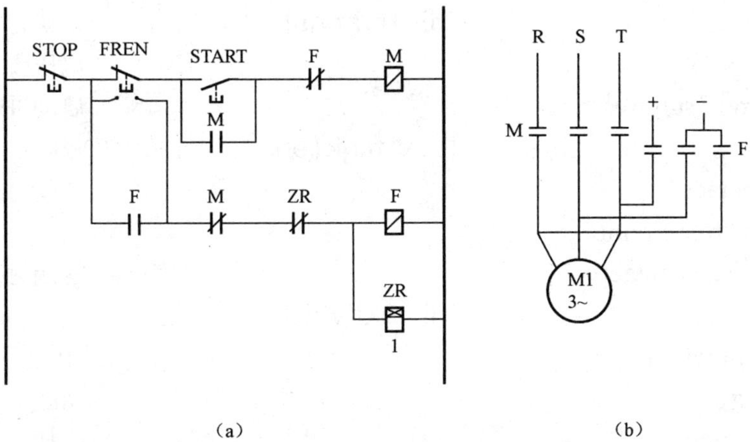

Fig.2.21 Optional dynamic braking

(a) Command Circuit; (b) Motor Circuit

11. Continuous and Discontinuous working motor circuit

The circuit shown in Fig.2.22 explains how control motor for continuous or discontinuous working. By pressing "START" button we make motor work continuously. Relay "M" is used to rotate motor and lock start button. By pressing "KS.CL" button we use relay "M" just for rotating motor. When we release "KS.CL" button "M" relay energy will be cut off and motor will stop. "STOP" button is used to stop motor in continuous working mode.

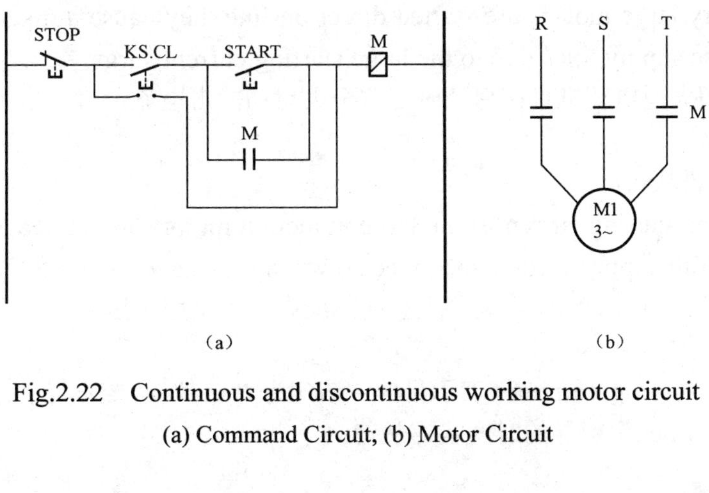

Fig.2.22 Continuous and discontinuous working motor circuit

(a) Command Circuit; (b) Motor Circuit

Technical Words and Expressions

contact	['kɔntækt]	n.	接触器
button	['bʌtn]	n.	按钮
timer	['taimə]	n.	定时器
auxiliary winding			辅助线圈
surge current			冲击（浪涌）电流
disturbance	[dis'təːbəns]	n.	干扰，骚乱，搅动
voltage dip			电压骤降
starting current surge			启动冲击电流
malfunction	[mæl'fʌŋkʃən]	n.	故障
auxiliary contact			辅助触点；联锁触点
Star-Delta starter circuit			星—三角启动器电路
normally closed contact			常闭触点
deactivate	[diː'æktiveit]	vt.	失电
in forward direction			［电子］正向
kinetic energy			动能
dynamic braking			能耗制动

Notes

[1] By pressing start button "A" and "M" relays are activated and motor starts to rotate.

译文为：按下启动按钮“A”，继电器“M”得电，电动机开始旋转。

此句中“and”连接了三个并列句，这三个句子间有因果次序关系。

[2] When timer finishes counting, relay "A" is cut off from energy by the contactor of time relay and motor continues to rotate without auxiliary winding.

译文为：当计数结束后，时间继电器的触点动作使继电器“A”断电，从而电动机在没有辅助线圈的情况下继续转动。

此句为“when”引导的时间状语从句，主句为“and”连接了两个并列句。

[3] When very large motors are started direct-on-line they cause a disturbance of voltage (voltage dip) on the supply lines due to the large starting current surge.

译文为：当超大型电动机直接启动时，这个大启动冲击电流，将会给供电线路带来电压扰动（电压骤降）。

when 引导状语从句。

[4] To limit the starting current some large induction motors are started at reduced voltage and then have the full supply voltage reconnected when they have run up to near rated speed.

译文为：为了限制启动电流，某些大型的感应电动机采用降压启动，当电动机接近额定转速后再给电动机加全压。

“To limit the starting current”表示目的，该句为“and”连接的两个并列句，其中第二个并列句带一个“when”引导的时间状语从句。

[5] While motor is rotating in one direction it is electrically impossible to rotate it in another direction without stopping it.

译文为：当电动机在一个方向上转动时，除非让它停下来，否则不可能在另一个方向上转动。“While”引倒条件状语从句，从句为“motor is rotating in one direction”，主句为“it is electrically…without stopping it”。“without”表示“除非”的意思。

Exercises

Ⅰ. Mark the following statements with T (true) or F (false) according to the text.

1. Button lock circuit is used to control motor from different locations. (   )

2. When very large motors are started direct-on-line they cause a disturbance of voltage (voltage dip) on the supply lines due to the large running current surge. (   )

3. High power motors always need starter circuit for starting to work. (   )

4. Star-Delta starter circuit is used to start motor working using delta connection for some period and then switch to star connection. (   )

5. When we cut off energy from motor it doesn't stop immediately. (   )

Ⅱ. Complete the following sentences.

1. In Remote control circuit all ______ connected ______ and start buttons connected ______ each other. We can start and stop motor by using any start and stop buttons from ______.

2. When the ______ of an induction motor are connected directly to its ______, a very large current (5～8 times ______) flows initially. This surge current reduces as the motor accelerates up to its ______.

3. To limit the starting current some large induction motors are started at ______ and then have the ______ reconnected when they have run up to near ______.

4. When we click on start button in Motor Starter circuit with single resistance, "M" ______ and "ZR" ______ ______. ______ of relay "M" connect motor to 3 phase power supply and ______ used to keep relay in power.

5. To stop motor immediately ______ circuit is used.

Reading 9 How to Wire a Motor Starter

A motor starter is a combination of devices used to start, run, and stop an induction motor based on commands from an operator or a controller. In North America, an induction motor will typically operate at 230V or 460V, 3-phase, 60 Hz and has a control voltage of 115 VAC or 24 VDC. Several other combinations are possible in North America and other countries, and are easily derived from the methods shown in this document.

The motor starter must have at least two components to operate: a contactor to open or close the flow of energy to the motor, and an overload relay to protect the motor against thermal overload. Other devices for disconnecting and short-circuit protection may be needed, typically a circuit breaker or fuses. Short-circuit protection will not be shown in the examples that follow.

The contactor is a 3-pole electromechanical switch whose contacts are closed by applying voltage to a coil. When the coil is energized, the contacts are closed, and remain closed, until the coil is de-energized. The contactor is specifically designed for motor control, but can be used for other purposes such as resistive and lighting loads. Since a motor has inductance, the breaking of the current is more difficult so the contactor has both a horsepower and current rating that needs to be adhered to.

The overload relay is a device that has three current sensing elements and protects the motor from an over current. Each phase going from the contactor to the motor passes through an overload relay current-sensing element. The overload relay has a selectable current setting based on the full load amp rating of the motor. If the overload current exceeds the setting of the relay for a sufficient length of time, a set of contacts opens to protect the motor from damage.

This article shows how to wire various motors using the FUJI series of contactors sold by Automation Direct. Other brands of contactors may be wired the same or similarly. Consult the manufacturer's wiring diagrams for other brands of contactors.

There are four basic wiring combinations:

(1) Full-voltage non-reversing 3-phase motors.

(2) Full-voltage reversing 3-phase motors.

(3) Single-phase motors.

(4) Wye-delta open transition 3-phase motors.

You must supply a disconnect switch, proper sized wire, enclosures, terminal blocks and any other devices needed to complete your circuit.

WARNING! Use the instructions supplied for each specific device. Failure to do so may result in electrical shock or damage.

The following components will be used (Fig.2.23).

(a) (b) (c) (d) (e) (f) (g)

Fig.2.23 Components

(a) Contactors; (b) Overload Relays; (c) Aux. Contacts; (d) Mechanical Interlock; (e) Normally Open Pushbutton; (f) Normally Closed Pushbutton; (g) 24 VDC Power Supply

Full-voltage non-reversing 3-phase motors

The following diagram depicts 3-phase non-reversing motor control with 24 VDC control voltage and manual operation (Fig.2.24). We will use a contactor, an auxiliary contact block, an overload relay, a normally open start pushbutton, a normally closed stop pushbutton, and a power supply with a fuse. The start and stop circuits can also be controlled using PLC inputs and outputs.

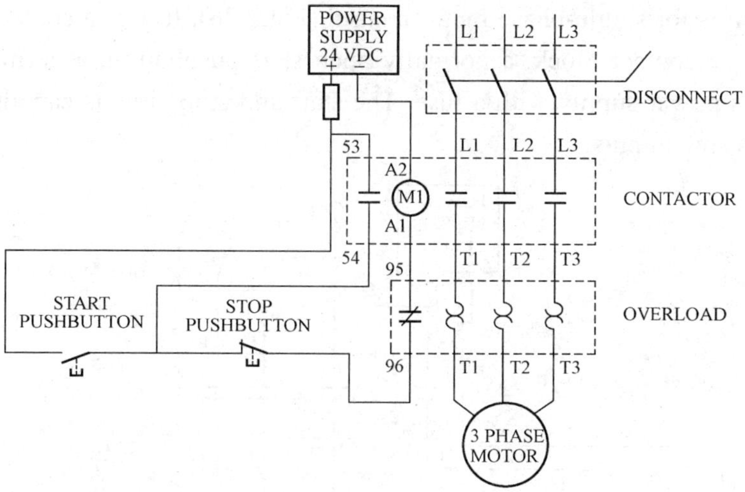

Fig.2.24 Full-voltage non-reversing 3-phase motors

Full-voltage reversing 3-phase motors

This diagram is for 3-phase reversing motor control with 24 VDC control voltage (Fig.2.25). It uses two contactors, two auxiliary contact blocks, an overload relay, a mechanical interlock, two normally open start pushbuttons, a normally closed stop pushbutton, and a power supply with a fuse. The forward, reverse, and stop circuits can also be controlled using PLC inputs and outputs.

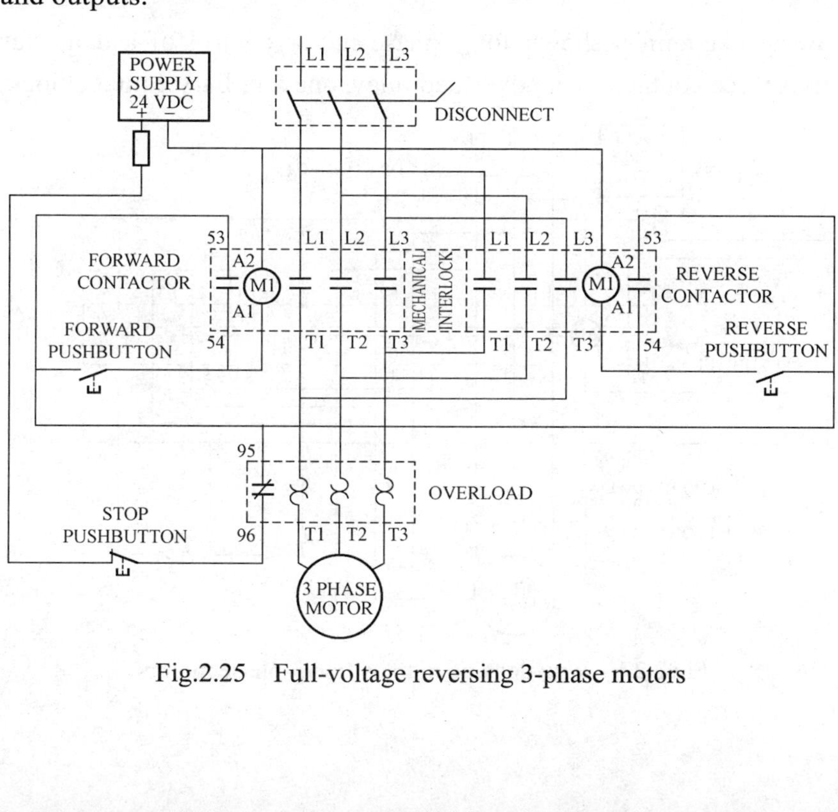

Fig.2.25 Full-voltage reversing 3-phase motors

Full-voltage single-phase motors

This diagram is for single-phase motor control (Fig.2.26). It uses a contactor, an overload relay, one auxiliary contact block, a normally open start pushbutton, a normally closed stop pushbutton, and a power supply with a fuse. The start and stop circuits can also be controlled using PLC inputs and outputs.

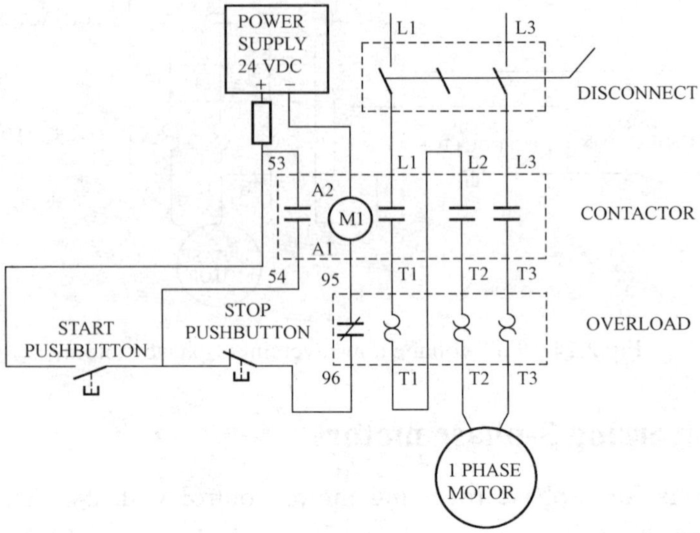

Fig.2.26　Full-voltage single-phase motors

Wye-delta open transition 3-phase motors

The following diagram is shown for 3-phase motor control of a delta-star connection (Fig.2.27). It uses three contactors, an overload relay, one auxiliary contact block, a normally

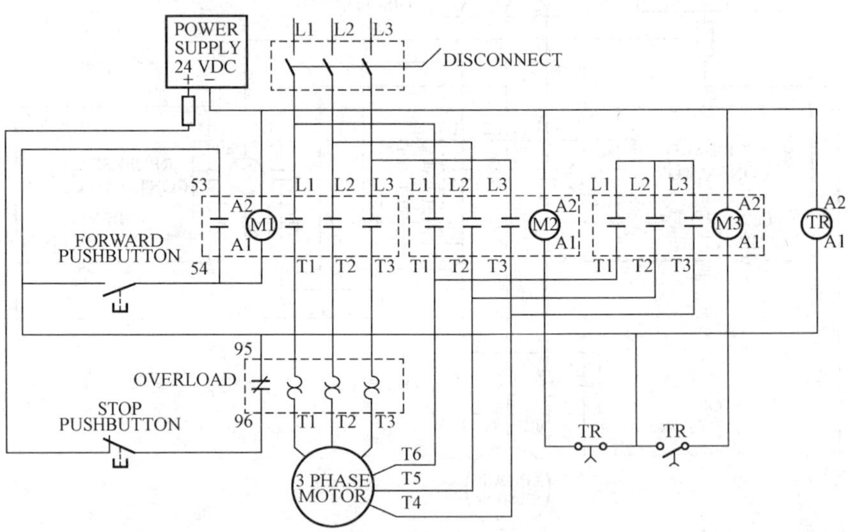

Fig.2.27　Wye-delta open transition 3-phase motors

open start pushbutton, a normally closed stop pushbutton, an on delay timer of 0～20 seconds and a power supply with a fuse. The start, stop, and timing circuits can also be controlled using PLC inputs and outputs.

Technical Words and Expressions

thermal overload		热过载
fuse	n.	熔丝
resistive and lighting load		阻性照明负载
over current		过电流
overload relay		过载继电器
mechanical interlock		机械连动装置，机械联锁装置

Comprehension

1. A motor starter is ______.
   A. used to control the speed of an induction motor
   B. an operator or a controller
   C. controlled by an operator or a controller
   D. a device which only has two components
2. When apply a voltage to the coil of a contactor, the normally open contact will ______ and the normally closed contact will ______.
   A. open, open B. open, close C. close, close D. close, open
3. The overload relay ______.
   A. is not necessary for motor start
   B. can sense voltage
   C. is a current-sensing element
   D. will cut the power supply to the motor in Fig.2.24 when there is over current
4. In Fig.2.25, when reverse contactor is pressed ______.
   A. the motor will run reversely B. the motor will run forwardly
   C. the contacts of M1 are closed D. the contacts of M2 are opened
5. In Fig.2.27, when forward pushbutton is pressed ______.
   A. coil of M2 is energized B. coil of delay timer is energized
   C. motor starts with full voltage. D. all above

Unit 10 Pulse Width Modulation Motor Control Theory

It is important to be able to control the speed of the robot motors so that you can accurately drive the robot in the direction you want. If you don't have fine enough speed control, the robot is likely to flit left and right and miss your target altogether!

With low powered motors that only consume just a few amps, you could use a variable resistor in series with the motor to vary the current, and therefore vary the speed of the motor[1]. For small motors the resulting power being dissipated in this variable resistor won't be too great and you won't have large heating problems to cope with. This method is often used on small toy models as it is the simplest form of speed control.

When you start to use motors capable of driving heavyweight robots that have stall currents in excess of 100 amps, a series variable resistor will need to dissipate large amounts of power. Apart from having to be a very low value resistor it is likely to also need extensive heat sinking if you are to stop it glowing red hot[2]! You are also simply wasting energy in heat that would otherwise allow you to keep the robot running for longer periods of time. For these applications, Pulse width modulation (PWM) motor control is a good choice.

PWM duty cycle

A better way of doing speed control is to switch the power to the motor on and off very quickly. The speed of a motor is proportional to the average voltage supplied across it, so if you switch the voltage on and off quickly enough, the motor only "sees" the average voltage. Because of the weight of the motor armature and its inertia, the motor speed won't vary noticeable between each on and off pulse, provided the pulses are short enough and close enough together[3]. To vary the speed of the motor, the duty cycle times of the on and off periods can be varied as shown in Fig.2.28.

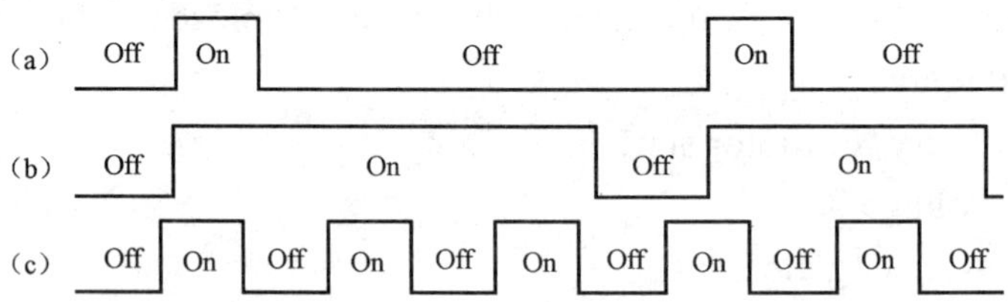

Fig.2.28 PWM duty cycles

On line (a) the on pulses are quite a bit shorter than the off pulses, so the motor will be moving relatively slowly.

To increase the motor speed you need to increase the on period relative to the off period so that the average voltage is increased. On line (b) this was done by making the on pulse longer while at the same time reducing the length of the off period. The time between the start of each successive on pulse remains the same, but the duty cycle has changed.

On line (c), the period of the on pulse remains the same, but the length of the off pulse is reduced. The effect is to increase the average voltage, but this also means there are more pulses per second than in line (b).

If the frequency of the pulses is low enough (less than say 20kHz) you are likely to hear the motors buzz as they run. There is nothing wrong with this, it is just the armature vibrating in sympathy with the pulses. You can observe this effect on modern day trains which buzz noticeably as they are driven, indicating that they too are using PWM as a speed control method. In contrast, the old "slam door" type trains that use resistors to drop the voltage, do not buzz, but are less efficient.

MOSFET devices

The devices normally used to switch the power "on" and "off" are Metal Oxide Semiconductor Field Effect Transistors or MOSFETs. These devices are used because they can switch very large currents under the control of a low signal level voltage.

The normal symbol of a MOSFET is shown below next to a relay type equivalent circuit (Fig.2.29). A purist may not agree that the relay is an exact equivalent circuit, but it does help to show how a MOSFET operates when it is used as a power switching device.

The device switches power between its Drain and Source terminals under control of the signal on the Gate terminal. The threshold at which the MOSFET will switch ON depends on the individual MOSFETs. Any Gate voltage above that "snaps" the MOSFET on faster. However, there is a significant input capacitance on the Gate terminal such that when you want to turn the device OFF again, you will have to discharge this input capacitance, which can slow down the switching time a bit[4]. You therefore have to choose the upper Gate voltage carefully so that you get reasonable ON and OFF switching times.

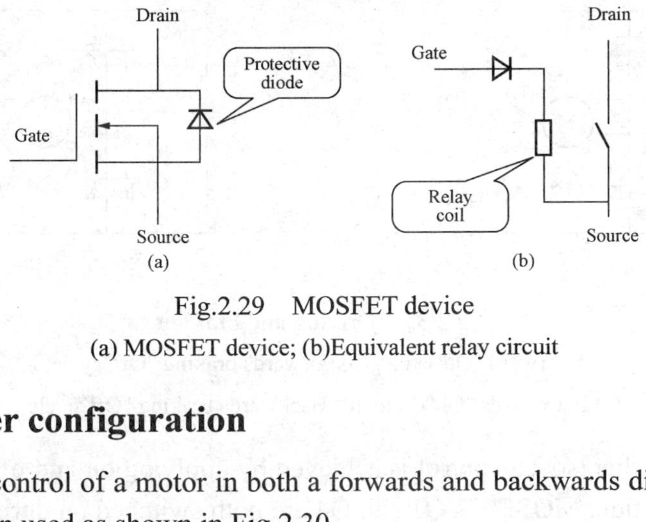

Fig.2.29 MOSFET device

(a) MOSFET device; (b)Equivalent relay circuit

H-Bridge driver configuration

To obtain full control of a motor in both a forwards and backwards direction, an H bridge configuration is often used as shown in Fig.2.30.

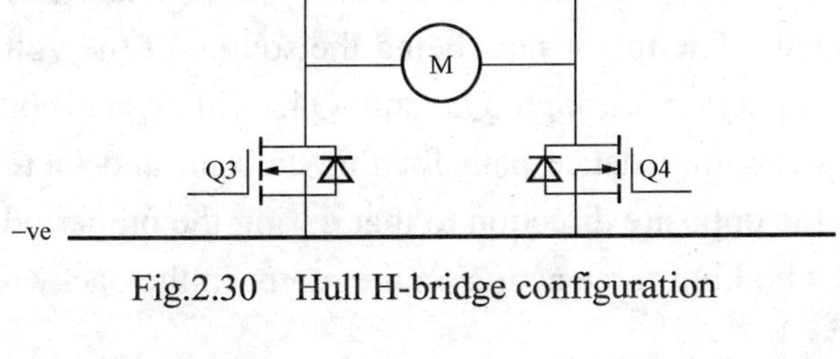

Fig.2.30 Hull H-bridge configuration

As the name suggests, the MOSFETs are configured around the motor in an H format, such that if Q1 and Q4 are switched on, the motor turns in one way, and if Q2 and Q3 are switched ON, then the motor turns in the other direction. If, for some peculiars reason you have Q1 and Q3 on together, or Q2 and Q4 on together, you have a smoke making machine as the MOSFET directly short the power rails together and will most likely self destruct in a matter of milliseconds[5]. This situation is normally called "shoot through" and should never be allowed to happen.

Driving ON cycles, and braking OFF cycles

As well as being able to drive a motor using an H-bridge configuration, you can also provide a braking action. The diagram in Fig.2.31 shows how this is achieved.

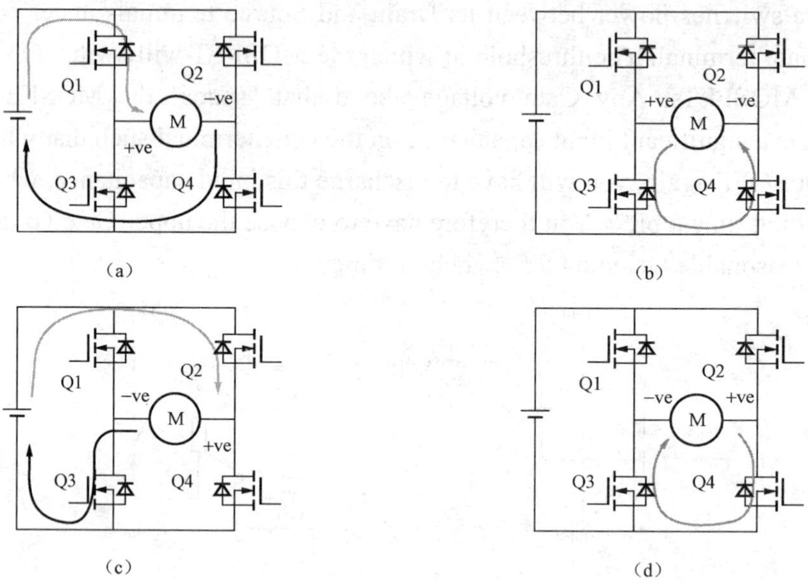

Fig.2.31　Driving and braking

(a) Forward "On"cycle; (b) Forwards braking "Off"cycle;

(c) Backwards "On"cycle; (d) Backwards braking "Off"cycle

As described earlier, speed control is achieved by applying on and off pulses to motor. In the top left configuration, MOSFETs Q1 and Q4 are both switched on during the on period and provide power to the motor to make it rotate in a forward direction. During the off period MOSFET Q1 is turned off, and Q3 is turned on in its place, removing the battery from the motor. With the power removed, the motor now acts as a generator and produced an induced voltage across its terminals. The motor now being the source of the voltage means the current flows in the opposite direction through Q3 and Q4, which are both turned on[6]. These MOSFETs offer a very low impedance path for this current, and therefore a strong "motor" force is experienced in the opposite direction to that during the on period. The net effect of this reverse motor action is a braking force acting on the motor in the backward direction.

The bottom left diagram shows the on cycle situation when the motor is driven in the backwards direction by turning on MOSFETs Q2 and Q3. During the off cycle, Q2 is turned off and Q4 on in its place, and again the motor acts as a generator with the induced currents again flowing through Q3 and Q4 as shown in the bottom right diagram. The MOSFETs once more offer a low impedance path for these induced currents and the net effect this time is a braking force in the forward direction.

Technical Words and Expressions

Pulse Width Modulation			脉宽调制
dissipate	['disipeit]	v.	消耗，浪费
heavyweight	['heviweit]		重负荷
stall current			堵转电流
average voltage			平均电压
inertia	[i'nəːʃjə]		惯性，惯量
duty cycle			占空因数，占空比
vibrate	[vai'breit]	v.	摆动，振动
in sympathy with			和……一致
buzz	[bʌz]	n.	蜂鸣，嗡嗡声
slam door			英国老旧车门式列车
threshold	['θreʃhəuld]	n.	上限，下限，阀值
H-Bridge driver		n.	桥式驱动器
power rail		n.	电源线
millisecond	['miliˌsekənd]	n.	毫秒
shoot through			直通
braking force			制动力

Notes

[1] With low powered motors that only consume just a few amps, you could use a variable resistor in series with the motor to vary the current, and therefore vary the speed of the motor.

译文为：对于仅仅消耗几安培的小功率电机，你可以通过在电机中串联可变电阻来改变电流，从而改变电机的速度。

“With”引导了一个复合结构在句中作状语，该结构中又含了一个“that”的定语从句修饰“motors”。

[2] Apart from having to be a very low value resistor it is likely to also need extensive heat sinking if you are to stop it glowing red hot!

译文为：如果你不想它热得发红，那么你除了要一个非常小的电阻外，它还可能要一个散热片。

该句为“if”引导的条件状语从句，表示“如果”，主句中“Apart from…resistor”部分为介词短语作主句的状语，主句为“it is likely to also need extensive heat sinking”。

[3] Because of the weight of the motor armature and its inertia, the motor speed won't vary noticeable between each on and off pulse, provided the pulses are short enough and close enough together.

译文为：假定脉冲足够短且距离足够近，那么由于电动机电枢的重量和它的惯性作用，电动机的转速在每个脉冲的通断间将不会明显变化。

该句为“provided”引导假设状语从句。

[4] However, there is a significant input capacitance on the Gate terminal such that when you want to turn the device OFF again, you will have to discharge this input capacitance, which can slow down the switching time a bit.

译文为：可是，栅极上有一个明显的输入电容，因此当你再次关断元件时，你必须给输入电容放电，这将会使你的关断时间稍微加长。

“such that”引导结果状语从句作“因此”解释，该句主句为“there is …terminal”，从句为“that when you …a bit”。而从句部分又是一个“when”引导时间状语从句，该时间状语从句部分又含有一个“which”引导的非限定性定语从句修饰“input capacitance”。

[5] If, for some peculiars reason you have Q1 and Q3 on together, or Q2 and Q4 on together, you have a smoke making machine as the MOSFET directly short the power rails together and will most likely self destruct in a matter of milliseconds.

译文为：如果由于某些特殊原因让 Q1 和 Q3 同时接通，或 Q2 和 Q4 同时接通，那么电源就会被烧坏，因 MOSFET 直接将电源线短接在一起从而很可能大概在几毫秒内损坏电源。

“If”引导条件状语从句，主句为“you have a smoke … milliseconds”。主句中“making machine”为“smoke”的定语直译为“围绕在电机周围的烟雾”，联系上下文该句可意译为“电源就会被烧坏”，“as”作为“出现烟雾”原因。

[6] The motor now being the source of the voltage means the current flows in the opposite direction through Q3 and Q4, which are both turned on.

译文为：电动机现在成了一个电压源，这就意味着 Q3、Q4 被同时接通后，电流通过 Q3、Q4 以反方向流动。

该句结构：主语部分“The motor now being the source of the voltage”＋谓语“means”＋宾语从句“the current … and Q4”。“which”引导非限定性定语从句，修饰“Q3 and Q4”。

Exercises

Ⅰ. Mark the following statements with T (true) or F (false) according to the text.

1. With high powered motors, you could use a variable resistor in series with the motor to vary the speed of the motor. (　　)

2. To increase the motor speed you need to increase the on period relative to the off period so that the average current is increased. (　　)

3. In contrast, the old "slam door" type trains that use resistors to drop the voltage, do not buzz, but are less efficient. (　　)

4. MOSFET switches power between its Gate and Source terminals under control of the signal on the Drain terminal. (　　)

5. In H-Bridge driver configuration speed control is achieved by applying on pulses to motor. ( )

Ⅱ. Complete the following sentences.

1. For small motors the resulting power being ______ in variable resistor won't be too great and you won't have large ______ to cope with.

2. A better way of doing speed control is to ______ to the motor on and off very quickly. The speed of a motor is proportional to ______ supplied across it, so if you switch the voltage on and off quickly enough, the motor only "sees" the average voltage.

3. Because of the weight of ______ and ______, the motor speed won't vary noticeable between each on and off ______, provided the pulses are short enough and close enough together.

4. If the ______ of the ______ is low enough (less than say 20kHz) you are likely to hear the motors ______ as they run. it is just ______.

5. To obtain full control of a motor in both ______ and ______ direction, ______ is often used.

Reading 10 Speed and Position Control of DC Motors

Closed loop vs Open loop control

In general open loop control means that you send electrical signals to an actuator to perform a certain action, like connecting a motor to a battery for example. In this scheme of control, there is no any mean for your controller to make sure the task was performed correctly and it often need human intervention to obtain accurate results. A very simple example of open loop control, is the remote controller of an RC toy car; you —— the human —— have to constantly check the position and the velocity of the car to adapt to the situation and move the car to the desired place.

But what if you could let the electronics handle a part, if not all of the tasks performed by a human in an open loop controller, while obtaining more accurate results with extremely short response time? This what is called closed loop control. In order to be able to build a closed loop controller, you need some mean of gaining information about the rotation of the shaft like the number of revolutions executed per second, or even the precise angle of the shaft. This source of information about the shaft of the motor is called "feed-back" because it sends back information from the controlled actuator to the controller.

Fig.2.32 shows clearly the difference between the two control schemes. Both types have a controller that gives orders to a driver, which is a power circuit (usually an H bridge) that drives the motor in the required direction. It is clear that the closed loop system is more complicated because it needs a "shaft encoder" which is a devise that will translate the rotation of the shaft into electrical signals that can be communicated to the controller.

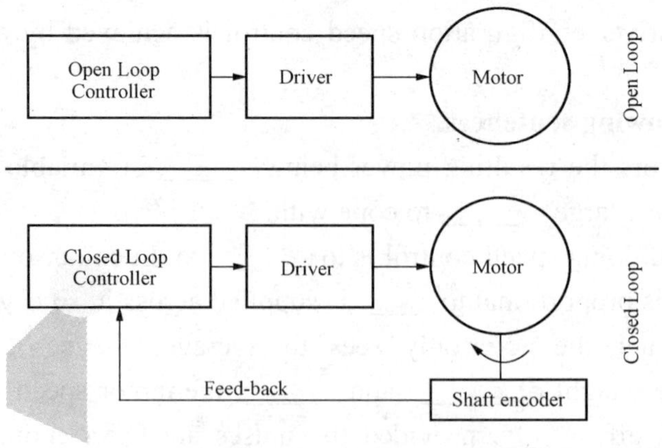

Fig.2.32 Closed loop vs Open loop

In other words, a closed loop controller will regulate the power delivered to the motor to reach the required velocity. If the motor is to turn faster than the required velocity, the controller will deliver less power to the motor. Controlling the electrical power delivered to the motor is usually done by Pulse Width Modulation.

The controller

A closed loop controller can be an analog circuit, a digital circuit made of logic gates, or a microcontroller. Generally, a microcontroller is the option that will provide more design flexibility. Recent microcontrollers running at very high clock rates can completely replace similar analog controllers, and can even be cheaper.

In a closed loop system, a microcontroller will have two main tasks:

1. constantly adjust the average power delivered to the motor to reach the required velocity.

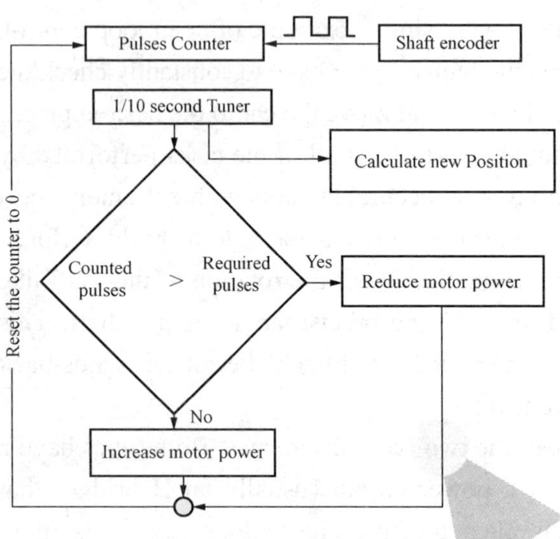

Fig.2.33 Schematic of motor speed control

2. Precisely calculate the position/angle of the motor's output shaft.

As you can see in Fig.2.33, the shaft encoder will provide the microcontroller's internal counter with a sequence of pulses that correspond to the rotation of the motor. A timer is set to execute two software routine every 1/10th of a second (which is just an arbitrary value). One of those software routines is to recalculate the actual angle of the shaft or the total number of revolutions.

Then, another software routine is executed to control the speed of the motor by comparing the number of counted pulses with a fixed number which is referred to as the "required pulses". The "required pulses" corresponds to the desired speed, and the "counted pulses" corresponds to the actual speed of the motor.

Finally, as you can notice in the schematic, it's all a matter of comparing those two values and constantly adjusting the power delivered to the motor. Note that choosing the right timing between each execution of this routine can dramatically improve overall system stability and performance, especially on low quality motors.

Controlling the power delivered to the motor to control its speed. Recalling the Fig.2.32, a closed loop system contains a controller and a driver. The driver on its own —— which is usually an H bridge —— cannot control the velocity of the motor. The most common technique to do so is to let the controller turn the driver ON and OFF at very high rates, changing the ratio between the ON and OFF time to control the speed of the motor (Fig.2.33). This is what is called PWM or pulse width modulation.

Technical Words and Expressions

open loop control		开环控制
intervention	n.	干涉
velocity	n.	速度，速率，迅速
response time		响应时间
closed loop control		闭环控制
shaft encoder		转轴编码器

Comprehension

1. General open loop control ______.
   A. sends electrical signals to a controller to perform a certain action
   B. has mean for your controller to make sure the task was performed correctly
   C. often needs human intervention to obtain accurate results
   D. needs some mean of gaining information about the rotation of the shaft

2. ______ obtains more accurate results with extremely short response time.
   A. Open loop circuit B. Closed loop control
   C. Open loop control D. Closed loop circuit

3. Which of the following about open loop and closed loop control of motor is not right? ______.
   A. Both have a controller that gives orders to a driver
   B. Both have a power circuit which usually is an H bridge that drives the motor in the required direction
   C. The open loop system is more complicated
   D. "Shaft encoder" is a devise that will translate the rotation of the shaft into electrical signals

4. A closed loop controller can be ______.

   A. an analog circuit　　B. a digital circuit made of logic gates

   C. a microcontroller　　D. all above

5. The "______" corresponds to the ______, and the "______" corresponds to the ______.

   A. required pulse, desired speed, actual speed of the motor, counted pulses

   B. counted pulse, desired speed, required pulses, actual speed of the motor

   C. desired speed, required pulses, counted pulses, actual speed of the motor

   D. required pulse, desired speed, counted pulses, actual speed of the motor

Unit 11　Variable-Frequency Drive

A variable-frequency drive (VFD in Fig.2.34) is a system for controlling the rotational speed of an alternating current (AC) electric motor by controlling the frequency of the electrical power supplied to the motor. A variable frequency drive is a specific type of adjustable-speed drive. Variable-frequency drives are also known as adjustable-frequency drives (AFD), variable-speed drives (VSD), AC drives, or inverter drives. Since the voltage is varied along with frequency, these are sometimes also called VVVF (variable voltage variable frequency) drives.

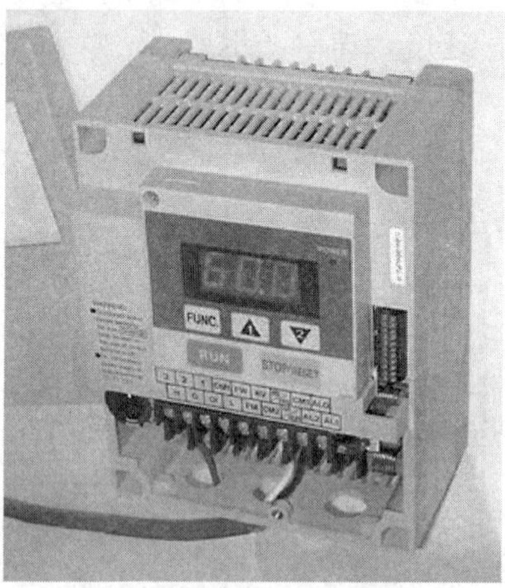

Fig.2.34　Small Variable Frequency Drive (VFD)

Variable-frequency drives are widely used. For example, in ventilations systems for large buildings, variable-frequency motors on fans save energy by allowing the volume of air moved to match the system demand. Variable frequency drives are also used on pumps and machine tool drives.

Operating principle

The synchronous speed of an AC motor is determined by the frequency of the AC supply and the number of poles in the stator winding, according to the relation:

$$RPM = \frac{120 \times f}{p}$$

Where:

RPM—— Revolutions per minute;

f—— AC power frequency (hertz);

p —— Number of poles (an even number).

The constant, 120, is 60 seconds per minute multiplied by 2 poles per pole pair. Sometimes 60 is used as the constant and p is stated as pole pairs rather than poles. By varying the frequency of the voltage applied to the motor, its speed can be changed.

Synchronous motors operate at the synchronous speed determined by the above equation. The speed of an induction motor is slightly less than the synchronous speed.

VFD types

Drives can be classified as: constant voltage, constant current, cycloconverter.

In a constant voltage converter, the intermediate DC link voltage remains approximately constant during each output cycle. In constant current drives, a large inductor is placed between the input rectifier and the output bridge, so the current delivered is nearly constant. A cycloconverter has no input rectifier or DC link and instead connects each output terminal to the appropriate input phase.

The most common type of packaged VF drive is the constant-voltage type, using pulse width modulation to control both the frequency and effective voltage applied to the motor load[1].

VFD structure

All VFDs have the same structure, which includes a rectifier, filter and inverter, as shown in Fig.2.35. The rectifier converts 3～0 AC line power to DC power. The components used in the rectifier are typically thyristors and/or diodes. The filter sits between the rectifier & inverter and provides harmonic and power ripple filtration using inductors and capacitors[2]. These components work to respectively smoothen and regulate the current and voltage supplied to the motor. The inverter portion typically consists of thyristors or IGBTs that are carefully controlled to sequence the proper voltage and current to the phase windings of the motor, depending on the speed and load required[3]. In case of IGBTs, control circuit is connected to the gate, but this circuitry is less complex and does not require polarity reversal.

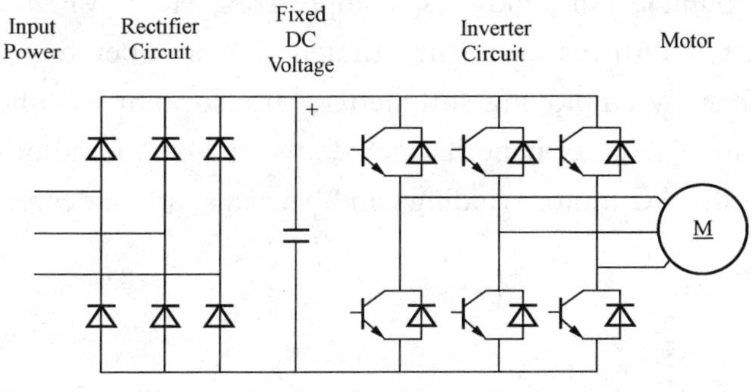

Fig.2.35 PWM AC variable speed drive

Inverters provide the user with tremendous flexibility by controlling two main elements of a three-phase induction motor, i.e., torque and speed. Motor speed and many operating parameters may be infinitely adjusted. Some of the other types of inverters include current source inverters, voltage source inverters; load commuted inverters, PWM inverters, vector control, etc. Each type of inverter has its own sets of advantages and disadvantages and should be selected according to particular requirements. The present economics favours PWM drive for applications under 200 HP.

VFD operator interface

The operator interface provides a means for an operator to start and stop the motor and adjust the operating speed. Additional operator control functions might include reversing and switching between manual speed adjustment and automatic control from an external process control signal[4]. The operator interface often includes an alphanumeric display and/or indication lights and meters to provide information about the operation of the drive. An operator interface keypad and display unit is often provided on the front of the VFD controller as shown in Fig.2.36. The keypad display can often be cable-connected and mounted a short distance from the VFD controller. Most are also provided with input and output (I/O) terminals for connecting pushbuttons, switches and other operator interface devices or control signals. A serial communications port is also often available to allow the VFD to be configured, adjusted, monitored and controlled using a computer.

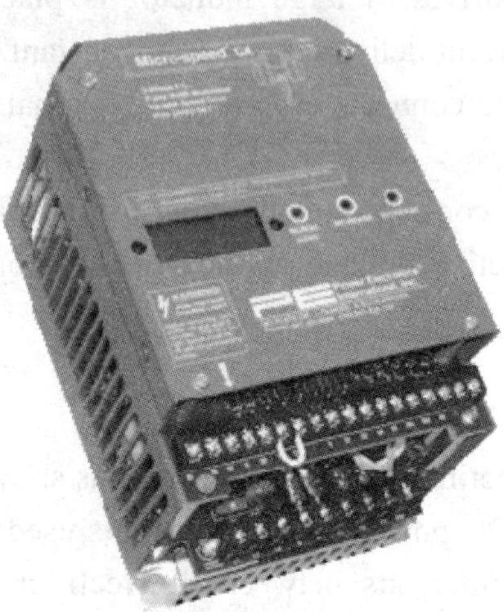

Fig.2.36 VFD operator interface

Advantages

VFDs eliminate the need for energy wasting throttling mechanisms like control valves and outlet dampers. These are mainly installed on loads where torque increases with speed including centrifugal pumps, fans, blowers, compressors, etc[5]. VFDs are used to improve process control, which in turn increases the efficiency of an operating system. These drives reduce mechanical stress by employing soft starters. It also improves the power factor of the whole electrical system. The other benefits include the reduction and/or elimination of motor starters, less stress on the AC motor windings and bearings, and a decrease in stress and wear on the pump or fan.

Disadvantages

The non-pure sine wave output power causes additional motor heating primarily because of harmonics. Depending upon the manufacturer and the type of variable frequency controller, the input voltage and current waveform to the motor will be distorted by varying degrees.

Harmonic currents generate no useful torque at the motor shaft. These create additional losses.

However, VFDs can be reliable and trouble-free if they are selected and installed properly. VFDs can cause damage to the motors they drive and cause a wide range of problems in the associated electrical system if they are not selected properly. Most of the problems arise from distortion of the voltage and current waveforms in the input and output of the drive, commonly called harmonic distortion.

Technical Words and Expressions

variable-frequency drive			变频器
rotational speed			转动速度，角速度
adjustable-speed drive			调速器
adjustable-frequency drive			调频器
variable-speed drive (VSD)			变速器
VVVF (variable voltage variable frequency) drive			变压变频器
ventilation	[ventiˈleiʃən]	n.	通风，流通空气
synchronous speed			同步速度，同步转速
stator winding			定子绕组
even number			偶数
constant voltage			恒压
constant current			恒流
cycloconverter	[ˌsaikləukənˈvəːtə]	n.	周波变换器，循环换流器，双向离子变频器
filtration	[filˈtreiʃən]	n.	过滤
inverter	[inˈvəːtə]	n.	逆变器
power ripple			电源纹波，电源脉动
smoothen	[ˈsmuːðən]	v.	使平滑，使平和
polarity reversal			极性变换
operating parameter			运行参数
load commuted inverter			负载换流逆变器
vector control			矢量控制
operator interface			操作界面
manual speed adjustment			手动调速
alphanumeric display			字母数字显示器
indication light			指示灯
meter	[ˈmiːtə]	n.	仪表
pushbutton		n.	按钮
throttling mechanism			节流装置
control valve			控制阀，调节阀
damper	[ˈdæmpə]	n.	风门；节气阀

centrifugal pump 离心泵，离心抽机
soft starter 软启动器
power factor 功率因素
non-pure sine wave 非正弦波
harmonic current 谐波（正弦）电流
trouble-free 无故障
harmonic distortion 谐波畸变（失真）

Notes

[1] The most common type of packaged VF drive is the constant-voltage type, using pulse width modulation to control both the frequency and effective voltage applied to the motor load.

译文为：最常见的封装式变频器是恒压型，它采用脉宽调制技术来控制频率及加在电机负载上的有效电压。

该句中“using…”部分为现在分词作方式状语，“applied to the motor load”部分则为“effective voltage”的定语。

[2] The filter sits between the rectifier & inverter and provides harmonic and power ripple filtration using inductors and capacitors.

译文为：滤波器位于整流器和逆变器之间，通过使用电感和电容来滤去谐波和电源纹波（电源脉动）。

第一个“and”连接了两个相同主语的并列句，第二个“and”连接了“provides”的两个宾语。而“using inductors and capacitors”为现在分词短语作条件状语。

[3] The inverter portion typically consists of thyristors or IGBTs that are carefully controlled to sequence the proper voltage and current to the phase windings of the motor, depending on the speed and load required.

译文为：逆变部分通常由晶闸管或 IGBT 组成，它将根据转速和负载的要求来恰当地控制晶闸管或 IGBT，从而给电动机各相绕组提供合适的电压和电流。

该句为“that”引导的定语从句修饰“thyristors or IGBTs”，但翻译时由于从句部分过长，因而把从句部分单独作为一句翻译。而从句中的“depending on…”部分为分词作独立成分。

[4] Additional operator control functions might include reversing and switching between manual speed adjustment and automatic control from an external process control signal.

译文为：此外它的操作控制功能还包括反转以及手动/自动调速间的切换，自动调速是由外部控制信号来控制的。

该句的翻译时把“from an external process control signal”部分单独作一句翻译，否则该部分放置在主句中翻译，会使主句显得冗长。

[5] These are mainly installed on loads where torque increases with speed including centrifugal pumps, fans, blowers, compressors, etc.

译文为：它们主要安装在转矩随转速变化而变化的负载上，如离心泵、风扇、吹风机、压缩机等。

该句为“where”引导的定语从句修饰“loads”。

Exercises

Ⅰ. Mark the following statements with T (true) or F (false) according to the text.

1. A variable-frequency drive (VFD) is a system for controlling the rotational speed of a direct current (DC) electric motor. (   )

2. Induction motors operate at the synchronous speed determined by the above equation. The speed of Synchronous motor is slightly less than the synchronous speed. (   )

3. In a constant voltage converter, the intermediate DC link voltage remains approximately constant during each output cycle. (   )

4. The pure sine wave output power causes additional motor heating primarily because of harmonics. (   )

5. The operator interface provides a means for an operator to start and stop the motor and adjust the operating speed. (   )

Ⅱ. Complete the following sentences.

1. A variable frequency drive is a specific type of ______. Variable-frequency drives are also known as ______, variable-speed drives (VSD), AC drives, or ______.

2. ______ of an AC motor is determined by the frequency of the AC supply and the number of ______ in the ______.

3. The most common type of packaged VF drive is ______ type, using ______ to control both the frequency and ______ applied to the motor load.

4. All VFDs have the same structure, which includes ______, filter and ______. The filter sits between the ______ and provides ______ filtration using ______ and capacitors.

5. VFDs are used to improve ______, which in turn increases the ______ of an operating system. These drives reduce mechanical stress by employing ______. It also improves ______ of the whole electrical system.

Reading 11 Vector Control (Motor)

Vector control (also called Field Oriented Control, FOC) is one method used in variable frequency drives to control the torque (and thus finally the speed) of three-phase AC electric motors by controlling the current fed to the machine.

Method

The Stator phase currents are measured and converted into a corresponding complex (space) vector. This current vector is then transformed to a coordinate system rotating with the rotor of the machine. For this the rotor position has to be known. Thus at least speed measurement is required. The position can then be obtained by integrating the speed.

Then the rotor flux linkage vector is estimated by multiplying the stator current vector with magnetizing inductance L_m and low-pass filtering the result with the rotor no-load time constant L_r/R_r, that is the ratio of the rotor inductance to rotor resistance.

Using this rotor flux linkage vector the stator current vector is further transformed into a coordinate system where the real x-axis is aligned with the rotor flux linkage vector.

Now the real x-axis component of the stator current vector in this rotor flux oriented coordinate system can be used to control the rotor flux linkage and the imaginary y-axis component can be used to control the motor torque.

Typically PI-controllers are used to control these currents to their reference values. However, bang-bang type current control, that gives better dynamics, is also possible.

With PI-controllers the outputs of the controllers are the x-y components of the voltage reference vector for the stator. Usually due to the cross coupling between the x- and y-axes a decoupling term is further added to the controller output in order to improve the control performance whcn big and rapid changes in speed, current and flux linkage take place. Usually the PI-controller also needs low-pass filtering of either the input or output of the controller in order to prevent the current ripple due to transistor switching from being amplified excessively and unstabilizing the control. Unfortunately, the filtering also limits the dynamics of the control system. Thus quite high switching frequency (typically more than 10 kHz) is required in order to allow only minimum filtering for high performance drives such as servo drives.

Next the voltage references are first transformed to the stationary coordinate system (usually through rotor d-q coordinates) and then fed into a modulator that using one of the many Pulse Width Modulation (PWM) algorithms defines the required pulse widths of the stator phase voltages and controls the transistors (usually IGBTs) of the inverter according to these.

This control method implies the following properties of the control (Fig.2.37):

Speed or position measurement or some sort of estimation is needed;

Torque and flux can be changed reasonably fast, in less than 5～10 milliseconds, by changing the references;

The step response has some overshoot if PI control is used;

The switching frequency of the transistors is usually constant and set by the modulator;

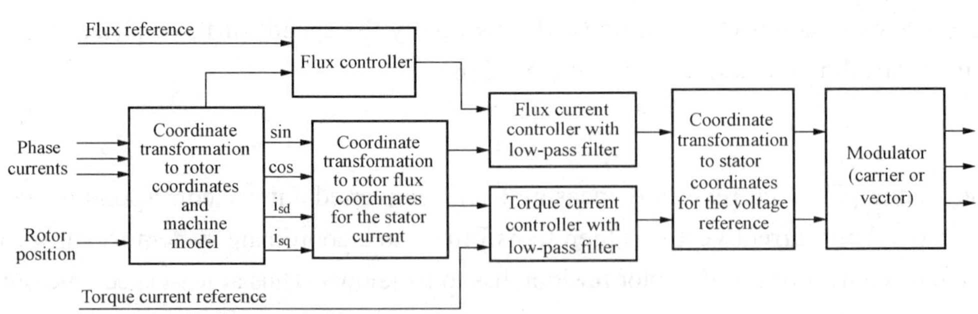

Fig.2.37 Vector control of motor

The accuracy of the torque depends on the accuracy of the motor parameters used in the control. Thus large errors due to for example rotor temperature changes often are encountered.

Reasonable processor performance is required, typically the control algorithm has to be calculated at least every millisecond.

Although the vector control algorithm is more complicated than the Direct Torque Control (DTC), the algorithm is not needed to be calculated as frequently as the DTC algorithm. Also the current sensors need not be the best in the market. Thus the cost of the processor and other control hardware is lower making it suitable for applications where the ultimate performance of DTC is not required.

Technical Words and Expressions

vector control		矢量控制
Field Oriented Control		磁场定向控制
coordinate system		坐标系
magnetizing inductance		磁化电感
multiply	v.	乘
low-pass filtering		低通滤波
orient	vt.	使适应，确定方向
reference value		参考值
bang-bang		继电器式控制
overshoot	n.	超调
Direct Torque Control		直接转矩控制
algorithm	n.	运算法则，算法

Comprehension

1. Vector control is ______.

   A. also called Field Oriented Control, FOC

   B. used to control the speed of three-phase AC electric motors

   C. used to control the torque of three-phase AC electric motors by controlling the input current

   D. all above

2. Which of the following is right? ______.

   A. To convert stator phase currents into a coordinate system rotating with the rotor of the motor, you have to know the rotor position

   B. Speed measurement can be used to obtain the rotor position by integrating the speed

   C. The rotor flux linkage vector is estimated by multiplying the stator current vector with magnetizing inductance L_m and low-pass filtering the result with the rotor no-load time the ratio of the rotor inductance to rotor resistance

   D. all above

3. In the process of Vector control, ______.
   A. PI-controllers are used to control voltage to their reference values
   B. the outputs of the PI controllers are the x-y components of the voltage reference vector for the stator
   C. usually the PI-controller also needs high-pass filtering of either the input or output of the controller in order to prevent the current ripple
   D. modulator uses PWM algorithms to define the required pulse widths of the rotor phase voltages
4. Vector control method has the properties that ______.
   A. speed or position measurement or some sort of estimation is not needed
   B. the step response has some overshoot if P control is used
   C. the switching frequency of the transistors is usually variable
   D. rotor temperature changes often result in the inaccuracy of the torque
5. Compared to Direct Torque Control, the vector control algorithm ______.
   A. is more complex
   B. needs to be calculated frequently
   C. needs the best current sensors in the market
   D. costs more

Chapter 3

Industry Computer Control Technology

Unit 12 Overview of Programmable Logic Controller (PLC)

What is a PLC?

Programmable logic controllers, also called programmable controllers or PLCs, are solid-state members of the computer family, using integrated circuits instead of electromechanical devices to implement control functions[1]. They are capable of storing instructions, such as sequencing, timing, counting, arithmetic, data manipulation, and communication, to control industrial machines and processes.

Programmable controllers have many definitions. However, PLCs can be thought of in simple terms as industrial computers with specially designed architecture. It is designed to read digital and analog inputs from various sensors, execute a user defined logic program, and write the resulting digital and analog output values to control industrial machines and processes (Fig.3.1).

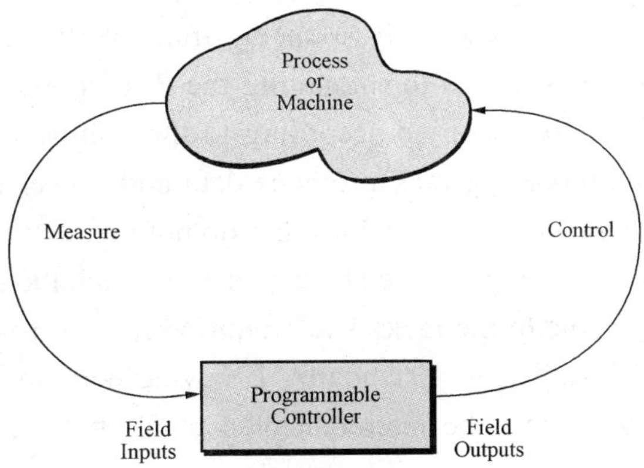

Fig.3.1 The principle of PLC

Now PLCs are used in many different industries and machines such as packaging and semiconductor machines. Well known PLC brands are Siemens, Allen-Bradley, ABB, Mitsubishi, Omron, and General Electric.

Components of the PLC

A schematic diagram of a programmable logic controller is presented in Fig.3.2. The basic components of the PLC are the following.

1. Processor

The processor (sometimes call a CPU), as in the self contained units, is generally specified according to memory required for the program to be implemented[2]. In the modularized versions, capability can also be a factor. This includes features such as higher math functions, PID control loops and optional programming commands. The processor consists of the microprocessor, system memory, and serial communication ports for printer, PLC LAN link and external programming device and, in some cases, the system power supply to power the processor and I/O modules.

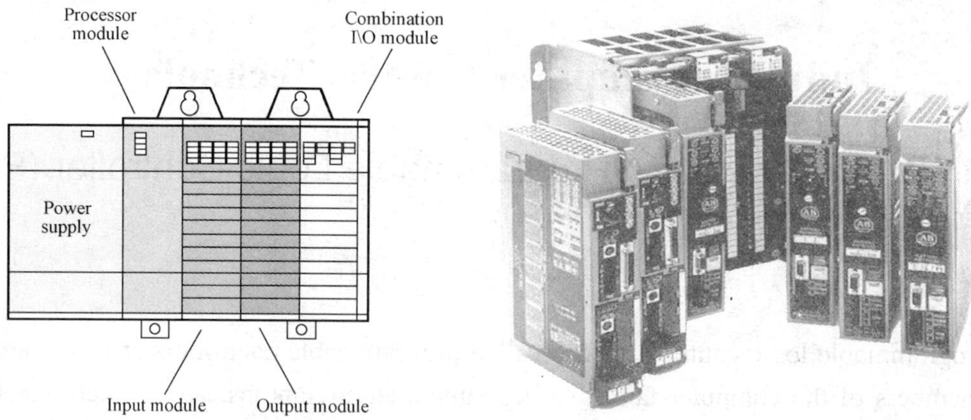

Fig.3.2 Diagram of the programmable logic controller

2. Mounting rack

This is usually a metal framework with a printed circuit board backplane which provides means for mounting the PLC input/output (I/O) modules and processor. Mounting racks are specified according to the number of modules required to implement the system. The mounting rack provides data and power connections to the processor and modules via the backplane. For CPUs that do not contain a power supply, the rack also holds the modular power supply. There are systems in which the processor is mounted separately and connected by cable to the rack. The mounting rack can be available to mount directly to a panel or can be installed in a standard "19" wide equipment cabinet. Mounting racks are cascadable so several may be interconnected to allow a system to accommodate a large number of I/O modules.

3. Input and output modules

Input/Output units are the interfaces between the internal PLC systems and the external processes to be monitored and controlled. Since the PLC is a logic based device with a typical operating voltage of 5 volts and the external processes usually demand higher powers and currents, the I/O modules are optically isolated[3]. The typical I/O operating voltages are 5V-240 V dc (or ac) and currents from 0.1A up to several amperes. The I/O modules are designed in this way to minimize or eliminate the need for any intermediate circuitry between the PLC and the process to be controlled. Small PLC units would have around 40 I/O connections with larger ones having more than 128 with either local or remote connections and extensive upgrade capabilities.

4. Power supply

The power supply specified depends upon the manufacturer's PLC being utilized in the application. As stated above, in some cases a power supply capable of delivering all required power for the system is furnished as part of the processor module[4]. If the power supply is a separate module, it must be capable of delivering a current greater than the sum of all the currents needed by the other modules. For systems with the power supply inside the CPU module, there may be some modules in the system which require excessive power not available from the processor either because of voltage or current requirements that can only be achieved through the addition of a second power source[5]. This is generally true if analog or external communication modules are present since these require ± DC supplies which, in the case of analog modules, must be well regulated.

5. Programming unit

The programming unit allows the engineer or technician to enter and edit the program to be executed. In it's simplest form it can be a hand held device with a keypad for program entry and a display device (LED or LCD) for viewing program steps or functions, as shown in Fig.3.3. More advanced systems employ a separate personal computer which allows the programmer to write, view, edit and download the program to the PLC. This is accomplished with proprietary software available from the PLC manufacturer. This software also allows the programmer or engineer to monitor the PLC as it is running the program. With this monitoring system, such things as internal coils, registers, timers and other items not visible externally can be monitored to determine proper operation. Also, internal register data can be altered if required to fine tune program operation. This can be advantageous when debugging the program. Communication with the programmable controller with this system is via a cable connected to a special programming port on the controller. Connection to the personal computer can be through a serial port or from a dedicated card installed in the computer.

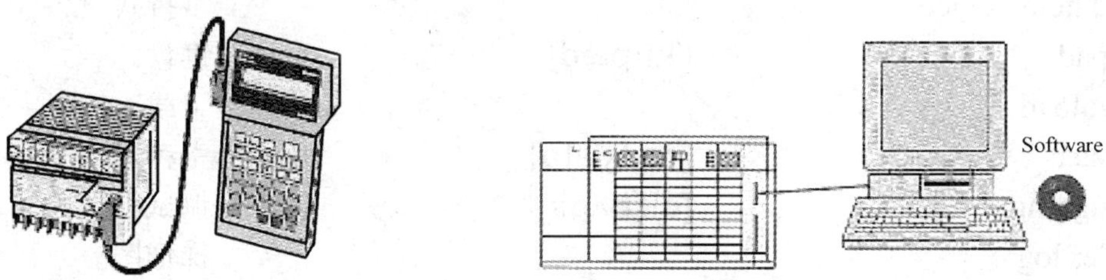

Fig.3.3 Programming Unit

Programming languages for PLC

Early PLCs were designed to replace relay logic systems. These PLCs were programmed in "ladder logic", which strongly resembles a schematic diagram of relay logic. Modern PLCs can be programmed in a variety of ways, from ladder logic to more traditional programming languages such as BASIC and C. Another method is State Logic, a Very High Level Programming Language designed to program PLCs based on State Transition Diagrams.

IEC 61131-3 currently defines five programming languages for programmable control systems: FBD (Function block diagram), LD (Ladder diagram), ST (Structured text, similar to the Pascal programming language), IL (Instruction list, similar to assembly language) and SFC (Sequential function chart).

Technical Words and Expressions

programmable logic controller			可编程控制器
electromechanical	[iˌlektrəumiˈkænikəl]	adj.	[机] 电动机械的，机电的，电机的
sequencing	[ˈsiːkwənsiŋ]	n.	先后顺序
timing	[ˈtaimiŋ]	n.	定时
counting	[ˈkauntiŋ]	n.	计算
data manipulation			数据操作
architecture	[ˈɑːkitektʃə]	n.	建筑，结构
brand	[brænd]	n.	商标，牌子
Siemen		n.	[德] 西门子
Allen-Bradley		n.	[美] 艾伦-布拉德利
Mitsubishi	[miˈtsubiʃi]	n.	[日] 三菱
Omron		n.	[日] 欧姆龙
processor	[ˈprəusesə]	n.	处理机，处理器
serial communication port			串行通信口
module	[ˈmɔdjuːl]	n.	组合部件，模块
mounting rack			机架
backplane			底板
hand held device			手持式设备
keypad	[ˈkiːpæd]	n.	键盘
download		vt.	下载
register	[ˈredʒistə]	n.	寄存器
debugging	[diːˈbʌgiŋ]	n.	调试
ladder logic			梯形图
Very High Level Programming Language			超高级编程语言
State Transition Diagram			状态转换图
FBD (Function block diagram)			功能块图
LD (Ladder diagram)			梯形图
ST (Structured text)			结构文本
IL (Instruction list)			指令表
SFC (Sequential function chart)			顺序功能图

Notes

[1] Programmable logic controllers, also called programmable controllers or PLCs, are solid-state members of the computer family, using integrated circuits instead of electromechanical devices to implement control functions.

译文为：可编程逻辑控制器，又称可编程控制器或PLC，是计算机家族的一员，它是用集成电路来执行控制任务，而不是机电设备。

“also called programmable controllers or PLCs”为过去分词作定语修饰“Programmable logic controllers”，“using…”部分为现在分词作状语修饰。

[2] The processor (sometimes call a CPU), as in the self contained units, is generally specified according to memory required for the program to be implemented.

译文为：处理器（有时又叫 CPU），整体式 PLC，通常根据执行程序所需的存储器的大小来指定的。

“required for the program”为过去分词作定语修饰“memory”，“to be implemented”为不定式作定语，修饰“program”。

[3] Since the PLC is a logic based device with a typical operating voltage of 5 volts and the external processes usually demand higher powers and currents, the I/O modules are optically isolated.

译文为：由于 PLC 是一个基于逻辑运算的设备，工作电压一般为 5V，而外部生产过程通常需要更高的电压和电流，因此输入/输出模块通常是光隔离的。

“Since”引导了一个原因状语从句，从句部分为“Since the PLC is...and currents”，主句部分为“the I/O modules are optically isolated”。从句为“and”连接的两个并列句，其中“with”表示“带有”的意思。

[4] As stated above, in some cases a power supply capable of delivering all required power for the system is furnished as part of the processor module.

译文为：如上所说，某些 PLC 的电源是作为处理器模块的一部分，它能够给系统提供各种所需电源。

“be furnished as”作为……提供，词句虽然是被动形式，但需按主动形式来翻译。

[5] For systems with the power supply inside the CPU module, there may be some modules in the system which require excessive power not available from the processor either because of voltage or current requirements that can only be achieved through the addition of a second power source.

译文为：对于电源内置在 CPU 模块中的 PLC，系统中可能存在一些模块，因为所需的电压或电流只能从附加的第二个电源上得到，这些模块所需的额外电源不能够从处理器上获得。

Which 引导定语从句修饰“modules”，该从句中“(which is) not available from the processor”为修饰“excessive power”的定语。

Exercises

Ⅰ. Mark the following statements with T (true) or F (false) according to the text.

1. PLCs use integrated circuits to implement control functions. (　　)

2. The processor (sometimes call a CPU), is generally specified according to memory required for the program to be implemented. (　　)

3. Mounting rack is usually a metal framework with a printed circuit board backplane which provides means for mounting the PLC input/output (I/O) modules only. (　　)

4. The typical I/O operating voltages are 5V-24V dc (or ac) and currents from 0.1A up to several amperes. (　　)

5. If the power supply is a separate module, it must be capable of delivering a current greater than the sum of all the currents needed by the other modules. (   )

Ⅱ. Complete the following sentences.

1. It is designed to read ______ from various ______, execute a user defined ______, and write the resulting digital and analog output values to control industrial machines and processes.

2. This includes features such as ______, ______ and ______.

3. The processor consists of the ______, system memory, ______ for printer, PLC LAN link and ______ and, in some cases, the system power supply to power the processor and ______.

4. More advanced systems of PLC employ a separate personal computer which allows the programmer to ______, ______, ______ and ______ the program to the PLC. This is accomplished with ______ available from the PLC ______.

5. Early PLCs were designed to replace _____. These PLCs were programmed in " _____ ", which strongly resembles a schematic diagram of relay logic. Modern PLCs can be programmed in a variety of ways, from ladder logic to ______ languages such as BASIC and C. Another method is ______.

Reading 12 Process Control System with PLC

Introduction

Generally speaking, process control system is made up of a group of electronic devices and equipment that provide stability, accuracy and eliminate harmful transition statuses in production processes. Operating system can have different form and implementation, from energy supply units to machines. As a result of fast progress in technology, many complex operational tasks have been solved by connecting programmable logic controllers and possibly a central computer. Beside connections with instruments like operating panels, motors, sensors, switches, valves and such, possibilities for communication among instruments are so great that they allow high level of exploitation and process coordination, as well as greater flexibility in realizing an process control system. Each component of a process control system plays an important role, regardless of its size. For example, without a sensor, PLC wouldn't know what exactly goes on in the process. In automated system, PLC controller is usually the central part of a process control system. With execution of a program stored in program memory, PLC continuously monitors status of the system through signals from input devices. Based on the logic implemented in the program, PLC determines which actions need to be executed with output instruments. To run more complex processes it is possible to connect more PLC controllers to a central computer. A real system could look like the one pictured in Fig.3.4.

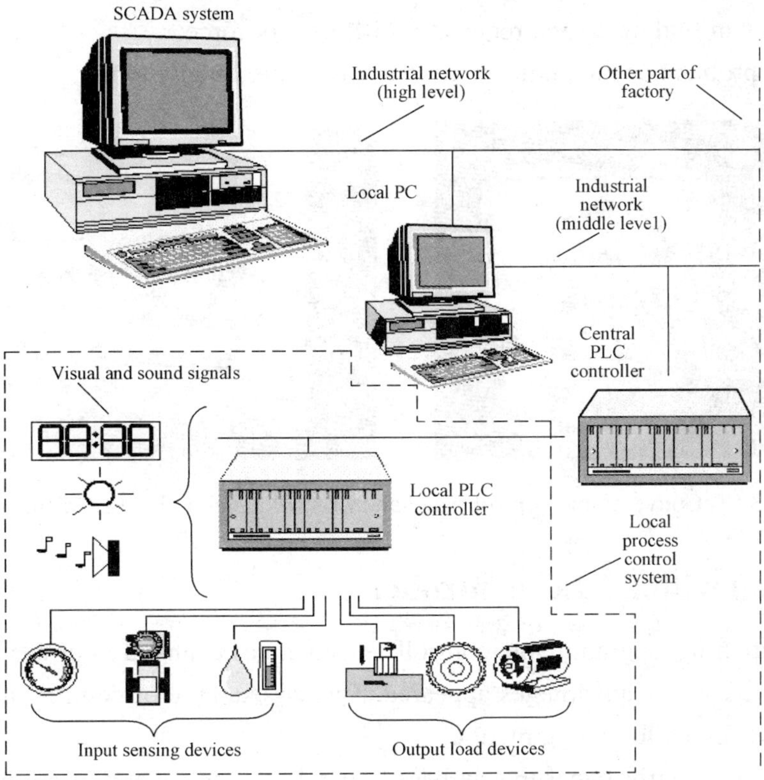

Fig.3.4 SCADA system

Conventional control panel

At the outset of industrial revolution, especially during sixties and seventies, relays were used to operate automated machines, and these were interconnected using wires inside the control panel. In some cases a control panel covered an entire wall. To discover an error in the system much time was needed especially with more complex process control systems. On top of everything, a lifetime of relay contacts was limited, so some relays had to be replaced. If replacement was required, machine had to be stopped and production too. Also, it could happen that there was not enough room for necessary changes. Control panel was used only for one particular process, and it wasn't easy to adapt to the requirements of a new system. As far as maintenance, electricians had to be very skillful in finding errors. In short, conventional control panels proved to be very inflexible. Typical example of conventional control panel is given in Fig.3.5.

In this photo you can notice a large number of electrical wires, time relays, timers and other elements of automation typical for that period. Pictured control panel is not one of the more "complicated" ones, so you can imagine what complex ones looked like.

Most frequently mentioned disadvantages of a classic control panel are:

- Too much work required in connecting wires;
- Difficulty with changes or replacements;

- Difficulty in finding errors; requiring skillful work force;
- When a problem occurs, hold-up time is indefinite, usually long.

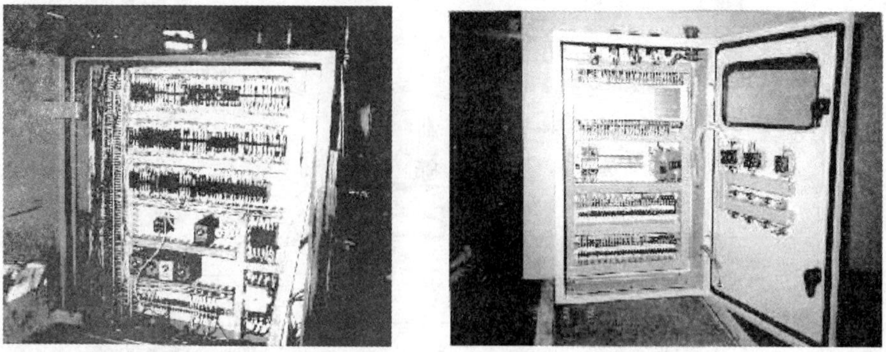

Fig.3.5 Conventional control panel and Control panel with a PLC controller

Control panel with a PLC controller

With invention of programmable controllers, much has changed in how a process control system is designed. Many advantages appeared. Typical example of control panel with a PLC controller is given in the following picture.

Advantages of control panel that is based on a PLC controller can be presented in few basic points:

1. Compared to a conventional process control system, number of wires needed for connections is reduced by 80%.

2. Consumption is greatly reduced because a PLC consumes less than a bunch of relays.

3. Diagnostic functions of a PLC controller allow for fast and easy error detection.

4. Change in operating sequence or application of a PLC controller to a different operating process can easily be accomplished by replacing a program through a console or using a PC software (not requiring changes in wiring, unless addition of some input or output device is required).

5. Needs fewer spare parts.

6. It is much cheaper compared to a conventional system, especially in cases where a large number of I/O instruments are needed and when operational functions are complex.

7. Reliability of a PLC is greater than that of an electro-mechanical relay or a timer.

Technical Words and Expressions

process control system	过程控制系统
operating panel	控制盘，控制面板
at the outset of	最初，开始
diagnostic function	诊断功能

1. In Process control system with PLC, the actions of output devices are determined by ______.

   A. the input signals of PLC　　B. the program in PLC

   C. the logic implemented in the computer　　D. A and B

2. which of the following is right? ______.

   A. At the beginner of industrial revolution, relays were used in conventional control panel

   B. The size of conventional control panel is very small

   C. Conventional control panel is easy to maintain

   D. Conventional control panel can be used for different process control system

3. The most disadvantage of a conventional control panel is ______.

   A. too much work required in connecting wires　　B. difficult in finding errors

   C. lifetime of relay contacts is limited　　D. all above

4. Compare to conventional control panel, control panel with a PLC controller ______.

   A. needs more wires

   B. maintenance is more complicated

   C. can be used to only one operating process easily

   D. is greater reliability

5. A PLC is much cheaper compared to an electro-mechanical relay or a timer, ______.

   A. when control functions are more complex

   B. when a control system needs a large number of input devices

   C. when a control system needs a large number of output devices

   D. all above

Unit 13 Applications of PLC

PLCs are industrial computers and able to interface with real-world devices such as switches, solenoids and so on. The actual logic of the control system is established inside the PLC by means of a computer program. This program dictates which output gets energized under which input conditions. Although the program itself appears to be a ladder logic diagram, with switch and relay symbols, there are no actual switch contacts or relay coils operating inside the PLC to create the logical relationships between input and output[1]. These are imaginary contacts and coils, if you will. The program is entered and viewed via a personal computer connected to the PLC's programming port.

Consider the circuit shown in Fig.3.6 and PLC program.

When the pushbutton switch is unactuated (unpressed), no power is sent to the X1 input of the PLC. Following the program, which shows a normally-open X1 contact in series with a Y1 coil, no "power" will be sent to the Y1 coil. Thus, the PLC's Y1 output remains de-energized, and the indicator lamp connected to it remains dark.

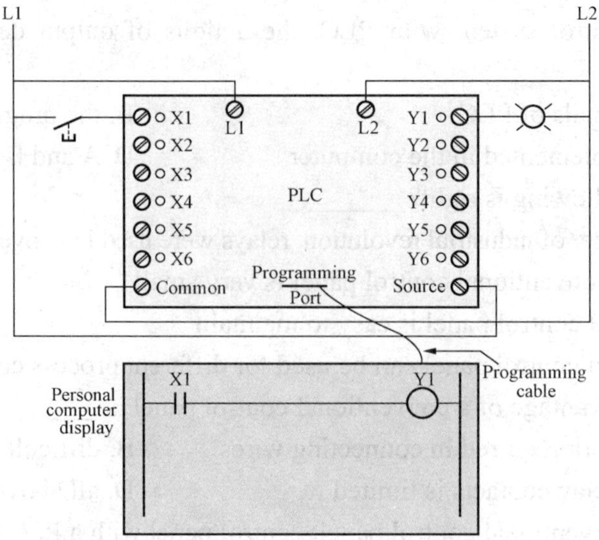

Fig.3.6 PLC circuit and PLC program

If the pushbutton switch is pressed, however, power will be sent to the PLC's X1 input. Any and all X1 contacts appearing in the program will assume the actuated (non-normal) state, as though they were relay contacts actuated by the energizing of a relay coil named "X1"[2]. In this case, energizing the X1 input will cause the normally-open X1 contact will "close," sending "power" to the Y1 coil. When the Y1 coil of the program "energizes", the real Y1 output will become energized, lighting up the lamp connected to it (Fig.3.7).

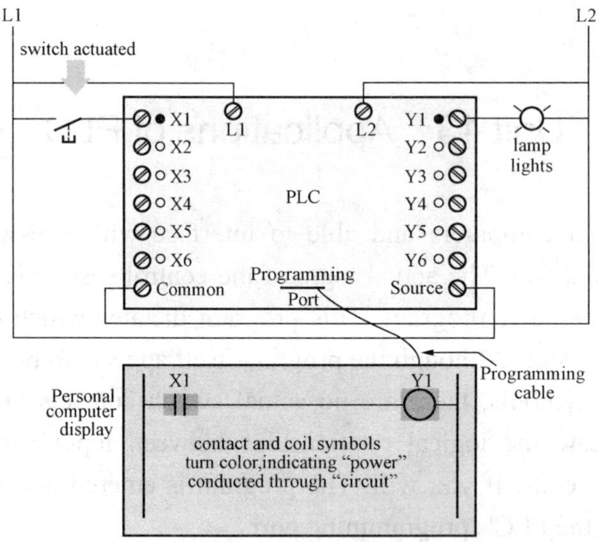

Fig.3.7 PLC circuit and PLC program

It must be understood that the X1 contact, Y1 coil, connecting wires, and "power" appearing in the personal computer's display are all virtual. They do not exist as real electrical components. They exist as commands in a computer program —— a piece of software only ——

that just happens to resemble a real relay schematic diagram.

Equally important to understand is that the personal computer used to display and edit the PLC's program is not necessary for the PLC's continued operation[3]. Once a program has been loaded to the PLC from the personal computer, the personal computer may be unplugged from the PLC, and the PLC will continue to follow the programmed commands. I include the personal computer display in these illustrations for your sake only, in aiding to understand the relationship between real-life conditions (switch closure and lamp status) and the program's status ("power" through virtual contacts and virtual coils)[4].

The true power and versatility of a PLC is revealed when we want to alter the behavior of a control system. Since the PLC is a programmable device, we can alter its behavior by changing the commands we give it, without having to reconfigure the electrical components connected to it.

One of the advantages of implementing logical control in software rather than in hardware is that input signals can be re-used as many times in the program as is necessary. For example, take the following circuit and program, designed to energize the lamp if at least two of the three pushbutton switches are simultaneously actuated (Fig.3.8).

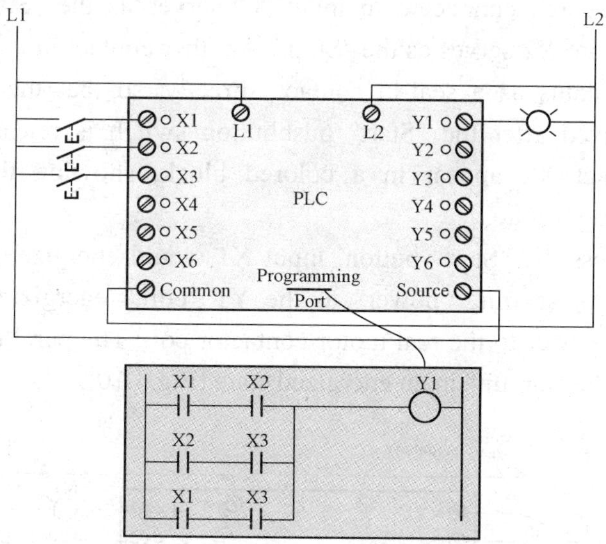

Fig.3.8 PLC circuit and PLC program

To build an equivalent circuit using electromechanical relays, three relays with two normally-open contacts each would have to be used, to provide two contacts per input switch. Using a PLC, however, we can program as many contacts as we wish for each "X" input without adding additional hardware, since each input and each output is nothing more than a single bit in the PLC's digital memory (either 0 or 1), and can be recalled as many times as necessary[5].

Furthermore, since each output in the PLC is nothing more than a bit in its memory as well, we can assign contacts in a PLC program "actuated" by an output (Y) status. Take for instance this next system, a motor start-stop control circuit (Fig.3.9).

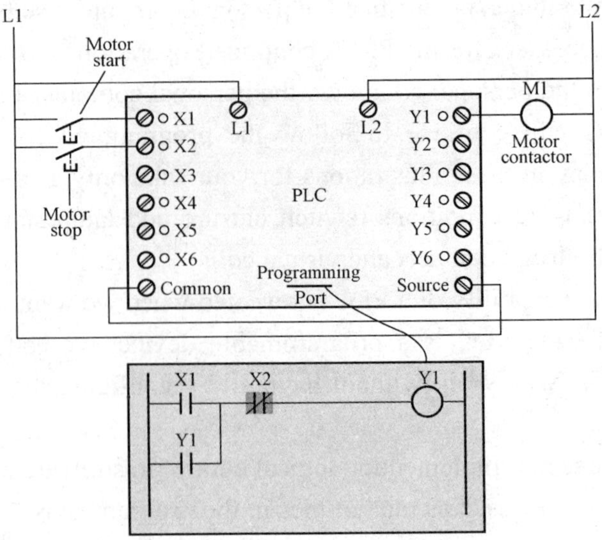

Fig.3.9 PLC circuit and PLC program

The pushbutton switch connected to input X1 serves as the "Start" switch, while the switch connected to input X2 serves as the "Stop." Another contact in the program, named Y1, uses the output coil status as a seal-in contact, directly, so that the motor contactor will continue to be energized after the "Start" pushbutton switch is released. You can see the normally-closed contact X2 appear in a colored block, showing that it is in a closed ("electrically conducting") state.

If we were to press the "Start" button, input X1 would energize, thus "closing" the X1 contact in the program, sending "power" to the Y1 "coil," energizing the Y1 output and applying 120 volt AC power to the real motor contactor coil. The parallel Y1 contact will also "close," thus latching the "circuit" in an energized state (Fig.3.10).

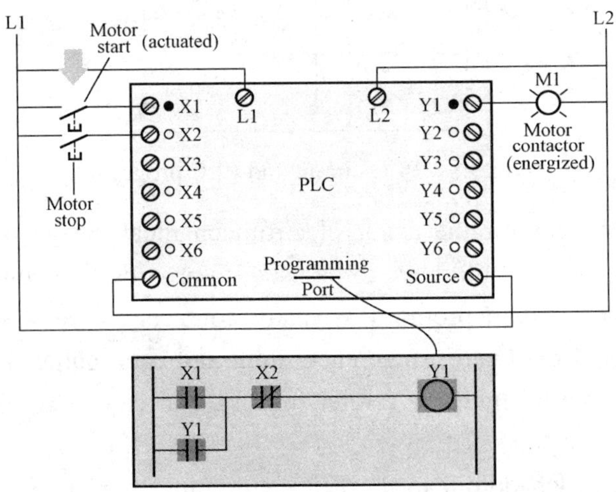

Fig.3.10 PLC circuit and PLC program

Now, if we release the "Start" pushbutton, the normally-open X1 "contact" will return to its "open" state, but the motor will continue to run because the Y1 seal-in "contact" continues to provide "continuity" to "power" coil Y1, thus keeping the Y1 output energized (Fig.3.11).

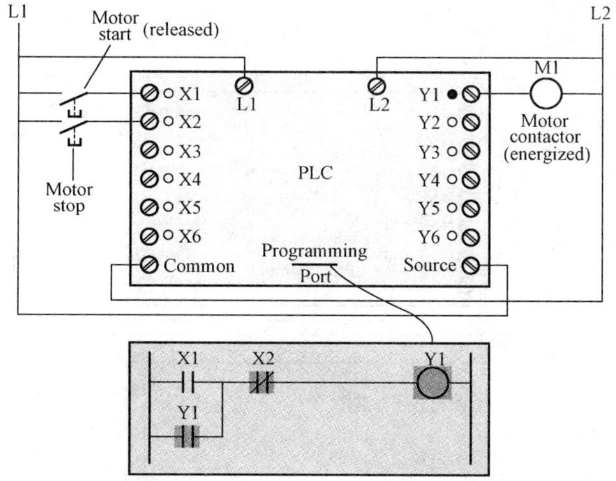

Fig.3.11 PLC circuit and PLC program

To stop the motor, we must momentarily press the "Stop" pushbutton, which will energize the X2 input and "open" the normally-closed "contact," breaking continuity to the Y1 "coil" (Fig.3.12).

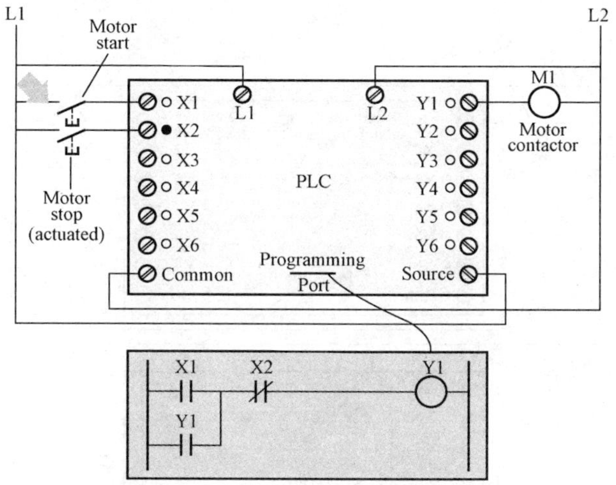

Fig.3.12 PLC circuit and PLC program

When the "Stop" pushbutton is released, input X2 will de-energize, returning "contact" X2 to its normal, "closed" state. The motor, however, will not start again until the "Start" pushbutton is actuated, because the "seal-in" of Y1 has been lost (Fig.3.13).

An important point to make here is that fail-safe design is just as important in PLC-controlled systems as it is in electromechanical relay-controlled systems. One should always consider the effects of failed (open) wiring on the device or devices being controlled. In this motor control circuit example, we have a problem: if the input wiring for X2 (the "Stop" switch) were to fail open, there would be no way to stop the motor!

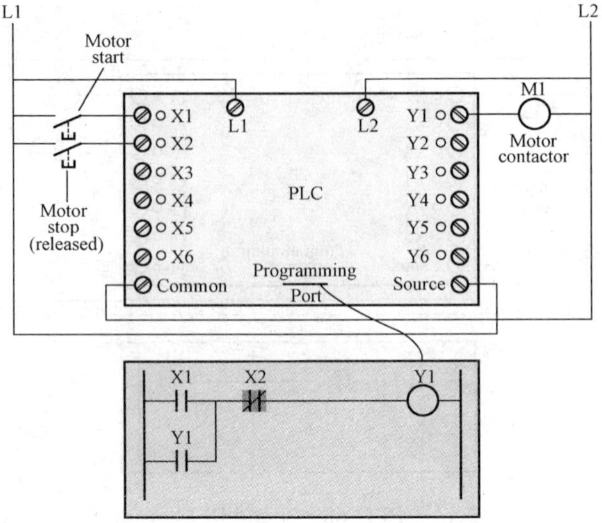

Fig.3.13 PLC circuit and PLC program

The solution to this problem is a reversal of logic between the X2 "contact" inside the PLC program and the actual "Stop" pushbutton switch (Fig.3.14).

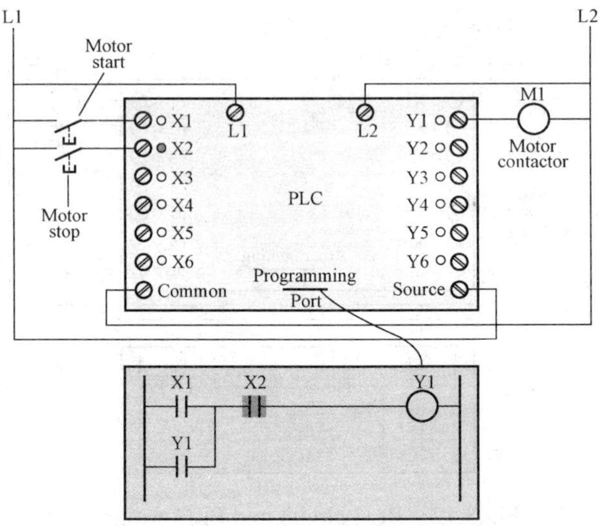

Fig.3.14 PLC circuit and PLC program

When the normally-closed "Stop" pushbutton switch is unactuated (not pressed), the PLC's X2 input will be energized, thus "closing" the X2 "contact" inside the program. This allows the motor to be started when input X1 is energized, and allows it to continue to run when the "Start" pushbutton is no longer pressed. When the "Stop" pushbutton is actuated, input X2 will de-energize, thus "opening" the X2 "contact" inside the PLC program and shutting off the motor. So, we see there is no operational difference between this new design and the previous design.

However, if the input wiring on input X2 were to fail open, X2 input would de-energize in the same manner as when the "Stop" pushbutton is pressed. The result, then, for a wiring failure on the X2 input is that the motor will immediately shut off. This is a safer design than the one previously shown, where a "Stop" switch wiring failure would have resulted in an inability to turn off the motor.

This section on programmable logic controllers illustrates just a small sample of their capabilities. As computers, PLCs can perform timing functions (for the equivalent of time-delay relays), drum sequencing, and other advanced functions with far greater accuracy and reliability than what is possible using electromechanical logic devices.

Technical Words and Expressions

solenoid	['səulinɔid]	n.	螺线管
dictate	[dik'teit]	n.	指令，指示，命令，规定
energize	['enədʒaiz]	vt.	使得电
programming port			编程口
normally-open contact			常开触点
indicator lamp			指示灯
non-normal			非正规的，非常态的
relay schematic diagram			继电器原理图
for…sake			为了……的缘故
reconfigure	[ˌri:kən'figə(r)]	v.	重新装配，改装
electromechanical relay			电磁继电器
digital memory			数字存储器
fail-safe design			可靠性设计
time-delay relay			延时继电器

Notes

[1] Although the program itself appears to be a ladder logic diagram, with switch and relay symbols, there are no actual switch contacts or relay coils operating inside the PLC to create the logical relationships between input and output.

译文为：尽管这个带有开关和继电器符号的程序看上去像梯形逻辑图，但 PLC 中并不是使用真实的开关或继电器线圈来建立输入输出间的逻辑关系的。

although 引导让步状语从句，主句中“operating…”为现在分词短语作定语修饰“actual switch contacts or relay coils”。

[2] Any and all X1 contacts appearing in the program will assume the actuated (non-

normal) state, as though they were relay contacts actuated by the energizing of a relay coil named "X1".

译文为：程序中所有 X1 的触点都将呈现激活（非常态）状态，它们就像继电器的触点一样被名为 X1 的继电器线圈激活。

appearing in the program 为现在分词短语作定语修饰主语“Any and all X1 contacts”。Though 引导状语从句，谓语用虚拟语气“were”，表示与事实相反，“actuated by…”部分为过去分词短语作定语修饰“relay contacts”。

[3] Equally important to understand is that the personal computer used to display and edit the PLC's program is not necessary for the PLC's continued operation.

译文为：同样重要的是，我们要明白用来显示和编辑 PLC 程序的个人电脑对于 PLC 的持续运行并不是必要的。

该句中含一个名词性 that 从句用作表语，该从句中“used”部分为过去分词短语作定语修饰从句主语“personal computer”。

[4] I include the personal computer display in these illustrations for your sake only, in aiding to understand the relationship between real-life conditions (switch closure and lamp status) and the program's status ("power" through virtual contacts and virtual coils).

译文为：为了帮助你理解实际环境（开关的闭合和电灯的状态）和程序状态（虚拟触点和线圈的通电情况）间的关系，我在图中加入了电脑的显示器部分。

“in aiding to”表示“为了”的意思。

[5] Using a PLC, however, we can program as many contacts as we wish for each "X" input without adding additional hardware, since each input and each output is nothing more than a single bit in the PLC's digital memory (either 0 or 1), and can be recalled as many times as necessary.

译文为：可是用 PLC 的话，我们就可在程序中为输入 X 编制任意多个触点而不需要增加额外的硬件，因为在 PLC 的数字存储器（0 或 1）中每个输入和输出只不过占一个位，并且可以被任意调用。

“Using”为现在分词置句首作条件状语从句，主句中含有一个“since”引导的原因状语从句“since each…necessary”。

Exercises

Ⅰ. Mark the following statements with T (true) or F (false) according to the text.

1. The actual logic of the control system is established inside the PLC by means of a computer program. (　　)

2. The contact, coil, connecting wires, and "power" appearing in the PLC's programming are all actual. (　　)

3. The personal computer used to display and edit the PLC's program is necessary for the PLC's continued operation. (　　)

4. One of the advantages of implementing logical control in software rather than in hardware is that input signals can be re-used as many times in the program as is necessary. (　　)

5. One should always consider the effects of failed (open) wiring on the device or devices being controlled. ( )

Ⅱ. Complete the following sentences.

1. Although the program of PLC appears to be a ______, with switch and relay ______, there are no actual switch ______ operating inside the PLC to create the logical relationships between input and output.

2. Since the PLC is ______, we can alter its behavior by changing ______ we give it, without having to ______ the electrical components connected to it.

3. ______ is just as important in PLC-controlled systems as it is in ______ -controlled systems.

4. Since each output in the PLC is nothing more than ______ in its ______ as well, we can assign ______ in a PLC program "actuated" by an ______.

5. As computers, PLCs can perform ________ (for the equivalent of time-delay relays), ______, and other advanced functions with far greater ______ and ______ than what is possible using electromechanical logic devices.

Reading 13 Ladder Diagram

Introduction

Programmable controllers are generally programmed in ladder diagram (or "relay diagram") which is nothing but a symbolic representation of electric circuits. Symbols were selected that actually looked similar to schematic symbols of electric devices, and this has made it much easier for electricians to switch to programming PLC controllers. Electrician who has never seen a PLC can understand a ladder diagram.

Ladder diagram

There are several languages designed for user communication with a PLC, among which ladder diagram is the most popular. Ladder diagram consists of one vertical line found on the left hand side, and lines which branch off to the right. Line on the left is called a "bus bar", and lines that branch off to the right are instruction lines. Conditions which lead to instructions positioned at the right edge of a diagram are stored along instruction lines. Logical combination of these conditions determines when and in what way instruction on the right will execute. Basic elements of a relay diagram can be seen in Fig.3.15.

Most instructions require at least one operand, and often more than one. Operand can be some memory location, one memory location bit, or some numeric value -number. In the example above, operand is bit 0 of memory location IR000. In a case when we wish to proclaim a constant as an operand, designation # is used beneath the numeric writing (for a compiler to know it is a constant and not an address.)

Based on the picture in Fig.3.15, one should note that a ladder diagram consists of two basic parts: left section also called conditional, and a right section which has instructions. When a condition is fulfilled, instruction is executed, and that's all!

Picture in Fig.3.16 represents a example of a ladder diagram where relay is activated in PLC controller when signal appears at input line 00. Vertical line pairs are called conditions. Each condition in a ladder diagram has a value ON or OFF, depending on a bit status assigned to it. In this case, this bit is also physically present as an input line (screw terminal) to a PLC controller. If a key is attached to a corresponding screw terminal, you can change bit status from a logic one status to a logic zero status, and vice versa. Status of logic one is usually designated as "ON", and status of logic zero as "OFF".

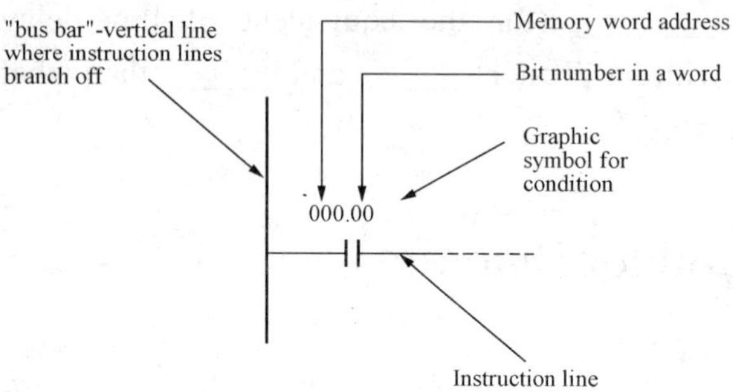

Fig.3.15 Basic elements of a relay diagram

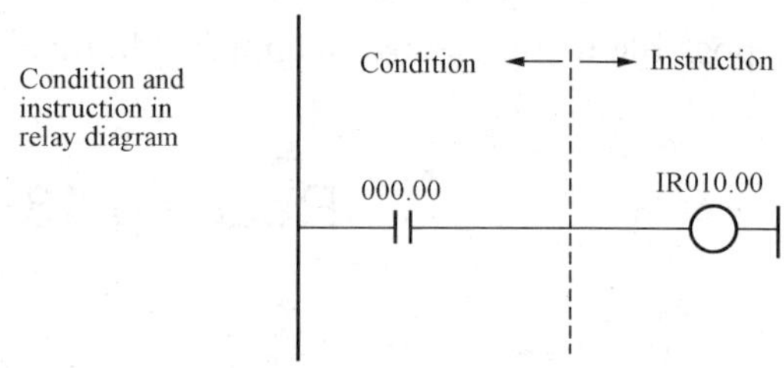

Fig.3.16 A example of a ladder diagram

Right section of a ladder diagram is an instruction which is executed if left condition is fulfilled. There are several types of instructions that could easily be divided into simple and complex. Example of a simple instruction is activation of some bit in memory location. In the example above, this bit has physical connotation because it is connected with a relay inside a PLC controller. When a CPU activates one of the leading four bits in a word IR010, relay contacts move and connect lines attached to it. In this case, these are the lines connected to a screw terminal marked as 00 and to one of COM screw terminals.

Brief example

Example below represents a basic program. Example consists of one input device and one output device linked to the PLC controller output. Key is an input device, and a bell is an output supplied through a relay 00 contact at the PLC controller output. Input 000.00 represents a condition in executing an instruction over 010.00 bit. Pushing the key sets off a 000.00 bit and satisfies a condition for activation of a 010.00 bit which in turn activates the bell. For correct program function another line of program is needed with END instruction, and this ends the program.

The picture in Fig.3.17 depicts the connection scheme for this example.

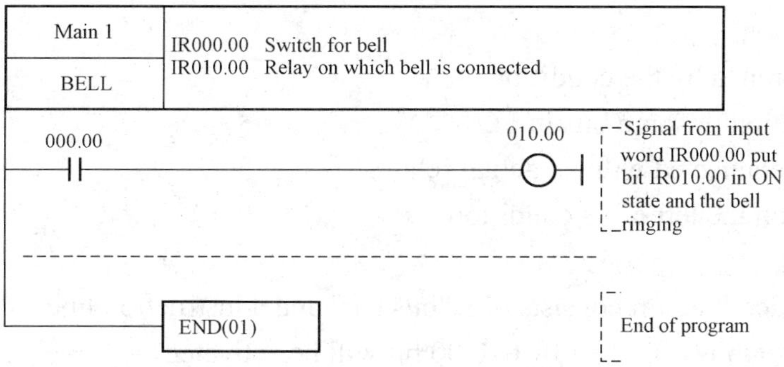

Fig.3.17 The connection scheme for this example

Technical Words and Expressions

vertical line		垂直线
branch off		分叉
bus bar		母线
instruction line		指令线
designation	n.	指示，指定
fulfill	vt.	实现，完成
screw terminal		螺纹接线端子

Comprehension

1. Why Electrician who has never seen a PLC can understand a ladder diagram? ______.
   A. A ladder diagram is a kind of assembler language
   B. A ladder diagram looks like actual circuit
   C. Symbols used in a ladder diagram look like actual electric devices
   D. Symbols used in a ladder diagram look like schematic symbols of electric devices
2. Which of the following is right? ______.
   A. PLCs are programmed in ladder diagram only
   B. A ladder diagram is a kind of electric circuits
   C. A ladder diagram is used to communication with a PLC
   D. Ladder diagram consists of a "bus bar" and a instruction line
3. In Fig.3.16 ______.
   A. if the Status of 000.00 is off , the condition is on
   B. if a key is attached to a corresponding screw terminal, you can change bit status from a logic zero status to a logic one status
   C. if a key is attached to a corresponding screw terminal, you can only change bit status from a logic one status to a logic zero status
   D. status of logic one must be designated as "ON", and status of logic zero as "OFF"

4. An instruction ______.
   A. is determined by the condition
   B. is activation of some bits in I/O
   C. may be connected with an actual relay
   D. locates on the left of its condition
5. In Fig.3.17, ______.
   A. the Ladder diagram consists of a "bus bar" and a instruction line
   B. if the switch is off , then IR 010.00 bit will be activated
   C. input device determines the state of IR000.00
   D. END instruction is not necessary

Unit 14 Introduction to Microcontrollers

A micro-controller can be compared to a small stand alone computer, it is a very powerful device, which is capable of executing a series of pre-programmed tasks and interacting with other hardware devices. Being packed in a tiny integrated circuit (IC) whose size and weight is usually negligible, it is becoming the perfect controller for robots or any machines requiring some kind of intelligent automation. A single microcontroller can be sufficient to control a small mobile robot, an automatic washer machine or a security system. Any microcontroller contains a memory to store the program to be executed, and a number of input/output lines that can be used to interact with other devices.

Nowadays, microcontrollers are so cheap and easily available that it is common to use them instead of simple logic circuits like counters for the sole purpose of gaining some design flexibility and saving some space[1]. Some machines and robots will even rely on a multitude of microcontrollers, each one dedicated to a certain task. Most recent microcontrollers are "In System Programmable", meaning that you can modify the program being executed, without removing the microcontroller from its place.

The 8051 microcontroller architecture

The 8051 is the name of a big family of microcontrollers. The device which we are going to use is the "AT89S52" (Fig.3.18) which is a typical 8051 microcontroller manufactured by AtmelTM[2].

A simpler architecture of 89S52 can be represented as the Fig.3.19. Fig.3.19 shows the main features and components that the designer can interact with. You can notice that the 89S52 has 4 different ports, each one having 8 input/output lines providing a total of 32 I/O lines. Those ports can be used to output DATA and orders do other devices, or to read the state of a sensor, or a switch. Most of the ports of the 89S52 have "dual function", meaning that they can be used for two different functions: the fist one is to perform input/output operations and the second one is used to implement special features of the microcontroller like counting external pulses, interrupting the execution of the program according to external events, performing serial data transfer or connecting the chip to a computer to update the software. Each port has 8 pins, and will be treated from the software point of view as an 8-bit variable called "register", each bit being connected to a different Input/Output pin[3].

Fig.3.18 AT89S52

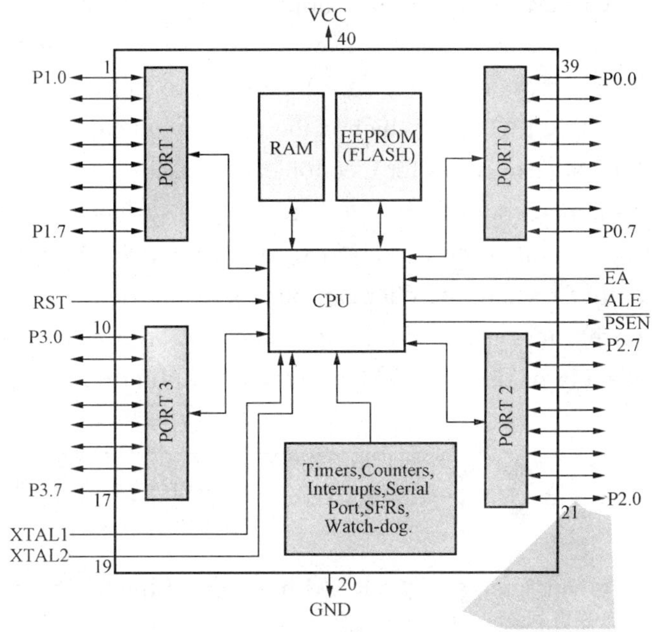

Fig.3.19 Architecture of 89S52

You can also notice two different memory types: RAM and EEPROM. Shortly, RAM is used to store variable during program execution, while the EEPROM memory is used to store the program itself, that's why it is often referred to as the "program memory".

The special features of the 89S52 microcontroller are grouped in the blue box at the bottom of Fig.3.19.

It is clear that the CPU (Central Processing Unit) is the heart of the microcontrollers. It is the CPU that will Read the program from the FLASH memory and execute it by interacting with the different peripherals discussed above.

Fig.3.20 shows the pin configuration of the 89S52, where the function of each pin is written next to it, and, if it exists, the dual function is written between brackets. The pins are written in

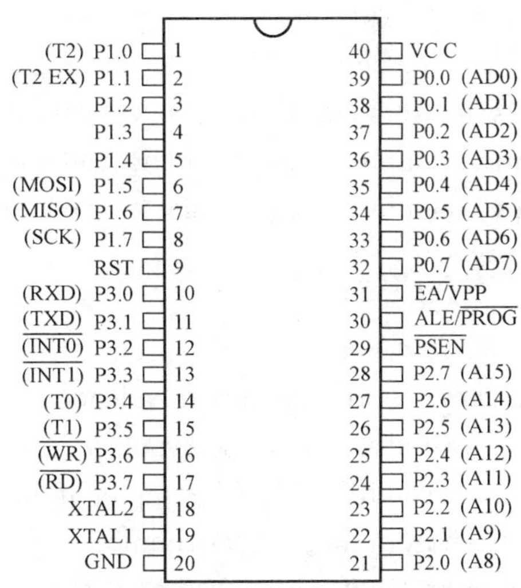

Fig.3.20 The pin configuration of the 89S52

the same order as in the block diagram of Fig.3.20, except for the VCC and GND pins which I usually note at the top and the bottom of any device. Note that the pin that have dual functions, can still be used normally as an input/output pin.

Memory organization

A RAM stands for Random Access Memory, it has basically the same purpose of the RAM in a desktop computer, which is to store some data required during the execution time of different programs. While an EEPROM, also called FLASH memory is a more elaborated ROM (Read Only Memory) which is the memory where the program being executed is stored[4]. The EEPROM term stands for Electronically Erasable and Programmable Read Only Memory.

In microcontrollers, like in any digital system, memory is organized in Registers, Which is the basic unit of construction of a memory. Each register is composed of a number of bits (usually 8) where the data can be stored. In the 8051 family of microcontrollers for example, most registers are 8-bit register, capable of storing values ranging from 0 to 255. Fig.3.21 shows a typical 8-bit registers, where the notation D0 to D7 stands for the 8 DATA bits of the register.

D7	D6	D5	D4	D3	D2	D1	D0

Fig.3.21 Typical register

As you shall see, the RAM memory of the 89S52, which contains 256 registers, is divided into to main parts, the GPR part, and the SFR part. GPR stands for "General Purpose Register" and are the registers that you can use to store any data during the execution of your program. SFRs (Special function Register) are registers used to control the functioning of the microcontroller and to assist the processor through the various operations being executed. For example, SFRs can be used to control Input/Output lines, to retrieve data transmitted through the serial port of a desktop computer, or to configure one of the on-chip counters and timers.

In a memory each register has a specific address which is used by the processor to read and write from specific memory location. The address is noted in Hexadecimal format as this notation simplifies digital logic calculations for the designers, 00 corresponds to the first location and FF which is equal to 256 corresponds to the last location.

Clock concept

The clock is a simple circuit that will generate pulses of electricity at a very specific frequency. Those pulses will cadence all the events happening inside a microcontroller, those pulses will also assure the synchronization of the events between various components inside the microcontroller. For example, if the CPU is waiting for some result of mathematical operation from the ALU (Arithmetic and Logic Unit), it will be known —— according to very specific protocol —— when and where the resulting data will be delivered to the CPU. The synchronization of those two devices is maintained because they share the same clock.

The clock has another very important role which is to enable the microcontroller to count timing. Without a precise clock, it would be impossible to build a "Real Time System", or any other device that relies on time measurements. It can be deduced that the precision of the timing of a microcontroller depends on the frequency of its clock.

In the 89S52 microcontroller, the clock can be fixed to different value by connecting a crystal to the pins 18 and 19. The maximum operating frequency of the AT89S52 is 33 MHz.

Technical Words and Expressions

micro-controller			微控制器
pre-programmed		adj.	预编程序的
negligible	['neglidʒəbl]	adj.	可以忽略的，不予重视的
intelligent	[in'telidʒənt]	n.	［计］智能的
security system			安全系统
multitude	['mʌltitjuːd]	n.	大量；众多
dedicate to			献身，用于
architecture	['ɑːkitektʃə]	n.	体系机构，结构；建筑
sensor	['sensə]		传感器
interrupt	[ˌintə'rʌpt]	n.	中断，中断信号
RAM (Random-access memory)			随机存储器
EEPROM			电可擦除只读存储器
FLASH memory			闪存
peripheral	[pə'rifərəl]	n.& adj.	外围设备；外围的
bracket	['brækit]	n.	括弧
elaborate	[i'læbərət]	adj.	精致的，精巧的
notation	[nəu'teiʃən]	n.	符号
GPR (General Purpose Register)			通用寄存器
SFR			特殊功能寄存器
serial port			［计］串行端口
on-chip			芯片内
memory location			存储单元
cadence	['keidəns]	n.	节奏，韵律
synchronization	[ˌsiŋkrənai'zeiʃən]	n.	同步
ALU (Arithmetic and Logic Unit)			算术逻辑部件，运算器
Real Time System			实时系统
fix	[fiks]	vi.	选定，确定
crystal	['kristl]	n.	石英晶振

Notes

[1] Nowadays, microcontrollers are so cheap and easily available that it is common to use

them instead of simple logic circuits like counters for the sole purpose of gaining some design flexibility and saving some space.

译文为：现在微控制器/单片机非常便宜且容易买到，因此为了增强设计的灵活性及节省空间，常用它们来替代一些像计数器这样简单的逻辑电路。

此句为 so…that…的结构。

[2] The device which we are going to use is the "AT89S52" which is a typical 8051 microcontroller manufactured by Atmel TM.

译文为：我们将使用的芯片是 AT89S52，它是 ATRNEL 公司制造的典型的 8051 系列微控制器/单片机。

该句结构为：The device（主语）＋is（谓语）＋the "AT89S52"（宾语），其中第一个 which 定语从句修饰"device"，第二个 which 定语从句修饰"AT89S52"，该从句中又有一个过去分词短语（manufactured by Atmel TM）作定语修饰"8051 microcontroller"。

[3] Each port has 8 pins, and will be treated from the software point of view as an 8-bit variable called "register", each bit being connected to a different Input/Output pin.

译文为：每个端口有 8 个引脚，在软件中它们被看作一个 8 位的变量，叫做寄存器，每一位都被连到不同的输入/输出引脚上。

and 引导两个主语相同的并列句，第二句的主语省略，其宾语"8-bit variable"带一个过去分词短语作定语 called "register".

[4] While an EEPROM, also called FLASH memory is a more elaborated ROM (Read Only Memory) which is the memory where the program being executed is stored.

译文为：而 EEPROM 又被称为闪存是一个更为复杂的 ROM（只读存储器），它是个用来存储被执行程序的存储器。

which 引导定语从句修饰"ROM"，该从句中有包含了一个 where 引导的定语从句修饰"memory"，而在 where 从句中"being executed"为现在分词作定语修饰"the program"。

Exercises

Ⅰ. Mark the following statements with T (true) or F (false) according to the text.

1. Nowadays, microcontrollers are cheap and easily available. (　　)

2. The 8051 is the name of a big family of microcontrollers. (　　)

3. 89S52 has 3 different ports, each one having 8 Input/output lines providing a total of 24 I/O lines. (　　)

4. There are two different memory types in89S52: RAM and EEPROM. (　　)

5. The ROM memory of the 89S52 contains 256 registers. (　　)

Ⅱ. Complete the following sentences.

1. Most recent microcontrollers are "______", meaning that you can ______ the program ______, without removing the microcontroller from its place.

2. Most of the ports of the 89S52 have "______", meaning that they can be used for two different ______: the fist one is to perform input/output operations and the second one is used to ______ of the microcontroller like counting external pulses, ______ the execution of the

program according to external events, performing ______.

3. It is the CPU that will Read the program from the ______ and execute it by interacting with ______.

4. A RAM stands for ______, which is to store some ______ required during the execution time of different programs. While an EEPROM, also called ______ is a more elaborated ROM (______) which is the memory where the program being executed is stored.

5. The ______ is a simple circuit that will generate ______ of electricity at a very specific ______. In the 89S52 microcontroller, the ______ can be ______ to different value by connecting ______ to the pins 18 and 19.

Reading 14 The Beginning...

As always, beginning is the most difficult. You have bought microcontroller, you have learned everything about its systems and registers, you have great idea how to apply all that in practice. The only thing left over to you is to start...

How to start working?

Microcontroller is a good-natured "giant from the bottle" and there is no need for extra knowledge in order to use it.

In order to create your first device under microcontroller's control, you need: the simplest PC, program for compiling into machine code and simple device for "transferring" that code from PC to chip itself.

The process itself is quite logical but dilemmas are anyway common, not because it is complicated but for the fact that there are numerous variations. Let's start...

Writing program in assembler

In order to write a program for the microcontroller, a specialized program in Windows environment may be used. It may, but it does not have to... On using such a software, there are numerous tools which facilitate operating (first of all simulator tool). This is a distinct advantage, but there are other ways too. Basically, text is the only important thing. Because of that any program for text processing can be used for writing program. The point is to write all instructions in order they should be executed by the microcontroller. The rules of assembly language are observed and instructions are written as they are defined. Program idea is followed. That's all!

```
RESET      VECTOR
           CSEG    AT      0
           JMP     XRESET              ; Reset vector
           CSEG
```

```
              ORG     100H
XRESET:       ORL     WMCON, #PERIOD      ; Defining of Watch-dog period
              ORL     WMCON, #WDTEN       ; Watch-dog timer is enabled
```

If a document is written for being used further by programmer then it has to have an extension, .asm in its name, for example: Program.asm.

If a program is written using a specialized program (mplab), this extension will be automatically added. If any other program for text processing (Notepad) is used then the document should be saved and additionally renamed. For example: Program.txt→Program.asm. This procedure is not necessary. The document may be saved in original format while its text may be copied to programmer for further use.

As seen, text of the program is the only thing that matters.

Compiling into machine code

Microcontroller "does not understand" assembly language. That is why this program should be compiled. If a specialized program is used —— nothing simpler —— a machine code compiler is a part of the software! Problem is solved by a click on the appropriate icon. The result is a new document which has extension .hex in its name. That is the same program you have already written, but compiled into machine language which microcontroller perfectly understands. The common name of this document is "hex code" and represents apparently meaningless series of numbers in hexadecimal numerical system.

```
:03000000020100FA1001000075813F
7590FFB29012010D80F97A1479D40
90110003278589EAF3698E8EB25B
A585FEA2569AD96E6D8FED9FAD
```

In case some other software for writing program in assembler is used, a software especially installed for compiling into machine code must be used. This compiler is activated, document with extension .asm is open and the appropriate command is executed. The result is the same —— a new document with extension .hex. The only problem is that it is stored in your PC.

Copy program to a microcontroller

A cable for serial communication and a special device called programmer are necessary to transfer "hex code" to the microcontroller. There are also several options on how to do it.

A great deal of programs and electronic circuits having this purpose can be found on Internet. Do as follows: open hex code document, adjust a few parameters and click on the icon for compiling. After a while, a series of zeros and units will be programmed into the microcontroller through the serial connection cable. The only thing left over is to transfer programmed chip to the final device. In case it is necessary to change something in the program, the previous procedure may be repeated.

The flowering pictures show steps of the beginning (Fig.3.22).

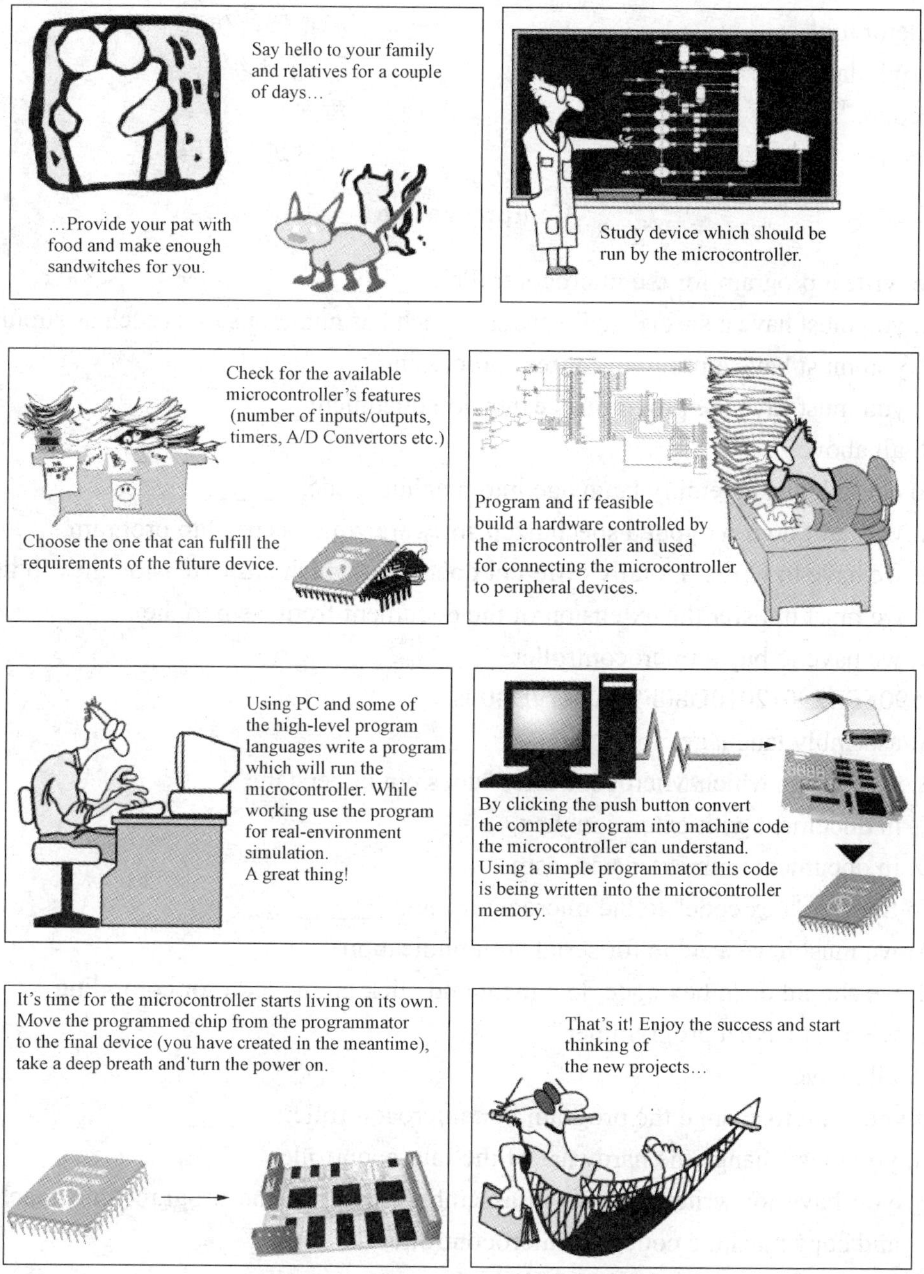

Fig.3.22 Programming for the beginners

Technical Words and Expressions

compile	vt.	编译，编辑，汇编
machine code		［计］机器代码
dilemma	n.	困境
assembler	n.	汇编程序
facilitate	vt.	使容易，使便利，推动

simulator tool		模拟器，仿真工具
assembly language		[计] 汇编语言
procedure	n.	程序
hex code		十六进制代码

Comprehension

1. To write a program for the microcontroller, ______.
   A. you must have a specialized software which has numerous tools such as simulator tool
   B. you must have a program for text processing
   C. you must save the program as extension document
   D. all above
2. To compile the assembly language into machine code, ______.
   A. we can't do it without a specialized software which is used to program
   B. we have to writer a totally different document which has extension .hex in its name
   C. we must transfer the extension of the document from .asm to .hex
   D. we have to buy a microcontroller
3. 7590FFB29012010D80F97A1479D40 is ______.
   A. assembly language
   B. a language which Microcontroller "does not understand"
   C. in document with extension .hex
   D. in document with extension .asm
4. To transfer "hex code" to the microcontroller, ______.
   A. we must have a cable for serial communication
   B. we should open hex code document and click on the icon for compiling
   C. we must have a programmer
   D. all above
5. If you want to change the program in a microcontroller, ______.
   A. you must change the hardware of the microcontroller
   B. you have to: write program in assembler, compile the program into machine code and copy machine code to a microcontroller
   C. you have to change the ASM file in the microcontroller
   D. all above

Unit 15 8051 Instruction Set

Introduction

Writing program for the microcontroller mainly consists of giving instructions (commands) in that order in which they should be executed later in order to carry out specific task[1]. As electronics can not "understand" what for example instruction "if the push button is pressed-turn the light on" means, then a certain number of simpler and precisely defined orders that decoder can recognize must be used. All commands are known as INSTRUCTION SET. All microcontrollers compatible with the 8051 have in total of 255 instructions, i.e. 255 different words available for program writing.

At first sight, it is imposing number of odd signs that must be known by heart. However, it is not so complicated as it looks like. Many instructions are considered to be "different", even though they perform the same operation, so there are only 111 truly different commands. For example: ADD A, R0, ADD A, R1... ADD A, R7 are instructions that perform the same operation (addition of the accumulator and register) but since there are 8 such registers, each instruction is counted separately! Taking into account that all instructions perform only 53 operations (addition, subtraction, copy etc.) and most of them are rarely used in practice, there are actually 20～30 shortened forms needed to be known, which is acceptable.

Types of instructions

Depending on operation they perform, all instructions are divided in several groups:

- Arithmetic Instructions;
- Branch Instructions;
- Data Transfer Instructions;
- Logical Instructions;
- Logical Instructions with bits.

The first part of each instruction, called MNEMONIC refers to the operation an instruction performs (copying, addition, logical operation etc.). Mnemonics commonly are shortened form of name of operation being executed. For example:

INC R1—means: Increment R1 (increment register R1).

Another part of instruction, called OPERAND is separated from mnemonic at least by one empty space and defines data being processed by instructions[2]. Some instructions have no operand, some have one, two or three. If there is more than one operand in instruction, they are separated by comma. For example:

RET—(return from sub-routine)—no operand.

ADD A, R3—(add R3 and accumulator)—two operand.

CJNE A, #20, LOOP—(compare accumulator with 20. If they are not equal, jump to address specified as LOOP)—three operand.

The operands listed below are written in shortened forms having the following meaning:

A—Accumulator.

Rn—Rn is one of R registers (R0～R7) in the currently active bank in RAM.

Rx—Rx is any register in RAM with 8-bit address. It can be a general-purpose register or SFR Register (I/O port, control register etc.).

@Ri—Ri is R0 or R1 register in the currently active bank. It contains register.

address—the instruction is referring to.

#X—X is any 8-bit number (0～255).

#X16—X is any 16-bit number (0～65535).

adr16—16-bit address is specified.

adr11—11-bit address is specified.

rel—The address of a close memory location is specified (−128 to +127 relative to the current one).

bit—Bit address is specified.

C—Carry bit in the status register (register PSW).

Arithmetic instructions

These instructions perform several basic operations (addition, subtraction, division, multiplication etc.). After execution, the result is stored in the first operand. For example:

ADD A, Rn—Instruction adds the number in the accumulator and the number in register Rn (R0～R7). After addition, the result is stored in the accumulator.

SUBB A,Rx

Description: Instruction performs subtract operation: A-Rx including the Carry bit as well which acts as borrow. If the higher bit is subtracted from the lower bit then the Carry bit is set. As it is direct addressing, Rx can be some of SFRs or general-purpose register with address 0～7FH. (0～127 dec.). The result is stored in the accumulator.

DEC Rx

Description: Instruction decrements value of the register Rx by 1. As it is direct addressing, Rx must be within the first 255 locations of RAM. If there is a 0 in the register, the result will be FFH.

Branch Instructions

There are two kinds of these instructions:

Unconditional jump instructions: after their execution a jump to a new location from where the program continues execution is executed[3]. For example:

ACALL adr11—Call subroutine located at address within 2 K byte Program Memory space.

RET—Return from subroutine.

Conditional jump instructions: if some condition is met—a jump is executed. Otherwise, the program normally proceeds with the next instruction. For example:

JBC bit, rel

Description: This instruction first check if the bit is set. If it is set, a jump to the specified address is executed and afterwards the bit is cleared. Otherwise, the program proceeds with the first next instruction. This is a short jump instruction, which means that the address of a new location must be relatively near the current position in the program (-129 to + 127 locations relative to the first following instruction).

Data Transfer Instructions

These instructions move the content of one register to another one. The register which content is moved remains unchanged. If they have the suffix "X" (MOVX), the data is exchanged with external memory. For example:

MOV A,@Ri

Description: Instruction moves the Rx register to the accumulator. Rx register address is stored in the Ri register (R0 or R1). After instruction execution, the result is stored in the accumulator. The Rx Register is not affected.

XCH A, Rx

Description: Instruction sets the contents of the accumulator into the register Rx. At the same time, the content of the Rx register is set into the accumulator. As it is direct addressing, the register Rx can be some of SFRs or general-purpose register with address 0～7FH (0～127 dec.).

Logical Instruction

These instructions perform logical operations between corresponding bits of two registers. After execution, the result is stored in the first operand.

ADD A, Rx

Description: Instruction adds the accumulator and Rx register. As it is direct addressing, Rx can be some of SFRs or general-purpose register with address 0～7 FH. The result is stored in the accumulator.

ORL A, #X

Description: Instruction performs logical-OR operation between the accumulator and number X. The result of this logical operation is stored in the accumulator.

CLR A/C

Description: Clear accumulator/Carry bit.

Logical Operations on Bits

Similar to logical instructions, these instructions perform logical operations. The difference is that these operations are performed on single bits.

ANL C, bit

Description: Instruction performs logical-AND operation between the addressed bit and Carry bit.

Technical Words and Expressions

execute	['eksikju:t]	vt.	执行，实行
instruction set			指令组（表），指令系统

compatible	[kəm'pætəbl]]	adj.	谐调的，一致的，兼容的
addition	[ə'diʃən]	n.	加法
subtraction	[səb'trækʃən]	n.	[数学] 减法
arithmetic instruction			算术运算指令
branch instruction			转移指令
data transfer instruction			数据传送指令
logical instruction			逻辑操作指令
logical instructions with bit			位操作逻辑指令
mnemonic	[ni(:)'mɔnik(əl)]	n.	操作码
operand	['ɔpəˌrænd]	n.	[计] 操作数
comma	['kɔmə]	n.	逗点，逗号
subroutine	[ˌsʌbru:'ti:n]	n.	[计] 子程序
accumulator	[ə'kju:mjuleitə]	n.	累加器，加法器
jump	[dʒʌmp]	n.	[计算机科学] 转移
general-purpose register			通用寄存器
status register			状态寄存器
division	[di'viʒən]	n.	除法
external memory			外存储器
direct addressing		n.	直接寻址

Notes

[1] Writing program for the microcontroller mainly consists of giving instructions (commands) in that order in which they should be executed later in order to carry out specific task.

译文为：对微处理器的编程主要是按顺序给出指令，然后执行指令，从而完成某一特定任务。

该句的主语为“Writing program for the microcontroller”，动名词“writing”作主语。in which 引导一个定语从句，修饰“order”。

[2] Another part of instruction, called OPERAND is separated from mnemonic at least by one empty space and defines data being processed by instructions.

译文为：指令的另一部分叫做操作数，它是通过至少一个空格与操作码进行隔离并对指令中处理的数据进行定义。

“and”引导两个主语相同的并列句，后一句省略主语，“being processed by instructions”为现在分词短语作定语修饰“data”。

[3] Unconditional jump instructions: after their execution a jump to a new location from where the program continues execution is executed.

译文为：无条件转移指令：当程序执行完该指令，程序将跳转到一个新的地址继续执行程序。

该句的主干为：a jump（主语）＋is executed（谓语）。其中，from where 引导一个定语从句。

Exercises

Ⅰ. Mark the following statements with T (true) or F (false) according to the text.

1. All microcontrollers compatible with the 8051 have in total of 111 instructions. (　　)
2. Many instructions are considered to be "same", if they perform the same operation. (　　)
3. Some instructions have no operand, some have one, two or three. (　　)
4. Arithmetic instructions perform several basic operations. After execution, the result is stored in the last operand. (　　)
5. Logical Instructions are performed on single bits. (　　)

Ⅱ. Complete the following sentences.

1. Depending on operation they perform, all instructions are divided in several groups: ______, ______, ______, ______ Logical Instructions with bits.
2. The first part of each instruction, called ______ refers to ______. Another part of instruction, called ______ is separated from mnemonic at least by one ______ and defines data being processed by instructions.
3. ADD A, Rn—Instruction adds the number in ______ and the number in ______ Rn (R0～R7). After addition, the result is stored in ______.
4. There are two kinds of ______: Unconditional jump instructions and ______.
5. XCH A, Rx—Instruction sets the contents of the ______ into the register Rx. At the same time, the content of the Rx register is set into the accumulator. As it is ______, the register Rx can be some of SFRs or ______ with address 0～7FH (0～127 dec.).

Reading 15　Basic Input/Output Operations of 8051

I/O port detailed structure

It is important to have some basic notions about the structure of an I/O port in the 8051 architecture. You will notice along this tutorial how this will affect our choices when it comes to connect I/O devices to the ports. Actually, the I/O ports configuration and mechanism of the 8051 can be confusing, due to the fact that a pin acts as an output pin as well as an input pin in the same time.

Fig.3.23 shows the internal diagram of a single I/O pin of port 1. The first thing you have to notice is that there are tow different direction for the data flow from the microcontroller's processor and the external pin: The Latch value and the Pin value. The latch value is the value that the microcontroller tries to output on the pin, while the pin value, is the actual logic state

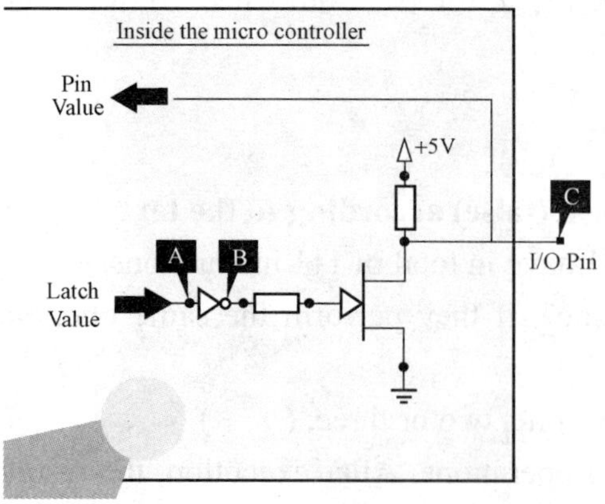

Fig.3.23 Basic I/O pin internal diagram

of the pin, regardless of the latch value that was set by the processor in the first place. The microcontroller reads the state of a pin through the Pin value line, and writes through the latch value line. If you imagine the behavior of the simple circuit in Fig.3.23, you'll notice that the I/O pin should follow the voltage change of the Latch value, providing 5V through the pull-up resistor, or 0V by connecting the pin directly to the GND through the transistor.

When the pin is pulled high by the pull-up resistor, the pin can output 5V but can also be used as an input pin, because there is no any risk of short-circuit due to the presence of a resistor. This can be easily verified by connecting the pin to 0V or to 5V, the tow possible outcomes are both unharmful for the microcontroller, and the PIN value line will easily follow the value imposed by the external connection.

Now imagine the opposite configuration, where the latch value would be low, causing the pin to provide 0V, being directly connected to GND through the resistor. If in this situation, an external device tries to raise the pin's voltage to 5V, a short circuit will occur and some damage may be made to the microcontroller's port or to the external device connected to that pin.

To summarize, in the 8051 architecture, to use a PIN as an input pin, you have to output "1", and the pin value will follow the value imposed by the device connected to it (switch, sensor, etc.). If you plan to use the pin as an output pin, then just output the required value without taking any of this in consideration.

Even if some ports like P3 and P0 can have a slightly different internal composition than P1, due to the dual functions they assure, understanding the structure and functioning of port 1 as described above is fairly enough to use all the ports for basic I/O operations.

A simple output project: Blinking a led

A first simple project to experiment with the output operations is to blink a LED. Assuming you have successfully written and compiled the code as explained in the previous part of the tutorial, now we are going to transfer the HEX file corresponding to that code on the 89S52 microcontroller. Let us recall that the HEX file is a machine language file, generated by the compiler, originally from a C code.

The code for blinking a LED is as follow:

```
 #include <REGX52.h>
#include <math.h>
delay(unsigned int y){
unsigned int i;
```

```
        for(i=0;i<y;i++){;}
    }
    main(){
        while(1){
         delay(30000);
         P1_0 = 0;
         delay(30000);
         P1_0 = 1;
        }
    }
```

Before transferring the HEX file to the target microcontroller, the hardware have to be constructed. First you have to provide a clean (noiseless) 5V power supply, by connecting the Vcc pin (40) to 5V and the GND pin (20) to 0V. Then you have provide a mean of regulating or generating the clock of the processor. The easiest and most efficient way to do this is to add a crystal resonator and 2 decoupling capacitors of approximately 30pF (see the crystal X1 and the capacitors C1 and C2 on Fig.3.23). Then, you have connect pin 31 (EA) to 5V. The EA pin is an active low pin that indicate the presence of an external memory. Activating this pin by providing 0V on it will tell the internal processor to use external memories and ignore the internal built-in memory of the chip. By providing 5V on the EA pin, its functionality is deactivated and the processor uses the internal memories (RAM and FLASH). At last, you have to connect a standard reset circuitry on pin 9 composed of the 10 kohm resistor R2 and the 10 μF capacitor C3, as you can see in the schematic. You can also add a switch to short-circuit pin 9 (RST) and 5V giving you the ability to reset the microcontroller by pressing on the switch (the processor resets in a high level is provided on the RST pin for more than 2 machine cycles).

Those were the minimum connections to be made for the microcontroller to be functional and able to operate correctly. According to the fact that we are going to use an ISP programmer, A connector is added by default to allow easy in system programming.

For our simple output project, a LED is connected to P1.0 through a 220 ohm resistor R1, as you can see in Fig.3.24 below. Note that there are other ways to connect the LED, but now that you understand the internal structure of the port, you can easily deduce that this is the only way to connect the LED so that the current is fully controlled by the external resistor R1. Any other connection scheme would involve the internal resistor of the port, which is "uncontrollable".

In order get rid of any confusion, a picture of the implementation of this simple project on a bread board is provided in Fig.3.25 to help you visualize the hardware part of the project:

Note that the reset switch and R/C filter are not present on this breadboard, the reset functionality of the ISP cable was used instead.

At this stage, you can finally connect your ISP programmer, launch the ISPprog software, browse the HEX file for programming the FLASH, and transfer it to the microcontroller, as described in the ISP page. You can eventually use any other available programming hardware and/or software.

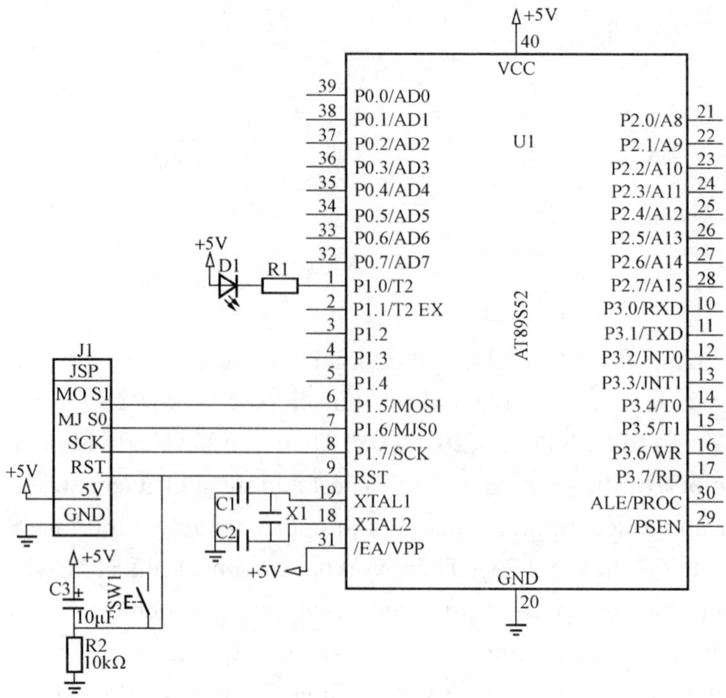

Fig.3.24 LED blinking project hardware

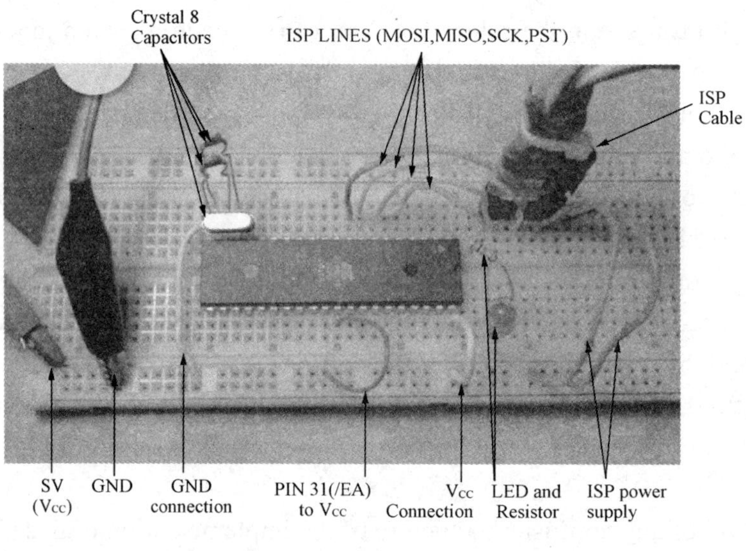

Fig.3.25 LED blinking project hardware implementation

If all your connections are correct, you should see the LED blinking as soon as the programming (transfer) is finished. You can experiment with different delay in the code to change the blinking frequency. Don't forget that for any change to take place, you have to rebuild your source code, generating a new hex file (replacing the old one) and retransfer the freshly generated HEX file to the microcontroller.

Technical Words and Expressions

notion	n.	概念，观念，想法，意见
I/O port		输入/输出口
tutorial	n.	指南
latch value		锁存值
pull-up resistor		上拉电阻
crystal resonator		晶体谐振器
decoupling capacitor		解耦电容
breadboard	n.	电路试验板，面包板
source code		原始（代）码，源程序

Comprehension

1. In Fig.3.23, if the latch value is high lever, I/O pin will be ______.
   A. 5V B. 0V C. 3V D. 7V
2. For basic I/O operations, the structure and functioning of port 1 is ______ port2.
   A. the same as B. more complicated than
   C. more simple than D. easier to understand than
3. In Fig.3.24, the circuit between pin 18 and pin19 ______.
   A. is used to provide reset circuitry to the processor
   B. is used to provide power to the processor
   C. is used to regulate power supply
   D. is used to provide a clock to the processor
4. If the EA pin is in low lever, ______.
   A. the processor will use external memories only
   B. the processor will use internal memories
   C. the processor will use RAM and FLASH
   D. the processor will use both external and internal memories
5. If you want to change the blinking frequency of LED, ______.
   A. you must change the hardware of the project
   B. you only have to change the C code of this project
   C. you have to change the HEX file in the microcontroller
   D. all above

Unit 16 Fieldbus

Fieldbus (or field bus) is the name of a family of industrial computer network protocols used for real-time distributed control, now standardized as IEC 61158.

A complex automated industrial system —— say a manufacturing assembly line —— usually needs an organized hierarchy of controller systems to function. In this hierarchy there is usually a Human Machine Interface (HMI) at the top, where an operator can monitor or operate the system. This is typically linked to a middle layer of programmable logic controllers (PLC) via a non time critical communications system (e.g. Ethernet). At the bottom of the control chain is the fieldbus which links the PLCs to the components which actually do the work such as sensors, actuators, electric motors, console lights, switches, valves and contactors.

Description

Fieldbus is an industrial network system for real-time distributed control. It is a way to connect instruments in a manufacturing plant. Fieldbus works on a network structure which typically allows daisy-chain, star, ring, branch, and tree network topologies. Previously computers were connected using RS-232 (serial connections) by which only two devices could communicate. This would be the equivalent of the currently used 4～20 mA communication scheme which requires that each device has its own communication point at the controller level, while the fieldbus is the equivalent of the current LAN-type connections, which require only one communication at the controller level and allow multiple (100's) of analog and digital points to be connected at the same time[1]. This reduces both the length of the cable required and the number of cables required. Furthermore, since devices that communicate through fieldbus require a Microprocessor, multiple points are typically provided by the same device[2]. Some fieldbus devices now support control schemes such as PID control on the device side instead of forcing the controller to do the processing...

History

Although fieldbus technology has been around since 1988, with the completion of the ISA S50.02 standard, the development of the international standard took many years. In 1999, the IEC SC65C/WG6 standards committee met to resolve difference in the draft IEC fieldbus standard. The result of this meeting was the initial form of the IEC 61158 standard with eight different protocol sets called "Types" as follows:

- Type 1 FOUNDATION Fieldbus H1;
- Type 2 ControlNet;
- Type 3 PROFIBUS;
- Type 4 P-Net;
- Type 5 FOUNDATION Fieldbus HSE (High Speed Ethernet);
- Type 6 SwiftNet (a protocol developed for Boeing, since withdrawn);
- Type 7 WorldFIP;
- Type 8 Interbus.

This form of "standard" was first developed for the European Common Market, concentrates less on commonality, and achieves its primary purpose —— elimination of restraint of trade between nations. Issues of commonality are now left to the international consortia that support each of the fieldbus standard types. Almost as soon as this "8-headed monster" was approved, the IEC standards development work ceased and the committee was dissolved. A new IEC committee SC65C/MT-9 was formed to resolve the conflicts in form and substance within the more than 4000 pages of IEC 61158. The work on the above protocol types is substantially complete. New protocols, such as for safety fieldbuses or realtime ethernet-based fieldbuses are being accepted into the definition of the international fieldbus standard during a typical 5-year maintenance cycle.

Recent additions or planned additions to IEC 61158 include but are not limited to:

- Type 10 PROFINET IO;
- Type 12 EtherCAT;
- Type 13 Ethernet Powerlink;
- Type 16 SERCOS_interface.

Both FOUNDATION Fieldbus and Profibus technologies are now commonly implemented within the process control field, both for new developments and major refits. In 2006, China saw the largest FF systems installations at NanHai and SECCO, each with around 15000 fieldbus devices connected.

Standards

There are a wide variety of concurring fieldbus standards. Some of the most widely used ones include:

- AS-Interface;
- CAN;
- Industrial Ethernet;
- Interbus;
- LonWorks;
- Modbus;
- PROFIBUS;
- BITBUS;
- CompuBus;
- SafetyBUS p.

Cost advantage

A major advantage of fieldbus implementation is the capital expenditure (CAPEX) savings associated with cable elimination; multiple devices share wire-pairs in order to communicate over the bus network and savings are also available through speedier commissioning.

Users have now found that ongoing maintenance and process control system performance are also very significantly enhanced through adopting fieldbus systems, which results in operations expense savings (OPEX)[3].

Disadvantages

There are disadvantages to using fieldbus compared to the 4～20 mA analog signal standard (or to 4～20 mA with HART):

- Fieldbus systems are more complex, so users need to be more extensively trained or more highly qualified.
- The price of fieldbus components is higher.
- Fieldbus test devices are more complex compared to a (high-spec) multimeter that can be used to read and simulate analog 4～20 mA signals.
- Slightly longer reaction times with fieldbus, depending on the system.
- Device manufacturers have to offer different versions of their devices (e.g. sensors, actuators) due to the number of different (incompatible) fieldbus standards. This can add to the cost of the devices and to the difficulty of device selection and availability.
- One or more fieldbus standards may predominate in future and others may become obsolete. This increases the investment risk when implementing fieldbus.

Current developments

In recent years a number of Ethernet-based industrial communication systems have been established, most of them with extensions for real-time communication. These have the potential to replace the traditional field buses in the long term. Currently the issue stopping most Ethernet fieldbus implementations is the availability of device power[4]. Most industrial measurement & control devices need to be powered from the bus and Power-over-Ethernet (PoE) does not deliver enough.

Here is a partial list of the new Ethernet-based industrial communication systems:

- EtherCAT;
- ETHERNET/IP;
- Ethernet Powerlink;
- Industrial Ethernet;
- PROFINET IO;
- SafetyNET p;
- SERCOS III;
- TTEthernet;
- VARAN.

Market

In process control systems, the market is dominated by FOUNDATION fieldbus and PROFIBUS PA. Both technologies use the same physical layer (2-wire manchester-encoded current modulation at 31.25 kHz) but are not interchangeable. As a general guide, applications which are controlled and monitored by PLCs (programmable logic controllers) tend towards PROFIBUS, and applications which are controlled and monitored by a DCS (digital/distributed control system) tend towards FOUNDATION Fieldbus. PROFIBUS technology is made available through Profibus International with headquarters in Karlsruhe, Germany. FOUNDATION Fieldbus technology is owned and distributed by the Fieldbus Foundation of Austin, Texas.

Technical Words and Expressions

fieldbus		n.	现场总线
protocol	['prəutəkɔl]	n.	协议
real time			[计] 实时
distributed control			分布式控制
assembly li			生产线，装配线
hierarchy	['haiərɑːki]	n.	层次，层级
Human Machine Interface (HMI)			人机界面
actuator	['æktjueitə]	n.	执行装置
console	[kən'səʊl]	n.	[计] 控制台
contactor	['kɔntæktə]	n.	接触器
daisy-chain		n.	菊花式链接
topology	[tə'pɔlədʒi]	n.	拓扑，布局；拓扑学
microprocessor	[maikrəʊ'prəʊsesə(r)]	n.	[计] 微处理器
FOUNDATION Fieldbus			基金会现场总线
consortia		n.	公会，银行团
Ethernet		n.	以太网
installation	[ˌinstə'leiʃən]	n.	[计] 安装，装置，就职
capital expenditure			资本支出，基本建设费用
commissioning	[kə'miʃəniŋ]	n.	试运转；试车
availability	[əˌveilə'biliti]	n.	可用性，有效性，实用性
obsolete	['ɔbsəliːt]	adj.	荒废的，陈旧的，过时的
interchangeable	[intə'tʃeindʒəb(ə)l]	adj.	可互换的
DCS (distributed control system)			集散式控制系统

Notes

[1] This would be the equivalent of the currently used 4～20 mA communication scheme which requires that each device has its own communication point at the controller level, while the fieldbus is the equivalent of the current LAN-type connections, which require only one communication at the controller level and allow multiple (100's) of analog and digital points to be connected at the same time.

译文为：这就和目前使用的 4～20mA 通信方式一样，它要求每个设备在控制器层上都有自己的通信接点，而现场总线和目前的局域网一样，它在控制器层上只需要一个通信接点并且可以同时连接多个（100）模拟和数字接点。

While 作为并列连词，引导并列句。Which 引导限定性定语从句修饰“4～20mA communication scheme”，“that each device...” that 引导一个宾语从句。

[2] Furthermore, since devices that communicate through fieldbus require a Microprocessor, multiple points are typically provided by the same device.

译文为：此外，由于通过现场总线进行通信的设备需要一个微处理器，同一设备通常会提供多个接点。

Since 引导原因状语从句，表示“由于”的意思，从句中 that 则引导了一个同谓语从句。

[3] Users have now found that ongoing maintenance and process control system performance are also very significantly enhanced through adopting fieldbus systems, which results in operations expense savings (OPEX).

译文为：现在用户发现采用现场总线系统后，日常维护也变得简单了，而且过程控制系统的性能也大大被增强，从而带来运行成本的下降。

That 后带一个宾语从句，该从句的主语是“ongoing maintenance ...performance”。Which 引导了一个非限定性定语从句。

[4] Currently the issue stopping most Ethernet fieldbus implementations is the availability of device power.

译文为：目前阻碍大多数以太网现场总线实施的问题在于总线无法给设备提供电源。

该句主语为“the issue stopping most Ethernet fieldbus implementations”，其中 stopping...为现在分词作定语修饰“the issue”。

Exercises

Ⅰ. Mark the following statements with T (true) or F (false) according to the text.

1. Fieldbus (or field bus) is used for real-time distributed control. (　　)

2. Fieldbus is a way to connect computer in a manufacturing plant. (　　)

3. Fieldbus only allows two devices to communicate. (　　)

4. The "standard" which was first developed for the European Common Market, concentrates on commonality. (　　)

5. Applications which are controlled and monitored by a DCS (digital/distributed control system) are dominated by FOUNDATION Fieldbus. (　　)

Ⅱ. Complete the following sentences.

1. In the hierarchy of automated industrial system, at the top is usually ______, where an operator can monitor or operate the system. This is typically linked to a middle layer of ______ via a non time critical communications system (e.g. Ethernet). At the bottom of the control chain is the ______.

2. Since devices that communicate through fieldbus require a Microprocessor, ______ are typically provided by the same device. Some fieldbus devices now support ______-such as

PID control on the device side.

3. Both ______ and ______ technologies are now commonly ______ within the process control field, both for new developments and major refits.

4. A major advantage of fieldbus implementation is ______ savings associated with ______; multiple devices share wire-pairs in order to communicate over the bus network and savings are also available through speedier commissioning.

5. In process control systems, the market is dominated by ______ and. Both technologies use the same ______ (2-wire manchester-encoded current modulation at 31.25 kHz) but are not interchangeable.

Reading 16 Profibus

PROFIBUS (Process Field Bus) is a standard for field bus communication in automation technology and was first promoted (1989) by BMBF (German department of education and research). It should not be confused with the PROFINET standard for industrial Ethernet.

The history of PROFIBUS goes back to a publicly promoted plan for an association started in Germany in 1987 and for which 21 companies and institutes devised a master project plan called "field bus". The goal was to implement and spread the use of a bit-serial field bus based on the basic requirements of the field device interfaces. For this purpose, respective company members agreed to support a common technical concept for production and process automation. First, the complex communication protocol Profibus FMS (Field bus Message Specification), which was tailored for demanding communication tasks, was specified. Subsequently in 1993, the specification for the simpler and thus considerably faster protocol PROFIBUS DP (Decentralized Peripherals) was completed. It replaced FMS.

The information technology played a decisive role in the development of the automation technology and changed the hierarchies and structures of offices. It now arrives to the industrial environment and its several sectors, from process and manufacture industries to buildings and logistic systems. The possibility of communication between devices and the use of standardized, open and transparent mechanisms are essential components of today's automation concept.

The communication expands rapidly in the horizontal direction at the field level, as well as in the vertical direction integrating all of the hierarchy levels of a system. According to the characteristics of the application and the maximum cost to reach, a gradual combination of different communication systems like Ethernet, PROFIBUS and AS-Interface are the ideal open networks conditions for industrial processes.

With respect to actuators/sensors the AS-Interface is the perfect data communication system, as the binary data signals are transmitted through an extremely simple and low-cost data bus, together with the 24VDC power supply required to feed those sensors and actuators.

Another important feature is that the data are transmitted in cycles, in a very efficient and fast way.

At field level, the peripherals distributed, like I/O modules, transducers, drives, valves and operation panels' work in automation systems, through an efficient, real-time communication system, the PROFIBUS DP or PA. The process data transmission is made in cycles, while alarms, parameters and diagnostics are transmitted only when necessary, in a non-cyclic way.

As to cells, the programmable controllers like the PLCs and the PCs communicate between themselves and so require that large data package be transferred in several and powerful communication functions. Furthermore, the efficient integration to the existing corporate communication systems, such as Intranet, Internet and Ethernet is absolutely mandatory. This need is met by PROFINet protocol.

The industrial communication revolution in the technology plays a vital role in the optimization of the process systems and has made a valuable contribution toward improving the use of resources. PROFIBUS is a central connecting link on the automation of data flow.

The PROFIBUS (Fig.3.26), in its architecture, is divided in three main variants:

PROFIBUS-DP: It is the high-speed solution for PROFIBUS. It was developed specifically for communication between automation systems and decentralized equipments. It is applicable on control systems where the access to I/O-distributed devices is emphasized and substitutes the conventional 4 to 20 mA, HART systems or in 24 Volts transmissions. It uses the RS-485 physical medium or fiber optics. It requires less than two minutes to transmit 1 I/O Kbyte and is largely used in critical time controls.

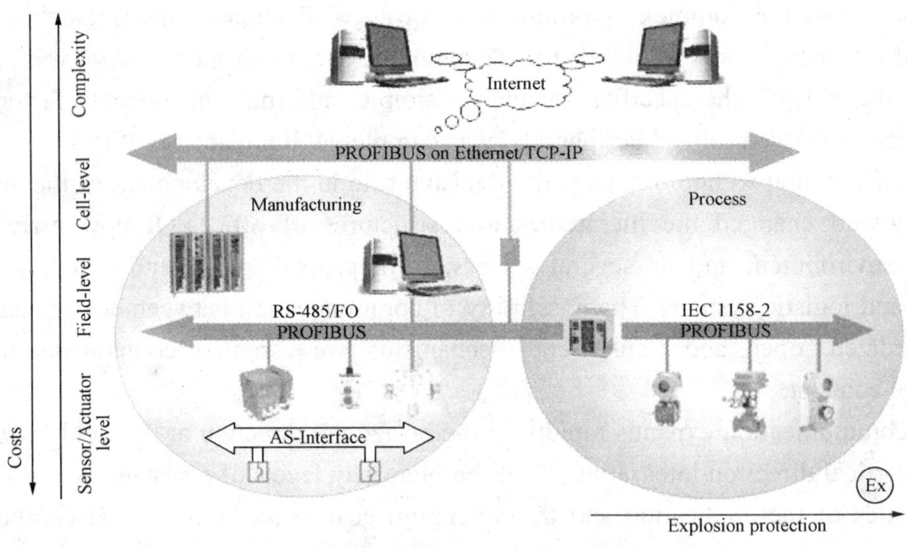

Fig.3.26 PROFIBUS

Currently, 90 percent of the applications involving slaves PROFIBUS utilize the PROFIBUS-DP. This variant is available in three versions: DP-V0 (1993), DP-V1 (1997), DP-V2 (2002). The origin of each version occurred alongside the technological advancement and the long-time growing demand for the applications.

PROFIBUS-FMS: The PROFIBUS-FMS provides the user with a wide selection of functions when compared to other variants. It is the solution in universal communication standard that may be used to solve complex communication tasks between PLCs and DCSs. This variant supports the communication between automation systems besides the exchange of data between intelligent equipments, generally used in control level. Recently, since its primary function is the peer-to-peer communication, it is being replaced by application in Ethernet.

PROFIBUS-PA: The PROFIBUS-PA is the solution PROFIBUS that attend to the requisites of process automation, where automation systems and process control systems connect with field equipments, like pressure and temperature transmitters, converters, positioners, etc. It may also replace the 4 to 20 mA standard.

There are potential advantages for using this technology, which carry functional advantages such as the transmission of reliable information, variable status dealing, failure safety systems, and the feature of auto-diagnosis equipment, equipment rangeability, measuring with high resolution, Integration with high speed discreet control, etc. In addition to the economical benefits pertinent to the installations (cost reduction up to 40% comparable to the conventional systems in some cases), maintenance costs reduction (up to 25% against the conventional systems), smaller startup time, it offers a significant increase in functionality and safety.

PROFIBUS-PA permits measurement and control through one line and two single cables. It also powers the field equipment in intrinsically safe areas. PROFIBUS-PA allows maintenance and connecting/disconnecting equipment even during operation without interfering in other stations in areas potentially explosive. PROFIBUS-PA was developed in cooperation with the Control and Process Industry (NAMUR), in compliance with the special requirements on this application area:

- The original application profile for the process automation and interoperability of field equipments from different manufacturers;
- Addition and removal of bus stations even in intrinsically areas without affecting other stations;
- A transparent communication through the couplers of the segment between the PROFIBUS-PA automation bus and the PROFIBUS-DP industrial automation bus.
- Power and data transmission on the same pair of cables based on the IEC 61158-2 technology;
- Use in potentially hazardous areas with "intrinsically safe" or "intrinsically unsafe" explosive-proof protection shield.

The connection of the transmitters, converters and positioners in a PROFIBUS-DP network is made by a DP/PA coupler. The twisted pair cable is used as power supply and data communication for each equipment, which makes the installation easier and lower the cost of hardware, thus resulting in less initiation time, problem-free maintenance, low engineering software cost and highly reliable operation.

Technical Words and Expressions

promote	vt.	促进，发扬
industrial Ethernet		工业以太网
communication protocol		通信协议
FMS (Field bus Message Specification)		现场总线信息规范
DP (Decentralized Peripheral)		分散的外围设备
transparent	adj.	透明的；透光的
AS-Interface		传感器/执行器接口
transducer	n.	传感器，变换器
substitute	v.	代替，替换，替代
twisted pair		双绞线

Comprehension

1. Which of the following is right? ______.
   A. PROFIBUS standard is a kind of industrial Ethernet
   B. Compared to Profibus FMS, PROFIBUS DP is the simpler and considerably faster protocol
   C. PROFIBUS is the ideal open networks conditions for industrial processes
   D. all above
2. The PROFIBUS DP or PA ______.
   A. is used at cell level B. can transfer large data package
   C. can realize real-time data transmission D. can realize all data transmission in cycles
3. PROFINet protocol ______.
   A. is a kind of PROFIBUS standard B. is a kind of industrial Ethernet
   C. supplies power for sensors and actuators D. all above
4. Which of the following is right? ______.
   A. PROFIBUS-PA may replace the 4 to 20 mA standard
   B. PROFIBUS-PA can supply power for the field device
   C. maintenance costs of PROFIBUS-PA are cheaper than the conventional systems
   D. all above
5. Which of the following is right? ______.
   A. PROFIBUS-DP is used for communication among decentralized equipments
   B. PROFIBUS-DP has already substituted the conventional 4 to 20 mA
   C. DP-V1 is a kind of PROFIBUS-DP
   D. the applications of PROFIBUS-DP are less than PROFIBUS-FMS

Chapter 4

Sensors and Transducers

Unit 17 Introduction to Sensor

A sensor is a device which measures a physical quantity and converts it into a signal which can be read by an observer or by an instrument[1]. For example, a mercury thermometer converts the measured temperature into expansion and contraction of a liquid which can be read on a calibrated glass tube. A thermocouple converts temperature to an output voltage which can be read by a voltmeter.

A sensor is composed of sense organ, transducer element, and conversion circuit (Fig.4.1).

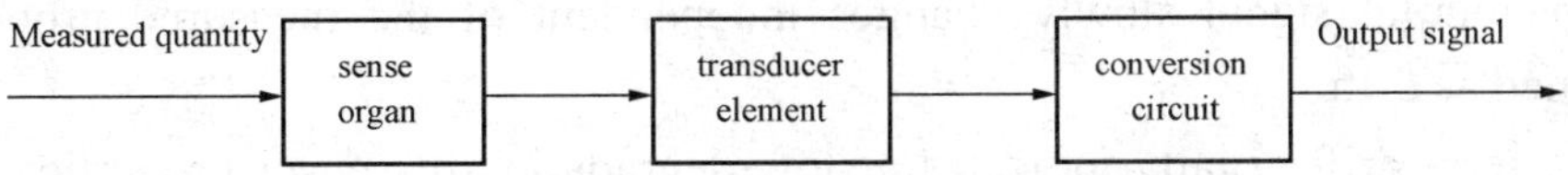

Fig.4.1 the comprising of a sensor

Sensors are used in everyday objects such as touch-sensitive elevator buttons and lamps which dim or brighten by touching the base. There are also innumerable applications for sensors of which most people are never aware. Applications include automobiles, machines, aerospace, medicine, industry, and robotics. Technological progress allows more and more sensors to be manufactured on a microscopic scale as micro-sensors using MEMS (Micro-Electro-Mechanical Systems) technology. In most cases, a micro-sensor reaches a significantly higher speed and sensitivity compared with macroscopic approaches. A good sensor obeys the following rules:

1. The sensor should be sensitive to the measured property.
2. The sensor should be insensitive to any other property.
3. The sensor should not influence the measured property.

Characteristics

A sensor's sensitivity indicates how much the sensor's output changes when the measured quantity changes. For instance, if the mercury in a thermometer moves 1cm when the temperature changes by 1°, the sensitivity is 1cm/1°. Sensors that measure very small changes must have very high sensitivities.

Ideal sensors are designed to be linear. The output signal of such a sensor is linearly proportional to the value of the measured property. The sensitivity is then defined as the ratio between output signal and measured property. For example, if a sensor measures temperature and has a voltage output, the sensitivity is a constant with the unit [V/K]; this sensor is linear because the ratio is constant at all points of measurement.

If the sensor is not ideal, several types of deviations can be observed:

- The sensitivity may in practice differ from the value specified. This is called a sensitivity error, but the sensor is still linear.

- Since the range of the output signal is always limited, the output signal will eventually reach a minimum or maximum when the measured property exceeds the limits. The full scale range defines the maximum and minimum values of the measured property.
- If the output signal is not zero when the measured property is zero, the sensor has an offset or bias. This is defined as the output of the sensor at zero input.
- If the sensitivity is not constant over the range of the sensor, this is called nonlinearity. Usually this is defined by the amount the output differs from ideal behavior over the full range of the sensor, often noted as a percentage of the full range[2].
- If the deviation is caused by a rapid change of the measured property over time, there is a dynamic error. Often, this behavior is described with a bode-plot showing sensitivity error and phase shift as function of the frequency of a periodic input signal.
- If the output signal slowly changes independent of the measured property, this is defined as drift.
- Long term drift usually indicates a slow degradation of sensor properties over a long period of time.
- Hysteresis is an error caused by when the measured property reverses direction, but there is some finite lag in time for the sensor to respond, creating a different offset error in one direction than in the other[3].
- If the signal is monitored digitally, limitation of the sampling frequency also can cause a dynamic error.
- The sensor may to some extent be sensitive to properties other than the property being measured. For example, most sensors are influenced by the temperature of their environment.
- The resolution of a sensor is the smallest change it can detect in the quantity that it is measuring. Often in a digital display, the least significant digit will fluctuate, indicating that changes of that magnitude are only just resolved.

All these deviations can be classified as systematic errors or random errors. Systematic errors can sometimes be compensated for by means of some kind of calibration strategy. Noise is a random error that can be reduced by signal processing, such as filtering, usually at the expense of the dynamic behavior of the sensor.

Technical Words and Expressions

sensor	['sensə]	n.	传感器
transducer	[trænz'dju:sə]	n.	传感器，变换器
mercury	['mə:kjuri]	n.	水银，汞
contraction	[kən'trækʃən]	n.	收缩，缩短，缩减
calibrate	['kælibreit]	v.	校准
thermocouple	['θə:məuˌkʌpl]	n.	［物］热电偶

elevator	['eliveitə]	n.	电梯，升降机
dim	[dim]	vt.	使暗淡，使失去光泽
aerospace	['ɛərəuspeis]	n.	航空宇宙
microscopic	[maɪkrə'skɔpɪk]	adj.	用显微镜可见的，精微的
MEMS			微型机电系统
deviation	[ˌdiːvi'eiʃən]	n.	偏差，误差
full scale range			量程
bode plot			波特图
phase shift			相移
drift	[drift]	n.	漂移
degradation	[ˌdegrə'deiʃən]	n.	降级，降格，退化
finite	['fainait]	adj.	有限的
calibration	[ˌkæli'breiʃən]	n.	标度，刻度，校准
resolution	[ˌrezə'ljuːʃən]	n.	分辨力，分辨率［度］
least significant digit			最低位数字
fluctuate	['flʌktjueit]	vi.	变动，波动

Notes

[1] A sensor is a device which measures a physical quantity and converts it into a signal which can be read by an observer or by an instrument.

译文：传感器是一种可以测量物理量并将被测量转化为观察者可读出或者仪器上显示的信号的装置。

“A sensor is a device”后面是“which”引导的定语从句。在定语从句中又引入了修饰“signal”的定语从句。“converts…into…”意为“将……转化为……”。

[2] Usually this is defined by the amount the output differs from ideal behavior over the full range of the sensor, often noted as a percentage of the full range.

译文：通常定义为在量程范围内传感器输出值与理想值之差，常用量程的百分比表示。

此处“this”指上文中的“nonlinearity”。“amount”后是一个省略了“that”的定语从句“the output differs from ideal behavior over the full range of the sensor”。

[3] Hysteresis is an error caused by when the measured property reverses direction, but there is some finite lag in time for the sensor to respond, creating a different offset error in one direction than in the other.

译文：滞后误差是由于被测变量改变方向引起的，由于传感器响应时在时间上存在一定的滞后，使得一个方向上的误差与另一方向上的误差不同。

句中“caused by when the measured property reverses direction”作“error”的定语。

Exercises

Ⅰ. Mark the following statements with T (true) or F (false) according to the text.

1. A good sensor should be sensitive to the measured property. (　　)

2. When a sensor measure very small changes, it must have very high sensitivities. (　　)

3. The output signal is still right when the measured property exceeds the limits. (　)

4. This sensor is linear when the sensitivity is a constant at all points of measurement. (　)

5. The sampling frequency has no influence on signal in digital monitor. (　　)

Ⅱ. Complete the following sentences.

1. A sensor is composed of ______, ______, ______.

2. The mercury in a thermometer moves 2cm when the temperature changes by 1°, the sensitivity is ______.

3. ______ indicates a slow degradation of sensor properties over a long period of time.

4. If the signal is monitored digitally, ______ can cause a dynamic error.

5. The smallest change a sensor can detect in the quantity that it is measuring is called ______.

Reading 17　Measurement and Error

Measurement is the process which uses a certain methods to obtain quantitative data of a certain objective things by drawing on the special technology and instruments. Making careful quantitative measurements are important if we want to claim that a particular physics theory explains something about the world around us.

Precision and the accuracy

Measurements represent some physical quantity. For example, 2.1 meter represents a distance, 7 kilograms represents a mass and 9.3 seconds represents a time. Notice that each of these quantities has a number (9.3) and a unit ("seconds"). The number tells you the amount and the unit tells you the thing that you are talking about. Both the number and the unit are required to specify a measured quantity.

If you measure your mass to be 120.317 kilograms, that is a very *precise* measurement because it is very specific. It also happens to be a very inaccurate measurement because you are not quite that fat. Your mass is considerably less, something like 65 kilograms. So, we should reduce the human error in scale reading. when we say that we have made a precise measurement we can also say that we have made a very specific measurement. When we say we have made an accurate measurement we are saying that our answer is close to the true value of the quantity. When we make measurements in the laboratory we should therefore distinguish between the precision and the accuracy of these measurements. The accuracy of a measurement is as important in science as the measurement itself. In fact, a measurement is essentially useless if we do not know its accuracy.

There is a certain inherent inaccuracy or variation in any measurement we make in the laboratory. This inherent inaccuracy or variation is called experimental "error" and the word is not meant to imply incompetence on the part of the experimenter. Error merely reflects the condition that our measuring instruments are imperfect. This lack of perfection in our measuring procedure is to be contrasted with mistakes like adding two numbers incorrectly or incorrectly writing down a number from an instrument. Those mistakes have nothing to do with what I mean by experimental error and everything to do with the competence of the experimenter! Understanding and quantifying measurement error is important in experimental science because it is a measure of how seriously we should believe (or not believe) our theories about how the physical universe works.

Error

There are basically two kinds of errors that enter scientific measurements: ① random errors; ② systematic errors. With careful planning of your experiment, the systematic errors can be minimized or avoided. Random errors, on the other hand, are always part of any measurement.

Perhaps you have had the experience of measuring something multiple times and not quite getting the same answer for each measurement. Your measured value could be a bit high or a bit low of the correct value. Perhaps you notice that the variations in your measurements have no fixed or predictable pattern. Your measured value could be as likely to be a bit too high as to be a bit to low. This variation in the measured quantity is called a random error. Indeed, with random errors an individual measurement of an object is just as likely to be a bit too high as to be a bit too low. For example, using a ruler often produces random errors because you will not consistently get the ruler's zero line exactly aligned with the edge of the measured object every time you make a measurement.

Measurements may display good precision but yet be very inaccurate. Often, you may find that your measurements are usually consistently too high or too low from the accurate value. The measurements are "systematically" wrong. For example, weighing yourself with a scale that has a bad spring inside of it will yield weight measurements that are inaccurate, either too high or too low, even though the weight measurements may seem reasonable. You might, for example, notice that you seem to gain weight after Thanksgiving holiday and lose weight after being ill. These observations may in fact be true but the actual value for your weight will be inaccurate. This is an example of a systematic error. Your measurements are systematically wrong. It is often very difficult to catch systematic errors and usually requires that you understand carefully the workings of your measuring device (s).

Taking the mean (average) value for a set of measurements is a good way of reducing the effects of random errors and is the preferred way to get your value. As you increase the number of measurements, the mean value of these measurements will more closely resemble the actual value of the quantity you are trying to measure, assuming there are no systematic errors present. This is because you are just as likely to measure a value that is slightly too high as one that is too low, so that the random errors will "average themselves out". The magnitude of the relative errors for the individual measurements gives you an idea of the uncertainty in your value.

Averaging your measurements will not help you when there are systematic errors present. In fact, there is no standard way to deal with systematic errors other than changing your measurement technique. Often you do not know you have systematic errors or you have trouble estimating them, which is why they are so troublesome.

Technical Words and Expressions

quantitative	adj.	数量（上）的
inherent	adj.	固有的；内在的
variation	n.	变化，变动（的程度）
incompetence	n.	无能力，不称职，不胜任
systematic	adj.	有系统的；有规则的
relative error		相对误差

Comprehension

1. In the following measurements, which is the most precise one? ______.
   A. 19cm B. 19.01cm C. 19.12cm D. 19.124cm
2. If your weight is 51kg, ______ is the most accurate measurement.
   A. 52.8kg B. 53.55kg C. 60.723kg D. 50kg
3. Which is not right about random errors? ______.
   A. Random errors have no fixed or predictable pattern
   B. With careful planning of your experiment, the random errors can be minimized or avoided
   C. Taking the mean (average) value for a set of measurements is a good way of reducing the effects of random errors
   D. The measured value could be likely a bit too high or a bit too low
4. Systematic errors ______.
   A. are usually consistently too high or too low from the accurate value
   B. are difficultly caught
   C. can be reduced by taking the mean (average) value for a set of measurements
   D. both A and B
5. From the text, we can know ______.
   A. there is difference between the precision and the accuracy
   B. the accuracy of a measurement is as important in science as the measurement itself
   C. averaging your measurements will not help you when there are systematic errors present
   D. all above

Unit 18 Temperature Sensor Overview

Temperature Sensing Methods

There are two temperature sensing methods:

—— Contact

—— Non-contact

Contact sensing brings the sensor in physical contact with a substance or object. It can be used with solids, liquids or gases. Non-contact (infrared) temperature sensing reads temperature by intercepting a portion of the infrared energy emitted by an object or substance, and detecting its intensity. Non-contact is used to sense the temperature of solids and liquids. Non-contact cannot be used on gases due to their transparent nature.

Contact Temperature Sensor Types and Comparisons

Contact sensors, aside from capillary/bulb thermometers and bi-metal sensors, use varying voltage signals or resistance values.

Voltage Signals

Thermocouple sensors generate varying voltage signals. The different metal and alloy combinations in the thermocouple's legs produce a predictable voltage for a given temperature.

Resistance Values

Resistance temperature detectors (RTDs) generate varying resistance values. RTDs as a class are divided into two types:

- Resistance wire RTD;
- Thermistor (thermally sensitive transistor).

RTDs work by producing a predictable resistance at a given temperature. Resistance wire RTDs (generally platinum) have a positive coefficient by increasing resistance with temperature increase. Thermistors are generally negative coefficient by decreasing resistance with temperature increase. Each of these three contact sensor types (RTDs, thermocouples, and thermistors) have advantages and disadvantages depending on application, desired response time and accuracy[1]. A presentation of general benefits can help determine the most suitable contact sensor type.

Thermocouple Advantages

- Extremely high temperatures: Noble metal thermocouples may be rated as high as 1700℃ (3100℉).
- Ruggedness: The thermocouples' inherent simplicity enables them to shock and vibration.
- Small size/fast response: Thermocouples with exposed or grounded junctions offer nearly immediate response to temperature changes.

RTD Advantages

- Wide temperature range: Watlow platinum sensors cover temperatures from −200 to 650℃ (−328 to 1200℉).
- High output: The current drop across an RTD provides a much larger signal than thermocouple voltage output.
- Linearity: Platinum and copper element RTDs follow a more linear curve than thermocouples or most thermistors.
- System wiring cost: Unlike a thermocouple, an RTD uses ordinary copper leads for extension wires and requires no cold junction compensation.
- Area sensing: Point measurements, while often desirable, may cause errors. An RTD element can be spread over a large area, improving control with area averaging.

Thermistor Advantages

Due to wide performance and cost variations among thermistors, generalized advantages and disadvantages may not always apply. Common benefits include:

- Low sensor cost: Most thermistors in their basic form cost much less than RTDs. When assembled in protective sheaths the price difference narrows.
- High resistance: Base resistance may be several thousand ohms. This provides a larger signal change compared to resistance wire RTDs with the same measuring current, negating leadwire resistance problems.
- Point sensing: Thermistor beads may be pinhead size for point sensing.

Contact Sensor Conclusions

- Thermocouples are best suited to high temperatures, environmental extremes, or applications requiring microscopic size sensors.
- RTDs are best for most industrial measurements over a wide temperature range, especially when sensor stability is essential for proper control.
- Thermistors are best for low cost applications over limited temperature ranges.

Non-Contact Sensors

A non-contact (infrared) sensor intercepts and converts emitted infrared heat into a voltage signal. Construction characteristics of non-contact sensors use a lens to concentrate radiated infrared energy onto a thermopile. The voltage signal produced by the thermopile is sent onto an electronics package for amplification and conditioning before being retransmitted as either a voltage or current signal[2]. Non-contact temperature sensors generally react and register (respond) faster than contact temperature sensors.

Non-Contact Temperature Sensor Advantages

The reasons for using non-contact over contact temperature sensing are:

- When physical contact with the object or substance would deface or contaminate;
- The process or object moves;
- A process requires a faster response than is possible with a contact sensor.

Contact vs. Non-contact Sensor Comparisons

Contact Temperature Sensors

Advantages

- Relatively rugged;
- Economical;
- Wide application range;
- Relatively accurate;
- Simple to apply.

Disadvantages

- Requires physical contact, may damage, mar or contaminate;
- Can cause wear on rotary components (slip rings);
- Slow to respond relative to non-contact sensing.

Non-contact Temperature Sensors

Advantages

- Relatively rugged;
- Remote mounting away from heat source;
- Ideal for measuring objects in motion;
- Faster response (milliseconds compared to seconds for contact sensing);
- Can sense temperature of irregular shaped objects;
- Will not deface, mar or contaminate.

Disadvantages

- Will not measure gas temperatures;
- Emissivity variations;
- Ambient temperature restrictions;
- Indicated temperature affected by environmental conditions (dust, smoke, etc.).

Technical Words and Expressions

intercepting	[ˌintəˈseptiŋ]	n.	截取（技术）；截接
capillary	[kəˈpiləri]	n.	毛细管
bulb	[bʌlb]	n.	球状物
thermometer	[θəˈmɔmitə(r)]	n.	温度计
alloy	[ˈælɔi]	n.	合金
thermistor	[θəːˈmistə]	n.	热敏电阻
bi-metal			双金属
platinum	[ˈplætinəm]	n.	铂
sheath	[ʃiːθ]	n.	鞘，护套，外壳
thermistor bead			球状热敏电阻

pinhead	['pinhed]	n.	针头
infrared	['infrə'red]	adj.& n.	红外线的；红外线
thermopile	['θə:məpail]	n.	温差电堆，热电堆
react	[ri'ækt]	vi.	起反应，起作用
deface	[di'feis]	vt.	磨损
contaminate	[kən'tæmineit]	vt.	把……弄脏，污染
mar	[mɑ:]	vt.	毁坏；损坏；玷污
emissivity	[ˌemi'siviti]	n.	[物] 发射率

Notes

[1] Each of these three contact sensor types (RTDs, thermocouples, and thermistors) have advantages and disadvantages depending on application, desired response time and accuracy.

译文为：这三种接触式测温计（热电阻、热敏电阻、热电偶）在应用场合、预期响应时间及精度方面各有优缺点。

"depending on..." 动名词短语在句中作状语。

[2] The voltage signal produced by the thermopile is sent onto an electronics package for amplification and conditioning before being retransmitted as either a voltage or current signal.

译文为：热电堆产生的电压信号发送到电子装置进行放大和调节，继而以电压或电流信号继续传送。

句中 "produced by the thermopile" 作主语 "the voltage signal" 的定语。

Exercises

Ⅰ. Mark the following statements with T (true) or F (false) according to the text.

1. Unlike a RTD, a thermocouple uses ordinary copper leads for extension wires and requires no cold junction compensation. (　　)

2. Platinum and copper element RTDs follow a more linear curve than thermocouples or most thermistors. (　　)

3. Thermocouple sensors generate varying current signals. (　　)

4. RTDs are best for most industrial measurements over a wide temperature range, especially when sensor stability is essential for proper control. (　　)

5. Noble metal thermocouples can measure extremely high temperature. (　　)

Ⅱ. Complete the following sentences.

1. Resistance wire RTDs (generally platinum) have a ______ coefficient by increasing resistance with temperature increase. Thermistors are generally ______ coefficient by decreasing resistance with temperature increase.

2. Non-contact sensors cannot be used on gases due to ______.

3. A non-contact (infrared) sensor intercepts and converts emitted infrared heat into ______.

4. RTDs work by producing a predictable ______ at a given temperature.

5. ______ are best suited to high temperatures, environmental extremes, or applications requiring microscopic size sensors.

Reading 18 Pressure Transducer

What is a pressure transducer? A pressure transducer is a transducer that converts pressure into an analog electrical signal. Although there are various types of pressure transducers, one of the most common is the strain-gage base transducer. The conversion of pressure into an electrical signal is achieved by the physical deformation of strain gages which are bonded into the diaphragm of the pressure transducer and wired into a wheat-stone bridge configuration. Pressure applied to the pressure transducer produces a deflection of the diaphragm which introduces strain to the gages. The strain will produce an electrical resistance change proportional to the pressure.

Pressure sensors are used for control and monitoring in thousands of everyday applications. Pressure sensors can also be used to indirectly measure other variables such as fluid/gas flow, speed, water level, and altitude. Pressure sensors can alternatively be called pressure transducers, pressure transmitters, pressure senders and pressure indicators, among other names.

Pressure sensors can vary drastically in technology, design, performance, application suitability and cost. for example, There are a category of pressure sensors that are designed to measure in a dynamic mode for capturing very high speed changes in pressure. Example applications for this type of sensor would be in the measuring of combustion pressure in an engine cylinder or in a gas turbine. These sensors are commonly manufactured out of piezoelectric materials such as quartz. Some pressure sensors, such as those found in speed cameras, function in a binary manner, i.e., when pressure is applied to a pressure sensor, the sensor acts to complete or break an electrical circuit. These types of sensors are also known as a pressure switches.

Types of pressure measurements

Pressure sensors can be classified in term of pressure ranges they measure, temperature ranges of operation, and most importantly the type of pressure they measure. In terms of pressure type, pressure sensors can be divided into five categories:

Absolute pressure sensor: This sensor measures the pressure relative to perfect vacuum pressure (0 PSI or no pressure). Atmospheric pressure is 101.325 kPa (14.7 PSI) at sea level with reference to vacuum.

Gauge pressure sensor: This sensor is used in different applications because it can be calibrated to measure the pressure relative to a given atmospheric pressure at a given location. A tire pressure gauge is an example of gauge pressure indication. When the tire pressure gauge reads 0 PSI, there is really 14.7 PSI (atmospheric pressure) in the tire.

Vacuum pressure sensor: This sensor is used to measure pressure less than the atmospheric pressure at a given location.

Differential pressure sensor: This sensor measures the difference between two or more pressures introduced as inputs to the sensing unit, for example, measuring the pressure drop across an oil filter. Differential pressure is also used to measure flow or level in pressurized vessels.

Sealed pressure sensor: This sensor is the same as the gauge pressure sensor except that it is previously calibrated by manufacturers to measure pressure relative to sea level pressure (14.7 PSI).

Applications

There are many applications for pressure sensors but we can narrow them down to three major categories:

Pressure sensing: This is the direct use of pressure sensors to measure pressure. This is useful in weather instrumentation, aircraft, cars, and any other machinery that has pressure functionality implemented.

Altitude sensing: This is useful in aircraft, rockets, satellites, weather balloons, and many other applications. All these applications make use of the relationship between changes in pressure relative to the altitude.

Flow sensing: This is the use of pressure sensors in conjunction with the venturi effect to measure flow. Differential pressure is measured between two segments of a venturi tube that have a different aperture. The pressure difference between the two segments is directly proportional to the flow rate through the venturi tube. A low pressure sensor is almost always required as the pressure difference is relatively small.

Technical Words and Expressions

strain-gage		应变计
deformation	n.	变形，畸变
bond	vt.	结合
turbine	n.	涡轮
sender	n.	发送器
differential pressure	n.	差压，压差
cylinder	n.	汽缸
piezoelectric	adj.	压电的
gauge pressure sensor		标准压力传感器
oil filter		（汽车等）机油滤清器
pressurize	vt.	密封

vessel	n.	导管
altitude	n.	高度
venturi	n.	文氏管，文丘里管
aperture	n.	孔径

Comprehension

1. A pressure transducer is ______.
   A. used for control and monitoring
   B. a transducer that converts pressure into an analog electrical signal
   C. used to indirectly measure other variables such as fluid/gas flow, speed, water level, and altitude
   D. all above
2. ______ measures the pressure relative to perfect vacuum pressure.
   A. Vacuum pressure sensor B. Gauge pressure sensor
   C. Absolute pressure sensor D. Differential pressure sensor
3. Which of the following pressure are usually measured with vacuum pressure sensor? ______.
   A. 15.6 PSI B. 10.2 PSI C. 14.7 PSI D. 101.3 PSI
4. When the sealed pressure sensor reads 14.7 PSI, the absolute pressure is ______.
   A. 14.7 PSI B. 0 PSI C. 29.4 PSI D. 44.1 PSI
5. Which of the following descriptions of pressure sensors is not right? ______.
   A. It can be used to measure pressure
   B. It is useful in aircraft, rockets, satellites, weather balloons
   C. Differential pressure is measured between two segments of a venturi tube that have the same aperture
   D. A low pressure sensor is almost always required as the pressure difference is relatively small

Unit 19 Hall-effect Sensors

Introduction

The Hall-effect has been known for over one hundred years, but has only been put to noticeable use in the last three decades. The first practical application (outside of laboratory experiments) was in the 1950s as a microwave power sensor. With the mass production of semiconductors, it became feasible to use the Hall-effect in high volume products. Micro-switch Sensing and Control revolutionized the keyboard industry in 1968 by introducing the first solid state keyboard using the Hall-effect. For the first time, a Hall-effect sensing element and its associated electronics were combined in a single integrated circuit. Today, Hall-effect devices are included in many products, ranging from computers to sewing machines, automobiles to aircraft, and machine tools to medical equipment.

Theory of the Hall Effect

Hall-effect sensors are a class of sensors that are used to detect the movement of ferrous items. The Hall-effect is a well known phenomenon occurring in conductors and semiconductor materials where in a current flowing generally perpendicular to a magnetic field induces a voltage perpendicular to both the field and current, which voltage is proportional to the product of the current and magnetic field[1]. The Hall-effect output voltage is the voltage produced across opposite edges of the conductor when placed in a magnetic field.

The Hall-effect comes about due to the nature of the current flow in a conductor. Moving charges experience a force, called the Lorentz Force, when a magnetic field is present that is not parallel to their motion (Fig.4.2). When such a magnetic field is absent, the charges follow an approximately straight, "line of sight" path. However, when a perpendicular magnetic field is applied, their path is curved so that moving charges accumulate on one face of the material. This leaves equal and opposite charges exposed on the other face, forming a Hall electric field. When electric field force equals Lorentz Force, the steady Hall voltage is generated.

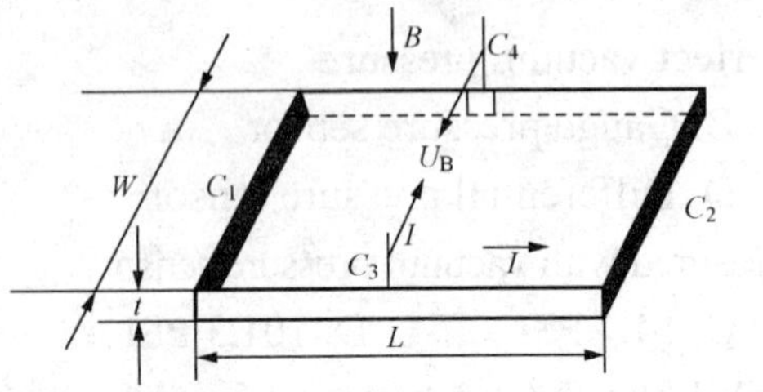

Fig.4.2 An illustration of the electromagnetic theory behind the Hall-effect

For a simple metal where there is only one type of charge carrier (electrons) the Hall voltage U_H is given by

$$U_H = K_H IB / d \tag{4-1}$$

Where I is the current across the plate length, B is the magnetic flux density, d is the depth of the plate, K_H is the Hall coefficient.

It can be seen that the Hall voltage is proportional to the product of the excitation current and magnetic flux density.

Basic Hall-effect sensors

The Hall element is the basic magnetic field sensor. It requires signal conditioning to make the output usable for most applications. The signal conditioning electronics needed are an amplifier stage and temperature compensation. Voltage regulation is needed when operating from an unregulated supply. Fig.4.3 illustrates a basic Hall-effect sensor. If the Hall voltage is measured when no magnetic field is present, the output is zero (Fig.4.3). However, if voltage at each output terminal is measured with respect to ground, a non-zero voltage will appear. This is the common mode voltage (CMV), and is the same at each output terminal. It is the potential difference that is zero. The amplifier shown in Fig.4.3 must be a differential amplifier so as to amplify only the potential difference – the Hall voltage. The Hall voltage is a low-level signal on the order of 30 micro-volts in the presence of a one gauss magnetic field[2]. This low-level output requires an amplifier with low noise, high input impedance and moderate gain. A differential amplifier with these characteristics can be readily integrated with the Hall element using standard bipolar transistor technology. Temperature compensation is also easily integrated. As was shown by equation (4-1), the Hall voltage is a function of the input current. The purpose of the regulator in Fig.4.3 is to hold this current constant so that the output of the sensor only reflects the intensity of the magnetic field. As many systems have a regulated supply available, some Hall effect sensors may not include an internal regulator.

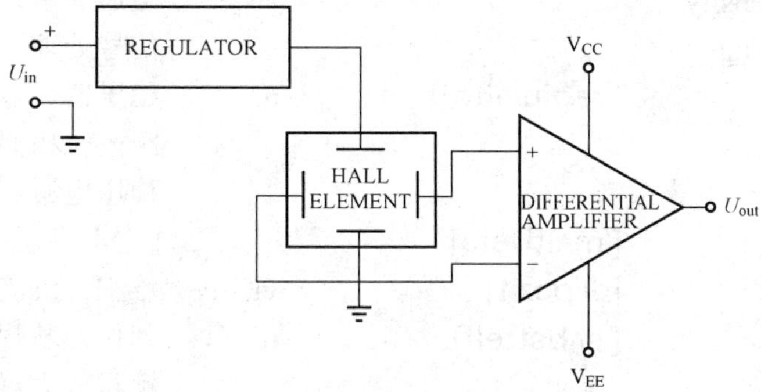

Fig.4.3 A basic Hall-effect sensor

Hall-effect sensors are constituted by a multilayer structure comprising a thin layer of a semiconductor material deposited on a substrate which is itself a semiconductor, with the two layers being electrically isolated from each other[3].

Depending on the application, the Hall voltage can be detected with an instrumentation amplifer (DC excitation current) or a lock-in amplifier (AC excitation current). A large range of Hall-effect sensors is available commercially, and facilitate the measurement of magnetic fields at frequencies from DC to about 100 kHz, and resolutions of about 10 μT.

Application of Hall-effect sensors

The high bandwidth and sensitivity of Hall-effect sensors can be exploited in many applications.

Hall sensors are employed in a wide variety of applications including, for example, automotive, medical, power electronics, computer sensors, transducers, material characterization and power meters. There have been known various types of sensing devices such as a position sensor, a current sensor, an angle sensor, a speed sensor and so on which utilize the Hall-effect. Hall-effect devices are becoming increasingly popular in industry for such purposes as sensing rotors of brushless motors and in other applications where the contact-less sensing of moving mechanical elements is desirable. Hall-effect current sensors offer several advantages over traditional current transformers.

Technical Words and Expressions

hall effect			霍尔效应
aircraft	[ˈɛəkrɑːft]	n.	飞行器
machine tool			机床
perpendicular	[ˌpəːpənˈdikjulə]	adj.	垂直的，正交的
Lorentz Force			洛伦兹力
ferrous	[ˈferəs]	adj.	铁的，含铁的，亚铁的
simple metal			纯金属
magnetic flux density			磁通（量）密度，磁感应强度
signal conditioning			信号处理
regulator	[ˈregjuleitə]]	n.	稳压器
on the order of…			跟……相似
regulated supply			稳压电源
multilayer	[ˈmʌltiˌleiə]		［电］多层
deposit	[diˈpɔzit]	vt.	堆积，沉淀
substrate	[ˈsʌbstreit]	n.	基件，基片
lock-in amplifier			锁相放大器
current transformer			电流互感器

Notes

[1] The Hall-effect is a well known phenomenon occurring in conductors and semiconductor materials where in a current flowing generally perpendicular to a magnetic field induces a voltage perpendicular to both the field and current, which voltage is proportional to the product of the current and magnetic field.

译文：霍尔效应是众所周知的现象：当导体或半导体中的电流垂直流过磁场时，产生一个既垂直于磁场又垂直于电流的电压，该电压与电流和磁场的乘积成正比。

“occurring in…”分词短语作定语，修饰 phenomenon; where 引导的状语从句修饰 materials；“be proportional to…”译为“与……成比例”。

[2] The Hall voltage is a low-level signal on the order of 30 micro-volts in the presence of a one gauss magnetic field.

译文：在高斯磁场中的霍尔电压是一个约 30μV 的低电平信号。

句中“on the order of 30 micro-volts”作定语修饰“low-level signal”，而“in the presence of a one gauss magnetic field”作状语。

[3] Hall-effect sensors are constituted by a multilayer structure comprising a thin layer of a semiconductor material deposited on a substrate which is itself a semiconductor, with the two layers being electrically isolated from each other.

译文：霍尔传感器是一个多层结构，是由一个薄的半导体层沉积在半导体基底上构成，并且两层是彼此电绝缘的。

"comprising..."现在分词短语作定语，其中又包含了一个定语从句，句中"with..."作状语。

Exercises

Ⅰ. Mark the following statements with T (true) or F (false) according to the text.

1. Hall-effect sensors are a class of sensors that are used to detect the movement of ferrous items. ( )

2. When electric field force doesn't equal Lorentz Force, the steady Hall voltage is generated. ( )

3. The Hall voltage is a high-level signal on the order of 30 micro-volts in the presence of a one gauss magnetic field. ( )

4. A large range of Hall-effect sensors is available commercially, and facilitate the measurement of magnetic fields at frequencies from DC to about 100 kHz, and resolutions of about 10 μT. ( )

5. Hall-effect sensors are constituted by a multilayer structure comprising a thin layer of a semiconductor material deposited on a substrate which is itself a semiconductor, with the two layers being electrically isolated from each other. ( )

Ⅱ. Complete the following sentences.

1. ______ sensors are a class of sensors that are used to detect the movement of ferrous items.

2. The Hall-effect comes about due to ______.

3. The Hall element is the basic magnetic field sensor. It requires signal conditioning to make the output usable for most applications. The signal conditioning electronics needed are ______ and ______.

4. Depending on the application, the Hall voltage can be detected with an ______ (DC excitation current) or a ______ (AC excitation current).

5. The high ______ and ______ of Hall-effect sensors can be exploited in many applications.

Reading 19 Overview of Fiber Optic Sensors

Over the past twenty years two major product revolutions have taken place due to the growth of the optoelectronics and fiber optic communications industries. The optoelectronics industry has brought about such products as compact disc players, laser printers, bar code scanners and laser pointers. The fiber optic communication industry has literally revolutionized the telecommunication industry by providing higher performance, more reliable telecommunication links with ever decreasing bandwidth cost. This revolution is bringing about the benefits of high volume production to component users and a true information superhighway built of glass.

Basic Concepts and Intensity Based Fiber Optic Sensors

Fiber optic sensors are often loosely grouped into two basic classes referred to as extrinsic or hybrid fiber optic sensors, and intrinsic or all fiber sensors. Fig.4.4 illustrates the case of an extrinsic or hybrid fiber optic sensor.

By arranging two optical fibers in line, a simple translation sensor can be configured as in Fig.4.5. The output from the two detectors can be proportioned to determine the translational position of the input fiber.

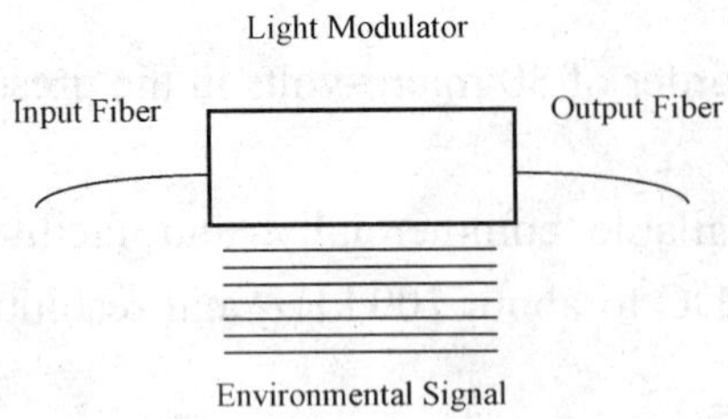

Fig.4.4 An extrinsic or hybrid fiber optic sensor

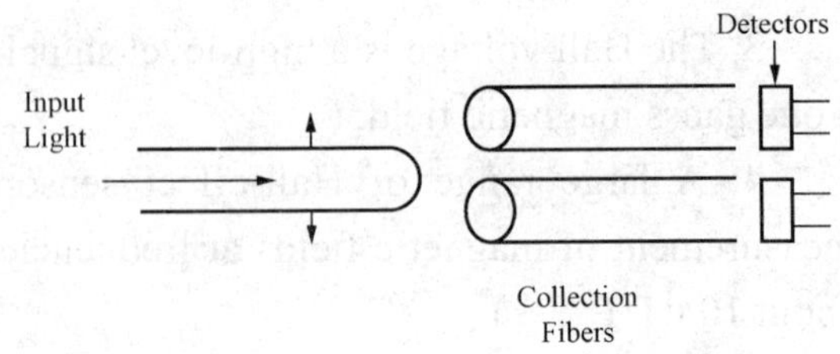

Fig.4.5 the collection fibers

A second common method of interrogating a position sensor using a single optical fiber is to use time division multiplexing methods. In Fig.4.6.a light source is pulsed. The light pulse then propagates down the optical fiber and is split into multiple interrogating fibers. Each of these fibers is arranged so that they have delay lines that separate the return signal from the encoder plate by a time that is longer than the pulse duration. When the returned signals are recombined onto the detector the net result is an encoded signal burst corresponding to the position of the encoded card.

Another class of intensity based fiber optic sensors is based on the principle of total internal reflection. In the case of the sensor in Fig.4.7, light propagates down the fiber core and hits the angled end of the fiber. If the medium into which the angled end of the fiber is placed has a low enough index of refraction then virtually all the light is reflected when it hits the mirrored surface and returns via the fiber. If however the index of refraction of the medium starts to approach that of the glass some of the light propagates out of the optical fiber and is lost resulting in an intensity modulation.

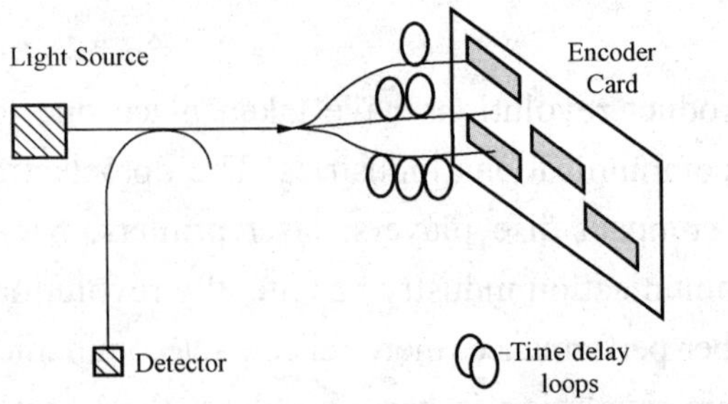

Fig.4.6 Time division multiplexing optical fiber

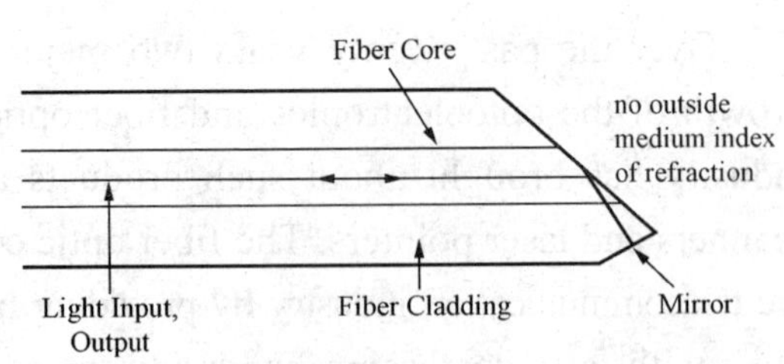

Fig.4.7 Total internal reflection optical fiber

Fiber optic sensors are being developed and used in two major ways. The first is as a direct replacement for existing sensors where the fiber sensor offers significantly improved performance, reliability, safety and/or cost advantages to the end user. The second area is the development and deployment of fiber optic sensors in new market areas.

Technical Words and Expressions

fiber optic		光纤
optoelectronics	n.	光电子学
compact disc		光盘
bar code scanner		条形码扫描器
laser pointer		激光指示器
literally	adv.	照字面意义，逐字地
superhighway	n.	超级高速公路
extrinsic	adj.	非本征的，非固有的
extrinsic fiber optic sensor		非本征光纤传感器
hybrid	adj.	混合的
hybrid fiber optic sensor		混合式激光传感器
intrinsic	adj.	（指价值、性质）固有的，内在的，本质的
interrogate	vt.	询问
multiplexing	n.	多路复用
propagate	v.	传送
encoder	n.	译码器，编码器
duration	n.	持续时间，为期
index	n.	指标，指数
refraction	n.	折射，折射度（转换角度）
deployment	n.	展开，配置

Comprehension

1. Which of the following descriptions of pressure sensors is not right? ______.

   A. The fiber optic communication industry has literally revolutionized the telecommunication industry

   B. The optoelectronics industry has brought about such products as compact disc players, laser printers, bar code scanners and laser pointers

   C. The revolution is bringing about the benefits of high volume production to component users and a true information superhighway built of glass

   D. Fiber optic communication grew up in the 19 century

2. Fiber optic sensors are often loosely grouped into ______.

   A. extrinsic and intrinsic

   B. hybrid fiber optic sensors and all fiber sensors

C. extrinsic or hybrid fiber optic sensors, and intrinsic or all fiber sensors

D. any one of above

3. Interrogating a position sensor using a single optical fiber is to use ______.

A. FDM B. TDM C. CDM D. GPRS

4. The fiber sensor offers ______.

A. improved reliability B. improved safety

C. cost advantages to the end user D. all

5. Due to the principle of total internal reflection, ______.

A. the light is split into interrogating fibers

B. the lights all propagate out of the optical fiber

C. the light is reflected when it hits the mirrored surface

D. there is no loss in intensity

Unit 20 Ultrasonic Sensor

An ultrasonic sensor typically utilizes a transducer that produces an electrical output in response to received ultrasonic energy. Ultrasonic sensors are designed for contact-less and wear-free detection of a variety of targets by means of sonic waves. It is not important whether the target is transparent or colored, metallic or non-metallic, firm, liquid or powdery. Environmental conditions such as spray, dust or rain seldom affect their function.

The normal frequency range for human hearing is roughly 20 to 20,000 Hz. Ultrasonic sound waves are sound waves that are above the range of human hearing and, thus, have a frequency above about 20,000 Hz[1]. Ultrasonic range finders typically use ultrasonic frequencies which are inaudible to the human ear. These high frequencies have inherently shorter wavelengths, which lead to greater positional accuracy than audible frequencies. Any frequency above 20,000 Hz may be considered ultrasonic.

The ultrasonic transducer produces ultrasonic signals. These signals are propagated through a sensing medium and the same transducer can be used to detect returning signals.

In most applications, the sensing medium is simply air. Transducers generally create ultrasonic vibrations through the use of piezoelectric materials such as certain forms of crystals or ceramic polymers.

Modes of Operation

There are two basic modes of operation: opposed mode and diffuse (echo) mode. In opposed mode (Fig.4.8), one sensor emits the sound wave and another, mounted opposite the emitter, receives the sound wave[2]. They "listen" to each other permanently. The ultrasonic sound is interrupted by an object between the emitter and receiver and the sensor generates a switching signal.

In diffuse mode (Fig.4.9), the same sensor emits the sound wave and then listens for the echo that bounces off an object. In other words, an object in front of the sensor is detected by its reflection of a part of the emitted sound. Ultrasonic sensors are mainly used in the diffuse mode.

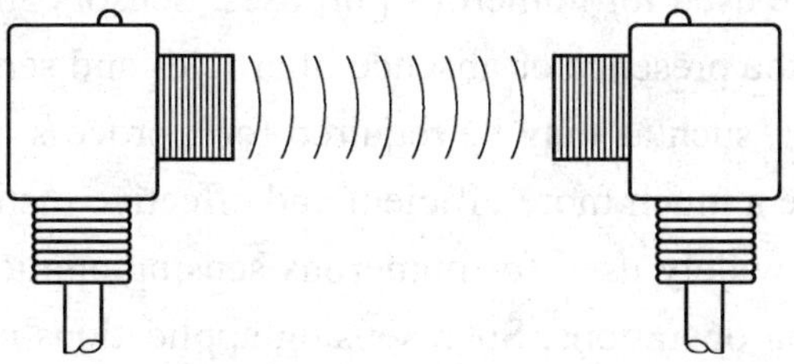

Fig.4.8 Opposed mode

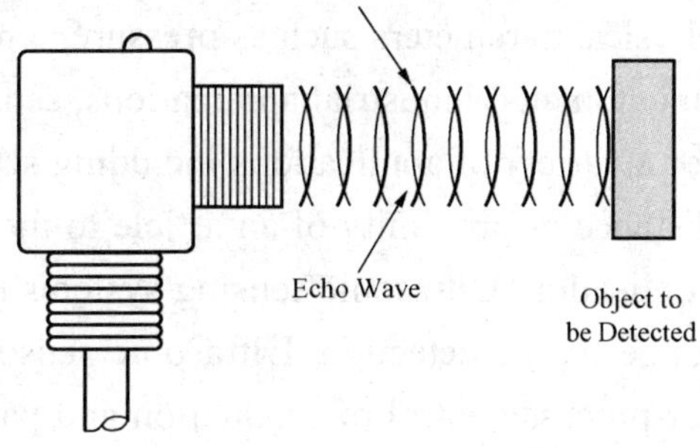

Fig.4.9 Diffuse mode

Because ultrasonic sensors depend on a reflected sound wave for proper operation, the shape, material, temperature and positioning of the target are important. These must be selected to return the strongest possible echo. Certain characteristic of targets must be considered when using ultrasonic sensors. These include target shape, material, temperature, size and positioning. Soft materials such as fabric or foam rubber are difficult to detect by diffuse ultrasonic technology because they are not sound-reflective[3].

Application

Ultrasonic sensors have typically been used in applications such as detecting and identifying solid objects, flow measurement (Fig.4.10), detecting possible collisions between objects to avoid the collisions, room surveillance, measuring the shape and orientation of a work-piece, and level measurement by measuring the absorption of sound (Fig.4.11). Ultrasonic sensors have been used for proximity or distance measurement. These devices typically transmit a short burst of ultrasonic sound toward a target which reflects the sound back to the sensor.

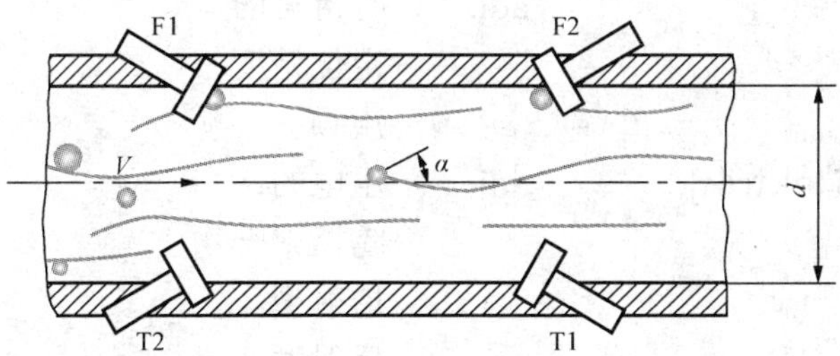

Fig.4.10 Flow measurement

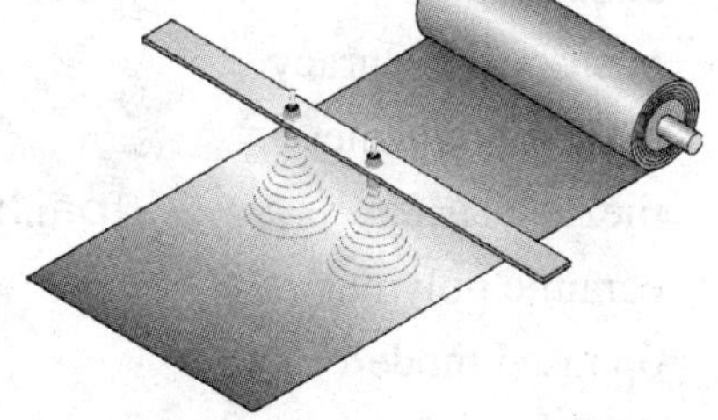

Fig.4.11 Level measurement

The system then measures the time for the echo to return to the sensor and computes the distance to the target using the speed of sound in the medium. Distance can be calculated by using the following equation:

$$Length=ct$$

where c is the speed of sound and t is the round-trip time-of-flight.

Sensors are devices which are designed so that they can detect or quantitatively determine physical parameters such as pressure, temperature, position or velocity over a measuring range. In automated industrial applications, sensors are used for numerous purposes. Sensors are used for a variety of applications including sensing the presence or absence of articles and sensing a distance or proximity of an article to the sensor, such as may be required for a process control application. Ultrasonic sensing systems provide a much more efficient and effective method of longer range detection. Ultrasonic sensors are widely used for numerous sensing applications for process control of production and packaging operations. Such sensing applications include container presence/absence detection, container size detection, product level detection, container orientation detection, container counting operations, material web control, tamper/safety seal detection, and surface coating detection.

Ultrasonic sensing techniques have earned a pre-eminent position in a variety of fields including medicine, nondestructive testing and process monitoring, geophysics, and sonar surveillance. Ultrasonic flow sensors have been employed for a number of years for performing intra-operative or extracorporeal blood flow measurements.

Technical Words and Expressions

ultrasonic	[ˈʌltrəˈsɔnik]	n.	超声波
roughly	[ˈrʌfli]	adv.	概略地，粗糙地
wear-free			无磨损的
sonic wave			声波
powdery	[ˈpaudəri]	adj.	粉状的
spray	[sprei]	n.	喷雾，飞沫
dust	[dʌst]	n.	灰尘，尘土
range finder			测距仪
audible	[ˈɔːdəbl]	adj.	听得见的
positional accuracy			定位精度
audible frequency			声频
piezoelectric	[paiˌiːzəuiˈlektrik]	adj.	压电的
ceramic polymer			陶器聚合物
opposed mode			透射型
diffuse mode			反射型
echo	[ˈekəu]	n.	回波
fabric	[ˈfæbrik]	n.	织物
foam rubber			海绵乳胶，泡沫乳胶
level measurement			物位测量

round trip			往返行程
quantitatively		adv.	数量上
packaging	[ˈpækidʒiŋ]	n.	包装
pre-eminent		adj.	卓越的
sonar	[ˈsəunɑː]	n.	声纳
extracorporeal	[ˌekstrəkɔːˈpɔːriəl]	adj.	身体外的

Notes

[1] Ultrasonic sound waves are sound waves that are above the range of human hearing and, thus, have a frequency above about 20,000 Hz。

译文：超声波是超过人耳所能听到的频率的波段，即 20kHz 以上。

“are sound waves that are above the range of human hearing and”和“have a frequency above about 20,000 Hz”并列。由“and”引导，“thus”为插入语，用于说明一种因果关系。

[2] In opposed mode, one sensor emits the sound wave and another, mounted opposite the emitter, receives the sound wave.

译文：在透射型时，一个传感器发射声波，安装在发射器对面的另一个接收声波。

“mounted opposite the emitter”作为“another”的定语。

[3] Soft materials such as fabric or foam rubber are difficult to detect by diffuse ultrasonic technology because they are not sound-reflective.

译文：一些像织物或海绵乳胶类的柔软物体很难用反射超声波技术检测，因为其对声音不反射。

句子主干为“Soft materials…are difficult to detect because…”。

Exercises

Ⅰ. Mark the following statements with T (true) or F (false) according to the text.

1. The normal frequency range for human hearing is roughly 20 to 20,000 Hz. (   )
2. Any frequency above 20,000 Hz may be considered ultrasonic. (   )
3. Soft materials such as fabric or foam rubber are easy to detect by diffuse ultrasonic technology. (   )
4. Ultrasonic sensing systems provide a much more efficient and effective method of longer range detection. (   )
5. Ultrasonic sensors are only used in the opposed mode. (   )

Ⅱ. Complete the following sentences.

1. ______ typically utilizes a transducer that produces an electrical output in response to received ultrasonic energy.
2. There are two basic modes of operation: ______ and ______ mode.
3. In ______, the same sensor emits the sound wave and then listens for the echo that bounces off an object.
4. A basic ultrasonic sensor system sends out a ultrasonic wave, which then ______ an

object and finally returns to the sensor system.

5. Ultrasonic sensors typically have ______ that converts an excitation electrical signal into ultrasonic energy bursts.

Reading 20 Infrared Sensors

Infrared sensors are designed to detect and measure thermal radiation emanating from remote objects. Being capable of acquiring temperature information of an object to be sensed, infrared sensors are adaptable to a variety of applications. IR systems have enabled night vision technology to be used widely in many military applications such as: target acquisition, missile seeker sensors, night driving, and search and track. Infrared detection systems have not only improved vision at night, but also improved vision through smoke, fog, dust, and haze and simple camouflage. Furthermore, because it is possible to obtain temperature information of objects, the infrared sensor is widely used as a surveillance camera and a fire-detecting camera. An infrared sensor basically comprises an infrared sensitive element for capturing infrared rays and a compensating element for obtaining a signal that is used as a basis for calculating the quantity of infrared rays detected. In an infrared sensor, a sensing element absorbs infrared rays emitted from an object to raise the temperature of itself, and temperature information of the object is obtained by detecting the change in characteristics of the sensing element according to the temperature rise. Infrared detecting elements for use in the infrared sensors have been generally classified into quantum type and thermal type. While the quantum type infrared detecting element is extremely high in the sensitivity, there have been such problems due to the necessity of using it at lower temperatures with the element itself cooled that the sensor is difficult to handle. Those classified as thermal type have a mechanism that the temperature of the temperature sensing part comprising a thermally insulated structure rises by the incidence of an infrared ray, and the temperature rise is converted into an electric signal by utilizing the pyroelectric effect, the thermoelectric effect, or the temperature coefficient of a resistor. The thermal type infrared detecting element is less sensitive than the quantum type but is not required to be cooled and simpler in the structure, and has been utilized widely in various practical ways of use, because of such advantages as low manufacturing costs, and minimized dimensions.

About Non-contact Infrared Temperature Sensor

Non-contact infrared temperature sensors absorb ambient infrared (IR) radiation emitted by a heated surface. They are used in a variety of applications where direct temperature measurement is not possible. With non-contact infrared temperature sensors, incoming light is converted to an electric signal that corresponds to a particular temperature. Although many different types of products are available, non-contact infrared temperature sensors can be thought of as belonging to general categories based on design and application. This category criteria attempts to distinguish unpacked devices that can be used as part of a larger sensor from, say, a gauge which can be read by simple examination. Categories for non-contact infrared temperature sensors include sensor elements or chips, sensors or transducers, gauges or indicators, and instruments or meters.

Passive Infrared sensor

A Passive Infrared sensor (PIR sensor) is an electronic device that measures infrared (IR) light radiating from objects in its field of view. PIR sensors are often used in the construction of PIR-based motion detectors. Apparent motion is detected when an infrared source with one temperature, such as a human, passes in front of an infrared source with another temperature, such as a wall.

All objects emit what is known as black body radiation. It is usually infrared radiation that is invisible to the human eye but can be detected by electronic devices designed for such a purpose. The term passive in this instance means that the PIR device does not emit an infrared beam but merely passively accepts incoming infrared radiation.

Technical Words and Expressions

infrared	adj. & n.	红外线的，红外线
missile	n.	导弹，发射物
missile seeker sensor		导弹跟踪传感器
fog	n.	雾
haze	n.	薄雾
quantum	n.	量子
incidence	n.	入射，入射角
pyroelectric	adj.	热电的
emanate	vt. & vi.	发散，放射
camouflage	n.	伪装，隐藏
pyroelectric effect		热电效应

Comprehension

1. Infrared system has improved night vision technology, such as ______.
   A. target acquisition　　B. missile seeker
   C. night driving　　D. all above
2. The thermal type infrared detecting element ______.
   A. is more sensitive than the quantum type
   B. has some problems to handle the cooled element at lower temperature
   C. is required to be cooled
   D. is simpler in the structure than the quantum type infrared detecting element

3. Which of the following is not right? ______.
   A. Non-contact infrared temperature sensors absorb ambient infrared radiation emitted by a heated surface
   B. Non-contact infrared temperature sensors are used in a variety of applications where direct temperature measurement is not possible
   C. Incoming light is converted to an electric signal that corresponds to a particular temperature
   D. Non-contact infrared temperature sensors is occasionally used
4. Passive infrared sensor ______.
   A. does not emit an infrared beam
   B. emits an infrared beam and accepts its reflection
   C. accepts incoming infrared radiation
   D. A and C
5. From this text, we can know ______.
   A. infrared sensors are designed to detect and measure thermal radiation emanating from remote objects
   B. the infrared sensor is widely used as a surveillance camera and a fire-detecting camera
   C. PIR sensors are often used in the construction of PIR-based motion detectors
   D. all above

Unit 21 Photoelectric Sensors

Introduction

A photoelectric sensor is an electrical device that responds to a change in the intensity of the light falling upon it[1]. Physical properties of light sensitive elements change their electrical features according to light intensity. The light intensity variation striking the receiver depends upon the presence or absence of the object to detect. This creates an electrical signal that, properly elaborated, activates a final amplifying stage that is capable of driving an external load. Photoelectric sensors have become a vital part in today's automation technology and our daily lives. Photoelectric sensors are used in many industries and applications to provide accurate detection of the objects without physical contacts. They are used for the non-contact detection, positioning, classification or counting of most diverse objects.

Basic components

There are three basic components of any photoelectric sensor:

Light source

A light emitting diode (LED) is a solid-state semiconductor that emits light when current is applied. LEDs are made to emit specific wavelengths or colors of light. Infrared, visible red, green, and blue LEDs are used as the light source (emitter) in most photoelectric sensors. Infrared LEDs are used in sensors where maximum light output is required for an extended sensing range.

Light detector

A photo detector is the component used to detect the light source. Photodiode or phototransistor is widely used depending on the intensity of light to be detected. Semiconductor photodiodes and avalanche photodiodes are the most suitable detectors in photoelectric sensors.

Lenses

Light sources emit light and light detector is sensitive to light over a broad area. Lenses are used with light sources and detector to narrow this area. Therefore, lenses are used to increase the sensing distance of the photoelectric sensor.

Features

Photoelectric sensors are highly insensitive to ambient light interference and can be used with or without fiber optic cables. They have high switching speed and optional time delay in selected modes. The sensors are available in high temperatures and can sense objects up to 25 meters distance.

Types of Photo Electric Sensors

Depending upon the mode of sensing, photoelectric sensor are three types: diffused beam sensor, through beam sensor, and retro-reflective sensor.

Diffused Beam sensor (Fig.4.12)

This device consists of a transmitter and receiver together. The emitter emits infrared rays which are reflected on the receiver through the object to be registered[2]. In the use of these sensors, it is important to bear in mind the color of the object, light color corresponds to the maximum distance and vice versa. In case of shiny object; the effect of surface of object is more important than the color. These sensors are particularly used for position sensing and counting non-metallic objects. It is also used for label sensing, level sensing, height sensing, plastic film sensing, edge detection of paper or sheet metallic etc.

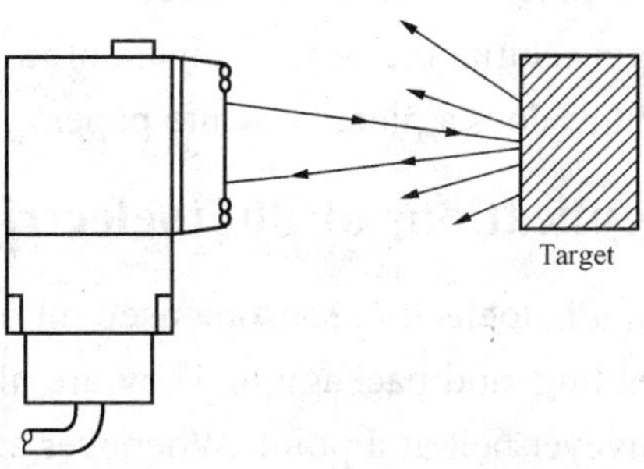

Fig.4.12 Diffused beam sensor

Through Beam Sensor (Fig.4.13)

It consists of two devices, a light emitter and a light receiver. These devices are kept apart facing each other. The Gallium-Aluminum-Arsenide-Luminescent diode integrated in the transmitter sends pulses of light in the infrared range which is invisible to the human eye.

The receiver opposite to the transmitter receives these rays. Sensing is achieved when these rays are interrupted by the object. Through beam sensors are used for sensing semi-transparent objects such as glass/plastic bottle, paper breakage detection and door opening / closing etc.

Retro-Reflective Sensor (Fig.4.14)

Retro-Reflective sensor consists of one device and a reflector. The device contains emitter and receiver. The rays emitted by the emitter are reflected by the reflector to the receiver. The sensing of the object occurs when the rays are interrupted. This sensor can be used when it is difficult to install Through Beam Sensor due to space constraints[3]. Further, simple wiring makes it suitable where sensing objects are bigger in size. Thus these sensors are used for loop control in de-coiler, edge detection in paper/sheet metal etc.

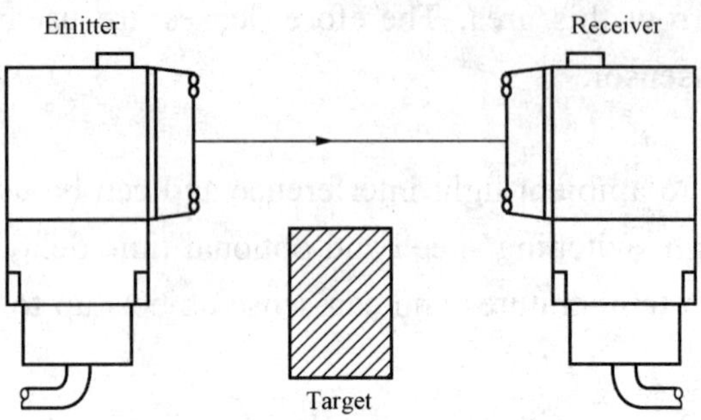

Fig.4.13 Through Beam Sensor

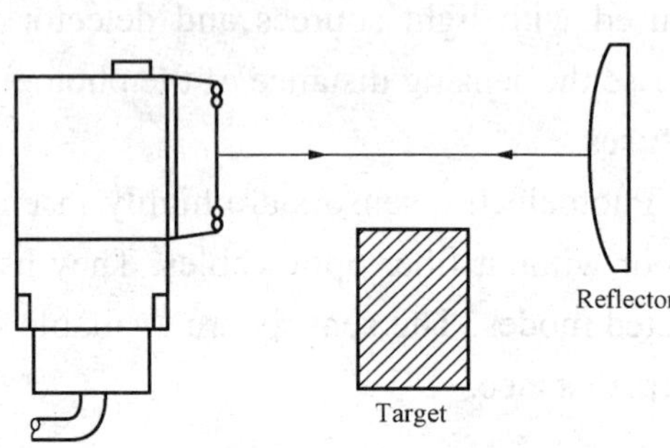

Fig.4.14 Retro-Reflective Sensor

Most retro-reflective targets are made up of many small corner-cube prisms, each of which has three mutually perpendicular surfaces. When a light beam enters a prism, the perpendicular surfaces reflect the beam back, parallel to the entering beam. In this way, the target returns the beam to its source. A good retro reflector returns about 3000 times as much light as does a piece of white paper.

Applications of Photoelectric sensors

Photoelectric sensors used in industries like food processing, transportation, material handling, and packaging. They are also used for counting the number of objects passing on a conveyer belt at a point. Whenever an object passes between the light source and detector, the light beam is interrupted, which gives out pulse, showing the presence of the object[4]. Thus by counting the number of pulses the number of objects passed through a point on the conveyer is known. Because of their high efficiency, small size, less weight, robust and effectiveness in all environments, photoelectric sensors are widely used in Control Industries.

Technical Words and Expressions

photoelectric	[ˌfəutəuiˈlektrik]	adj.	光电的
diffusion beam sensor			反射型光束传感器

through beam sensor			透过型光束传感器
retro-reflective sensor			回归反射型传感器
breakage	['breikidʒ]	n.	破坏，破损，破损量
decoiler	[diː'kɔilə]	n.	开卷机，拆卷机
prism	[' prizəm]	n.	棱镜
corner-cube prism			三面直角棱镜
conveyer		n.	运输机
robust	[rə'bʌst]	adj.	坚固耐用的
belt	[belt]	n.	带子

Notes

[1] A photoelectric sensor is an electrical device that responds to a change in the intensity of the light falling upon it.

译文：光电传感器是一种对照在其上面的光强度变化作出响应的器件。

此句中包含一个“that”引导的定语从句，由于“that”在从句中作主语，所以不能省略。

[2] The emitter emits infrared rays which are reflected on the receiver through the object to be registered.

译文：发射器发出红外光，光通过要对准的物体反射到接收器上。

“which are reflected on the receiver …”中 which 引导定语从句，“to be registered”作“the object”的定语。

[3] This sensor can be used when it is difficult to install Through Beam Sensor due to space constraints.

译文：当由于空间限制安装透射型传感器比较困难的时候可以使用这类传感器。

主句为被动形式，后跟“when”引导的时间状语从句。从句中“it”为形式主语，真正的主语为不定式短语“to install Through Beam Sensor…”，“due to…”表原因。

[4] Whenever an object passes between the light source and detector, the light beam is interrupted, which gives out pulse, showing the presence of the object.

译文：每当有物体通过光源和检测器之间时，光束被阻挡，就给出一个脉冲表示物体出现。

句中“Whenever”表示“无论何时，随时”，引导时间状语从句。“which”代表“the light beam is interrupted”，“showing the presence of the object”在句中作状语。

Exercises

Ⅰ. Mark the following statements with T (true) or F (false) according to the text.

1. Physical properties of light sensitive elements change their electrical features according to light intensity. (　　)

2. A photoelectric sensor can't be used for the non-contact detection. (　　)

3. Lenses are used to increase the sensing distance of the photoelectric sensor. (　　)

4. Through Beam Sensor consists of a transmitter and receiver together. (　　)

5. When the retro-Reflective Sensor is used, the sensing of the object occurs when the rays are interrupted. (   )

Ⅱ. Complete the following sentences.

1. ______ is the component used to detect the light source.
2. ______ consists of emitter and receiver and a reflector.
3. Photoelectric sensors are widely used because of ______.
4. In case of shiny object; the effect of surface of object is ______ than the color.
5. Most retro-reflective targets are made up of many small corner-cube prisms, each of which has ______.

Reading 21 Overview on Transducer

Transducers are electric or electronic devices that transform energy from one manifestation into another. Most people, when they think of transducers, think specifically of devices that perform this transformation in order to gather or transfer information, but really, anything that converts energy can be considered a transducer.

Transducers that detect or transmit information include common items such as microphones, Geiger meters, potentiometers, pressure sensors, thermometers, and antennae. A microphone, for example, converts sound waves that strike its diaphragm into an analogous electrical signal that can be transmitted over wires. A pressure sensor turns the physical force being exerted on the sensing apparatus into an analog reading that can be easily represented. While many people think of transducers as being some sort of technical device, once you start looking for them, you will find transducers everywhere in your everyday life. It is commonly used in two senses; the sensor, used to detect a parameter in one form and report it in another (usually an electrical or digital signal), and the audio loudspeaker, which converts electrical voltage variations representing music or speech, to mechanical cone vibration and hence vibrates air molecules creating sound. In this text, we mainly introduce the audio transducers.

About Audio Transducers and Buzzers

Audio transducers and buzzers are used in electronic equipment, toys and various warning devices as sounding components. They can be either electromagnetic or piezoelectric in operation. Electromagnetic transducers generate either a single continuous sound or intermittent tones and are available with either self-contained or external drive circuitry. Piezoelectric transducers include a metal plate that vibrates with the expansion or contraction of a piezoceramic element. Some audio transducers can transmit signals, some can receive signals, and some can both transmit and receive signals.

Audio transducers and buzzers vary according to tone, frequency, and sound pressure. Some devices have an alarm with a continuous tone, while others have an alarm with a pulsed or non-continuous tone. The frequency measures the number of events or cycles that occur in a time period, usually one second, in Hertz (Hz). The sound pressure level (SPL) measures the loudness or volume in decibels (dB). A 10 dB increase in SPL represents a doubling in volume. In terms of electrical specifications, audio transducers and buzzers also vary by operating voltage rating, maximum operating current, and operating temperature.

There are several ways to terminate audio transducers and buzzers. Some devices use pre-wired leads or screw terminals. Others use multi-pin connectors called PC pins or plugs called quick connects. Solder tabs are flat pieces of metal to which operators can solder wires. Surface mount technology (SMT) connects the element to the surface by wave soldering, but does not use terminations.

There are several ways to mount audio transducers and buzzers. Panel mounted devices have a partially threaded body, a matching nut, and can be either flush or flange. Screw-down devices have flanges with holes. Socket mounted devices plug into a receptacle, typically an integrated circuit (IC). Surface mounted components are soldered to a flat pad on the face of a printed circuit board. Typically, this pad is coated with a paste-like formulation of solder and flux. With careful placement, components mounted in this way remain in place until elevated temperatures, usually from an infrared oven, melt the paste and solder the mount's flat terminals to the circuit board's pad.

Some audio transducers and buzzers are programmable, provide volume control, or include a visual alarm to alert employees who work in areas with high noise levels. Internally driven transducers use self-contained circuitry with inductively coupled coils, and produce an average sound output of 85 dB or 10 cm/min. Externally driven transducers have a single coil and a magnetic circuit composed of a permanent magnet, an iron core, a highly permeable metal disk, and a vibrating diaphragm.

There are a variety of applications for audio transducers and buzzers. Examples include measuring equipment, industrial sensors, industrial equipment and machines, computers and peripherals, medical equipment, and audio and video equipment.

Technical Words and Expressions

manifestation	n.	表现形式
potentiometer	n.	电位计，分压计
exerted	adj.	外露的
buzzer	n.	蜂鸣器
Geiger meter		盖革计量表
cone	n.	锥形物，圆锥体
screw-down device		螺旋装置
threaded body		螺纹体
matching nut		匹配的螺母
flange	n.	凸缘，法兰

receptacle	n.	插座
paste	n.	浆糊
diaphragm	n.	膜片

Comprehension

1. Transducers that detect or transmit information include ______.
   A. microphones B. potentiometers C. pressure sensors D. all above
2. ______ turn the physical force being exerted on the sensing apparatus into an analog reading that can be easily represented.
   A. Thermometers B. Microphones
   C. Pressure sensors D. Antennae
3. Which of the following about audio transducers and buzzers is not right? ______.
   A. They can be either electromagnetic or piezoelectric in operation
   B. Audio transducers and buzzers vary according to tone, frequency, and sound pressure
   C. All of them have an alarm with a continuous tone
   D. Some of them can both transmit and receive signals
4. ______ plug into a receptacle, typically an integrated circuit (IC).
   A. Panel mounted devices B. Screw-down devices
   C. Socket mounted devices D. None of them
5. From the text, we can know ______.
   A. anything that converts energy can be considered a transducer.
   B. a microphone converts sound waves that strike its diaphragm into an analogous electrical signal that can be transmitted over wires
   C. audio transducers and buzzers have a variety of applications
   D. all above

Chapter 5

Automatic Control System

Unit 22 An Introduction to Control Systems

Overview

Control theory is

- a theory that deals with influencing the behavior of dynamical systems;
- an interdisciplinary subfield of science, which originated in engineering and mathematics, and evolved into use by the social sciences, like psychology, sociology and criminology[1].

An example

Consider an automobile's cruise control, which is a device designed to maintain a constant vehicle speed; the desired or reference speed, provided by the driver. The system in this case is the vehicle. The system output is the vehicle speed, and the control variable is the engine's throttle position which influences engine torque output.

A simple way to implement cruise control is to lock the throttle position when the driver engages cruise control. However, on hilly terrain, the vehicle will slow down going uphill and accelerate going downhill. In fact, any parameter different than what was assumed at design time will translate into a proportional error in the output velocity, including exact mass of the vehicle, wind resistance, and tire pressure. This type of controller is called an open-loop controller because there is no direct connection between the output of the system (the engine torque) and the actual conditions encountered; that is to say, the system does not and can not compensate for unexpected forces.

In a closed-loop control system, a sensor monitors the output (the vehicle's speed) and feeds the data to a computer which continuously adjusts the control input (the throttle) as necessary to keep the control error to a minimum (to maintain the desired speed). Feedback on how the system is actually performing allows the controller (vehicle's on board computer) to dynamically compensate for disturbances to the system, such as changes in slope of the ground or wind speed. An ideal feedback control system cancels out all errors, effectively mitigating the effects of any forces that may or may not arise during operation and producing a response in the system that perfectly matches the user's wishes.

History

Although control systems of various types date back to antiquity, a more formal analysis of the field began with a dynamics analysis of the centrifugal governor, conducted by the physicist James Clerk Maxwell in 1868 entitled On Governors. This described and analyzed the phenomenon of "hunting", in which lags in the system can lead to overcompensation and unstable behavior. This generated a flurry of interest in the topic, during which Maxwell's classmate Edward John Routh generalized the results of Maxwell for the general class of linear systems. Independently, Adolf Hurwitz analyzed system stability using differential equations in 1877. This result is called the Routh-Hurwitz theorem.

A notable application of dynamic control was in the area of manned flight. The Wright Brothers made their first successful test flights on December 17, 1903 and were distinguished by their ability to control their flights for substantial periods (more so than the ability to produce lift from an airfoil, which was known). Control of the airplane was necessary for safe flight.

By World War Ⅱ, control theory was an important part of fire-control systems, guidance systems and electronics. The Space Race also depended on accurate spacecraft control. However, control theory also saw an increasing use in fields such as economics .

People in systems and control

Many active and historical figures made significant contribution to control theory, including, for example:

Alexander Lyapunov (1857—1918) in the 1890s marks the beginning of stability theory.

Harold S. Black (1898—1983), invented the concept of negative feedback amplifiers in 1927. He managed to develop stable negative feedback amplifiers in the 1930s.

Harry Nyquist (1889—1976), developed the Nyquist stability criterion for feedback systems in the 1930s.

Richard Bellman (1920—1984), developed dynamic programming since the 1940s.

Norbert Wiener (1894—1964) co-developed the Wiener-Kolmogorov filter and coined the term Cybernetics in the 1940s.

John R. Ragazzini (1912—1988) introduced digital control and the z-transform in the 1950s.

Classical control theory

To avoid the problems of the open-loop controller, control theory introduces feedback. A closed-loop controller uses feedback to control states or outputs of a dynamical system. Its name comes from the information path in the system: process inputs (e.g. voltage applied to an electric motor) have an effect on the process outputs (e.g. velocity or torque of the motor), which is measured with sensors and processed by the controller; the result (the control signal) is used as input to the process, closing the loop.

Closed-loop controllers have the following advantages over open-loop controllers:

- disturbance rejection (such as unmeasured friction in a motor);
- guaranteed performance even with model uncertainties, when the model structure does not match perfectly the real process and the model parameters are not exact;
- unstable processes can be stabilized;

- reduced sensitivity to parameter variations;
- improved reference tracking performance.

In some systems, closed-loop and open-loop control are used simultaneously. In such systems, the open-loop control is termed feedforward and serves to further improve reference tracking performance.

A common closed-loop controller architecture is the PID controller.

Closed-loop transfer function

The output of the system $y(t)$ is fed back through a sensor measurement F to the reference value $r(t)$. The controller C then takes the error e (difference) between the reference and the output to change the inputs u to the system under control P. This is shown in the Fig.5.1. This kind of controller is a closed-loop controller or feedback controller.

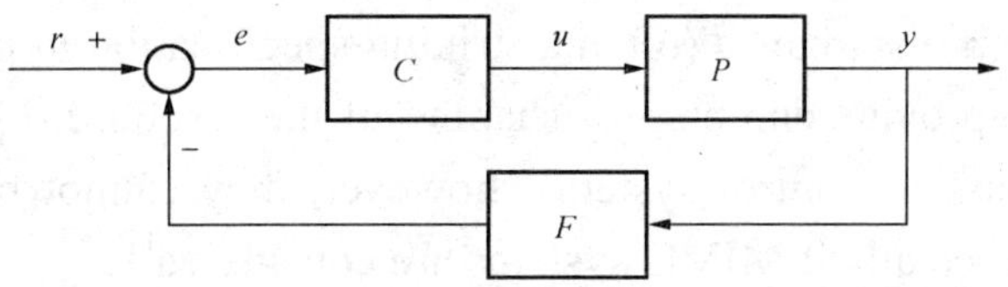

Fig.5.1 Closed-loop control system

This is called a single-input-single-output (SISO) control system; MIMO (i.e. Multi-Input-Multi-Output) systems, with more than one input/output, are common. In such cases variables are represented through vectors instead of simple scalar values. For some distributed parameter systems the vectors may be infinite-dimensional (typically functions).

If we assume the controller C, the plant P, and the sensor F are linear and time-invariant (i.e., elements of their transfer function, $P(s)$, and $F(s)$ do not depend on time), the systems above can be analyzed using the Laplace transform on the variables. This gives the following relations:

$$Y(s)=P(s)U(s)$$
$$U(s)=C(s)E(s)$$
$$E(s)=R(s)-F(s)Y(s)$$

Solving for $Y(s)$ in terms of $R(s)$ gives:

$$Y(s)=\left[\frac{P(s)C(s)}{1+F(s)P(s)C(s)}\right]R(s)=H(s)R(s)$$

The expression $H(s)=\dfrac{P(s)C(s)}{1+F(s)P(s)C(s)}$ is referred to as the closed-loop transfer function of the system. The numerator is the forward (open-loop) gain from r to y, and the denominator is one plus the gain in going around the feedback loop, the so-called loop gain. If$|P(s)C(s)|>>1$, i.e. it has a large norm with each value of s, and if $|F(s)|=1$, then $Y(s)$ is approximately equal to $R(s)$. This means simply setting the reference controls the output.

PID controller

The PID controller is probably the most-used feedback control design, being the simplest one[2]. "PID" means Proportional-Integral-Derivative, referring to the three terms operating on the error signal to produce a control signal. If $u(t)$ is the control signal sent to the system, $y(t)$ is the measured output and $r(t)$ is the desired output, and tracking error $e(t)=r(t)-y(t)$, a PID controller has the general form:

$$u(t)=K_{\mathrm{P}}e(t)+K_{\mathrm{I}}\int e(t)\mathrm{d}t+K_{\mathrm{D}}\frac{\mathrm{d}}{\mathrm{d}t}e(t)$$

The desired closed loop dynamics is obtained by adjusting the three parameters K_{P}, K_{I} and K_{D}, often iteratively by "tuning" and without specific knowledge of a plant model. Stability can often be ensured using only the proportional term. The integral term permits the rejection of a step disturbance (often a striking specification in process control). The derivative term is used to provide damping or shaping of the response. PID controllers are the most well established class of control systems; however, they cannot be used in several more complicated cases, especially if MIMO systems are considered[3].

Modern control theory

In contrast to the frequency domain analysis of the classical control theory, modern control theory utilizes the time-domain state space representation, a mathematical model of a physical system as a set of input, output and state variables related by first-order differential equations. To abstract from the number of inputs, outputs and states, the variables are expressed as vectors and the differential and algebraic equations are written in matrix form (the last one can be done when the dynamical system is linear and time invariant). The state space representation (also known as the "time-domain approach") provides a convenient and compact way to model and analyze systems with multiple inputs and outputs. With inputs and outputs, we would otherwise have to write down Laplace transforms to encode all the information about a system. Unlike the frequency domain approach, the use of the state space representation is not limited to systems with linear components and zero initial conditions. "State space" refers to the space whose axes are the state variables. The state of the system can be represented as a vector within that space.

Technical Words and Expressions

interdisciplinary	[ˌintəːˈdisiplinəri]	adj.	各学科间的
psychology	[saiˈkɔlədʒi]	n.	心理学，心理，心理特点
sociology	[ˌsəusiˈɔlədʒi]	n.	社会学
criminology	[ˌkrimiˈnɔlədʒi]	n.	犯罪学，刑事学
throttle	[ˈθrɔtl]	n.	油门
open-loop controller			开环控制器
closed-loop controller			闭环控制器
feedback	[ˈfiːdbæk]	n.	反馈，反应
mitigate	[ˈmitigeit]	vt.	减轻，缓和

centrifugal governor			离心调速器，离心式传感器
dynamical	[daiˈnæmikəl]	adj.	动力（学）的
Nyquist stability criterion			奈奎斯特稳定判据
differential equation			微分方程（式）
stability criterion			稳定性判据
infinite-dimensional			无限维的
numerator	[ˈnju:məreitə]	n.	（分数的）分子
tracking error			跟踪误差
encode	[inˈkəud]	vt.	编码；编制成计算机语言
frequency domain			频域
state space			状态空间
first-order differential equation			一阶微分方程
vector	[ˈvektə]		矢量
matrix	[ˈmeitriks]		矩阵

Notes

[1] Control theory is an interdisciplinary subfield of science, which originated in engineering and mathematics, and evolved into use by the social sciences, like psychology, sociology and criminology.

译文为：控制理论是一个跨学科的子科学，它产生于工程学和数学中，并逐渐被其他社会科学所利用，如心理学、社会学和犯罪学。

该句是由 which 引导的非限制性定语从句，修饰 control theory，originate in 的意思是“产生于”；evolve into 的意思是“逐渐发展成”。

[2] The PID controller is probably the most-used feedback control design, being the simplest one.

译文为：PID 控制器可能是使用最广泛和最简单的反馈控制器。

系动词 be 的现在分词 being 作状语。选择现在分词还是过去分词，关键看主句的主语。如分词的动作是主句的主语发出，分词选用现在分词，反之用过去分词。

[3] PID controllers are the most well established class of control systems; however, they cannot be used in several more complicated cases, especially if MIMO systems are considered.

译文为：众所周知，PID 控制器能够构建成一流的控制系统，然而，对一些更加复杂的系统，例如多输入多输出系统，它们还不适用。

该句是由 however 连接的并联句。

Exercises

Ⅰ. Mark the following statements with T (true) or F (false) according to the text.

1. A simple way to implement cruise control is to lock the throttle position when the driver engages cruise control. (　　)

2. The closed-loop and open-loop control can not be used simultaneously. (　　)

3. In MIMO systems variables are represented through simple scalar values. (　　)

4. For some distributed parameter systems the vectors may be infinite-dimensional. (　　)

5. The state space representation provides a convenient and compact way to model and analyze systems with multiple inputs and outputs. (　　)

Ⅱ. Complete the following sentences.

1. Control theory is ______, which originated in engineering and mathematics, and ______, like psychology, sociology and criminology.

2. In a closed-loop control system, a sensor monitors the output and ______ which continuously adjusts the control input as necessary to ______.

3. To avoid the problems of the open-loop controller, control theory ______. A closed-loop controller uses feedback to ______.

4. The PID controller is probably the most-used feedback control design, ______. "PID" ______, referring to the three terms operating on the error signal to produce a control signal.

5. Unlike ______, the use of the state space representation is not limited to systems with ______.

Reading 22 Topics in Control Theory

Stability

Stability (in control theory) often means that for any bounded input over any amount of time, the output will also be bounded. This is known as BIBO stability. If a system is BIBO stable then the output cannot "blow up" (i.e., become infinite) if the input remains finite.

Mathematically, this means that for a causal linear system to be stable all of the poles of its transfer function must satisfy some criteria depending on whether a continuous or discrete time analysis is used:

- In continuous time, the Laplace transform is used to obtain the transfer function. A system is stable if the poles of this transfer function lie strictly in the closed left half of the complex plane (i.e. the real part of all the poles is less than zero).
- In discrete time the Z-transform is used. A system is stable if the poles of this transfer function lie strictly inside the unit circle (i.e. the magnitude of the poles is less than one).

When the appropriate conditions above are satisfied a system is said to be asymptotically stable: the variables of an asymptotically stable control system always decrease from their initial value and do not show permanent oscillations. Permanent oscillations occur when a pole has a real part exactly equal to zero (in the continuous time case) or a modulus equal to one (in the discrete time case). If a simply stable system response neither decays nor grows over time, and has no oscillations, it is marginally stable: in this case the system transfer function has non-repeated poles at complex plane origin (i.e. their real and complex component is zero in the continuous time case). Oscillations are present when poles with real part equal to zero have an imaginary part not equal to zero.

Differences between the two cases are not a contradiction. The Laplace transform is in Cartesian coordinates and the Z-transform is in circular coordinates, and it can be shown that:

- the negative-real part in the Laplace domain can map onto the interior of the unit circle;
- the positive-real part in the Laplace domain can map onto the exterior of the unit circle.

If a system in question has an impulse response of

$$x(n) = 0.5^n u[n]$$

then the Z-transform (see this example), is given by

$$X(z) = \frac{1}{1-0.5z^{-1}}$$

which has a pole in z=0.5 (zero imaginary part). This system is BIBO (asymptotically) stable since the pole is inside the unit circle.

However, if the impulse response was

$$x(n) = 1.5^n u[n]$$

then the Z-transform is

$$X(z) = \frac{1}{1-1.5z^{-1}}$$

which has a pole at z=1.5 and is not BIBO stable since the pole has a modulus strictly greater than one.

Numerous tools exist for the analysis of the poles of a system. These include graphical systems like the root locus, Bode plots or the Nyquist plots.

Controllability and observability

Controllability and observability are main issues in the analysis of a system before deciding the best control strategy to be applied, or whether it is even possible to control or stabilize the system. Controllability is related to the possibility of forcing the system into a particular state by using an appropriate control signal. If a state is not controllable, then no signal will ever be able to control the state. If a state is not controllable, but its dynamics are stable, then the state it is termed stabilizable. Observability instead is related to the possibility of "observing", through output measurements, the state of a system. If a state is not observable, the controller will never be able to determine the behaviour of an unobservable state and hence cannot use it to stabilize the system. However, similar to the stabilizability condition above, if a state cannot be observed it might still be detectable.

From a geometrical point of view, looking at the states of each variable of the system to be controlled, every "bad" state of these variables must be controllable and observable to ensure a good behaviour in the closed-loop system. That is, if one of the eigenvalues of the system is not both controllable and observable, this part of the dynamics will remain untouched in the closed-loop system. If such an eigenvalue is not stable, the dynamics of this eigenvalue will be present in the closed-loop system which therefore will be unstable. Unobservable poles are not present in the transfer function realization of a state-space representation, which is why sometimes the latter is preferred in dynamical systems analysis.

Solutions to problems of uncontrollable or unobservable system include adding actuators and sensors.

Control specifications

Several different control strategies have been devised in the past years. These vary from extremely general ones (PID controller), to others devoted to very particular classes of systems (especially robotics or aircraft cruise control).

A control problem can have several specifications. Stability, of course, is always present: the controller must ensure that the closed-loop system is stable, regardless of the open-loop stability. A poor choice of controller can even worsen the stability of the open-loop system, which must normally be avoided. Sometimes it would be desired to obtain particular dynamics in the closed loop: i.e. that the poles have $\mathrm{Re}[\lambda] < -\overline{\lambda}$, where $\overline{\lambda}$ a fixed value is strictly greater than zero, instead of simply ask that $\mathrm{Re}[\lambda] < 0$.

Another typical specification is the rejection of a step disturbance; including an integrator in the open-loop chain (i.e. directly before the system under control) easily achieves this. Other classes of disturbances need different types of sub-systems to be included.

Other "classical" control theory specifications regard the time-response of the closed-loop system: these include the rise time (the time needed by the control system to reach the desired value after a perturbation), peak overshoot (the highest value reached by the response before reaching the desired value) and others (settling time, quarter-decay). Frequency domain specifications are usually related to robustness.

Modern performance assessments use some variation of integrated tracking error (IAE, ISA, CQI).

Technical Words and Expressions

bounded	adj.	有界限的，有限制的
causal linear system		因果线性系统
oscillation	n.	摆动，振动
marginally	adv.	在边上
interior	n.	内部
exterior	n.	外部
unit circle		单位圆

root locus		根轨迹
eigenvalue	n.	特征值
dynamics	n.	动态
state-space representation		空间状态表示法
actuator	n.	执行器
cruise	n.	巡航
step disturbance		阶跃扰动
overshoot	n.	超调量
robustness	n.	鲁棒性
cartesian coordinate		笛卡儿坐标，直角坐标（系）
tracking error		跟踪误差
asymptotically	adv.	渐近地
controllability	n.	可控性；能控性
observability	n.	可观测性

Comprehension

1. If a system is BIBO stable, then the output ______ if the input remains finite.
   A. can not become infinite B. can not become finite
   C. can not equal the input D. can "blow up"
2. A system is stable if ______.
   A. the zeros of this transfer function lie strictly in the closed left half of the complex plane
   B. the zeros of this transfer function lie strictly in the closed right half of the complex plane
   C. the poles of this transfer function lie strictly in the closed left half of the complex plane
   D. the poles of this transfer function lie strictly in the closed right half of the complex plane
3. A discrete system is stable if ______.
   A. the magnitude of the poles is more than one
   B. the magnitude of the poles is less than one
   C. the magnitude of the poles is equal to one
   D. the magnitude of the poles is not equal to one
4. Permanent oscillations occur when ______ in the continuous time case.
   A. a zero has a real part exactly equal to zero
   B. a zero has a real part exactly not equal to zero
   C. a pole has a real part exactly equal to zero
   D. a pole has a real part exactly not equal to zero
5. Which is not a tool existing for the analysis of the poles of a system? ______.
   A. the root locus
   B. Bode plot
   C. the Nyquist plot
   D. the Laplace transform

Unit 23 Transfer Function

Overview

A transfer function is a mathematical representation, in terms of spatial or temporal frequency, of the relation between the input and output of a (linear time-invariant) system. With optical imaging devices, for example, it is the Fourier transform of the point spread function (hence a function of spatial frequency), i.e. the intensity distribution caused by a point object in the field of view.

Explanation

The transfer function is commonly used in the analysis of single-input single-output electronic filters, for instance. It is mainly used in signal processing, communication theory, and control theory. The term is often used exclusively to refer to linear, time-invariant systems (LTI), as covered in this article. Most real systems have non-linear input/output characteristics, but many systems, when operated within nominal parameters (not "over-driven") have behavior that is close enough to linear that LTI system theory is an acceptable representation of the input/output behavior[1].

In its simplest form for continuous-time input signal $x(t)$ and output $y(t)$, the transfer function is the linear mapping of the Laplace transform of the input $X(s)$ to the output $Y(s)$:

$$Y(s)=H(s)X(s)$$

or

$$H(s)=\frac{Y(s)}{X(s)}=\frac{L\{y(t)\}}{L\{x(t)\}}$$

where $H(s)$ is the transfer function of the LTI system.

In discrete-time systems, the function is similarly written as $H(z)=\frac{Y(z)}{X(z)}$ and is often referred to as the pulse-transfer function.

Direct derivation from differential equations

Consider an inhomogeneous linear differential equation with constant coefficients

$$L[u]=\frac{\mathrm{d}^n u}{\mathrm{d}t^n}+a_1\frac{\mathrm{d}^{n-1}u}{\mathrm{d}t^{n-1}}+\cdots+a_{n-1}\frac{\mathrm{d}^n u}{\mathrm{d}t^n}+a_n\frac{\mathrm{d}^n u}{\mathrm{d}t^n}=r(t)$$

where u and r are suitably smooth functions of t, and L is the operator defined on the relevant function space, which transforms u into r. That kind of equations can be used to constrain the output function u in terms of the forcing function r. The transfer function, written as an operator $F[r]=u$, is the right inverse of L, since $L[F[r]]=r$.

Solutions of the homogeneous equation $L[u]=0$ can be found by trying $u=e^{\lambda t}$. That substitution yields the characteristic polynomial

$$p_L(\lambda)=\lambda^n+a_1\lambda^{n-1}+\cdots+a_{n-1}\lambda^n+a_n$$

The inhomogeneous case can be easily solved if the input function r is also of the form $r(t)=e^{st}$. In that case, by substituting $u=H(s)e^{st}$ one finds that $L[H(s)e^{st}]=e^{st}$ if and only if

$$H(s)=\frac{1}{p_L(s)},\qquad p_L(s)\neq 0$$

Taking that as the definition of the transfer function requires to carefully disambiguate between complex vs. real values, which is traditionally influenced by the interpretation of abs $H(s)$ as the gain and arctan $H(s)$ as the phase lag.

Signal processing

Let $x(t)$ be the input to a general linear time-invariant system and $y(t)$ be the output, and the Laplace transform of $x(t)$ and $y(t)$ be

$$X(s)=L\{x(t)\}=\int_{-\infty}^{\infty}x(t)e^{-st}dt$$

$$Y(s)=L\{y(t)\}=\int_{-\infty}^{\infty}y(t)e^{-st}dt$$

Then the output is related to the input by the transfer function $H(s)$ as

$$Y(s)=H(s)X(s)$$

and the transfer function itself is therefore

$$H(s)=\frac{Y(s)}{X(s)}$$

In particular, if a complex harmonic signal with a sinusoidal component with amplitude $|X|$, angular frequency ω and phase arg (X)

$$x(t)=Xe^{j\omega t}=|X|e^{j(\omega t+\arg X)}$$

where

$$X=|X|e^{j\arg X}$$

is input to a linear time-invariant system, then the corresponding component in the output is:

$$y(t)=Ye^{j\omega t}=|Y|e^{j(\omega t+\arg Y)}$$

and

$$Y=|Y|e^{j\arg Y}$$

Note that, in a linear time-invariant system, the input frequency ω has not changed; only the amplitude and the phase angle of the sinusoid have been changed by the system. The frequency response $H(\mathrm{j}\omega)$ describes this change for every frequency ω in terms of gain:

$$G(\omega)=\frac{|Y|}{|X|}=|H(\mathrm{j}\omega)|$$

and phase shift:

$$\phi(\omega)=\arg(Y)-\arg(X)=\arg(H(\mathrm{j}\omega))$$

The phase delay (i.e., the frequency-dependent amount of delay introduced to the sinusoid by the transfer function) is:

$$T_{\phi}(\omega)=-\frac{\phi(\omega)}{\omega}$$

The group delay (i.e., the frequency-dependent amount of delay introduced to the envelope of the sinusoid by the transfer function) is found by computing the derivative of the phase shift with respect to angular frequency ω,

$$T_{g}(\omega)=-\frac{\mathrm{d}\phi(\omega)}{\mathrm{d}\omega}$$

The transfer function can also be shown using the Fourier transform which is only a special case of the bilateral Laplace transform for the case where $s=\mathrm{j}\omega$[2].

Common transfer function families

While any LTI system can be described by some transfer function or another, there are certain "families" of special transfer functions that are commonly used. Typical infinite impulse response filters are designed to implement one of these special transfer functions.

Control engineering

In control engineering and control theory the transfer function is derived using the Laplace transform.

The transfer function was the primary tool used in classical control engineering. However, it has proven to be unwieldy for the analysis of multiple-input multiple-output (MIMO) systems, and has been largely supplanted by state space representations for such systems. In spite of this, a transfer matrix can be always obtained for any linear system, in order to analyze its dynamics and other properties: each element of a transfer matrix is a transfer function relating a particular input variable to an output variable.

Technical Words and Expressions

transfer function			传递函数
temporal	['tempərəl]	adj.	暂时的，瞬间的
linear time-invariant system			线性时不变系统
intensity distribution			强度分析，亮度分布
Fourier transform			傅里叶变换

point spread function			点扩散函数，点分布函数
spatial frequency			空间频率
discrete-time system			离散时间系统
Laplace transform			拉普拉斯变换
polynomial	[pɔli'nəumjəl]	adj. & n.	多项式的，多项式
inhomogeneous linear differential equation			非齐次线性微分方程
smooth function			平滑函数
characteristic polynomial			特征多项式
disambiguate	[dis,æmbi'gjueit]	vt.	消除……的歧义
phase lag			相位滞后
derivative	[di'rivətiv]	n.	导数
bilateral	[ˋbai'lætərəl]	adj.	双边的，双方的
unwieldy	[ʌn'wi:ldi]	adj.	难控制的
supplant	[sə'plɑ:nt]	vt.	取代
control engineering			控制工程
multiple-input multiple-output (MIMO) system			多输入—多输出系统

Notes

[1] Most real systems have non-linear input/output characteristics, but many systems, when operated within nominal parameters have behavior that is close enough to linear that LTI system theory is an acceptable representation of the input/output behavior.

译文为：大多数实时系统具有非线性输入/输出的特点，但许多系统在标定参数范围内运行时，其特性近似线性，这时 LTI 系统理论可以运用到输入/输出的特性分析中。

这是由 but 连接的并联句；but 后的分句中，主语是 many systems，when 引导了一个条件状语从句，其中又包含了一个由 that 引导的定语从句。

[2] The transfer function can also be shown using the Fourier transform which is only a special case of the bilateral Laplace transform for the case where $s=j\omega$.

译文为：也可以通过傅里叶变换来表示传递函数，傅里叶变换是 $s=j\omega$ 时的双边拉普拉斯变换的一个特例。

谓语为被动时，经常可译成主动句，把主语译成宾语，构成无主语的动宾结构，句子中包含一个由 which 引导的定语从句，修饰 the fourier transform。

Exercises

Ⅰ. Mark the following statements with T (true) or F (false) according to the text.

1. The Bode plot is the primary tool used in classical control engineering. (　　)
2. The transfer function can also be shown using the Fourier transform. (　　)
3. While any LTI system can be described by some transfer function or another, there are certain "families" of special transfer functions that are commonly used. (　　)
4. In control engineering and control theory the transfer function is derived using the

Laplace transform. ( )

5. Each element of a transfer matrix is not a transfer function relating a particular input variable to an output variable. ( )

Ⅱ. Complete the following sentences.

1. A transfer function is ______, in terms of spatial or temporal frequency, of the relation between the input and output of a ______ system.

2. Most real systems have ______, but many systems, when operated within nominal parameters have behavior ______ to linear that LTI system theory is an acceptable representation of the input/output behavior.

3. The transfer function can also be shown using ______ which is only a special case of the bilateral Laplace transform for ______.

4. ______was the primary tool used in classical control engineering. However, it has proven to be unwieldy for ______, and has been largely supplanted by state space representations for such systems.

5. In spite of this, a transfer matrix can be always obtained for ______, in order to analyze its dynamics and other properties: ______ is a transfer function relating a particular input variable to an output variable.

Reading 23 PID Controller

The PID control scheme is named after its three correcting terms, whose sum constitutes the manipulated variable (MV). Hence:

$$MV(t) = P_{\text{out}} + I_{\text{out}} + D_{\text{out}}$$

where P_{out}, I_{out}, and D_{out} are the contributions to the output from the PID controller from each of the three terms, as defined below.

Proportional term

The proportional term makes a change to the output that is proportional to the current error value. The proportional response can be adjusted by multiplying the error by a constant K_p, called the proportional gain.

The proportional term is given by:

$$P_{\text{out}}=K_p e(t)$$

where

- P_{out}: Proportional output;
- K_p: Proportional Gain, a tuning parameter;
- e: $Error=SP-PV$;
- t: Time or instantaneous time (the present).

A high proportional gain results in a large change in the output for a given change in the error. If the proportional gain is too high, the system can become unstable. In contrast, a small gain results in a small output response to a large input error, and a less responsive (or sensitive) controller. If the proportional gain is too low, the control action may be too small when responding to system disturbances.

In the absence of disturbances, pure proportional control will not settle at its target value, but will retain a steady state error that is a function of the proportional gain and the process gain. Despite the steady-state offset, both tuning theory and industrial practice indicate that it is the proportional term that should contribute the bulk of the output change.

Integral term

The contribution from the integral term is proportional to both the magnitude of the error and the duration of the error. Summing the instantaneous error over time (integrating the error) gives the accumulated offset that should have been corrected previously. The accumulated error is then multiplied by the integral gain and added to the controller output. The magnitude of the contribution of the integral term to the overall control action is determined by the integral gain K_i.

The integral term is given by:

$$I_{out} = K_i \int_0^t e(t)\mathrm{d}t$$

where

- I_{out}: Integral output;
- K_i: Integral Gain, a tuning parameter;
- e: *Error=SP−PV*;
- t: Time in the past contributing to the integral response.

The integral term (when added to the proportional term) accelerates the movement of the process towards setpoint and eliminates the residual steady-state error that occurs with a proportional only controller. However, since the integral term is responding to accumulated errors from the past, it can cause the present value to overshoot the setpoint value (cross over the setpoint and then create a deviation in the other direction).

Derivative term

The rate of change of the process error is calculated by determining the slope of the error over time (i.e. its first derivative with respect to time) and multiplying this rate of change by the derivative gain K_d. The magnitude of the contribution of the derivative term to the overall control action is termed the derivative gain K_d.

The derivative term is given by:

$$D_{out} = K_d \frac{\mathrm{d}e}{\mathrm{d}t}$$

where

- D_{out}: Derivative output;
- K_d: Derivative Gain, a tuning parameter;
- e: $Error=SP-PV$;
- t: Time or instantaneous time (the present).

The derivative term slows the rate of change of the controller output and this effect is most noticeable close to the controller setpoint. Hence, derivative control is used to reduce the magnitude of the overshoot produced by the integral component and improve the combined controller-process stability. However, differentiation of a signal amplifies noise and thus this term in the controller is highly sensitive to noise in the error term, and can cause a process to become unstable if the noise and the derivative gain are sufficiently large.

Summary

The output from the three terms, the proportional, the integral and the derivative terms are summed to calculate the output of the PID controller. Defining $u(t)$ as the controller output, the final form of the PID algorithm is:

$$u(t) = MV(t) = K_p e(t) + K_i \int_0^t e(t)\mathrm{d}t + K_d \frac{\mathrm{d}e}{\mathrm{d}t}$$

and the tuning parameters are:

(1) K_p: Proportional Gain —— Larger K_p typically means faster response since the larger the error, the larger the Proportional term compensation. An excessively large proportional gain will lead to process instability and oscillation.

(2) K_i: Integral Gain —— Larger K_i implies steady state errors are eliminated quicker. The trade-off is larger overshoot: any negative error integrated during transient response must be integrated away by positive error before we reach steady state.

(3) K_d: Derivative Gain —— Larger K_d decreases overshoot, but slows down transient response and may lead to instability due to signal noise amplification in the differentiation of the error.

Technical Words and Expressions

manipulated variable		操纵变量
tuning parameter		调整参数
retain	vt.	保持，保留
bulk	n.	大部分，大多数
setpoint value		设定值
trade-off		折中方案
instability	n.	不稳定，不稳固
differentiation	n.	微分

Comprehension

1. The proportional term makes a change to the output that is ______.
   A. proportional to the slope of the error over time
   B. proportional to the current error value
   C. proportional to both the magnitude of the error and the duration of the error
   D. proportional to the duration of the error
2. If the proportional gain is too high, ______.
   A. the system can become unstable
   B. it results in a small output response to a large input error
   C. the control action may be too small when responding to system disturbances
   D. the system can not become unstable
3. The integral term makes a change to the output that is ______.
   A. proportional to the slope of the error over time
   B. proportional to the current error value
   C. proportional to both the magnitude of the error and the duration of the error
   D. proportional to the duration of the error
4. The integral term ______.
   A. accelerates the movement of the process towards setpoint
   B. eliminates the residual steady-state error that occurs with a proportional only controller
   C. can cause the present value to overshoot the setpoint value
   D. all of the above
5. The term derivation ______.
   A. slows the rate of change of the controller output
   B. can cause the present value to overshoot the setpoint value
   C. accelerates the movement of the process towards setpoint
   D. eliminates the residual steady-state error that occurs with a proportional only controller

Unit 24 Bode Plot

A Bode plot, named after Hendrik Wade Bode, is usually a combination of a Bode magnitude plot and Bode phase plot:

A Bode magnitude plot is a graph of log magnitude versus frequency, plotted with a log-frequency axis, to show the transfer function or frequency response of a linear, time-invariant system[1].

The magnitude axis of the Bode plot is usually expressed as decibels, that is, 20 times the common logarithm of the amplitude gain. With the magnitude gain being logarithmic, Bode plots make multiplication of magnitudes a simple matter of adding distances on the graph (in decibels), since

$$\log ab = \log a + \log b$$

A Bode phase plot is a graph of phase versus frequency, also plotted on a log-frequency axis, usually used in conjunction with the magnitude plot, to evaluate how much a frequency will be phase-shifted. For example a signal described by: $A\sin(\omega t)$ may be attenuated but also phase-shifted. If the system attenuates it by a factor x and phase shifts it by $-\Phi$ the signal out of the system will be $(A/x)\sin(\omega t-\Phi)$. The phase shift Φ is generally a function of frequency.

Phase can also be added directly from the graphical values, a fact that is mathematically clear when phase is seen as the imaginary part of the complex logarithm of a complex gain.

The magnitude and phase Bode plots can seldom be changed independently of each other —— changing the amplitude response of the system will most likely change the phase characteristics and vice versa[2]. For minimum-phase systems the phase and amplitude characteristics can be obtained from each other with the use of the Hilbert transform.

If the transfer function is a rational function with real poles and zeros, then the Bode plot can be approximated with straight lines. These asymptotic approximations are called straight line Bode plots or uncorrected Bode plots and are useful because they can be drawn by hand following a few simple rules. Simple plots can even be predicted without drawing them.

The approximation can be taken further by correcting the value at each cutoff frequency. The plot is then called a corrected Bode plot.

Rules for hand-made Bode plot

The premise of a Bode plot is that one can consider the log of a function in the form:

$$f(x) = A\prod(x+c_n)^{a_n}$$

as a sum of the logs of its poles and zeros:

$$\log f(x) = \log A + \sum a_n \log(x+c_n)$$

This idea is used explicitly in the method for drawing phase diagrams. The method for drawing amplitude plots implicitly uses this idea, but since the log of the amplitude of each pole or zero always starts at zero and only has one asymptote change (the straight lines), the method can be simplified.

Straight-line amplitude plot

Amplitude decibels is usually done using the $20\log_{10}(X)$ version. Given a transfer function in the form

$$H(s) = A\prod\frac{(s+x_n)^{a_n}}{(s+y_n)^{b_n}}$$

where x_n and y_n are constants, $s=\mathrm{j}\omega$, $a_n, b_n>0$, and H is the transfer function:

- at every value of s where $\omega = x_n$(a zero), increase the slope of the line by $20a_n$dB per decade.
- at every value of s where $\omega = y_n$(a pole), decrease the slope of the line by $20b_n$dB per decade.
- The initial value of the graph depends on the boundaries. The initial point is found by putting the initial angular frequency ω into the function and finding $H(\mathrm{j}\omega)$.
- The initial slope of the function at the initial value depends on the number and order of zeros and poles that are at values below the initial value, and are found using the first two rules.

To handle irreducible 2nd order polynomials, ax^2+bx+c can, in many cases, be approximated as $\left(\sqrt{a}x+\sqrt{c}\right)^2$.

Note that zeros and poles happen when ω is equal to a certain x_n or y_n. This is because the function in question is the magnitude of $H(\mathrm{j}\omega)$, and since it is a complex function, $|H(\mathrm{j}\omega)|=\sqrt{H \bullet H^*}$. Thus at any place where there is a zero or pole involving the term $(s+x_n)$, the magnitude of that term is $\sqrt{(x_n+\mathrm{j}\omega)\bullet(x_n-\mathrm{j}\omega)}=\sqrt{x_n^2+\omega^2}$.

Corrected amplitude plot

To correct a straight-line amplitude plot:

- at every zero, put a point $3a_n$dB above the line,
- at every pole, put a point $3b_n$dB below the line,
- draw a smooth curve through those points using the straight lines as asymptotes (lines which the curve approaches).

Note that this correction method does not incorporate how to handle complex values of x_n or y_n. In the case of an irreducible polynomial, the best way to correct the plot is to actually calculate the magnitude of the transfer function at the pole or zero corresponding to the irreducible polynomial, and put that dot over or under the line at that pole or zero.

Straight-line phase plot

Given a transfer function in the same form as above:

$$H(s)=A\prod\frac{(s+x_n)^{a_n}}{(s+y_n)^{b_n}}$$

The idea is to draw separate plots for each pole and zero, then add them up. The actual phase curve is given by $-\arctan(\mathrm{Im}[H(s)]/\mathrm{Re}[H(s)])$.

To draw the phase plot, for each pole and zero:

- if A is positive, start line (with zero slope) at 0 degrees;
- if A is negative, start line (with zero slope) at 180 degrees;
- at every (for stable zeros $-\mathrm{Re}(z)<0$), increase the slope by $45a_n$ degrees per decade,

beginning one decade before $\omega = x_n$ (E.g., $\frac{x_n}{10}$);

- at every $\omega = y_n$ (for stable poles–Re(p)<0), decrease the slope by $45b_n$ degrees per decade, beginning one decade before $\omega = y_n$ (E.g., $\frac{y_n}{10}$);
- "unstable" (right half plane) poles and zeros [Re(s) > 0] have opposite behavior;
- flatten the slope again when the phase has changed by $90a_n$ degrees (for a zero) or $90b_n$ degrees (for a pole);
- After plotting one line for each pole or zero, add the lines together to obtain the final phase plot; that is, the final phase plot is the superposition of each earlier phase plot.

Magnitude plot

The magnitude (in decibels) of the transfer function above, (normalized and converted to angular frequency form), given by the decibel gain expression A_v dB:

$$A_v\text{dB} = 20\log|H(\text{j}\omega)| = 20\log\frac{1}{\left|1+\text{j}\frac{\omega}{\omega_c}\right|} = -20\log\left|1+\text{j}\frac{\omega}{\omega_c}\right| = -10\log\left[1+\frac{\omega^2}{\omega_c^2}\right]$$

when plotted versus input frequency ω on a logarithmic scale, can be approximated by two lines and it forms the asymptotic (approximate) magnitude Bode plot of the transfer function:

- for angular frequencies below ω_c it is a horizontal line at 0 dB since at low frequencies the $\frac{\omega}{\omega_c}$ term is small and can be neglected, making the decibel gain equation above equal to zero,
- for angular frequencies above ω_c it is a line with a slope of −20dB per decade since at high frequencies the $\frac{\omega}{\omega_c}$ term dominates and the decibel gain expression above simplifies to $-20\log\frac{\omega}{\omega_c}$ which is a straight line with a slope of −20dB per decade.

These two lines meet at the corner frequency. It can be seen that for frequencies well below the corner frequency, the circuit has an attenuation of 0 dB, corresponding to a unity pass band gain, i.e. the amplitude of the filter output equals the amplitude of the input. Frequencies above the corner frequency are attenuated —— the higher the frequency, the higher the attenuation.

Phase plot

The phase Bode plot is obtained by plotting the phase angle of the transfer function given by

$$\varphi = -\arctan\frac{\omega}{\omega_c}$$

versus ω, where ω and ω_c are the input and cutoff angular frequencies respectively. For input frequencies much lower than corner, the ratio $\frac{\omega}{\omega_c}$ is small and therefore the phase angle is close to zero. As the ratio increases the absolute value of the phase increases and becomes −45 degrees when $\omega=\omega_c$. As the ratio increases for input frequencies much greater than the corner frequency, the phase angle asymptotically approaches −90 degrees. The frequency scale for the phase plot is logarithmic.

Normalized plot

The horizontal frequency axis, in both the magnitude and phase plots, can be replaced by the normalized (nondimensional) frequency ratio $\frac{\omega}{\omega_c}$. In such a case the plot is said to be normalized and units of the frequencies are no longer used since all input frequencies are now expressed as multiples of the cutoff frequency ω_c.

Technical Words and Expressions

Bode plot			波德图
frequency response			频率响应
logarithmic	[ˌlɔgəˈriθmik]	adj.	对数的
common logarithm			自然对数
log-frequency axis			对数频率坐标轴
attenuate	[əˈtenjueit]	vt.	衰减
minimum-phase system			最小相位系统
Hilbert transform			希耳伯特变换
rational function			有理函数
asymptote	[ˈæsimptəut]	n.	渐近线
incorporate	[inˈkɔːpəreit]	vt.	把……合并，使并入
polynomial	[ˌpɔliˈnəumjəl]	n.	多项式
irreducible polynomial			不可约多项式
cutoff angular frequency			转折频率
corner frequency			转折频率
corrected Bode plot			修正波德图
hand-made Bode plot			手工绘制波德图
straight-line amplitude plot			直线幅值图
premise	[ˈpremis]	n.	前提
decibel	[ˈdesibel]	n.	分贝

irreducible [,iri'dju:sibl] adj. 不能约的

magnitude plot 幅值图

phase plot 相位图

normalized plot 标准化图

Notes

[1] A Bode magnitude plot is a graph of log magnitude versus frequency, plotted with a log-frequency axis, to show the transfer function or frequency response of a linear, time-invariant system.

译文为：波德幅值图是不同频率对应的对数幅值图，在对数—频率坐标轴上表示，表示线性非时变系统的传递函数或频率响应。

plotted…过去分词作定语，修饰 bode magnitude plot，to show…是动词不定式作状语。

[2] The magnitude and phase Bode plots can seldom be changed independently of each other——changing the amplitude response of the system will most likely change the phase characteristics and vice versa.

译文为：幅值和相位波德图的变化常相互影响——系统幅值响应的变化很可能会改变相位特性，反之亦然。

changing…为现在分词作主语，and vice versa 翻译成"反之亦然"。

Exercises

Ⅰ. Mark the following statements with T (true) or F (false) according to the text.

1. A Bode magnitude plot is a graph of magnitude versus frequency. (   )

2. The magnitude and phase Bode plots can be changed independently of each other. (   )

3. A Bode phase plot is a graph of phase versus frequency. (   )

4. For minimum-phase systems the phase and amplitude characteristics can be obtained from each other with the use of the Hilbert transform. (   )

5. The phase Bode plot is obtained by plotting the phase angle of the transfer function. (   )

Ⅱ. Complete the following sentences.

1. A Bode phase plot is a graph of phase ______, also plotted on a log-frequency axis, usually used ______, to evaluate how much a frequency will be phase-shifted.

2. The horizontal frequency axis, in ______, can be replaced by ______.

3. In the case of an irreducible polynomial, the best way to correct the plot is ______ ______ at the pole or zero corresponding to the irreducible polynomial, and put that dot ______.

4. Phase can also be added directly ______, a fact that is mathematically clear when phase is seen as ______.

5. If the transfer function is a rational function with ______, then the Bode plot can be approximated ______.

Reading 24 Microphone Frequency Response

Frequency response refers to the way a microphone responds to different frequencies. It is a characteristic of all microphones that some frequencies are exaggerated and others are attenuated (reduced). For example, a frequency response which favours high frequencies means that the resulting audio output will sound more trebly than the original sound.

Frequency Response Charts

A microphone's frequency response pattern is shown using a chart like the one below and referred to as a frequency response curve. The x axis shows frequency in Hertz, the y axis shows response in decibels. A higher value means that frequency will be exaggerated; a lower value means the frequency is attenuated. In this example, frequencies around 5 kHz are boosted while frequencies above 10 kHz and below 100 Hz are attenuated. This is a typical response curve for a vocal microphone.

Which Response Curve is Best?

An ideal "flat" frequency response means that the microphone is equally sensitive to all frequencies. In this case, no frequencies would be exaggerated or reduced (the chart above would show a flat line), resulting in a more accurate representation of the original sound. We therefore say that a flat frequency response produces the purest audio.

In the real world a perfectly flat response is not possible and even the best "flat response" microphones have some deviation.

More importantly, it should be noted that a flat frequency response is not always the most desirable option. In many cases a tailored frequency response is more useful. For example, a response pattern designed to emphasise the frequencies in a human voice would be well suited to picking up speech in an environment with lots of low-frequency background noise.

The main thing is to avoid response patterns which emphasise the wrong frequencies. For example, a vocal mic is a poor choice for picking up the low frequencies of a bass drum.

Frequency Response Ranges

You will often see frequency response quoted as a range between two figures. This is a simple (or perhaps "simplistic") way to see which frequencies a microphone is capable of capturing effectively. For example, a microphone which is said to have a frequency response of 20 Hz to 20 kHz can reproduce all frequencies within this range. Frequencies outside this range will be reproduced to a much lesser extent or not at all.

This specification makes no mention of the response curve, or how successfully the various frequencies will be reproduced. Like many specifications, it should be taken as a guide only.

Condenser vs Dynamic

Condenser microphones generally have flatter frequency responses than dynamic. All other things being equal, this would usually mean that a condenser is more desirable if accurate sound is a prime consideration.

Technical Words and Expressions

microphone	n.	扩音器，麦克风
exaggerate	v.	使增大
trebly	adv.	高声地
boost	v.	提高，增强
flat frequency response		平坦的频率响应
quote	v.	引用
bass drum		低音鼓，大鼓
condenser	n.	冷凝器，电容器

Comprehension

1. From the article, we can know ______.
   A. frequency response refers to the way a microphone responds to different frequencies
   B. an ideal "flat" frequency response means that the microphone is equally sensitive to all frequencies
   C. in the real world a perfectly flat response is not possible
   D. it should be noted that a flat frequency response is not always the most desirable option
2. A frequency response which favours high frequencies means ______.
   A. the resulting audio output will sound more twice than the original sound
   B. the resulting audio output will sound less trebly than the original sound
   C. the resulting audio output will sound more trebly than the original sound
   D. the resulting audio output will sound less twice than the original sound
3. For the frequency response curve, ______.
   A. the x axis shows frequency in decibels
   B. the y axis shows response in Hertz
   C. a higher value means that frequency will be exaggerated
   D. a lower value means the frequency is exaggerated
4. For an ideal "flat" frequency response, ______.
   A. it means that the microphone is not equally sensitive to all frequencies
   B. frequencies would be exaggerated or reduced
   C. it will result in a more accurate representation of the original sound
   D. it produces the purest audio

5. Which is not TRUE? ______.

A. In the real world a perfectly flat response is not possible

B. Condenser microphones generally have flatter frequency responses than dynamic

C. A microphone's frequency response pattern is shown using a chart like the one below and referred to as a frequency response curve

D. A flat frequency response is not always the most desirable option

Unit 25 Process Control System

Process control system

Automatic process control is concerned with maintaining process variables, temperatures, pressures, flows, compositions, and the like at some desired operationvalue. Processes are dynamic in nature. Changes are always occurring, and if actions are not taken, the important process variables —— those related to safety, product quality, and production rates-will not achieve design conditions.

In order to fix ideas, let us consider a heat exchanger in which a process stream is heated by condensing steam[1]. The process is sketched in Fig.5.2.

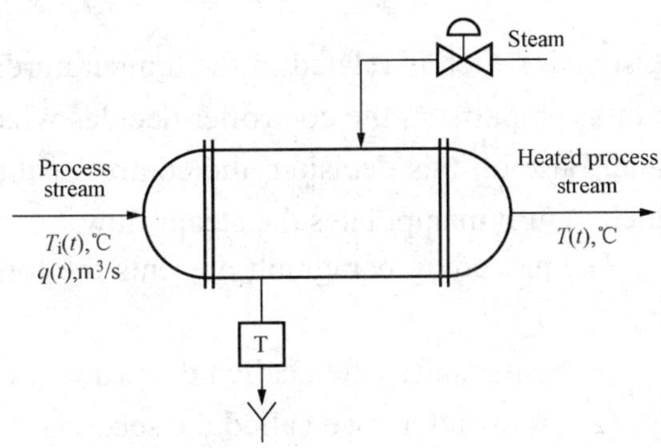

Fig.5.2 Heat exchanger

The purpose of this unit is to heat the process fluid from some inlet temperature, $T_i(t)$ up to a certain desired outlet temperature, $T(t)$. As mentioned, the heating medium is condensing steam.

The energy gained by the process fluid is equal to the heat released by the steam, provided there are no heat losses to surroundings, that is, the heat exchanger and piping are well insulated.

In this process there are many variables that can change, causing the outlet temperature to deviate from its desired value[2]. If this happens, some action must be taken to correct for this deviation. That is, the objective is to control the outlet process temperature to maintain its desired value.

One way to accomplish this objective is by first measuring the temperature $T(t)$, then comparing it to its desired value, and, based on this comparison, deciding what to do to correct for any deviation. The flow of steam can be used to correct for the deviation. This is, if the temperature is above its desired value, then the steam valve can be throttled back to cut the steam flow to the heat exchanger. If the temperature is below its desired value, then the steam valve could be opened some more to increase the steam flow to the exchanger. All of these can be done manually by the operator, and since the procedure is fairly straightforward, it should present no problem. However, since in most process plants there are hundreds of variables that must be maintained at some desired value, this correction procedure would required a tremendous number of operators. Consequently, we would like to accomplish this control automatically. That is, we want to have instruments that control the variables without requiring intervention from the operator. This is what we mean by automatic process control.

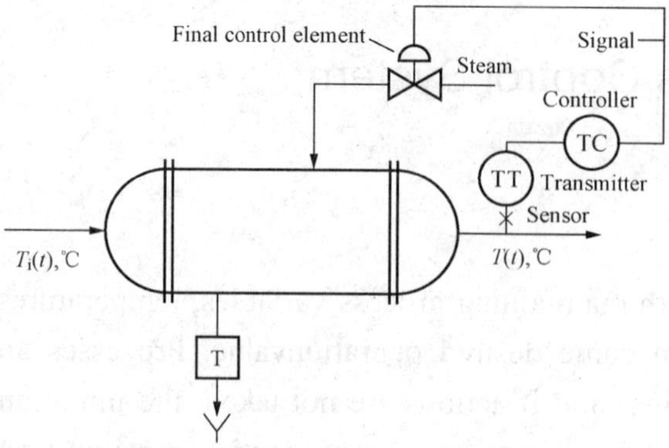

Fig.5.3 Heat exchanger control loop

To accomplish this objective a control system must be designed and implemented. A possible control system and its basic components are shown in Fig.5.3. The first thing to do is to measure the outlet temperature of the process stream. A sensor (thermocouple, thermistors, etc.) does this. This sensor is connected physically to a transmitter, which takes the output from the sensor and converts it to a signal strong enough to be transmitter to a controller. The controller then receives the signal, which is related to the temperature, and compares it with desired value. Depending on this comparison, the controller decides what to do to maintain the temperature at its desired value. Base on this decision, the controller then sends another signal to final control element, which in turn manipulates the steam flow.

The preceding paragraph presents the four basic components of all control systems. They are:

(1) Sensor, also often called the primary element.

(2) Transmitter, also called the secondary element.

(3) Controller, the "brain" of the control system.

(4) Final control system, often a control valve but not always. Other common final control elements are variable speed pumps, conveyors, and electric motors.

The importance of these components is that they perform the three basic operations that must be present in every control system. These operations are:

(1) Measurement (M): Measuring the variable to be controlled is usually done by the combination of sensor and transmitter.

(2) Decision (D): Based on the measurement, the controller must then decide what to do to maintain the variable at its desired value.

(3) Action (A): As a result of the controller's decision, the system must then take an action. This is usually accomplished by the final control element.

As mentioned, these three operations, M, D, and A, must be present in every control system. The decision-making operation in some system is rather simple, while in others it is more complex. The engineer designing a control system must be sure that the action taken affects the variable to be controlled, that is, that the action taken affects the measured value [3]. Otherwise, the system is not controlling and will probably do more harm than good.

Important terms of automatic process control

It is necessary to define some terms used in the field of automatic process control. The first term is controlled variable. This is the variable that must be maintained or controlled at some desired value. In the preceding example, the process outlet temperature $T(t)$ is the controlled variable. The second term is set point, the desired value of controlled variable. The manipulated variable is the variable used to maintain the controlled variable at its set point. In the example, the flow of steam is the manipulated variable. Finally, any variable that can cause the controlled variable to deviate away from set point is defined as a disturbance or upset. In most process there are a number of different disturbances. As an example, in the heat exchanger shown in Fig.5.2, possible disturbances are inlet process temperature $T_i(t)$, the process flow $q(t)$, the quality of the energy of the steam, ambient conditions, process fluid composition, fouling, and so on. What is important here is to understand that in the process industries, most often it is because of this disturbance that automatic process control is needed. If there were no disturbances, design-operating conditions would prevail and there would be no necessity of continuously "policing" the process.

The following additional terms are also important. Open loop refers to the condition in which the controller is disconnected from the process. That is, the controller is not making the decision of how to maintain the controlled variable at set point. Another instance in which open-loop control exists is when the action (A) taken by controller does not affect the measurement (M). This is indeed a major flaw in the control system design. Closed-loop control refers to the condition in which the controller is connected to the process, comparing the set point to the controlled variable and determining corrective action.

With these terms defined, the objective of an automatic process control system can be stated as follows: the objective of an automatic process control system is to use the manipulated variable to maintain the controlled variable at its point in spite of disturbances.

Regulatory and servo control

In some processes the controlled variable deviates from a constant set point because of disturbance. Regulatory control refers to systems designed to compensate for these disturbances. In some other instances the most important disturbance is the set point itself. That is the set point may be changed as a function of time (typical of this are batch processes), and therefore the controlled variable must follow the set point. Servo control refers to control systems designed for this purpose.

Regulatory control is by far more common than servo control in the process industries. However, the basic approach to designing either of them is essentially the same. Thus, the many principles in automatic process control apply to both cases.

Background needed for process control

To be successful in practice of automatic process control, the engineer must first understand the principles of process engineering. For the study of process automatic control it is also important to understand how processes behave dynamically. Consequently, it is necessary to develop the set of equations that describe different processes. This is called modeling. To do this, the knowledge of the basic principles mentioned in the previous paragraph and of mathematics through differential is needed. In process control the Laplace transforms are used heavily. This greatly simplifies the solution of differential equations and the dynamic analysis of processes and their control systems.

Another important "tool" for the study and practice of process control is computer simulation. Many of the equations developed to describe process are nonlinear in nature and, consequently, the most exact way to solve them is by numerical methods; this means computer solution. The computer solution of process models is called simulation.

Technical Words and Expressions

process control system			过程控制系统
heat exchanger			热交换器
sketch	[sketʃ]	v.	（给……）绘草图
inlet	['inlet]	n.	入口
outlet	['autlet, -lit]	n.	出口
piping	['paipiŋ]	n.	管道，管线
condensing	[kən'densiŋ]	n.	冷凝
fouling	['fauliŋ]	n.	（水管、枪筒等中的）污垢
prevail	[pri'veil]	vi.	占优势
numerical method			计算方法，数值法

Notes

[1] In order to fix ideas, let us consider a heat exchanger in which a process stream is heated by condensing steam.

译文为：为了说明问题，让我们来看一下热交换器。流体在这个过程中被过热蒸汽加热。

主句是一个祈使句，which 引导了一个定语从句，修饰 heat exchanger。

[2] In this process there are many variables that can change, causing the outlet temperature to deviate from its desired value.

译文为：很多变量在这个过程中会发生变化，继而导致出口温度偏离期望值。

句中 that 引导定语从句，修饰 many variables，分词结构 causing…作伴随状语。

[3] The decision-making operation in some system is rather simple, while in others it is more complex. The engineer designing a control system must be sure that the action taken affects the variable to be controlled, that is, that the action taken affects the measured value.

译文为：有些系统的决策任务简单，而有些很复杂。设计控制系统的工程师必须确保所采取的操作能影响被控变量，也就是说，该操作要影响测量值。

连词“while”表示转折，连接两个并列句，“be sure that the…”是由 that 引导的宾语从句。

Exercises

Ⅰ. Mark the following statements with T (true) or F (false) according to the text.

1. This controller is connected physically to a transmitter. (　　)
2. Sensor is often called the primary element. (　　)
3. Based on the measurement, the controller must then decide what to do to maintain the variable at its desired value. (　　)
4. In some processes the controlled variable deviates from a constant set point because of disturbance. (　　)
5. Regulatory control is by far more common than servo control in the process industries. (　　)

Ⅱ. Complete the following sentences.

1. The decision-making operation in some system is ______, while in others it is ______.
2. The engineer designing a control system must be sure that the action ______, that is, that ______.
3. In some instances the most important disturbance is ______. That is the set point may be changed as a function of time, and therefore ______ must follow the set point.
4. ______ refers to the condition in which the controller is connected to the process, comparing the set point to the controlled variable and ______.
5. It is necessary to develop the set of equations that ______. This is called ______.

Reading 25 Control Engineering

Control engineering is the engineering discipline that focuses on mathematical modeling of systems of a diverse nature, analyzing their dynamic behavior, and using control theory to create a controller that will cause the systems to behave in a desired manner.

Modern control engineering is closely related to electrical, electronic and computer engineering, as electronic circuits can often be easily described using control theory techniques. At many universities, control engineering courses are primarily taught by electrical or electronics faculty members; in others it is connected to computer science, as most control techniques today are implemented through computers, often as embedded systems (as in the automotive field). Previous to modern electronics, process control devices were devised by mechanical engineers using mechanical feedback along with pneumatic and hydraulic control devices, some of which are still in use today.

The field of control within chemical engineering is often known as process control. It deals primarily with the control of variables in a chemical process in a plant. It is taught as part of the undergraduate curriculum of any chemical engineering program, and employs many of the same principles in control engineering.

Other engineering disciplines also overlap with control engineering, as it can be applied to any system for which a suitable model can be derived.

Control engineering has diversified applications that include science, finance management, and even human behaviour. Students of control engineering may start with a linear control system course which requires elementary mathematics and Laplace transforms (called classical control theory). In linear control, the student does frequency and time domain analysis. Digital control and nonlinear control courses require Z Transformations and algebra respectively, and could be said to complete a basic control education. From here onwards there are several sub branches.

Control engineering is the engineering discipline that focuses on the modelling of a diverse range of dynamic systems (e.g. mechanical systems) and the design of controllers that will cause these systems to behave in the desired manner. Although such controllers need not be electrical many are and hence control engineering is often viewed as a subfield of electrical engineering. However, the falling price of microprocessors is making the actual implementation of a control system essentially trivial. As a result, focus is shifting back to the mechanical engineering discipline, as intimate knowledge of the physical system being controlled is often desired.

Electrical circuits, digital signal processors and microcontrollers can all be used to implement control systems. Control engineering has a wide range of applications from the flight and propulsion systems of commercial airliners to the cruise control present in many modern automobiles.

In most of the cases, control engineers utilize feedback when designing control systems. For example, in an automobile with cruise control the vehicle's speed is continuously monitored and fed back to the system which adjusts the motor's torque accordingly. Where there is regular feedback, control theory can be used to determine how the system responds to such feedback. In practically all such systems stability is important and control theory can help ensure stability is achieved.

Although feedback is an important aspect of control engineering, control engineers may also work on the control of systems without feedback. This is known as open loop control. A classic example of open loop control is a washing machine that runs through a pre-determined cycle without the use of sensors.

Technical Words and Expressions

discipline	n.	学科
faculty member	n.	教职员，教职工

curriculum	n.	课程
pneumatic control		气动控制
hydraulic control		液压控制
overlap	v.	（与……）交叠
onwards	adv.	向前地，在先地
subfield	n.	子域
trivial	adj.	细小的
intimate	adj.	密切的
propulsion system		推进系统，动力装置
pre-determined cycle		预订循环

Comprehension

1. Control engineering ______.

A. focuses on mathematical modeling of systems of a diverse nature

B. is the engineering discipline

C. uses control theory to create a controller that will cause the systems to behave in a desired manner

D. all of above

2. Why are control engineering courses primarily taught by electrical or electronics faculty members? ______.

A. Because students like control engineering courses

B. Because teachers like control engineering courses

C. Because control engineering courses is easy to learn

D. Because control engineering courses are useful for electrical or electronics faculty students

3. Other engineering disciplines also overlap with control engineering because ______.

A. we can apply control engineering disciplines to get a suitable model which is useful

B. control engineering disciplines are suitable for other engineering

C. control engineering disciplines are simple

D. other engineering disciplines are simple

4. Which can not be used to implement control systems? ______.

A. Electrical circuits

B. Digital signal processors

C. Microcontrollers

D. Embedded systems

5. Which is not TRUE? ______.

A. In most of the cases, control engineers utilize feedback when designing control systems

B. Control engineers can not work on the control of systems without feedback

C. Students of control engineering may start with a linear control system course which requires elementary mathematics and Laplace transforms

D. Control engineering is the engineering discipline that focuses on the modelling of a diverse range of dynamic systems and the design of controllers

Unit 26 Distributed Control System

A distributed control system (DCS) refers to a control system usually of a manufacturing system, process or any kind of dynamic system, in which the controller elements are not central in location (like the brain) but are distributed throughout the system with each component sub-system controlled by one or more controllers[1]. The entire system of controllers is connected by networks for communication and monitoring.

DCS is a very broad term used in a variety of industries, to monitor and control distributed equipment:

- Electrical power grids and electrical generation plants;
- Environmental control systems;
- Traffic signals;
- Water management systems;
- Oil refining plants;
- Chemical plants;
- Pharmaceutical manufacturing;
- Sensor networks.

Elements

A DCS typically uses custom designed processors as controllers and uses both proprietary interconnections and protocols for communication. Input & output modules form component parts of the DCS. The processor receives information from input modules and sends information to output modules. The input modules receive information from input instruments in the process (a.k.a. field) and transmit instructions to the output instruments in the field. Computer buses or electrical buses connect the processor and modules through multiplexers/demultiplexers. Buses also connect the distributed controllers with the central controller and finally to the Human-Machine Interface (HMI) or control consoles.

Elements of a distributed control system may directly connect to physical equipment such as switches, pumps and valves or may work through an intermediate system such as a SCADA system.

Applications

Distributed Control Systems (DCSs) are dedicated systems used to control manufacturing processes that are continuous or batch-oriented, such as oil refining, petrochemicals, central station power generation, pharmaceuticals, food & beverage manufacturing, cement production, steelmaking, and papermaking[2]. DCSs are connected to sensors and actuators and use setpoint control to control the flow of material through the plant. The most common example is a setpoint control loop consisting of a pressure sensor, controller, and control valve. Pressure or flow measurements are transmitted to the controller, usually through the aid of a signal conditioning Input/Output (I/O) device. When the measured variable reaches a certain point, the controller instructs a valve or actuation device to open or close until the fluidic flow process reaches the desired setpoint. Large oil refineries have many thousands of I/O points and employ very large DCSs. Processes are not limited to fluidic flow through pipes, however, and can also include things like paper machines and their associated variable speed drives and motor control centers, cement kilns, mining operations, ore processing facilities, and many others.

A typical DCS consists of functionally and/or geographically distributed digital controllers capable of executing from 1 to 256 or more regulatory control loops in one control box. The input/output devices (I/O) can be integral with the controller or located remotely via a field network. Today's controllers have extensive computational capabilities and, in addition to proportional, integral, and derivative (PID) control, can generally perform logic and sequential control.

DCSs may employ one or several workstations and can be configured at the workstation or by an off-line personal computer. Local communication is handled by a control network with transmission over twisted pair, coaxial, or fiber optic cable. A server and/or applications processor may be included in the system for extra computational, data collection, and reporting capability.

History

Early minicomputers were used in the control of industrial processes since the beginning of the 1960s. The DCS was introduced in 1975. Both Honeywell and Japanese electrical engineering firm Yokogawa introduced their own independently produced DCSs at roughly the same time, with the TDC 2000 and CENTUM systems, respectively. US-based Bristol also introduced their UCS 3000 universal controller in 1975. In 1980, Bailey (now part of ABB) introduced the NETWORK 90 system. Also in 1980, Fischer & Porter Company(now also part of ABB) introduced DCI-4000 (DCI stands for Distributed Control Instrumentation).

The DCS largely came about due to the increased availability of microcomputers and the proliferation of microprocessors in the world of process control. Computers had already been applied to process automation for some time in the form of both Direct Digital Control (DDC) and Set Point Control. In the early 1970s Taylor Instrument Company, (now part of ABB) developed the 1010 system, Foxboro the FQX1 system and Bailey Controls the 1055 systems. All of these were DDC applications implemented within mini-computers (DEC PDP 11, Varian

Data Machines, MODCOMP etc.) and connected to proprietary Input/Output hardware. Sophisticated (for the time) continuous as well as batch control was implemented in this way. A more conservative approach was Set Point Control, where process computers supervised clusters of analog process controllers. A CRT-based workstation provided visibility into the process using text and crude character graphics. Availability of a fully functional graphical user interface was a way away.

Central to the DCS model was the inclusion of control function blocks. Function blocks evolved from early, more primitive DDC concepts of "Table Driven" software. One of the first embodiments of object-oriented software, function blocks were self contained "blocks" of code that emulated analog hardware control components and performed tasks that were essential to process control, such as execution of PID algorithms. Function blocks continue to endure as the predominant method of control for DCS suppliers, and are supported by key technologies such as Foundation Fieldbus today.

Digital communication between distributed controllers, workstations and other computing elements (peer to peer access) was one of the primary advantages of the DCS. Attention was duly focused on the networks, which provided the all-important lines of communication that, for process applications, had to incorporate specific functions such as determinism and redundancy. As a result, many suppliers embraced the IEEE 802.4 networking standard. This decision set the stage for the wave of migrations necessary when information technology moved into process automation and IEEE 802.3 rather than IEEE 802.4 prevailed as the control LAN.

The Network Centric Era of the 1980s

The DCS brought distributed intelligence to the plant and established the presence of computers and microprocessors in process control, but it still did not provide the reach and openness necessary to unify plant resource requirements. In many cases, the DCS was merely a digital replacement of the same functionality provided by analog controllers and a panelboard display. This was embodied in The Purdue Reference Model (PRM) that was developed to define Manufacturing Operations Management relationships. PRM later formed the basis for ISA95 standards activities today.

In the 1980s, users began to look at DCSs as more than just basic process control. A very early example of a Direct Digital Control was completed by the Australian business Midac in 1981～1982 using R-Tec Australian designed hardware. The system installed at the University of Melbourne used a serial communications network, connecting campus buildings back to a control room "front end". Each remote unit ran 2 Z80 microprocessors whilst the front end ran 11 in a Parallel Processing configuration with paged common memory to share tasks and could run up to 20,000 concurrent controls objects.

It was believed that if openness could be achieved and greater amounts of data could be shared throughout the enterprise that even greater things could be achieved[3]. The first attempts to increase the openness of DCSs resulted in the adoption of the predominant operating system of the day: UNIX. UNIX and its companion networking technology TCP/IP were developed by the Department of Defense for openness, which was precisely the issue the process industries were looking to resolve.

As a result suppliers also began to adopt Ethernet-based networks with their own proprietary protocol layers. The full TCP/IP standard was not implemented, but the use of Ethernet made it possible to implement the first instances of object management and global data access technology. The 1980s also witnessed the first PLCs integrated into the DCS infrastructure. Plant-wide historians also emerged to capitalize on the extended reach of automation systems. The first DCS supplier to adopt UNIX and Ethernet networking technologies was Foxboro, who introduced the I/A Series system in 1987.

The Application Centric Era of the 1990s

The drive toward openness in the 1980s gained momentum through the 1990s with the increased adoption of Commercial-Off-The-Shelf (COTS) components and IT standards. Probably the biggest transition undertaken during this time was the move from the UNIX operating system to the Windows environment. While the realm of the real time operating system (RTOS) for control applications remains dominated by real time commercial variants of UNIX or proprietary operating systems, everything above real-time control has made the transition to Windows.

The invasion of Microsoft at the desktop and server layers resulted in the development of technologies such as OLE for Process Control (OPC), which is now a de facto industry connectivity standard. Internet technology also began to make its mark in automation and the DCS world, with most DCS HMI supporting Internet connectivity. The '90s were also known for the "Fieldbus Wars", where rival organizations competed to define what would become the IEC fieldbus standard for digital communication with field instrumentation instead of 4～20 milliamp analog communications. The first fieldbus installations occurred in the 1990s. Towards the end of the decade, the technology began to develop significant momentum, with the market consolidated around Foundation Fieldbus and Profibus PA for process automation applications. Some suppliers built new systems from the ground up to maximize functionality with fieldbus, such as ABB with System 800xA, Emerson Process Management with the DeltaV control system, Siemens with the Simatic PCS7.

The impact of COTS, however, was most pronounced at the hardware layer. For years, the primary business of DCS suppliers had been the supply of large amounts of hardware, particularly I/O and controllers. The initial proliferation of DCSs required the installation of prodigious amounts of this hardware, most of it manufactured from the bottom up by DCS suppliers. Standard computer components from manufacturers such as Intel and Motorola, however, made it cost prohibitive for DCS suppliers to continue making their own components, workstations, and networking hardware.

As the suppliers made the transition to COTS components, they also discovered that the hardware market was shrinking fast. COTS not only resulted in lower manufacturing costs for the supplier, but also steadily decreasing prices for the end users, who were also becoming increasingly vocal over what they perceived to be unduly high hardware costs. Some suppliers that were previously stronger in the PLC business, such as Rockwell Automation, Schneider and Siemens, were able to leverage their expertise in manufacturing control hardware to enter the DCS marketplace with cost effective offerings. The traditional DCS suppliers introduced new generation DCS System based on the latest Communication and IEC Standards, which resulting in a trend of combining the traditional concepts/functionalities for PLC and DCS into a one for all solution —— named "Process Automation System/Controller".

Technical Words and Expressions

distributed control system (DCS)			分布式控制系统，集散控制系统
sub-system			子系统
electrical power grid			电力网
pharmaceutical	[ˌfɑːməˈsjuːtikəl]	adj.	制药的；配药的
input module			输入模块
transmit instruction			传输指令
proprietary	[prəˈpraiətəri]	adj.	专用的
multiplexer	[ˈmʌltiˌpleksə]	n.	多路（复用）器
demultiplexer	[diˈmʌltipleksə]	n.	信号分离器，多路输出选择器
control console			控制台
batch-oriented			批处理
petrochemical	[petrəuˈkemikəl]	n.	石化产品
beverage	[ˈbevəridʒ]	n.	饮料
fluidic	[fluːˈidik]	adj.	流体的，液体的，射流的
cement kiln			水泥窑
sequential control	[siˈkwenʃəl]	adj.	顺序控制
coaxial	[kəuˈæksəl]	adj.	同轴的，共轴的
fiber optic cable			光缆
direct digital control (DDC)			直接数字控制
set point control (SPC)			设定点控制
embodiment	[ˋimˈbɔdimənt]	n.	体现
predominant	[priˈdɔminənt]	adj.	占主导地位的，显著的
redundancy	[riˈdʌndənsi]	n.	冗余
parallel processing			并行处理
commercial-off-the-shelf			商用现货的

consolidate	[kən'sɔlideit]	adj.	使加固，使联合
proliferation	[prəu,lifə'reiʃən]	n.	扩散
prodigious	[prə'didʒəs]	adj.	异常的，惊人的，巨大的
perceive	[pə'si:v]	vt.	感觉，察觉，理解
leverage	['li:vəridʒ]	vt.	促使……改变

Notes

[1] A distributed control system (DCS) refers to a control system usually of a manufacturing system, process or any kind of dynamic system, in which the controller elements are not central in location (like the brain) but are distributed throughout the system with each component sub-system controlled by one or more controllers.

译文为：集散控制系统是指制造系统、过程或者其他类型的动态系统的控制系统，在这些系统中，控制器并不处于中央位置，而是分散在系统的各个部分，每个元件的子系统由一个或多个控制器控制。

该句中，由 which 引导了一个非限制性定语从句，在从句中，由连接词 but 连接了两个并联句，两者之间是转折关系。

[2] Distributed Control Systems (DCSs) are dedicated systems used to control manufacturing processes that are continuous or batch-oriented, such as oil refining, petrochemicals, central station power generation, pharmaceuticals, food & beverage manufacturing, cement production, steelmaking, and papermaking.

译文为：集散控制系统属于专用系统，用来控制连续或间歇型的生产过程，如石油炼制，石油化工，发电总厂，制药，食品及饮料制造，水泥生产，炼钢和造纸。

used to…是过去分词作定语，修饰 dedicated systems，that 引导了一个限制性定语从句。

[3] It was believed that if openness could be achieved and greater amounts of data could be shared throughout the enterprise that even greater things could be achieved.

译文为：我们相信如果开放性可以实现，企业中更多的数据可以共享的话，那么可以实现更具成就的事情。

句子中第一个 that 引导了一个主语从句，it 是形式主语，真正的主语是 that 后面的句子，第二个 that 引导了一个结果状语从句。

Exercises

Ⅰ. Mark the following statements with T (true) or F (false) according to the text.

1. DCS is a very broad term used in a variety of industries, to monitor and control distributed equipment. (   )

2. DCSs may employ only one workstation and can be configured at the workstation or by an off-line personal computer. (   )

3. A DCS refers to a control system usually of a manufacturing system, process or any kind of dynamic system. (   )

4. Elements of a distributed control system can not directly connect to physical equipment. (   )

5. The processor receives information from input modules and sends information to output modules in DCS. (   )

Ⅱ. Complete the following sentences.

1. A DCS refers to a control system usually of a manufacturing system, process or any kind of dynamic system, in which ______ are not central in location but are distributed throughout the system with each component sub-system controlled ______.

2. DCSs are connected to ______ and use ______ to control the flow of material through the plant.

3. A typical DCS consists of functionally and/or geographically _______ capable of executing ______ regulatory control loops in one control box.

4. The DCS largely came about due to ______ and ______ in the world of process control.

5. The drive _______ in the 1980s gained momentum through the 1990s with the increased adoption of ______ components and IT standards.

Reading 26 Simulation of Control Systems

Simulink is a graphical extension to MATLAB for modeling and simulation of systems. In Simulink, systems are drawn on screen as block diagrams. Many elements of block diagrams are available, such as transfer functions, summing junctions, etc., as well as virtual input and output devices such as function generators and oscilloscopes. Simulink is integrated with MATLAB and data can be easily transferred between the programs.

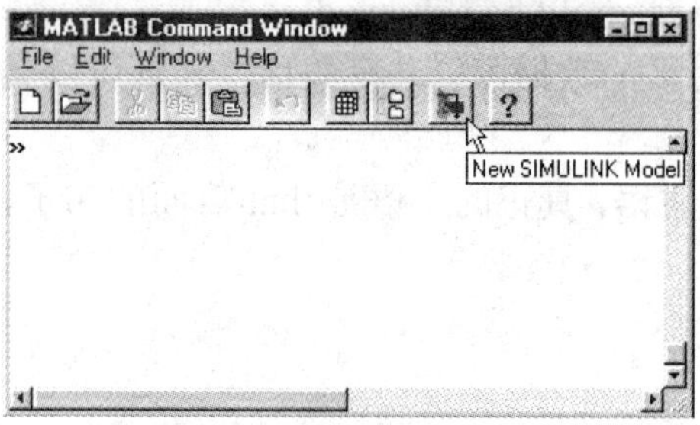

Fig.5.4 Starting Simulink

Starting Simulink

Simulink is started from the MATLAB command prompt by entering the following command: simulink; Alternatively, you can hit the New Simulink Model button at the top of the MATLAB command window as shown in Fig.5.4.

When it starts, Simulink brings up a blank, untitled, model window. This is the window into which a new model can be drawn.

Basic Elements

There are two major classes of items in Simulink: blocks and lines. Blocks (Fig.5.5) are used to generate, modify, combine, output, and display signals. Lines are used to transfer signals from one block to another.

Blocks

There are several general classes of blocks:

Sources: Used to generate various signals.

Sinks: Used to output or display signals.

Discrete: Linear, discrete-time system elements (transfer functions, state-space models, etc.).

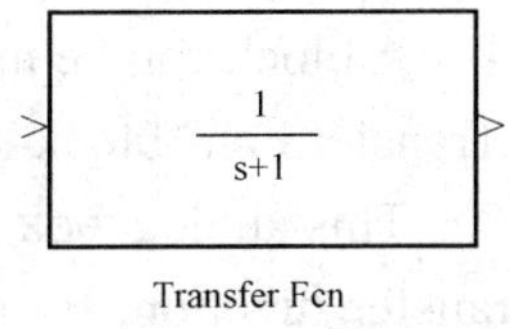

Fig.5.5 Block

Linear: Linear, continuous-time system elements and connections (summing junctions, gains, etc.).

Nonlinear: Nonlinear operators (arbitrary functions, saturation, delay, etc.).

Connections: Multiplex, Demultiplex, System Macros, etc.

Blocks have zero to several input terminals and zero to several output terminals. Unused input terminals are indicated by a small open triangle. Unused output terminals are indicated by a small triangular point. The block shown in Fig. 5.5 has an unused input terminal on the left and an unused output terminal on the right.

Lines

Lines transmit signals in the direction indicated by the arrow. Lines must always transmit signals from the output terminal of one block to the input terminal of another block. On exception to this is a line can tap off of another line, splitting the signal to each of two destination blocks, as shown in Fig.5.6.

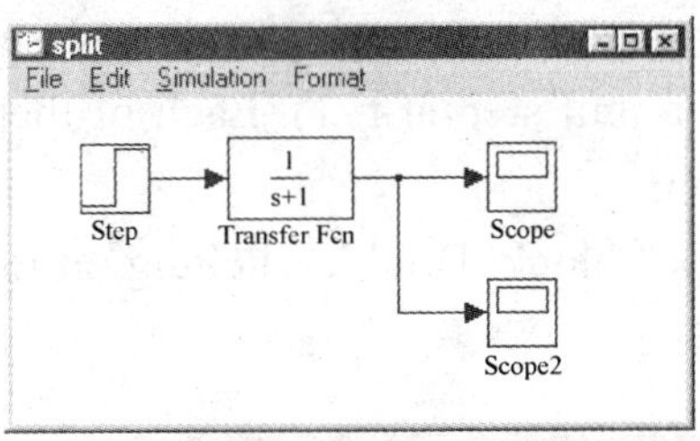

Fig.5.6 The use of line

Lines can never inject a signal into another line; lines must be combined through the use of a block such as a summing junction.

A signal can be either a scalar signal or a vector signal. For Single-Input, Single-Output systems, scalar signals are generally used. For Multi-Input, Multi-Output systems, vector signals are often used, consisting of two or more scalar signals. The lines used to transmit scalar and vector signals are identical. The type of signal carried by a line is determined by the blocks on either end of the line.

Simple Example

The simple model in Fig.5.7 consists of three blocks: Step, Transfer Fcn, and Scope. The Step is a source block from which a step input signal originates. This signal is transferred through the line in the direction indicated by the arrow to the Transfer Function linear block. The Transfer Function modifies its input signal and outputs a new signal on a line to the Scope. The Scope is a sink block used to display a signal much like an oscilloscope.

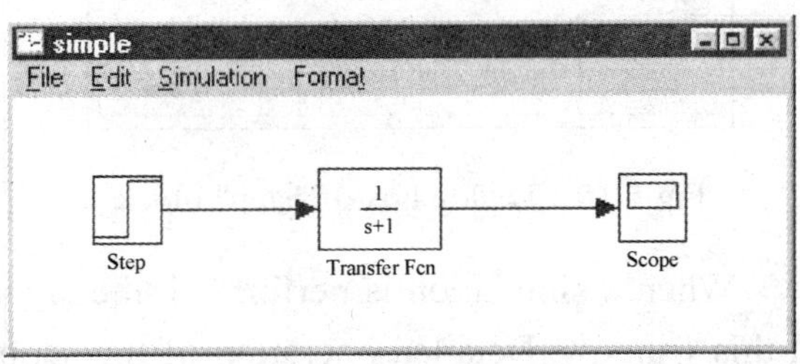

Fig.5.7 Simple model example

Modifying Blocks

A block can be modified by double-clicking on it. For example, if you double-click on the "Transfer Fcn" block in the simple model, you will see the dialog box in Fig.5.8.

This dialog box contains fields for the numerator and the denominator of the block's transfer function. By entering a vector containing the coefficients of the desired numerator or denominator polynomial, the desired transfer function can be entered. For example, to change the denominator to s^2+2s+1, enter the following into the denominator field: [1 2 1], and hit the close button, the model window will change to Fig.5.9, which reflects the change in the denominator of the transfer function.

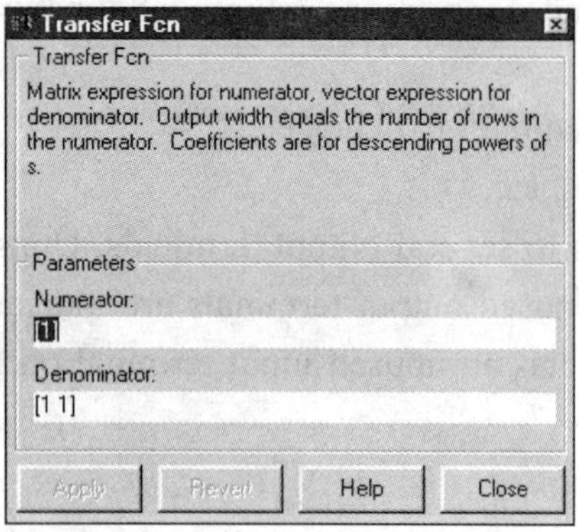

Fig.5.8 Dialog box of Transfer Fcn

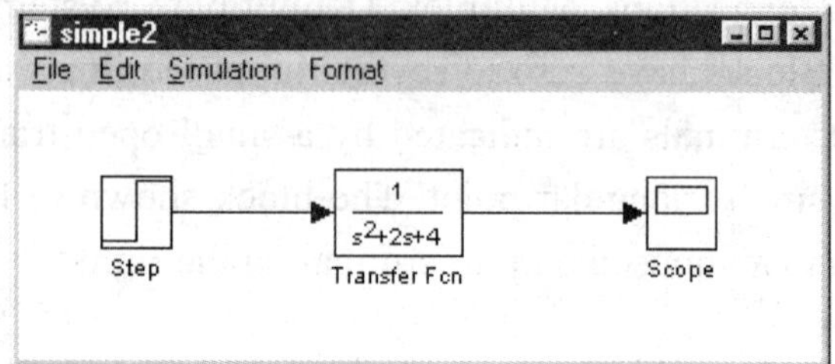

Fig.5.9 Window of simple

The "step" block can also be double-clicked, bringing up the dialog box in Fig.5.10.

The default parameters in this dialog box generate a step function occurring at time=1 sec, from an initial level of zero to a level of 1 (in other words, a unit step at t=1). Each of these parameters can be changed. Close this dialog before continuing.

The most complicated of these three blocks is the "Scope" block. Double clicking on this brings up a blank oscilloscope screen in Fig.5.11.

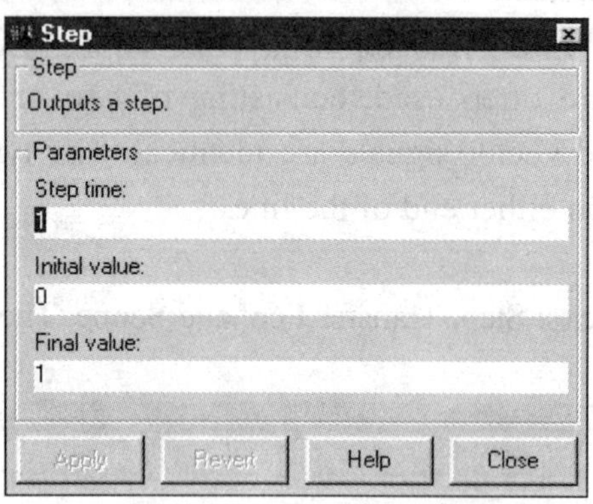

Fig.5.10 Dialog box of "step" block

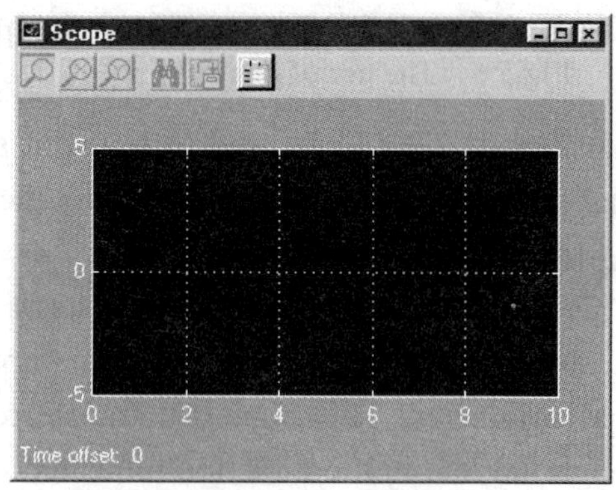

Fig.5.11 a blank oscilloscope screen

When a simulation is performed, the signal which feeds into the scope will be displayed in this window. Detailed operation of the scope will not be covered in this tutorial. The only function we will use is the auto scale button, which appears as a pair of binoculars in the upper portion of the window.

Running Simulations

Before running a simulation of this system, first open the scope window by double-clicking on the scope block. Then, to start the simulation, either select Start from the Simulation menu (as shown in Fig.5.12) or hit Ctrl-T in the model window.

The simulation should run very quickly and the scope window will appear as shown in Fig.5.13.

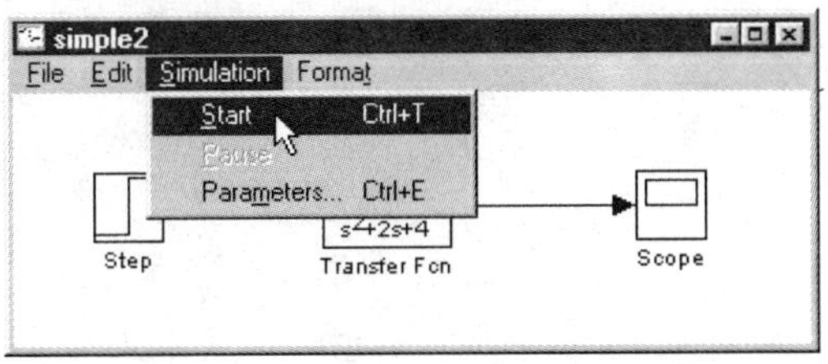

Fig.5.12 Running Simulations

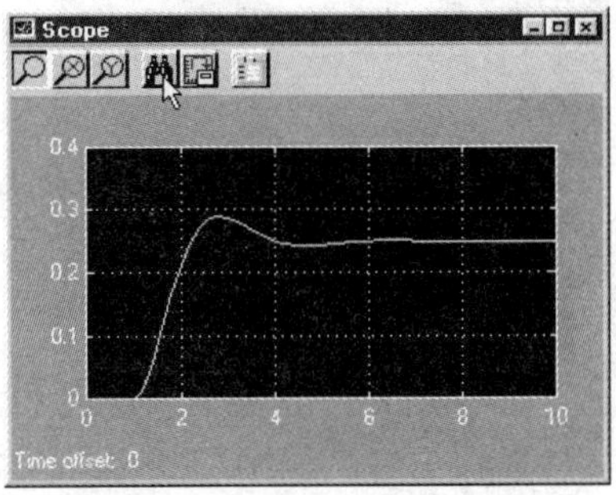

Fig.5.13 Scope window

Technical Words and Expressions

simulink	n.	仿真
function generator		函数发生器
tap off		分接
sink block		接收框
denominator	n.	[数] 分母
numerator	n.	[数] 分子
binocular	n.	双筒望远镜

Comprehension

1. Which of the following is not the block of Simulink? ______.

   A. Step B. Summing junction C. Multiplex D. Dialog box

2. Which of the following line in Simulink is not right? ______.

   A. 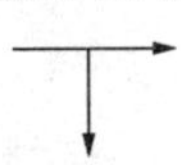 B.  C. 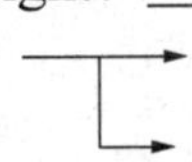 D. 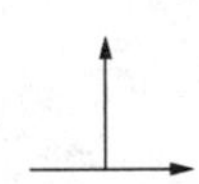

3. If you enter [1 2 3] into the denominator field and enter [1 1] into the numerator field, the Transfer Function is ______.

   A. $\dfrac{s+1}{s^2+2s+3}$ B. $\dfrac{s^2+2s+3}{s+1}$ C. $\dfrac{s+1}{3s^2+2s+1}$ D. $\dfrac{3s^2+2s+1}{s+1}$

4. Which of the following is most complicated block? ______.

   A. Line B. "Transfer Fcn" block

   C. "Step" block D. "Scope" block

5. To running a simulation, ______.

   A. you must open the scope window by double-clicking on the scope block

   B. you can select Start from the Simulation menu

   C. you must hit Ctrl-T in the model window

   D. B and C

第一章 电工电子技术基础

第1单元 电气元件与网络

电路元件的概念被用在电网络分析中。任何电网络都可分解为原理图或电路图中多个、相互连接的电气元件，来建立模型。每个电路元件会以某种方式影响网络的电压或流过网络的电流。通过分析网络受到各个元件作用的方式，就可以估计出实际的网络如何在大范围内起作用。

元件与组件

根据各自的代表意义，实际的电气或电子组件和理想的电气元件之间存在着差别：

- 电气元件并不存在，根据集总元件模型假设其具有理想特性。
- 相反地，实际组件确实存在，不具有理想特性，其数值具有不确定性，具有一定程度的非线性，需要多个理想电路元件组合来近似表示。

用电气元件进行电路分析对理解由实际组件组成的许多实用电气网络很有用。

元件

四个基本的电路变量是电流 I，电压 U，电荷 Q 和磁通 Φ_m。使用这四个变量，只需要5个元件就可以表示任一个组件或网络。

两种电源：

- 电流源，测量单位为安培，会在导体中产生电流。根据关系式 $dQ=-Idt$ 确定电荷。
- 电压源，测量单位为伏特，会在两个点之间产生电位差。根据关系式 $d\Phi_m=Udt$ 确定磁通。

三种无源元件：

- 电阻 R，单位为欧姆——产生的电压与流过电阻的电流成正比。根据关系式 $dU=RdI$ 把电压与电流联系起来。
- 电容 C，单位为法拉——产生的电流与电容端电压变化率成正比。根据关系式 $dQ=CdU$ 把电荷与电压联系起来。
- 电感 L，单位为亨利——产生的电压与电感上电流变化率成正比。根据关系式 $d\Phi_m=LdI$ 把磁通与电流联系起来。

例子

下面是用理想元件来表示实际元件的例子。

- 一次近似中，用电压源表示电池。为了表示电池的内阻（该电阻导致电池使用过程中发热和电压下降），更精确的模型用电阻与电压源的串联表示，可以并联一个电流源来表示电池的漏电（电流源在很长的时间内使电池放电）。
- 一次近似中，电阻器用电阻表示。更精确的模型中含有串联电感，用来表示导线中的电感效应（螺线型电阻具有更大的电感），可以再并联一个电容来表示电阻导线之间的近似电容效应。导线可以用低阻值的电阻表示。

- 表示半导体时更常使用电流源。例如，在一次近似中，双极性晶体管可以用一个受输入电压控制的可变电流源表示。

电气网络

电气网络是由电阻、电感、电容、传输线、电压源、电流源和开关相互连接而成的。

电路是闭合的网络，给电流提供返回的路径（图 1.1）。网络是两个或多个元件组成的，网络不一定是电路。

仅有电源（电压源或电流源）、线性集总元件（电阻、电容、电感）和线性分布元件组成的网络可以通过代数变换法去确定直流响应、交流响应和瞬态响应。

还含有有源电子元件的网络被称为电子电路。这样的网络通常是非线性的，需要更复杂的设计分析工具。

第 2 单元 网 络 分 析

网络在电子学中是指相互连接的元件的集合。网络分析是求解网络中每个元件的端电压、流过元件的电流的方法。有许多不同的方法来完成此任务。但是，在绝大多数电路分析中，假定网络中的元件都是线性的。除了明确说明外，本文中介绍的方法只适用于线性网络分析。

定义

元件：有两个或多个端点，电荷可流入或流出。

节点：两个以上元件的连接点。为了分析方便，阻值为零的导线可看作节点。

支路：连接两个节点间的元件。

网孔：网络内的各支路连接起来所形成的闭合回路。

端口：从一端流入的电流等于从另一端流出电流的二端网络。

等效电路

网络分析的一个有效方法是通过减少元件数来简化网络。其可以通过用具有相同作用的抽象元件代替实际元件来实现。某些特殊方法可以直接减少元件数，例如把串联阻抗合并。另一方面可以仅仅把电路结构转化为通过运算可以使元件数减少的电路结构。例如，使用诺顿定理可以把电压发生器转换为电流发生器，这样就可以把发生器的内阻和并联的阻抗负载合并。

电阻电路仅含有电阻、理想电流源和理想电压源。如果电源是恒值的电源（直流电源），那就是直流电路。电路的分析是指求解电路中电压和电流的过程。这儿提到的方法原理也可用于交流电路的相量分析。

如果一个网络的端电压和流过端点间的电流之间的关系与另一个网络端点间的电压和电流关系相同，这两个电路可以说成是（图 1.4 中的电路 1 和电路 2）等效的。

对于所有的 U_1 值，如果 $U_2=U_1$ 能推出 $I_2=I_1$，那么端点 ab 间的电路 1 与端点 xy 间的电路 2 是等效的。

上面是关于只有一个端口的网络的充分说明。对于含有一个端口以上的网络，应该定义所有相应的端口间具有相同的电流、电压关系。例如，星形和三角形网络是三端口网络，因此需要三个联立的方程来充分说明其等效。

串联阻抗和并联阻抗

任何二端口网络间的阻抗通过连续地应用阻抗的串联或并联最终简化为单个阻抗。

阻抗串联：$Z_{eq}=Z_1+Z_2+\cdots+Z_n$。

阻抗并联：$\dfrac{1}{Z_{eq}}=\dfrac{1}{Z_1}+\dfrac{1}{Z_2}+\cdots+\dfrac{1}{Z_n}$。

应用上面的公式两个并联阻抗可简化为：$Z_{eq}=\dfrac{Z_1Z_2}{Z_1+Z_2}$。

电源变换

具有内阻的发电机（例如非理想发电机）可以表示为理想电压源或理想电流源与阻抗的连接。这两种形式是等效的，其变换公式如下。如果端点 ab 间的两个网络等效，那么两个网络中的 U 和 I 是完全相同的。因此：

$$U_S = RI_S \quad 或 \quad I_S = \frac{U_S}{R}$$

第 3 单元 二 极 管

在电子学中，二极管是一种二端元件。二极管有两个电极，可以让想要的电信号通过。绝大多数是使用二极管的单向导通电流特性。变容二极管可用作电子式的可调电容器。

电流流过大多数二极管所显示的方向性一般被称为整流。二极管的共同功能是可以让电流从一个方向流过（称为正偏），反方向则阻断电流（称为反偏）。因此二极管可以被看作单向电子阀。

实际的二极管不会具有如此完美的通—断特性，而是具有更复杂的非线性电气特性，该特性由二极管的类型决定。二极管还有其他的功能，这些功能没有利用这种通—断方式。

早期的二极管包含触须晶体和真空管。现在最通用的二极管是由半导体材料制成的，比如硅和锗。

半导体二极管

现代绝大多数二极管是基于半导体 PN 结的，在 PN 型二极管中，电流可以从 P 型侧流到 N 型侧，但不会反方向流动。另一种类型的二极管是肖特基二极管，其由金属和半导体之间的接触面形成而不是由 PN 结构成。

电流—电压特性

半导体二极管的电流—电压特性，即 I–U 曲线，与载流子流过的耗散层或耗散区有关，耗散层或耗散区位于不同类型半导体间形成的 p–n 结上。被称为耗散层或耗散区有关。当 PN 结刚形成时，N 型掺杂区的移动电子扩散进入 P 型掺杂区，在 P 型掺杂区存在大量的空穴，在这里电子与空穴“复合”。当移动电子与空穴复合时，空穴和电子都消失了，在 N 侧留下静止的带正电的供体，在 P 侧留下带负电的受体。PN 结所在的区域形成电荷载流子耗尽，因而可作为绝缘体。

但是，耗尽层的宽度不会无限地变宽。对于每一对复合的电子－空穴来说，带正电的掺杂离子被留在N型掺杂区，带负电的掺杂离子被留在P型掺杂区。随着复合的继续，产生了更多的离子，耗尽区的电场强度增加，该电场使复合变慢，最终使复合停止。这时候，在耗尽区存在一个内电场。

如果二极管上的外加电压极性与内电场极性相同的话，耗尽区仍然可作为绝缘体，阻碍任何电流通过。这是反偏现象。但是，如果外加电压极性和内电位相反的话，复合再次进行，使得电流持续流过PN结。对于硅二极管来说，内电位大约为0.6V。因此，如果外电流流过二极管，二极管上大约有0.6V电压，所以P掺杂区电压比N掺杂区高，由于二极管正偏，我们认为二极管“导通”。

二极管的I–U特性可以被近似分成4个工作区域（图1.8）。

当反偏电压很大时，超过最大反向电压或PIV时，产生反向击穿，这时电流会急剧增加，通常会永久损坏器件。雪崩二极管专门工作在雪崩区。对于稳压管，不存在PIV概念。稳压管含有一个大量掺杂的PN结，可以让电子从P型材料的价电子带穿过到达N型材料的传导带，这样反向电压就被箝制在一个确定的值，并且不会出现雪崩。这两种元件被箝位在反向电压区域时，都存在最大电流和最大功率限制。

第二个区域，反偏电压大于PIV，只有一个很小的反向饱和电流。对于一个处于反偏区域的普通整流二极管来说，流过它的电流很低（处于μA级）。

第三个区域为正向微偏，这种情况下只有很小的正向电流流过。

当电位差增加到大于“阈值电压”、“导通电压”或“二极管正向压降”时，二极管电流开始变大，二极管呈现出很低的电阻。

电流—电压曲线是呈指数关系。普通的硅二极管在额定电流时，阈值电压定义为0.6～0.7V。对于其他类型的二极管，这个值是不同的，肖特基二极管只有0.2V那么低，红色发光二极管的阈值电压可以达到1.4V以上，蓝色发光二极管可以达到4.0V。

电流较高时，二极管的正向压降增加。功率二极管在满额定电流时，压降一般为1～1.5V。

半导体二极管类型

有几种类型的结型二极管（图1.9），或者通过几何尺寸、掺杂程度来强调二极管的不同物理性质，或者像耿氏二极管、激光二极管和MOSFET那样确实属于不同的元件。选择二极管正确的极性，是二极管在特殊电路中的应用。

普通二极管，工作方式如上所述，通常是由掺杂的硅制成的，很少是由锗制成的。在开发出硅功率整流二极管之前，二极管由氧化铜构成，后来用硒构成，其较低的效率使得其正向压降要高得多，并且需要一个大的散热片（通常为二极管金属衬底的延伸），要比通过相同额定电流的硅二极管所需的散热片大得多。CMOS集成电路中的二极管绝大多数为PN二极管，集成电路的每个引脚上都有两个二极管，内部还包含许多二极管。

应用

无线电解调

二极管最初是用作对AM无线电广播进行解调。探索的历史在无线电文章中详细分析。

总的来说，AM 信号由正、负交流电压峰值组成，其幅值或“包络线”与初始的音频信号成正比。二极管（最初为晶体二极管）对 AM 高频信号检波，得到音频信号，该音频信号为初始的音频信号。使用简单的滤波器对音频信号进行滤波，然后加到音频放大器或传感器上，可以产生声波。

能量转换

整流器由二极管构成，在整流器中，二极管用来把交流电转换为直流电。机动车交流发电机是一个常用的例子，其中二极管把交流变为直流，比早期的发电机换向器提供更好的性能。类似地，二极管也可以用在科克罗夫－瓦尔电压倍增器上，把 AC 变为较高的 DC 电压。

过电压保护

二极管经常用来传导具有破坏性的高电压来保护敏感电子器件。在正常环境下，二极管通常反偏。当电压升高到超出正常范围时，二极管变为正偏（导通）。例如，二极管用在（步进电动机和 H 桥）电动机控制器和继电器电路中对线圈进行快速地去激励时，避免了那种具有破坏性的电压尖峰的发生（在该种应用中所用的任何二极管被称为回扫二极管）。许多集成电路也把二极管接在引脚上防止外电压损坏敏感的三极管。在功率较大时，专用的二极管可以用来进行过电压保护（看图 1.9 所示的二极管类型）。

第 4 单元 运算放大器

运算放大器，常称为运放，是差动输入式直接耦合高增益电压放大器，通常为单端输出。运放的输出端受负反馈或正反馈控制，负反馈在很大程度上决定输出电压的大小，正反馈可以提高增益并产生振荡。高输入阻抗及低输出阻抗是其重要的典型特征。

如今运放是最广泛使用的电子器件，被广泛应用在家电、工业和科学仪器领域中。中等生产规模的许多标准集成电路运放的价格只需几美分；但是一些具有特殊性能指标的集成或混合运放，因生产数量少，价格在 100 美元以上。

现代电子式的设计比早期的坚固耐用，一些运放可以承受输出端的直接短路而不会损坏。

电路符号

运放的电路符号如图 1.14 所示。

其中：U_+：同相输入；

U_-：反相输入；

U_{out}：输出；

U_{S+}：正电源；

U_{S-}：负电源。

电源接线端（U_{S+}和 U_{S-}）可以用不同的方式标记。虽然标法不同，其功能保持不变。为了清晰，这些接线端经常不在图中标出，电源的结构在电路中描述。反相输入端和同相输入端的位置，如果合适的话，在图上可以颠倒；电源的接线端通常不颠倒。例如，IC741 是一种运放，可在模拟计算机、仪表及其他控制系统中进行算术运算。运算放大器是一类线性集成电路。线性的特性是可以像模拟方式一样放大连续的电压信号。因为运放的可靠性高、价格便宜，如今被广泛地使用。主要用作电压放大器。基本的运算放大器工作类似于以下顺序：

输入级→中间级→电平转换器→输出级

输入级由高输入阻抗组成，可以放大给定输入信号的差。中间级由串联放大器组成，放大输入信号。由于放大倍数高，信号的直流电平增加。为了使其降到额定值，使用了电平转换器。输出级由甲乙类或乙类功率放大器组成，用来放大输出信号的功率。

理想运放的工作原理

放大器的差动输入由反相输入端和同相输入端组成，运算放大器放大的只是两个信号间的电压差。这种放大器被称为差分放大器。在普通使用情况下，运放的输出电压是通过把输出电压的一部分反馈到输入端来实行控制的。这种反馈被称为负反馈。如果反馈系数为零，即不存在负反馈，放大器处于开环运行，输出为差分输入电压乘以放大器的总增益，如下面等式表示：

$$U_{out} = (U_+ - U_-)G$$

这里 U_+为同相端电压，U_-为反相端电压，G 为放大器的总开环增益。

因为开环增益值通常很大，而且不太受制造工艺的控制，因此不加负反馈时运放很少使用。除非差分输入电压非常小，否则开环运行会使运放进入饱和状态。加负反馈时，如何计算输出电压，以下面的基本同相放大器电路为例说明。

运放的另一种典型结构是加正反馈，把输出信号的一部分回送到同相输入端。关于正反馈一个重要的应用是迟滞型比较器。

对于任何输入电压，理想运放具有：无穷大的开环增益，无穷大的带宽，无穷大的输入阻抗（使输入电流为零），零偏移电压，无穷大的转换速率，零输出阻抗，零干扰。

应用

在电子系统设计中的应用

不管所用的放大器是集成的还是离散的，把运放当作电路模块使用要比把它们都看作单个的电路元件（晶体管，电阻等）要容易和清楚得多。在第一级近似中，运放可用作理想的差动放大模块。后一级的极限值应该处于每个运放允许的参数取值范围内。

所有电子电路的设计都遵循相同的规则。电路所需的技术要求在图上给出。例如，要求增益为 100，在规定的温度范围，误差为 5%，漂移小于 1%；输入阻抗小于 1MΩ 等。

在电路建模的帮助下，一个简单的电路就设计出来了。工业上所要用的特殊的运放和元件在选择时应该满足设计标准，在可接受的价格上，误差应该在规定的范围。如果所有的标准不能全部满足，技术要求需要修正。

简单同相放大器电路

一般运放有两个输入端、一个输出端。输出电压是两个输入差的倍数。

$$U_{out} = G(U_+ - U_-)$$

G 是运放的开环增益。假定输入端有很高的阻抗，流入或流出输入端的电流可以忽略。运放输出端有非常低的源阻抗。

如果输出接到反相输入端（图 1.15），经电压分配器 $K=R_1/(R_1+R_2)$换算后，得到：

$$U_+=U_{in}$$

$$U_{-}=K\,U_{out}$$
$$U_{out}=G\,(U_{in}-KU_{out})$$

要求 U_{out}/U_{in}，结果为：

$$U_{out}/U_{in}=G/(1+G\,K)$$

如果 G 很大，U_{out}/U_{in} 接近于 $1/K$，等于 $1+(R_2/R_1)$。

负反馈连接是运放的最典型应用，但是可能有很多种不同的结构，使得其成为最通用的电子模块之一。

当按照负反馈结构连接时，运放使 U_{out} 为所需的电压从而使输入端电压尽可能相等。这一点和高输入阻抗，有时被称为运放设计的两条“黄金法则”（对于采用负反馈的电路）。

1. 没有电流流入输入端。

2. 输入端电压近似相等。

绝大多数单、双、四路运放都有标准化的引脚输出，这使得不需要改变接线就可以用一种类型代替另一种类型。选择某种运放要考虑开环增益、带宽、噪声、输入阻抗、功率消耗，或者折中考虑这些因素。

第5单元 数字逻辑门

逻辑门的介绍

数字逻辑门，也称为组合逻辑门或简称逻辑门，是一种数字集成电路，它的输出在任何时候由当时的输入状态决定。由于逻辑门是数字集成电路，其输入和输出信号只能为两种数字状态之一，也就是逻辑“0”或逻辑“1”。因此，逻辑门的输出状态由每个输入端的逻辑状态决定。

逻辑门的主要应用是实现数字电路中数字信号流的逻辑，逻辑的本意是定义成为处理真和假的哲学分支，真和假由其他事情的真和假决定。本质上这是数字电路中逻辑门的功能——给定一组为真（逻辑 1）或假的（逻辑 0）输入，确定输出为真或假。

逻辑门的任何输入组合所对应的输出被制成被称为真值表的表格。真值表给出了逻辑门的每一种可能的输入组合以及组合的相应输出。表 1.2 描述了各种类型的逻辑门，并给出了每一种逻辑门所对应的真值表。

表 1.2　　逻辑门及其性质

<table>
<tr><th>门</th><th>说　明</th><th colspan="3">真 值 表</th></tr>
<tr><td rowspan="5">与门</td><td rowspan="5">与门是一种逻辑门，只有当输入都为‘1’时，输出才为‘1’。因此，只要有一个输入为‘0’，输出就为‘0’。用数学公式表示为：Q=A·B</td><td>A</td><td>B</td><td>输出 Q</td></tr>
<tr><td>0</td><td>0</td><td>0</td></tr>
<tr><td>0</td><td>1</td><td>0</td></tr>
<tr><td>1</td><td>0</td><td>0</td></tr>
<tr><td>1</td><td>1</td><td>1</td></tr>
<tr><td rowspan="5">或门</td><td rowspan="5">或门是一种逻辑门，只有当输入都为‘0’时，输出才为‘0’。因此，只要有一个输入为‘1’，输出就为‘1’。用数学公式表示为：Q=A+B</td><td>A</td><td>B</td><td>输出 Q</td></tr>
<tr><td>0</td><td>0</td><td>0</td></tr>
<tr><td>0</td><td>1</td><td>1</td></tr>
<tr><td>1</td><td>0</td><td>1</td></tr>
<tr><td>1</td><td>1</td><td>1</td></tr>
</table>

续表

门	说明	真值表
非门	非门是一种逻辑门，其输出与输入状态相反。用数学公式表示为：$Q=\overline{A}$	A 输出Q 0 1 1 0
与非门	与非门是在与门后加一个非门。因此，对于相同的输入组合，与非门的输出与与门相反。用数学公式表示为：$Q=\overline{A\cdot B}$	A B 输出Q 0 0 1 0 1 1 1 0 1 1 1 0
或非门	或非门是在或门后加一个非门。因此，对于相同的输入组合，或非门的输出与或门相反。用数学公式表示为：$Q=\overline{A+B}$	A B 输出Q 0 0 1 0 1 0 1 0 0 1 1 0
异或门	异或门是一种逻辑门，当只有一个输入为‘1’时，输出才为‘1’	A B 输出Q 0 0 0 0 1 1 1 0 1 1 1 0

有趣的是，逻辑门相互之间的运算可以使用称之为布尔代数的数学分支来表示和分析，像普通代数一样，布尔代数可以对要求的表达式进行运算或对等式进行化简。布尔代数中所用的表达式被称为布尔表达式。

逻辑门的类型

目前有几种类型的逻辑门，每一种逻辑门都可以实现某种逻辑功能。它们是：①与门；②或门；③非门；④与非门；⑤或非门；⑥异或门。上面的表 1.1 给出了这些逻辑门及其特性。

逻辑门可以被看作是开关的组合。例如，与门，如果它所有的输入为‘1’，输出才为‘1’，每个开关表示一个输入，那么其可以被表示为开关的串联。电流要流过电路负载（等效于与门输出为逻辑‘1’），所有的开关都需要导通（等效于与门输入为逻辑‘1’）。

另一方面，或门可以用开关的并联来表示，所以要给电路负载供电，只需要接通一个并联开关。

在布尔代数中，与运算可以用乘来表示，如果所有的输入都为‘1’，乘积的结果将为‘1’。乘数只要出现‘0’，乘积将为‘0’。‘A 与 B’的布尔表达式类似于乘法表达式，例如 $A\cdot B$。

另一方面，或运算可以用布尔代数中的加法表示。这是因为要使加法的结果为‘0’，所有的输入必须为‘0’，这基本上可以表示或运算。‘A 或 B’的布尔表达式为 A+B。

非运算通常可以用要取非的符号上加一条线表示：$\overline{A}$=NOT(A)。与非运算为与运算后面带个非运算。或非运算为或运算后带非运算。电子电路中所用的逻辑门符号如图 1.16 所示。

布尔代数中最有用的定理之一为摩根定理，该定理表达了运用非运算，如何将与运算转化为或运算。摩根定理通常可以表示为下面的两个等式：

$$\overline{A\cdot B}=\overline{A}+\overline{B}$$

$$\overline{A+B}=\overline{A}\cdot\overline{B}$$

摩根定理在数字电子学中有实际的意义：设计者不必添加过多的集成电路，只要可能，可以用其他门的等效组合来代替。由于与非门和或非门可以用作非门，摩根定理隐含任何布尔运算都可以用与非门或或非门实现。这就是为什么与非门和或非门被称为通用门的原因。

第6单元 触 发 器

在数字电路中，触发器这个术语，指的是有两个稳定状态，能够用作一位存储器的电子电路。触发器通常由一个或两个控制信号，以及门或时钟信号控制。输出包括反码和正常输出。由于触发器用电子电路实现，因此需要电源和接地。

实现

触发器可以是简单的或钟控的。简单的触发器由一对交叉耦合的反相元件组成，真空管、双极性晶体管、场效应晶体管、反相器和反相逻辑门都被用在实际电路中——也许可以通过门控机制来增强（使能端或禁止端）。更先进的时钟型器件专门设计用于同步系统，那样的器件除了专用的时钟信号跃变时，可忽略其输入。在跃变时，根据输入信号，触发器可以改变或维持输出信号。一些触发器在时钟上升沿改变输出，其他的在下降沿改变输出。

钟控型触发器一般为主－从触发器，主从触发器由两个基本触发器组成，使得触发器对短时钟跃变期间所出现的尖峰和噪声不敏感。然而它们通常也包含异步清零和置位，这样在与时钟无关的情况下，可以改变当前的输出。

触发器可进一步分为既适用于异步又适用于时序系统的类型：SR、D、T 以及 JK 都属于这样的系统；所有这些都可以通过几个逻辑门由其他类型组合得到。某种类型的性质可以用特征方程中的术语描述，根据当前输入信号和当前输出 Q 推出下一个输出 Q_{next}。

SR 触发器

基本的锁存器是简单的 SR 触发器，其中 S 和 R 分别表示置位和复位。该触发器可以用一对交叉耦合的或非逻辑门构成，存储位为标以 Q 的输出端。

通常在存储模式，S 和 R 输入端都为低电平，反馈保持 Q 和 $\overline{Q}$ 输出恒定，$\overline{Q}$ 为 Q 的反码。如果 S 端脉冲为高电平而 R 维持为低电平，那么输出端变为高电平，即使 S 变为低电平，输出仍维持高电平；类似地，如果 R 为高电平而 S 为低电平，那么输出为低电平，即使 R 变为低电平，输出仍维持低电平。

JK 触发器

JK 触发器通过把 S=R=1 当成翻转或触发指令，增强了 SR 触发器的功能。明确地说，J=1，K=0 是触发器置位指令；J=0，K=1 是触发器复位指令；J=1，K=1 是触发器翻转指令，即，把输出改变为当前值的反码，使 J=K=0 对 D 触发器没有影响，而是维持当前的值。要得到 D 触发器，设置 K 等于 J 的反码就可以了。JK 触发器是通用型触发器，因为其可以设置为 SR 触发器、D 触发器或 T 触发器。注意：在所示的时序图中触发器为上升沿触发。

JK 触发器的特征方程是

$$Q_{next} = J\overline{Q}+\overline{K}Q$$

相应的真值表如下。

使用

- 一个触发器可以存储一位或两位数，看预先设置。
- 任何一种触发器类型都可以用来构成其他任一种触发器。
- 许多逻辑合成工具除了 D 触发器和 D 锁存器外，不使用其他任何类型。
- 许多 FPGA 器件只含有边沿触发 D 触发器。
- 几个触发器内包含的值可以表示程序装置的状态，计数器的值，计算机存储器中的 ASCII 字符或其他任何信息。
- 一种用法是根据电子逻辑构成有限状态机。触发器可以记住机器以前的状态，数字逻辑用这些状态算出下一个状态。

触发器集成电路

集成电路可以提供一个或多个触发器。例如，7400 系列的 7473 双 JK 主从触发器或 74374 八进制 D 触发器。

第二章 电机和电机控制

第 7 单元 电动机和直流电动机

电动机基础

电动机是一种将电能转换为机械能的机械设备。电动机对现代生活极其重要，电动机被广泛地应用在许多不同的地方，如真空吸尘器、洗碗机、电脑打印机、传真机、盒式录像机、机床、印刷机、汽车、地铁、污水处理厂及水泵站。

电动机运行的主要物理原理是安培定律和法拉第定律。安培定律指出：对于处在磁场中的带电导体，如果流过导体的电流的某一分量与磁场成直角，那么该导体将受到力的作用。将电流或磁场任意一个量反向，都将会产生作用方向相反的力。法拉第定律指出：如果导体在磁场中运动，那么任何与磁场垂直的运动分量都会在导体两端产生电位差。

电动机由两个基本部分组成。第一部分被称为定子，由导磁材料和导线组成，用来产生所需形状的磁场。第二部分被称为转子，同样由导磁材料和导线组成，用来产生某种形状的磁场，该磁场与定子产生的磁场相互作用。转子为电动机中的运动部分，转子有一根转轴与被驱动机械相连，并有一些装置维持转子与电动机外壳间的电气接触（通常是炭刷与滑环的接触)。运行时，供给电动机的电流可以在转子和定子中产生磁场。这两个磁场的相互作用使转子受到转矩作用，从而转动。

根据电动机所加电源的类型，电动机分成两大类——直流电动机和交流电动机。

1821 年麦克尔·法拉第在英国演示了第一台直流电动机。由于当时只有直流电源，所以第一批商用电动机是直流电动机，并在 19 世纪 80 年代开始普及。这些直流电动机既可用在小功率场合，也可用于大功率场合，如市内电车。直到 19 世纪 90 年代，有了交流电能后，交流电动机才首先由威斯丁豪斯和通用电气公司共同研制出。

直流电动机

一个简单的直流电动机有一个可在磁场中旋转的线圈。线圈中的电流通过与滑环滑动连接的两个电刷来提供。线圈处于稳定的磁场中。图 2.2 中施加在带电导线上的力在线圈上产生一个转矩。

长为 L 且所带电流为 i 的导线在磁场强度为 B 的磁场中所受的力 F 等于 iLB 乘上 B 与 i 间夹角的正弦值，如果磁场是均匀垂线，那么 B 与 i 夹角为 90°。F 的方向可由右手定则来判断，如图 2.2（a）所示。图上所示的两个力 F 大小相等方向相反，但由于它们被垂直放置，故它们将产生一个转矩。（线圈另外两边的力作用在同一条水平线上，因而不会产生转矩）。

线圈也可被看成是一个磁偶极子或一个小电磁铁，如图 2.2（b）中 NS 箭头所示：将你的右手顺着电流的方向卷起来，你的大拇指朝向为 N 极，如右图所示，把由转子线圈产生的磁体看成一个永磁体，我们将会看到同样的转矩（N 极吸引 S 极）。

我们来看一下滑环上电刷的作用。当旋转的线圈面到达水平位置时，电刷将断开连接（不会丢失什么能量，因为这是转矩为零的点——作用力的方向朝里）。线圈的角动量推动线圈越过这个断点，然后电流在相反的方向上流动，这使得转子磁极的方向反向。因而，过了断点后，转子继续逆时针转动并且两个力开始作用在一条直线上，但方向相反。

在一个周期中，产生的转矩随着两个力在垂直方向上分量改变而改变。因此转矩的大小取决于线圈轴线和磁场夹角的正弦值。然而，由于滑环的存在，转矩总是为同一个方向，图 2.3 就是转矩随时间的变化情况。

直流电动机的分类

直流电动机的应用比我们想象的更为普遍。一辆汽车上有多达 20 台直流电动机，用来驱动风扇、座椅和窗户。根据所使用的电路来分类，直流电动机可分为三种类型。在并励电动机中，电枢和励磁绕组并联，因此流过它们的电流是相互独立的。流过励磁绕组的电流可用励磁变阻器（可变电阻）控制，因此电动机可在很宽的范围内调速。这种类型的电动机用来驱动机床或风扇，因为它们都需要较宽的调速范围。

在串励电动机中，励磁绕组与电枢绕组串联，这就导致启动转矩非常高，因为启动时电枢电流和磁场强度都为最大值。然而，一旦电枢开始转动，反电动势会使电路中的电流减小，从而减小磁场强度。串励电动机用于需要大启动转矩的场合，如用在汽车启动电动机、起重机和升降机。

复励电动机是串励和并励电动机的组合，它有并联励磁绕组和串联励磁绕组。这种电动机具有大启动转矩和很强的变速能力，被用于同时需要这两种特性的场合如冲床、传送带和电梯。

第 8 单元　感 应 电 动 机

每个现代家庭都有一台或多台感应电动机。你将会在很多地方发现感应电动机的身影，如风扇、冰箱、真空吸尘器、洗衣机、洗碗机、衣服干燥机中，及鱼缸中用来防止水变绿和鱼死亡的水循环泵。空调中可能也会有一个——除非它是特殊的高科技空调。

优点：便宜，噪声小，运行时间长，无干扰。

缺点：需要以恒转速（50Hz 除以极对数）转动；转速无法超过 1500r/min（4 极电动机）；启动电流大，或效率低，或两者兼有；它消耗的能量有点大。

图 2.5 就是一个风扇中的感应电动机。

实际上，电动机的轴承和端盖已被拿走。我们可以把转子拿走，图 2.6（b）就是剩下部分。它有四个绕组，这些绕组简单的串联。

喔，事实并不是如此简单——电流从白线中流入，然后在第一个绕组［图 2.6（a）右上角］中逆时针流动，下一个绕组［图 2.6（a）右下角］中顺时针流动，左下角绕组中又逆时针流动，左上角绕组顺时针流动，最后从另一根白线中流出。因此，想象一下在电源的正半周，电流实际上从第一根线中流入。第一组绕组将产生一个北磁极向内的磁场；第二组产生南磁极向内的磁场；以此类推，结果是：N-S-N-S。

半个电源周期（10ms）后电流反向，因此磁场的极向也反向，现在磁极方向为：S-N-S-N。现在定子磁场的方向转动了 90°。转子是导电体，因此转子要跟随定子磁场转动。为了跟随上定子磁场，转子必需旋转 90°。因此转子旋转一圈需要花费二个电源周期（40ms），从而转子以 1500r/min 的速度旋转。如果转子能跟上这个旋转磁场，转子为这个转速。但是转子和旋转磁场的转速不完全一致，事实上正是因为转子转速比旋转磁场低，才使得转矩产生。因此，转子以稍低于 1500r/min 的速度（通常为 1440r/min）旋转，转速具体值的大小将根据转矩大小决定。

注意一下，到目前为止我们所讨论的电动机可以顺时针方向也可逆时针方向转动。因此，这种电动机需要一些内部的装置来确保电动机只在正确的方向上旋转。在此电动机中，该功能是通过使用罩极来实现的。

注意看图 2.7 中绕组的顶端。看在远离主磁极的左边是否有一个很小的附加的磁极（或一叠铁迭片）。这个附加磁极与主磁极一样，都是通过绕组激励产生磁极的，但它被一个很厚的铜圈“罩”起来与主磁极隔离，这个铜片将叠片整个包起来，就像一个短路线圈。磁场在铜片中感应出电流，这个电流产生一个相位移，因此罩极能够给主磁场增加一个向右的小磁场分量，由于有正确的相位，可确保风扇按正确的方式旋转（否则风扇将吸风，而不是吹风了）。

因而实际上我们的感应电动机已在使用感应原理了，我们还没开始讨论转子呢！

现在我们来看一下转子（图 2.8）。这真让人失望——它看上去一点也不像课本中的“松鼠的笼子”！对于命名者，松鼠这种假想是怎么来的呢？

实际上转子是由一叠圆形软铁叠片做成的。是的——它是固体。它将磁场（由定子绕组产生的）集中到磁场真正发挥作用的区域（转子的导条）。

实际上你可以看到导条的边缘，它们分布在转子轴的周围，但它们与转轴大概成 30°。这是怎么了？工厂里制造坏了？事实是它就是这样设计的，目的是减小齿槽效应转矩。如果导条与转轴平行，那么当每个导条经过绕组下方时，转矩将会上下波动。通过将导体倾斜，就可以让转矩在转子转动时更加保持一致。

现在我们来看一下另外一种感应电动机（图 2.9）。

这是来自于天文望远镜的感应电动机。它是摄影胶片输出机构的一部分，并且要求能够实现正反转。因此它有两个独立的绕组及 4 根输出线。一根绕组与电源线（美国同行称其

“line”）直接相连；另一根通过电容与电源相连，电容可以提供一个必要的 90°相位移。将绕组交换，或将其中一个绕组反向连接，那么电动机将反向运行。

当我们把它拆开时，虽然我们看到一个与前面电动机不同的绕组结构，但没什么好奇怪的。它有更多的磁极，因而转速更慢。

同样，转子是固体，因而我们看不到里面的情况。在转子的末端贴有铝片，而且这些铝片被卷成一组小的扇片做成了一个简单的冷却扇（图 2.10）。（这对于我们介绍的第一种电动机是没必要的——将它放置在风扇的中间就可冷却了）

由于天文望远镜不再使用胶片，我们可以将它切成两半，然后看看是否有一只松鼠在里面。

没有松鼠，但有一大组铝导条，就像教科书上一样。如果你把转子的导条看成变压器的单匝二次绕组（通过端环），每极下的一次绕组大概有 50～100 匝，很明显流过转子导条的电流非常大——对于一个 240W 的电动机有 100A。这就说明了为什么需要这么粗短的导条。

罩极式电动机的一个缺点是它的启动转矩非常低。对于像风扇这类稳态时负载几乎为零的场合这没什么大碍。但对于某些应用场合，如洗衣机，这就无法正常工作了。因此这样的电动机通过使用电容来给正交磁绕组产生一个所需的相位移，就像本例中那样。

感应电动机有许多种类，但以上讨论的两种是家庭中最常用的。

但对于负荷大的场合，你需要三相感应电动机。它利用了商用三相电源的优点：三相电源通过三相导线传送，每相为 50Hz 的正弦波，并且每相彼此相位差为 120°。一个三相电动机在机壳中放置间隔为 120°的三相绕组，因而自动产出一个旋转的磁场。三相感应电动机是工业生产中的“大负荷电动机”，有些三相感应电动机的额定功率已超过了兆瓦。

第 9 单元　简单电动机控制电路

本文将介绍一些简单的交流电动机控制电路。

1. 按钮自锁电路

图 2.12 所示电路表示了如何使用继电器触点来锁住按钮状态。当按下“开始”按钮，“M”继电器得电，电动机开始转动。同时继电器“M”的一个触点锁住开始按钮，从而电流可以持续流过继电器“M”。停止按钮用来切断继电器“M”的电源，从而切断电动机的电源。

2. 远程控制电路

图 2.13 所示电路可在多地控制电动机。所有的停止按钮串联连接且开始按钮相互并联。我们可以通过使用任何一个地点的开始和停止按钮来启动和停止电动机。

3. 单相异步电动机的启动电路

图 2.14 所示电路用来起动单相异步电动机。按下启动按钮“A”，继电器“M”得电，电动机开始旋转。同时，时间继电器“ZR”得电，开始计数。当计数结束后，时间继电器的触点动作使继电器“A”断电，从而电动机在没有辅助线圈的情况下继续转动。

4. 单电阻电动机启动电路

当感应电动机的定子绕组与三相电源直接相连，开始时流过一个非常大的电流（满载电流的5～8倍）。在电动机转速达到正常转速前，这个冲击电流将随着电动机的加速而下降。当超大型电动机直接启动时，这个大启动冲击电流将会给供电线带来电压扰动（电压骤降）。这个电压扰动将会给其他和这个电源连接的电气设备造成故障。为了限制启动电流，某些大型的感应电动机采用降压启动，当电动机接近额定转速后再给电动机加全压。

图2.15中所示电路用来启动大功率的感应电动机。当我们按下启动按钮，“M”继电器和“ZR”时间继电器得电。“M”继电器的主触点将三相电源接到电动机上，它的辅助触点用来保证继电器处于通电状态。串联在电动机上的电阻使得电动机的电压降低。时间继电器“ZR”开始倒计时。当时间继电器结束计数后，时间继电器“ZR”的触点使得继电器“A”得电。继电器“A”的主触点将电动机电路中的电阻短路掉，电动机全压运行。在电动机达到额定转速前，时间继电器“A”的定时器必须被设置在计数工作状态。停止按钮用来切断电动机和所有控制电路中继电器的电源。

5. 电动机双电阻启动电路

大功率电动机通常需要启动电路来启动。在图2.16中，当按下启动按钮，由于使用了双电阻故电动机开始低压启动。第一个定时器开始计数到指定的时间。当计数结束继电器“A”得电，它将电动机电路中的第一个电阻短路掉并启动第二个定时器。当第二个定时器计数结束继电器“B”得电，电路中的两个电阻都被短路掉。

6. 星－三角启动电路

图2.17中电路使用星—三角启动电动机：先采用星型连接，然后再切换到三角形连接。这种方法用于启动大功率电动机。当我们按下“启动”按钮，继电器“A”得电，它的触点动作使继电器“M”得电，“M”的主触点将电动机与电源相连。继电器“A”的其他触点使电动机绕组以星形的方式相连。电动机在低压状态下开始转动。“开始”按钮也使时间继电器“ZR”得电。当时间继电器结束计数，它的常闭触点动作，继电器“A”失电，从而使继电器“B”得电。继电器“B”将电动机的连接方式转换成三角形。继电器“B”的辅助触点使时间继电器“ZR”失电。当我们按下“停止”按钮，所有的继电器失电且电动机电源被切断。

7. 带互锁的电动机换向

在图2.18中我们用两个按钮让电动机在两个不同的方向上转动。“ILERI”按钮使控制电动机正转的继电器“I”得电，而“GERI”按钮使控制电动机反转的继电器“G”得电。同时按钮“ILERI”又用来切断继电器“G”的电源，防止继电器“I”通电前“G”得电。这就防止电动机电路中出现短路。按钮“GERI”也是同样的作用。“STOP 按钮”用来同时切断继电器“I”和“G”，从而切断电动机电源。

8. 带电气互锁的电动机换向

在图2.19中，按下按钮“ILERI”或“GERI”从而让电动机在指定的方向上转动。当电动机在一个方向上转动时，除非让它停下来，否则不可能在另一个方向上转动。如果你试图在电动机在某个方向上旋转时改变它的转向，控制电路的安全触点是不会让相应的继电器得电的。例如我们按下“ILERI”按钮来让电动机正转。继电器“I”得电，电动机开始转动。位于继电器“G”前的继电器“I”的常闭触点将会防止继电器“G”得电。因此如果要让电动机反转，我们必须按下“停止”按钮使电动机停转及继电器“I”失电。

9. 能耗制动

当我们切断电动机电源时，电动机不会立即停转。它将继续旋转直到它的动能全部耗尽。为了让电动机快速停止，我们采用了能耗制动。

在控制电路中（图.2.20），当我们按下开始按钮，继电器“M”和断电延时时间继电器“ZR”得电。电动机通过继电器“M”的主触点接到电源上。当我们按下停止按钮，继电器“M”和断电延时时间继电器“ZR”失电。电动机电源被切断。断电延时时间继电器的计数器开始倒计数。在计数器倒计数期间断电延时时间继电器“ZR”的触点保持得电状态。“ZR”的触点使得连接电动机和制动电路的继电器“F”得电。当断电延时时间继电器结束计数，它的常开触点断开，从而使继电器“F”失电。电动机从制动电路中断开，电动机完全停止转动。

10. 选择性能耗制动

图 2.21 电路有一个能耗制动选择按钮“FREN”。按下“启动”按钮电动机开始旋转。我们有两种方法使电动机停止。第一种方法：按下“FREN”按钮从而将切断主电源并短时将制动电路加到电动机上。第二种方法：按下“停止”按钮从而仅切断电动机上的电源。

11. 电动机的连续和断续工作电路

图 2.22 电路说明了如何来控制电动机让它连续或断续工作。按下“启动”按钮，我们让电动机连续工作。继电器“M”用来使电动机旋转并使开始按钮自锁。按下“KS.CL”按钮，我们仅用继电器“M”来控制电动机转动。当我们松开“KS.CL”按钮，继电器“M”的电源被切断，电动机将停转。“停止”按钮用来让连续工作模式下的电动机停转。

第 10 单元 直流电动机的脉宽调制理论

直流电动机速度的控制是非常重要，它可以让你精确地驱动机器人，让它在你所希望的方向上运行。如果你的速度控制不够精确，那么你的机器人就可能会左右摆动甚至完全失去目标。

对于仅仅消耗几安培的小功率电动机，你可以通过在电动机中串联可变电阻来改变电流，从而改变电动机的速度。对于小电动机而言，最终在可变电阻中损耗的能量不会太大而且你也不必去处理发热大的问题。这种方法通常使用在小玩具模型中，因为这是最简单的速度控制方式。

当你开始使用堵转电流超过 100A 的电动机来驱动大型机器人时，一个串联可变电阻将会损耗大量能量。如果你不想它热的发红，那么你除了要一个非常小的电阻外，它还可能要一个大散热片。你同时还要损失热能，而这部分能量可以让你的机器人运行更长时间。对于这些应用场合，PWM 电动机控制技术是一个很好的选择。

脉宽调制的占空比

一种更好的速度控制方法是将电动机的电源在通断间快速切换。电动机的速度与提供给电动机的平均电压成正比，所有只要你足够快地使电压通断，那么电动机仅能“看”到平均电压的作用效果。假定脉冲足够短且距离足够近，那么由于电动机电枢的重量和它的惯性作用，电动机的转速在每个脉冲的通断间将不会明显变化。要改变电动机的速度，如图 2.28 所示改变一个周期中通断的占空比就可。

在图 2.28（a）中通的脉宽要比断的脉宽短得多，因此电动机将相对较慢地旋转。

为了提高电动机转速，你需要将接通与关断的时间比提高，从而增大平均电压。在图 2.28（b）中这点是通过将通的脉宽加长同时将断的脉宽缩短来实现的。两个连续脉冲的起点间的时间间隔保持不变，但是占空比改变了。

在图 2.28（c）中，通脉冲的时间长度保持不变，但是断脉冲的时间长度缩短。结果提高了平均电压，但这也意味着它每秒中的脉冲个数要比图 2.28（b）中多了。

如果脉冲的频率足够低（小于 20kHz），那么电动机运行时你可能会听到电动机发出的嗡嗡声。这没关系，这只是电枢随着脉冲的变化而均匀的振动。这种效果你在现代列车可看到，当列车在运行时发出明显的嗡嗡声，这表明它们都是使用 PWM 作为速度控制方式的。相反，电阻降压调速的英国老式车门式列车，不会发出嗡嗡声，但是效率较低。

金属氧化物半导体场效应晶体管元件

通常用来切换电源通断的器件是金属氧化物半导体场效应晶体管或 MOSFET。之所以使用这些器件是因为它们可以用一个小的电压信号来控制大电流的通断。

下面给出了 MOSFET 的常用符号，它的边上是一个继电器式等效电路。某些专业的人士可能认为继电器模型不是准确的等效电路，但是它可以帮助我们显示 MOSFET 用作电源转换器件时是如何工作的。

该器件在栅极信号的控制下，来接通漏极和源极间的电能。MOSFET 的阈值电压取决于 MOSFET 本身。任何一个高于阈值电压的栅极电压将使 MOSFET 快速导通。可是，栅极上有一个重要的输入电容，因此当你想再次关断器件时，你必须给输入电容放电，这将会使你的关断时间稍微加长。因此你需要仔细地选择一个合适的最大栅极电压以便你可以得到合适的开和关的转换时间。

H 桥式驱动器的结构

为了能够完全控制电动机的正反转，通常使用 H 桥式结构，如图 2.30 所示。

顾名思义，MOSFET 以 H 形状分布在电动机周围，这样如果 Q1 和 Q4 接通，电动机在一个方向上转动，如果 Q2 和 Q3 接通，那么电动机将在另一个方向上转动。如果，由于某些特殊原因你让 Q1 和 Q3 同时接通，或 Q2 和 Q4 同时接通，那么电动机就会被烧坏，因 MOSFET 直接将电源线短接在一起，从而很可能大概在几毫秒内损坏电源。这种情况通常被称为“直通”并且决不允许发生。

通周期运行，断周期制动

H 桥式结构电路既可以驱动电动机，同样也可以提供制动的作用。图 2.31 显示了它是如何实现制动的。

就像前面所描述的那样，电动机的速度控制是通过给电动机施加通断脉冲来实现的。在上面左图的结构中，MOSFET Q1 和 Q4 在导通期间内全部导通，从而给电动机提供电能使它正转。在关断时间内 Q1 被切断，此时 Q3 被导通，从而将电动机的电源切断。电源被切断后，电动机就作为发电机运行，它的两端产生感应电压。电动机现在成了一个电压源，这就意味着 Q3、Q4 被同时接通后，电流通过 Q3、Q4 的反方向流动。这些 MOSFET 对电流有一个很小的阻抗，因此在导通期间在电流的反方向上有一个强大的“电动机”力。这个反向电动机力的作用是给正向运行的电动机一个反向的制动力。

左下图显示了 MOSFET Q2 和 Q3 接通后电动机反向运行时的接通的电流回路。在关断期间，Q2 被切断，此时 Q4 被接通，从而电动机再次作为发电机运行，它的感应电流再次流过 Q3 和 Q4 如右下图所示。MOSFET 同样给感应电流提供一个低阻抗通路，因此这次的最终效果是产生一个正向的制动力。

第 11 单元 变 频 器

变频器（VFD）是通过控制加在电动机上电源的频率从而来控制交流电动机转速的一种装置。变频器是一种特殊的调速驱动装置。变频器被称为调频器（AFD）、变速器（VSD）、交流驱动器或变换器。由于它的电压随着频率的变化而变化，因此它又被称作变压变频驱动器。

变频器得到广泛应用。例如，在大型建筑物的通风系统中，风扇上的变频电动机通过将流动空气的量与系统的要求相匹配从而来节约能源。变频器还应用于泵和机床中。

工作原理

根据公式知，交流电动机的同步转速是由交流电源的频率及定子绕组的极数决定的。公式：

$$RPM=\frac{120\times f}{p}$$

其中：RPM=转数/分；f=交流电源的频率（赫兹）；p=极数（偶数）。

常数 120，是 60（每分钟 60s）×2（每对极有 2 个极）。有时这个常数是 60，这时 p 表示的是极对数而不是极数。改变加在电动机上电压的频率，就可以改变电动机的转速。

同步电动机的同步转速由上式确定。感应电动机的转速比同步转速略低。

变频器的种类

变频器可被分成恒压型变频器、恒流型变频器和双向离子变频器。

在恒压型变频器中，中间直流回路的电压在每个输出周期中基本保持不变。在恒流型变频器中，一个大电感被置于整流输入装置和输出电桥装置之间，这样传送的电流就近似为常数。双向离子变频器没有整流输入或直流回路部分，而是将每个输出端连到相应的输入相上。

最常见的封装式变频器是恒压型，它采用脉宽调制技术来控制频率及加在电动机负载上的有效电压。

变频器结构

所有的变频器都有相同的结构，包含了整流器、滤波器及逆变器，如图 2.35 所示。整流器将三相交流线电压转变为直流电。整流器中用的典型器件是晶闸管和/或二极管。滤波器位于整流器和逆变器之间，通过电感和电容来滤去谐波和电源纹波（电源脉动）。这些元件分别对加到电动机上的电流和电压进行滤波和稳压。逆变部分通常由晶闸管或 IGBT 组成，根据转速和负载的要求来恰当地控制晶闸管或 IGBT，从而给电动机各相绕组提供合适的电压和电流。如果使用 IGBT，栅极要与控制电路相连，但是这种电路比较简单并且不需要极性变换。

通过控制三相感应电动机的两个主要参数，也就是转矩和速度，逆变器给使用者带来了很大的灵活性。电动机的速度和许多运行参数可以被随意调整。一些其他类型的逆变器包括电流源型逆变器、电压源型逆变器、负载换流逆变器、PWM 逆变器、矢量控制等，每一种逆变器都有其优点和缺点，必须根据实际需要来选择。对于 200 马力以下的应用场合，当前最经济的选择是 PWM 逆变器。

变频器的操作界面

操作界面为操作者启动、停止及调整电动机转速提供了一个平台。此外它的操作控制功能还包括反转以及手动/自动调速间的切换，自动调速是由外部控制信号来控制的。操作界面通常包括一个文字数字显示屏和/或指示灯及仪表，它们将提供变频器运行的相关信息。操作界面键盘和显示装置通常在变频器的前面，如图 2.36 所示。键盘通常可以通过电缆线连接并安装在离变频器不远的地方。大多数变频器都配有输入、输出端可以连接按钮，开关、其他操作设备及控制信号。变频器还有一个串行通信口，该口可以让计算机来设定、调整及监控变频器。

优点

变频器可以减小节流装置如控制阀和输出节气阀上的能源浪费。它们主要安装在转矩随转速变化而变化的负载上，如离心泵、风扇、吹风机、压缩机等。变频器用来改善过程控制，从而提高操作系统的效率。变频器通过使用软启动减小了机械应力，同时也提高了整个电气系统的功率因素。其他的优点包括减小和/或省略电动机启动器，减小交流电动机绕组和轴承的压力，以及减少泵或风扇的压力和磨损。

缺点

由于输出电源不是纯粹的正弦波，它含有谐波，这导致电动机产生额外的热量。根据制造商和变频器的种类，输入到电动机上的电压和电流波形将产生不同程度的失真。谐波电流将在电动机轴上产生无用的转矩，这些将产生额外的损耗。

然而，如果变频器的选择和安装正确的话，那么它就可以可靠和无故障地运行。如果变频器选择不当的话，它们就会对其所驱动的电动机造成损坏，并且使得与其相连的电气系统发生一系列的问题。变频器的输入输出电压和电流波形畸变［失真］所引起的问题我们通常称为谐波畸变［失真］。

第三章 工业计算机控制技术

第12单元 可编程控制器综述

什么是PLC？

可编程逻辑控制器，又称可编程控制器或PLC，是计算机家族的一员，通过使用集成电路而不是机电设备来完成控制任务。它可以存储如顺序、定时、计数、算术、数据操作及通信等指令，并通过这些指令来控制工业机械和工业过程。

可编程控制器的定义有很多种。简单的说，PLC可以被认为是具有特殊设计结构的工业计算机。它们被设计成可以从各种传感器读取数字或模拟的输入信号，然后执行用户编制的逻辑程序，并将最后的数字和模拟输出值输出，从而来控制工业机器和工业过程（如图 3.1 所示）。

目前PLC被应用于各个工业领域和生产机器中，如包装和半导体机器。知名的PLC品牌有西门子、艾伦-布拉得利（AB）、ABB、三菱、欧姆龙和通用电气。

PLC的组成部分

图3.2是PLC的示意图。PLC的基本组成部件如下。

1．处理器

处理器（有时又叫CPU），整体式PLC，通常根据执行程序所需的存储器的大小来指定。在模块式PLC中，容量同样也是一个要素。它的特点包含了如高速数学运算功能、PID控制回路和选择编程指令。处理器由以下部分组成：微处理器、系统存储器、用于打印的串行通信口、PLC的局域网连接块和外部编程器，此外在某些PLC中还有给处理器和输入/输出模块提供电能的电源。

2．机架

机架通常是一个金属的框架，带有印刷电路板底板，用来安装PLC的输入/输出模块和处理器。机架的类型是根据运行系统所需的模块数来确定的。机架通过底板给处理器和模块提供数据和电源的连接。对于无内置电源的CPU，机架同样给CPU提供模块化电源。有些PLC系统中的处理器是独立安装的，并通过电缆连到机架上。机架可直接安装到面板上或者安装在标准的19寸机柜中。机架是可以扩展的，因此可将几个机架连接起来从而使得系统可容纳更多的输入/输出模块。

3．输入输出模块

输入输出单元是联接PLC内部系统和外部被监控过程的接口。由于PLC是一个基于逻辑运算的设备，工作电压一般为5V，而外部生产过程通常需要更高的电压和电流，因此输入/输出模块通常是光隔离的。典型的输入/输出模块的工作电压是5～240V直流（或交流），电流从0.1A到几安培。输入/输出模块采用这种设计方法是为了使PLC与被控过程间的中间电路最小化或消除。小型 PLC 单元大约有 40 个输入/输出接口，而大型 PLC 则有 128 个以上本地或远程接口，这大大提升了 PLC 的容量。

4．电源

电源的选择取决于实际应用中所选制造商的 PLC。如上所说，某些 PLC 的电源封装在处理器模块中作为处理器模块的一部分，能够给系统提供各种所需电源。如果电源是一个独立的模块，那么它必须能够提供一个比其他模块所需电流之和还要大的电流。对于电源内置在 CPU 模块中的 PLC，系统中可能存在一些模块，因为所需的电压或电流只能从附加的第二个电源上得到，这些模块所需的额外电源不能够从处理器上获得。一般来说，这种情况通常出现在 PLC 系统中包含模拟或外部通信模块时，因为这些模块需要直流电源，就拿模拟模块为例，这个直流电源必须很稳定。

5．编程单元

编程单元可让工程师或技术人员输入和编辑要执行的程序。最简单的编程器可以是一个手持式编程器（指令编程器），有一个键盘用来输入程序，还有一个显示器（发光二极管或液晶的）用来查看程序步骤和功能，如图 3.3 所示，更先进的编程系统采用一台单独的个人电脑，它可让编程者在计算机上写、检查、编辑程序并将程序下载到 PLC 中。这些都是通过 PLC 制造商提供的专业软件来完成的。该软件还可让编程者或工程师来监视 PLC 运行程序时的状态。有了监控系统后，就可监控那些外部无法看见的东西，如内部线圈、寄存器、定时器及其他参量，从而得出合适的操作方法。在进行程序微调时，还可改变内部寄存器的数据。在调试程序时，这是非常有用的。与可编程控制器的通信是通过连在 PLC 特殊编程端口上的电缆线来实现的。与个人电脑的连接可通过串口或计算机内置的专用通信卡来实现。

PLC 的编程语言

早期的 PLC 是用来替代继电器逻辑系统。这些 PLC 用“梯形逻辑图”来编程，这种图与继电器逻辑示意图非常相似。现代 PLC 的编程方式可谓是多种多样，从梯形逻辑图发展到多种传统编程语言，如 BASIC 语言和 C 语言。另一种方法是状态逻辑，这种用于 PLC 编程的语言是一种基于状态转换图的超高级编程语言。

IEC61131-3 目前为可编程控制系统定义了 FBD（功能块图）、LD（梯形图）、ST（结构文本，与 Pascal 编程语言类似）、IL（指令表，与汇编语言类似）和 SFC（顺序功能图）5 种编程语言。

第13单元 PLC 的 应 用

PLC 是一种工业计算机，它能够与现实世界中的设备如开关、线圈等进行连接。控制系统的实际逻辑关系通过计算机程序在 PLC 中建立。程序规定了在哪几个输入作用下，哪个输出得电。尽管这个带有开关和继电器符号的程序看上去像梯形逻辑图，但 PLC 中并不是使用真实的开关或继电器线圈来建立输入输出间的逻辑关系的。如果你愿意，可以把它们想象成接触器和线圈。所有程序的输入和检查都是通过与 PLC 编程口相连的个人电脑来完成。

让我们来看一下图 3.6 所示电路和 PLC 程序：

当按钮开关没激活（没按下）时，PLC 的输入 X1 无法通电。按照下面的程序，X1 的常开触点与 Y1 线圈串联，则出线圈 Y1 将不会通电。因此，PLC 的输出 Y1 将保持失电状态，与它相连的指示灯维持不亮。

但是，如果按下按钮开关，PLC 的 X1 输入端将得电。程序中所有 X1 的触点都将处于得电（非常态）状态，它们就像继电器的触点一样由名为 X1 的继电器线圈激活。在这种情况下，让输入 X1 得电将使 X1 的常开触点闭合，将电能传送到线圈 Y1，使其得电。当程序中的线圈 Y1“得电”，实际输出 Y1 将通电，与之相连的灯被点亮。

有一点必须明白，个人电脑上出现的触点 X1、线圈 Y1、连接线及电源都是虚拟的。它们并不是作为真实的电气元件存在的。它们只是作为计算机程序中的指令而存在——仅是一种软件——它只是恰好与实际的继电器原理图相似而已。

同样重要的是，我们要明白用来显示和编辑 PLC 程序的个人电脑对于 PLC 的持续运行并不是必要的。一旦程序从电脑中下载到了 PLC 中后，个人计算机可以从 PLC 上拔掉，PLC 将会继续根据程序的指令运行。为了帮助理解实际环境（开关的闭合和电灯的状态）和程序状态（虚拟触点和线圈的通电情况）间的关系，我在图中为你加入了电脑的显示器部分。

当我们想要去改变某控制系统的特性时，PLC 真正的功能和多样性就会得到体现。由于 PLC 是一种可编程器件，因此我们只需改变输入的指令就可以改变它的功能，而不需要重新布置与之相连的电气元件。

与使用硬件相比，使用软件来实现逻辑控制的优势之一就是，只要有必要，输入信号就可在程序中多次使用，例如，就以下的电路和程序来说，作用是如果三个按钮开关中有两个被同时激活，那么灯泡通电。

如果用电磁继电器建立与上图等效的电路，我们必须要三个继电器，每个继电器带两个常开触点，为每个输入开关提供两个触点。可是用 PLC 的话，只要有必要我们就可在程序中为输入 X 编制任意多个触点而不需要增加额外的硬件，因为在 PLC 数字存储器（0 或 1）中，每个输入和输出只不过占一位（0 或 1），并且可以被任意调用。

此外，由于 PLC 的每个输出在存储器中也只占一个比特（位），我们可在 PLC 程序中指定由输出 Y 的状态“控制”的触点。以下一个系统为例，电动机启—停控制电路：

这时与输入 X1 相连的按钮开关作为启动开关，与输入 X2 相连的开关作为停止开关。程序中的另一个触点 Y1，直接用输出线圈的状态作自锁触点，这样当松开“开始”按钮开关，电动机接触器继续通电。你可以看到 X2 的常闭触点为彩色块，表示它此时处于闭合（导电）状态。

如果我们按下开始按钮，输入 X1 将通电，然后使程序中 X1 的触点闭合，将电能传送到线圈 Y1，输出 Y1 通电并且将 120V 的交流电加到实际电动机的接触器线圈上。并联的 Y1 触点也将同时“闭合”，从而将电路锁定在通电状态。

现在，如果我们松开“开始”按钮，X1 的常开触点将重新回到“断开”状态，但是电动机仍将继续运转，因为 Y1 的自锁触点将继续给线圈 Y1 提供“持续”的“电能”，因此使输出 Y1 保持通电。

为了让电动机停转，我们必须立刻按下“停止”按钮，这将会使输入 X2 通电，并使其常闭触点“断开”，从而断开电能与线圈 Y1 的连接。

当“停止”按钮被放开，输入 X2 将断电，使 X2 的触点返回常态——“闭合”状态。然而，电动机将不会重新启动直到“开始”按钮被激活，因为 Y1 的自锁功能失去。

这里要指出的一个重点是，可靠性设计在 PLC 控制系统中与在继电器控制系统中同样重要。我们始终需要考虑到与元件或被控设备相连的导线断开的影响。以这个电动机控制电路为例，我们有一个问题：如果 X2 的输入接线（“停止”开关）自动断开，那么就无法使电动机停转！

这个问题的解决方法是对 PLC 程序中触点 X2 和实际“停止”按钮开关之间进行反逻辑处理：

当常闭的“停止”按钮开关未被激活（没按下），PLC 的输入 X2 将通电，因而程序中 X2 的触点“闭合”。这样当输入 X1 通电时电动机就可以启动，并且在“开始”按钮不再按下时电动机可继续运行。当“停止”按钮被激活，输入 X2 将失电，因而 PLC 程序中 X2 的触点将“断开”并且电动机失电。因此，我们可以看到这种新的设计方案与之前的设计方案在运行操作上没有差别。

然而，如果与输入 X2 相连的输入接线断开，当“停止”按钮被按下时，输入 X2 将同样失电。那么，X2 输入的连接线断开的结果是电动机将立即关断。这种设计比之前所示的设计更安全，在之前的设计中，“停止”开关接线的断开将会导致无法关断电机。

这部分关于可编程控制器的阐述仅仅是其功能的一个小小的说明。和计算机一样，PLC 能够执行定时功能（相当于时间继电器延时）、鼓型排序控制功能以及其他先进功能，它的精度和稳定性要比使用机电逻辑控制设备所能达到的精度和稳定性要高得多。

第 14 单元　微控制器/单片机介绍

微控制器/单片机可与一个标准的小型独立计算机相媲美，它是一种功能非常强大的器件，可以执行一系列预先编制好的程序任务，且还可与其他硬件设备进行通信。微控制器/单片机被封装在一个尺寸和重量都非常小的集成电路中，对于机器人或任何需要智能自动控制的机器而言，它是一个完美的控制器。单个微控制器/单片机就足以控制一个小型可移动机器人，一台自动洗碗机或一个安全系统。所有的微控制器/单片机都包含一个存储器用来存储要执行的程序，还有一些用于连接外部设备的输入/输出线。

现在微控制器/单片机非常便宜且容易买到，因此为了增强设计的灵活性及节省空间，常用它们来替代一些像计数器这样简单的逻辑电路。一些机器和机器人将依赖多块微控制器/单片机，每一块都用于某一特定的任务。目前大多数的微处理器/单片机都是“在线编程/在系统编程”，这就意味着你可以在不将微处理器/单片机移出的情况下改变它所执行的程序。

8051 微控制器/单片机的结构

8051 是一个大微处理器/单片机系列的名称。我们将使用的芯片是 AT89S52，它是 ATMEL 公司制造的典型 8051 系列微控制器/单片机。

图 3.19 是 AT89S52 的一个简单的结构图。该图显示了设计者所接触到的 AT89S52 的主要特征和组成成分。你可以看到 AT89S52 有 4 个不同的端口，每个端口有 8 根输入/输出线，共提供 32 根输入/输出线。这些端口可以用来输出数据和指定作为其他功能，或用来读传感器或开关的状态。AT89S52 的大多数端口都有“双重功能”，也就是说它们可用作两种不同的功能：第一种是用来执行输入/输出操作，第二种是用来执行微控制器/单片机的特殊功能，如对外部脉冲计数，根据外部事件中断所执行的程序，执行串行数据传输或将该芯片与计算

机相连对软件升级。每个端口有 8 个引脚，在软件中它们被看作一个 8 位的变量，即寄存器，每一位都被连到不同的输入/输出引脚上。

此外你还可看到两个不同类型的存储器：RAM 和 EEPROM。简单的说，RAM 是在程序执行过程中用来存储变量的，而 EEPROM 存储器是用来存储程序本身的，这就是为什么它经常被称作“程序存储器”的原因。

89S52 微控制器/单片机的一些特殊功能被列在图 3.19 底部的蓝色方框中。

很显然，CPU（中央处理器）是微控制器/单片机的核心部分。正是 CPU 从闪存中读取程序，然后通过与上面讨论的不同外围设备协作来执行程序。

图 3.20 显示了 89S52 的引脚结构，每个引脚的功能被标注在它边上，而且，如果有双重功能，第二种功能就被标准在括号内。除了电源 VCC 和地 GND 引脚，引脚的顺序和框图 3.20 的引脚标法是相同的，VCC 和 GND 引脚通常标注在元件的顶部和底部。注意有双重功能的引脚，通常仍然被用作输入/输出脚。

存储器结构

RAM 表示随机存储器，它与台式电脑中 RAM 的作用基本相同，用来存储不同程序执行过程中所需要的数据。而 EEPROM 又被称为闪存，是一个更为复杂的 ROM（只读存储器），它是用来存储被执行程序的。EEPROM 是电擦除可编程只读存储器的缩写。

和任何数字系统一样，微控制器中存储器是由寄存器组成的，寄存器是存储器的基本构成单元。每个寄存器有一些位组成（通常是 8 位），每个位中可存储数据。在 8051 微控制器/单片机系列中大多数寄存器是 8 位寄存器，可以存储的数值范围从 0 到 255。图 3.21 显示了一个典型的 8 位寄存器，符号 D0 到 D7 表示寄存器的 8 个数据位。

正如你将看到的那样，89S52 的随机存储器包含 256 个寄存器，它们被分成两个主要部分：通用寄存器和特殊功能寄存器。GPR 表示通用寄存器，它可用来存储程序执行过程中的任何数据。SFR（特殊功能寄存器）是用来控制微控制器/单片机的操作及协作处理器来执行各种操作。例如，SFR 可以用来控制输入/输出线，检索通过台式电脑串行通信口传输的数据，或设置芯片内的计数器和定时器参数。

在存储器中，每个寄存器都有一个指定的地址，处理器可用该地址从指定的存储器区间中读写该寄存器内容。地址使用十六进制表示，因为对设计者来说这种符号简化了数字逻辑运算，00 代表第一个单元，FF 即 256 表示最后一个单元。

时钟概念

时钟是一个能产生指定频率的电脉冲的简单电路。这些脉冲将控制着微控制器/单片机内发生的所有事件的节奏，同时这些脉冲还将确保微控制器/单片机内各个部件之间同步。例如，如果 CPU 在等待 ALU（算术逻辑部件）的数学运算结果，根据特定的协议，CPU 将知道运算的结果在何时何地传送给 CPU，这两个部件的同步性是通过共享同一个时钟来实现的。

时钟还有一个很重要的任务：它使得微控制器/单片机可以实现计数。没有一个精确的时钟，就不可能建立一个实时系统，或其他依赖时间测量的元件。由此可推知，微控制器/单片机的定时精度取决于时钟的频率。

在 89S52 微控制器/单片机中，时钟可根据与 18、19 引脚相连的晶振来设定不同的值。

AT89S52 最大的工作频率是 33MHz。

第 15 单元 8051 指令系统

介绍

对微处理器的编程主要是按顺序给出指令，然后执行指令，从而完成某一特定任务。由于电子器件无法明白如“如果按下按钮—灯亮”此类语句的意思，那么就必须使用一些解码器能够认识的更为简单和精确定义的指令。所有的命令被通称为指令系统。与 8051 相兼容的单片机总共有 255 条指令，即程序编写可用到 255 种不同的命令。

首先，必须牢记大量特殊符号。这并不像看上去那么复杂。虽然许多指令被认为是不同的，但它们执行的却是相同的操作，这样真正不同的指令只有 111 条。例如：ADD A，R0，ADD A，R1 ... ADD A，R7 都是执行相同操作（将累加器和寄存器相加）的指令。但是由于有 8 个寄存器，因此每一条指令都是单独运算的。这样来看的话，所有指令一共才执行了 53 种操作（加，减，复制等）并且大多数在实际中很少使用，实际上只有 20～30 条简短的指令需要记住，这是可以记住的。

指令的类型

根据指令所执行的操作的不同，所有指令可分为以下几类：

- 算术运算类指令；
- 转移类指令；
- 数据传送类指令；
- 逻辑运算类指令；
- 位操作逻辑指令。

每条指令的第一部分叫做操作码，它指出了指令所执行的操作（复制、加、逻辑运算等）。操作码通常是所执行操作名称的简写。例如：

INC R1——意思：将 R1 加 1（寄存器 R1 增加 1）。

指令的另一部分叫做操作数，它是通过至少一个空格与操作码进行隔离并对指令中处理的数据进行定义。有些指令没有操作数，有些有一个，有些有两个或三个。如果指令中的操作数超过一个，那就用逗号将它们分开。例如：

RET——（从子程序中返回）——无操作数。

ADD A,R3——（将 R3 和累加器相加）——两个操作数。

CJNE A,#20，LOOP——（将累加器内容与 20 比较。如果它们不相等，那么跳转到指定的 loop。）——三个操作数。

下表中列出的一些简写的操作数的意思如下：

A——累加器。

Rn——Rn 是 RAM 中当前工作寄存器（R0-R7）中的一个。

Rx——RAM 中任意一个 8 位地址寄存器，它可以是一个通用寄存器或 SFR 寄存器（I/O 端口，控制寄存器等）。

@Ri——Ri 是当前工作寄存器中 R0 或 R1 寄存器。它包含寄存器。

Address——指令所指地址。

#X——8 位立即数（0～255）。

#X16——16 位立即数（0～65 535）。

adr16——16 位的目的地址。

adr11——11 位的目的地址。

rel——相对偏移量（在-128～127 之间）。

bit——所指定的位地址。

C——状态寄存器中的进位标志（程序状态寄存器）。

算术运算指令

这些指令将执行一些基本运算操作（加、减、除、乘等）。执行完后，结果将存储在第一个操作数中。例如：

ADD A,Rn——该指令将累加器中内容和寄存器 Rn（R0～R7）中的数据进行加运算。加完后，结果存储在累加器中。

SUBB A,Rx

描述：该指令执行减运算：累加器 A 减去 Rx 且进位位作为借位参与运算。如果低位从高位中减去，那么进位位置 1。由于是直接寻址，Rx 可以是特殊功能寄存器或地址在 0～7F 的通用寄存器。结果存储在累加器中。

DEC Rx

描述：该指令将寄存器 Rx 中的数减 1。由于它是直接寻址，Rx 必须是位于 RAM 中开始的 255 区域中。如果寄存器中的数是 0，那么结果将是 FFh。

转移指令

转移指令有两种：

无条件转移指令：当程序执行完该指令，程序将跳转到一个新的地址继续执行程序。例如：

ACALL adr11——调用子程序，该子程序必须位于程序寄存器 2KB 范围内。

RET——从子程序中返回。

条件转移指令：如果满足某些条件——执行跳转。否则，程序继续执行下条指令。例如：

```
JBC bit,rel
```

描述：这条指令首先检查 bit 位是否置 1。如果是，跳转到指定的地址并将 bit 位清零。否则顺序执行下条指令。这是一条短跳转指令，这就意味着地址所指的位置必须与程序的当前位置相近（与下一条指令的相对位置为-129～+127 之间）。

数据传送指令

这些指令将某一寄存器的内容传送到另一个中。内容被传送的寄存器保持不变。如果这些指令带有“x”的后缀，那么就是与外部存储器进行数据交换。例如：

MOU A,@Ri

描述：该指令将寄存器 RX 的内容传送到累加器中。寄存器 RX 的地址存储在工作寄存器 Ri 中（R0 或 R1）。该指令执行完后，结果存储在累加器中。寄存器 Rx 的内容不变。

XCH A,Rx

描述：该指令将累加器中的内容提出放入寄存器 RX 中。同时，寄存器 RX 中的内容被放入累加器。由于它是直接寻址，寄存器 RX 可以是一些特殊功能寄存器或地址位于 0～7Fh 之间的通用寄存器。

逻辑指令

该指令将两个寄存器相对应的位进行逻辑运算。该指令执行完后，结果存储在第一个操作数中。

ADD A,Rx

描述：该指令将累加器和寄存器 Rx 的内容相加。由于是直接寻址，寄存器 Rx 可以是一些特殊功能寄存器或地址位于 0～7Fh 之间的通用寄存器。结果被存储在累加器中。

ORL A,#X

描述：该指令将累加器的内容和立即数 X 进行逻辑或运算。逻辑运算的结果被存储在累加器中。

CLR A/C

描述：将累加器/进位位清零。

逻辑位操作指令

与逻辑指令相似，这些指令执行逻辑运算。差别在于，这些运算是在一个位之间执行。

ANL C,bit

描述：该指令在指定位和进位间执行逻辑与运算。

第 16 单元　现　场　总　线

现场总线是用于实时分布式控制的一类工业计算机网络协议的名称，目前采用的标准是 IEC 61158。

一个复杂的自动化工业系统——就拿工业生产线来说——通常需要一个有序的分层控制系统来使其运行。在这个分层体系中，顶层通常是一个人机界面（HMI），可以让操作者来监控或操作系统。通常通过使用实时性要求不高的通信系统（如以太网）将 HMI 连接到位于中间层的可编程控制器上。控制系统的底层是现场总线，它将 PLC 与传感器、执行装置、电动机、控制灯、开关、阀门及接触器之类的现场装置连接起来。

描述

现场总线是一种用于实时分布式控制的工业网络系统。它是工厂设备的一种连接方式。现场总线的网络结构可以是菊花链、星形、环形、分支形及树形拓扑结构。以前的计算机用 RS-232 进行连接（串行连接），这种连接方式只允许两个设备间进行通信。这就和目前使用的 4～20mA 通信方式一样，它要求每个设备在控制器层上都有自己的通信接点，而现场总线和目前的局域网一样，它在控制器层上只需要一个通信接点并且可以同时连接多个（100）模拟和数字接点。这就减少了所需电缆的长度及根数。此外，由于通过现场总线进行通信的设备需要一个微处理器，同一设备通常可提供多个接点。目前有些现场总线设备还支持 PID 等控制策略，从而不需控制器来处理。

发展史

尽管现场总线技术从 1988 年左右就产生，然而到 ISA S50.02 标准形成，花了许多年时间才形成这一国际性的标准。1999 年，IEC SC65C/WG6 标准委员会召开会议解决对国际电工委员会起草的现场总线标准的不同意见。这次会议产生了最初的 IEC 61158 标准，它有 8 种不同类型的协议，如下所示：

类型 1：现场总线基金会的 H1 总线；
类型 2：设备网络总线；
类型 3：过程现场总线；
类型 4：多主控制器主从式总线；
类型 5：高速以太网总线；
类型 6：SwiftNet 现场总线；
类型 7：工厂仪表总线；
类型 8：传感器/调节器总线系统。

这种“标准”最初是为欧洲市场开发的，不是面向普通用户的，并且实现了它的初衷——消除国家间的贸易限制。这一普及化任务就落到了支持各种总线标准的国际性组织身上。几乎在这“8 种主要标准”通过的同时，IEC 标准的研究工作停止了并且解散了委员会。一个新的 IEC 委员会 SC65C/MT-9 形成，它用超过 4000 页的 IEC 61158 来解决各种标准形式和实质上的冲突。上面的标准已经很完整了。在通常的 5 年修改周期中，新的协议如安全现场总线或基于以太网的实时现场总线，被纳入国际现场总线标准的定义。

最近加入及计划加入 IEC 61158 的协议包括但不限于以下几种：

类型 10：分散式现场设备技术；
类型 12：以太网控制自动化技术；
类型 13：实时工业以太网；
类型 16：sercos 总线（串行实时通信总线）。

目前基金会现场总线和 PROFIBUS 总线（过程现场总线）被广泛应用于过程控制领域，并都作出了大量改进。在 2006 年，南海壳牌石油（Nanhai petrochemical）以及中国上海赛科（SECCO）安装了最大的 FF（基金会现场总线）总线系统，每个系统可连接 15 000 个现场总线设备。

标准

现在并存的现场总线标准有很多种。其中使用最为广泛的有 AS-Interface 总线、can 总线、工业以太网、Interbus、现场操作网络、Modbus、过程现场总线 PROFIBUS、BITBUS 总线、CompuBus 总线和 SafetyBUS p 总线。

成本优势

实施现场总线的主要优点在于电缆的减少节省了成本的支出。在总线网络上实现通信的多个设备共享同一对电缆线，同时其快速的调试过程也节省了开支。

现在用户发现采用现场总线系统后，日常维护也变得简单了，而且过程控制系统的性能也大大被增强，从而带来运行成本的下降。

缺点

与 4～20mA 的模拟信号通信标准相比较，现场总线有以下缺点：

现场总线系统更复杂，因此使用者需要进行更多的训练或具有更高的技术；现场总线设备的价格较高；与用万用表来读和模拟 4～20mA 的模拟信号相比，现场总线的测试设备更为复杂。现场总线的通信速度要稍微慢点，其快慢由系统决定；根据现场总线标准的不同，设备制造商需提供不同型号的设备（如传感器、执行器）。这将增加设备成本，增加设备选择和应用的难度；未来将有一个或几个现场总线标准成为主流，其他的标准将被淘汰。这就提高了现场总线实施时的投资风险。

目前的发展状况

近几年产生了许多基于以太网的工业通信系统，它们大多都带有扩展的实时通信功能。从长远来看，它们具有取代传统现场总线的潜力。目前阻碍大多数以太网现场总线实施的问题在于总线无法给设备提供电源。大多数工业测量和控制设备需要由总线提供电能，而通过以太网来传送电能的技术还未发展成熟。

下面列出了部分新型的基于以太网的工业通信系统：EtherCAT 总线、ETHERNET/IP 总线、Ethernet Powerlink 总线、Industrial Ethernet 总线、PROFINET IO 总线、SafetyNET p 总线、SERCOS III 总线、TTEthernet 总线和 UARAN 总线。

市场

在过程控制系统中，市场被基金会现场总线和 PROFIBUS PA 主宰。这两种技术使用相同的物理层，但无法替换。作为一般的规则，在 PLC 监控系统的应用中一般采用 PROFIBUS 总线，而在由 DCS 监控系统的应用一般中采用基金会现场总线。PROFIBUS 技术由总部在德国卡尔斯鲁厄的 PROFIBUS 国际拥有，基金会现场总线技术由得克萨斯州的奥斯汀现场总线基金会所有。

第四章　传　感　器

第 17 单元　传 感 器 简 介

传感器是一种可以测量物理量并将被测量转化为观察者可读出或者仪器上能显示的信号

的装置。例如：水银温度计，它利用水银热胀冷缩的性质，将测得的温度显示在标有刻度的玻璃管上。热电偶将温度转化成可在伏特表上读出的电压值等。

传感器一般由敏感元件、传感元件及测量转换电路三部分组成。

传感器在我们日常生活中随处可见。例如，触摸式电梯按钮和触摸式电灯等，通过触摸底座就可以实现灯的开关。传感器还有无数的应用，其中大部分人们从来没有意识到，包括应用到汽车、机械、航空、医疗、工业及机器人等方面。技术的进步使越来越多的传感器能通过微机电系统技术制造成微型传感器。在多数情况下，微型传感器与大型传感器相比具有更高的速度和灵敏度。一个好的传感器应遵循以下三个原则：

1. 传感器对被测特性敏感。
2. 传感器对其他特性不敏感。
3. 传感器不能影响被测特性。

特性

传感器的灵敏度是指当被测量变化时，传感器输出变化的多少。例如，当温度变化 1°时，如果温度计中的水银改变 1cm，灵敏度就为 1cm/1°。测量微弱变化的传感器要求其具有很高的灵敏度。

理想的传感器都是线性的，即输出信号与被测量成线性比例关系。灵敏度被定义为输出信号与被测信号的比值。例如，如果传感器测量温度，输出为电压，其灵敏度是单位为 V/K 的常数，这个传感器是线性的，因为对于所有的测量值，比值为常数。

如果传感器是非理想的，就会存在几种偏差：

- 在实践中，灵敏度与给定值不同，这种偏差称为灵敏度误差，但传感器依然是线性的。
- 由于传感器输出信号的范围是有限的，当被测量超出这个极限时，输出信号将最终为最大值或最小值。所以将被测信号的最大值与最小值之间的范围定义为量程。
- 如果被测量为零时输出信号不为零，该传感器存在着误差，误差的定义是传感器输入为零时的输出值。
- 如果灵敏度在传感器的测量范围内不为常数，称为非线性。通常定义为在量程范围内传感器输出值与理想值之差，常用量程的百分比表示。
- 如果偏差是以时间为函数，被测量快速变化引起的，则称为动态误差。其性质经常以周期信号的频率为函数，用波特图表示灵敏度误差和相移之间的关系。
- 如果输出信号变化缓慢，与被测量无关，这称为漂移。
- 长期漂移通常表示传感器由于长时间使用性能慢慢下降。
- 变差是由于被测变量改变方向引起的，由于传感器响应在时间上存在一定的滞后，使得一个方向上的误差与另一方向上的误差不同。
- 如果信号是以数字形式检测的，采样频率的限制也会引起动态误差。
- 传感器对被测量以外的特性存在一定程度的敏感性。例如，大多数传感器都会受到周围环境温度的影响。
- 分辨率是指传感器在测量的量中所能检测到的最小变化。在数字显示中，最低位数字通常是变化的，表明量值的变化正好被分辨。

所有的误差可分为系统误差和随机误差。系统误差有时可以通过一些校准措施进行补偿。

而像噪声引起的随机误差可以通过滤波等信号处理技术进行减少，但以牺牲传感器的动态性能为代价。

第18单元　温度传感器概述

测温方法

测温方法可分为接触式、非接触式两类。

接触式测温法是指传感器与被测物直接接触，可用于测固体、液体或气体的温度。非接触式（红外）测温法是通过截取部分被测物发射的红外能量并检测其强度而测温。非接触式测温仪经常用来测固体和液体，而不能测气体，因为气体具有透明性。

接触式温度传感器的类型及比较

接触式传感器除了毛细管/球管温度计和双金属温度计之外，还有利用电压信号或电阻信号测温的。

电压信号

热电偶可以产生不同的热电势信号，不同金属合金做成的热电偶的两端可以产生与温度对应的热电势。

电阻信号

电阻式温度检测器能产生不同的电阻值，分为两种类型：

- 电阻丝绕制的热电阻；
- 热敏电阻（热敏晶体管）。

热电阻工作时，能产生与温度对应的电阻值。热电阻（通常是铂）有正的温度系数，温度升高，阻值增大。热敏电阻则有负的温度系数，温度升高，阻值减小。这三种接触式测温计（热电阻、热敏电阻、热电偶）在应用场合、所需响应时间及精度方面各有优缺点。掌握它们的优点有助于选出最合适的接触型传感器类型。

热电偶的优点：

- 测高温：贵重金属热电偶测温可达1700℃（3100℉）。
- 坚固耐用：热电偶固有的简单结构使得它具有良好的抗震性。
- 尺寸小/响应速度快：热电偶裸露的或接地的端使其对温度的变化几乎会立即作出响应。

热电阻的优点

- 测温范围广：Watlow生产的铂电阻测温范围为-200～650℃（-328～1200℉）。
- 输出信号大：热电阻的压降远比热电偶的输出的电压信号大。
- 线性度：与热电偶和多数热敏电阻相比，铂电阻和铜电阻的线性度更好。
- 配线成本：与热电偶不同，热电阻仅使用普通铜导线作延长导线，并且不需要冷端温度补偿。
- 测温区域：尽管经常需要点测，但它可能会带来误差。用热电阻可测量多个点，取其平均值来提高测量准确度。

热敏电阻优点：

由于热敏电阻的性能和成本不同，不能对其优缺点一概而论，但共有的优点如下：

- 成本低：多数普通热敏电阻比热电阻便宜的多，装有保护套的则价格差别不大。
- 电阻值高：基极阻值可能高达几千欧，忽略导线的阻值时，对于同样的测量电流，热敏电阻的信号改变比热电阻大得多。
- 测温点：球状热敏电阻由于只有针头大小，可用于点测量。

接触式传感器总结：

- 热电偶最适合测高温或环境要求使用微小传感器等极端的环境。
- 热电阻最适合温度变化范围大的工业环境，特别是控制要求稳定性高的环境。
- 热敏电阻最适合成本要求低，温度变化范围不大的环境。

非接触式传感器

非接触式（红外线）传感器截取被测物发射的红外线能量，并将其转化为电压信号。这类传感器的结构特点是用透镜把辐射的红外线能量聚集到热电堆。热电堆产生的电压信号发送到电子装置进行放大和调节，继而以电压或电流信号继续传送。一般情况下，非接触式温度传感器的反应和响应速度比接触式快。

非接触式传感器的优点

选用非接触式温度传感器的理由：

- 直接接触会损坏或污染传感器。
- 被测物移动。
- 生产过程中物理量测量需要更快的响应速度。

接触式和非接触式比较：

接触式温度传感器

优点

- 相对坚固耐用；
- 经济；
- 测温范围广；
- 相对精度高；
- 应用简单。

缺点

- 需要直接接触，可能损坏、污染；
- 可造成活动部件（滑环）磨损；
- 相比非接触式温度计，响应速度慢。

非接触式温度传感器

优点

- 相对坚固耐用；
- 可远离热源安装；
- 更适合测移动物体；

- 响应速度快（微秒级，而接触式为秒级）；
- 能测不规则形状的物体温度；
- 不会损毁、损坏或污染。

缺点

- 不能测气体温度；
- 热辐射率变化；
- 受限环境温度；
- 显示的温度受环境条件（粉尘、烟雾等）影响。

第19单元 霍尔传感器

介绍

霍尔效应被人们了解已有一百多年了，但真正大量的使用只有三十来年。第一次实际应用是在20世纪50年代用作微波功率传感器。随着半导体的大规模生产，把霍尔效应用在大量的产品中变得可行。1968年引入了利用霍尔效应制造的第一个固态键盘，微型开关传感与控制掀起了键盘工业的革命。霍尔传感元件及其相关的电子器件首次与单个集成电路组合。如今，霍尔效应器件已被用在许多产品中，从计算机到缝纫机、汽车到飞机、机床到医疗器械。

霍尔效应

霍尔传感器是用来测量铁类物质运动的传感器，霍尔效应是众所周知的现象：当导体或半导体中的电流垂直流过磁场时，产生一个既垂直于磁场又垂直于电流的电压，该电压与电流与磁场的乘积成正比。霍尔电压存在于放置在磁场中导体的端面之间。

霍尔效应是由于电流在导体中的流动而产生的。在一个磁场中，当该磁场与电荷移动的方向不平行时，移动的电荷受到一个力，这个力称为洛仑兹力。当磁场不存在时，电荷会沿着一个近似直线的方向流动。然而，在一个正交的磁场中，电荷的路径将发生弯曲，以至于移动的电荷在导体表面累积。导体的另一表面会产生等量但是极性相反的电荷聚集，形成霍尔电场。当电场力等于洛仑磁力时，就产生了稳定的霍尔电压。

纯金属中只有一种类型的载流子（电子），霍尔电压 U_H 为

$$U_H=K_H IB/d$$

式中，I 为流过金属板的电流；B 为磁感应强度；d 为金属板的厚度；K_H 为霍尔系数。

从上式可以看出，霍尔电压与激励电流和磁感应强度成比例关系。

简单的霍尔传感器

霍尔元件是简单的磁场传感器。它需要经过信号处理使输出稳定才能大量应用。所需的信号处理器件是放大级和温度补偿。如果电源不稳定，还需要稳压。图4.3是一个简单的霍尔传感器，当没有磁场时，霍尔电压为零。但每个输出端如果对地测量的话，电压不为零，该电压为共模电压，每个输出端的共模电压相同，为零的是电位差。图4.3所示的放大器是差动放大器，只用来放大电位差——霍尔电压。在高斯磁场中的霍尔电压是一个约30μV的低电平信号，所以需要一个噪声低、阻抗高、增益合适的放大器。具有这些特点的差动放大

器运用标准双极晶体管技术，可以与霍尔元件集成。而且温度补偿也容易集成。从式（4-1）可以看出，霍尔电压是输入电流的函数。图 4.3 中稳压器的作用是保持电流恒定，传感器的输出仅反应磁场强度。许多系统都带有稳压电源，所以一些霍尔传感器不带内置稳压器。

霍尔传感器是个多层结构，是由一个薄的半导体材料层沉积在一个半导体基底上构成，并且两层是彼此电绝缘的。

根据应用不同，霍尔电压可通过仪器放大器（直流励磁电流）或锁相放大器（交流励磁电流）测得。霍尔传感器在商业上应用范围很广，可用于从直流到 100kHz 的磁场强度的测量，分辨率大约为 10μT。

霍尔传感器的应用

霍尔传感器的带宽和灵敏度高使它得到了广泛的应用。

霍尔传感器在很多领域得到了应用，如汽车、医疗、电力电子、计算机传感器、变送器、材料品质鉴定及功率表等。我们熟悉的各种传感设备如位置传感器、电流传感器、角度传感器和速度传感器等都是利用了霍尔效应。由于可以检测无刷电动机的转子，以及可实现运动机械元件的非接触检测，霍尔装置在工业上的应用越来越普及。霍尔电流传感器在许多方面优于传统的电流互感器。

第 20 单元　超 声 波 传 感 器

超声波传感器可以把接收到的超声波能量转换为电信号输出。超声波传感器利用声波可以对各种类型的目标进行非接触、无磨损的检测。目标是透明的还是有色的、金属的还是非金属的、是固态还是液体或粉末都不重要。周围的环境如喷雾、灰尘或下雨对它几乎没有影响。

人耳所能听到的频率范围大概为 20～20 000Hz。超声波是超过人耳所能听到的频率的声波，即 20kHz 以上。超声波测距仪一般所用的超声波频率是人耳所听不到的。这些高频本身波长较短，这使得其具有比声频更高的定位精度，任何频率超过 20kHz 的都可以认为是超声波。

超声波传感器产生超声波信号。这些信号经传输介质传播后，再用同一个传感器检测返回信号。在多数应用中，传输介质为空气，通过采用像晶体或陶瓷聚合物这样的压电材料，传感器可产生超声波振动。

工作模式

超声波有透射型和反射型两种基本的工作类型。在透射型时，一个传感器发射声波，安装在发射器对面的另一个接收声波。它们永远“倾听”对方的声音。当超声波被发射器和接收器间的物体阻挡时，传感器产生一个开关信号。

在反射型模式下，同一个传感器发射声波并接收由目标反射回的声波。换句话说，传感器通过接收部分反射回的声波检测到前方的目标物体。超声波传感器主要以反射模式工作。

由于超声波传感器要正常运行取决于反射波，所以目标物体的形状、材质、温度以及位置等都很重要。这些都要仔细选择以保证接收到最强的回波。在使用超声波传感器时，必须考虑目标的某些特性，如目标形状、材质、温度以及位置。一些像织物或海绵乳胶类的柔软物体很难用反射超声波技术检测，因为其对声音不反射。

应用

超声波传感器一般用于检测和识别固态物体、流量测量（图 4.10），检测出物体间可能发生的要避免的碰撞，房屋监测、形状测量及工件的定位、物位测量都可通过测量声音的吸收完成（图 4.11）。超声波传感器还用于近程或远程测量。这些设备一般会对把声音反射给传感器的目标发射一个短超声波脉冲。

系统测量回波返回传感器的时间，利用介质中的声速可计算出距离。距离可以用下面的公式表示：

$$Length=ct$$

式中，c 为介质中的声速；t 为往返行程时间。

传感器在量程范围内检测像压力、温度、位置、速度这样的参数。在自动化工业应用中，传感器有很多用途。传感器可用来检测物体是否存在，检测距离或检测物体到传感器的近程，也可以用于过程控制。超声波传感器可以对远距离检测提供更高效、更有效的方法。超声波传感器被广泛地用于生产和包装的过程控制，包括集装箱有无检测、箱内容量检测、物位检测、集装箱定位检测、集装箱计数运算、物料网络控制、受损/安全密封检测、表面覆层检测。

超声波传感器在各个领域都取得了重要地位，包括医疗、无损检测、过程监控、地理物理学和声纳监测等。超声波传感器还可以进行体内、体外血流量测量。

第 21 单元　光 电 传 感 器

介绍

光电传感器是一种对照在其上面的光强度变化作出响应的器件。光敏元件的物理性质使其根据光强度的不同变化电信号。到达接收器上的光强度变化程度取决于被检测的目标是否存在。产生的电信号相互精细，可触发末级放大部分，进而驱动外负载。光电传感器已成为自动化技术及我们日常生活中很重要的一部分。它广泛应用于许多工业生产中，提供精确的不需要直接接触的物体检测。它们还可以用于绝大多数类型物体的非接触检测、定位、分类及计数。

基本构成

光电传感器一般包括三部分。

光源

发光二极管是一种当有电流通过时会发光的固态半导体器件。发光二极管能发出特定波长或颜色的光。红外光，可见的红光、绿光、蓝光 LED 作为光源（发射器）应用于大多数光电传感器中。红外 LED 用在扩展检测范围时，需要最大量光输出的传感器中。

光检测器

光检测器是检测光源的器件。根据要检测的光强度，光电二极管或光电晶体管被广泛使用。半导体光电二极管和雪崩光电二极管是光电传感器中最合适的检测器。

透镜

光源发射光，光检测器在很宽的区域内对光很敏感。将透镜与光源和检测器一起使用可使这个区域变窄。所以，透镜可用来增加光电传感器的检测距离。

特点

光电传感器对周围光线的干扰非常不敏感，有没有光缆都可以使用。它们在选定的模式下具有高开关速度和可选的时间延迟。这些传感器能够在高温环境下使用，而且可以检测到远达 25m 的物体。

光电传感器的类型

根据检测模式的不同，光电传感器可分为以下三类：反射型光束传感器、透射式光束传感器、回归反射式光电传感器。

反射型光束传感器

这种传感器由装在一起的发射器和接收器组成。发射器发出红外光，光通过要对准的物体反射到接收器上。使用这类传感器时，记住物体的颜色非常重要，浅色对应的距离最远，反之亦然。对于发光物体，物体表面的影响比颜色更重要。这些传感器尤其可用于位置检测和非金属物体的计数。它也可以用作标签、物位、高度的感应，以及塑料薄膜的检测和纸张或金属薄板的边缘检测。

透射型光束传感器

这类传感器由光发射器和光接收器两个器件组成，它们以相对的方式分开放置。发冷光的砷化镓铝二极管集成在发射器中发射出人眼看不到的红外光脉冲。发射器对面的接收器接收光线。当光线受到被检测物的阻挡时，检测就实现了。透射式光束传感器被用于检测半透明物体，比如玻璃/塑料瓶检测、纸张破损和门的开关等检测。

回归反射型光电传感器

回归反射式光电传感器包含了一套装置和一个反射器。这套装置包括发射器和接收器。发射器发出的光线经反射器反射到接收器。当光线被阻挡时产生感应信号。当由于空间限制安装透射型传感器比较困难的时候可以使用这类传感器。此外，简单的布线就使其适用于尺寸较大的物体的检测。因此，这类传感器可用于开卷机的闭环控制以及纸张和金属薄片的边缘检测等。

多数回归反射对象都是由许多小的三面直角棱镜组成，每个棱镜有三个相互垂直的表面。当光束射入棱镜，垂直的表面反射回光束，与入射光束平行。通过这种方式，目标将光束反射到光源。一个好的回归反射器可以反射大约 3000 次，其重量和一张白纸一样轻。

光电传感器的应用

光电传感器应用于食品加工、运输、材料处理以及包装等工业中。它还可对传输带上某点通过的物体进行计数。每当有物体通过光源和检测器之间时，光束被阻挡，就给出一个脉冲表示物体出现。因此，通过计算脉冲的个数就可以得知传输带上这点通过的物体数目。光电传感器因其效率高、体积小、重量轻以及在各种环境下的坚固性和有效性被广泛应用于控制工业中。

第五章 自动控制系统

第22单元 控制系统介绍

概述

控制理论是：

- 用来处理影响动态系统特性的理论；
- 一个跨学科的子科学，它产生于工程学和数学中，并逐渐被其他社会科学所利用，如心理学，社会学和犯罪学。

举个例子

考虑汽车的速度控制系统，通过该装置使汽车速度恒定，与驾驶员设定的期望或参考速度相等。在这种情况下，控制系统是汽车，系统输出是汽车速度，控制变量是发动机油门位置，其影响发动机的扭矩输出。

操作速度控制系统的一个简单方法是驾驶员在驾驶时，锁定住油门位置。然而，在丘陵地区，车辆上坡时速度变慢，下坡时速度加快。事实上，实际参数值与设计时的假定值会有所不同，从而导致输出速度形成了相对误差，包括汽车的确切重量、风的阻力以及轮胎气压。这种类型的控制器称为开环控制器，因为系统输出和实际情况没有直接的联系，也就是说，系统没有也无法补偿不可预知的影响。

闭环控制系统中，传感器监视着系统的输出，并把输出数据送到计算机中，计算机不断地调整控制输入，这个对保证控制误差达到最小值来讲很有必要。反映系统实际工作状态的反馈信息允许控制器动态补偿系统受到的干扰，如地面坡度的改变或风速。一个理想的反馈控制系统能克服所有的误差，有效地减轻在系统运行过程中可能会造成的影响，使系统的输出完全满足使用者的意愿。

历史

虽然各种类型的控制系统可以追溯到古代，但是对该领域比较正式的分析开始于物理学家 James Clerk Maxwell 对离心调速器的动态分析，其在 1868 年任州长，他描述和分析了“摆动”现象，在该过程中，系统的滞后可能会导致系统过度补偿和不稳定。这引起了一系列感兴趣的研究课题，在此期间，Maxwell 的同学 Edward John Routh 解出了广义线性系统范围内 Maxwell 问题的结果。另外，在 1877 年 Adolf Hurwitz 利用微分方程分析了系统的稳定性，该结论被称为 Routh-Hurwitz 定理。

动态控制方面一个著名的应用是载人飞行。Wright 兄弟在 1903 年 12 月 17 号成功地进行了首次试飞，这次飞行的显著特征是其具有飞行相当长的一段时间，飞机的可控性对安全飞行具有必要性。

到第二次世界大战，控制理论已经成为消防控制系统、导航系统及电子学的重要组成部分。太空行走也取决于准确的航天器控制。然而，控制理论在如经济学等领域中的运用也越来越多。

与系统及控制相关的人

当今和历史上许多人在控制理论发展方面作出了重大贡献，例如包括：

稳定性理论的产生标志是 Alexander Lyapunov（1857—1918）在 19 世纪 90 年代的研究。

Harold S. Black（1898—1983）于 1927 年提出了负反馈放大器的概念，并于 20 世纪 30 年代成功地设计出稳定的负反馈放大器。

Harry Nyquist（1889—1976）在 20 世纪 30 年代提出了适用于反馈系统的 Nyquist 稳定性判据。

Richard Bellman（1920—1984）在 20 世纪 40 年代提出了动态规划理论。

Norbert Wiener（1894—1964）在 20 世纪 40 年代与人合作设计出了 Wiener-Kolmogorov 滤波器，并创造出控制论这一专业术语。

John R. Ragazzini（1912—1988）在 20 世纪 50 年代引入了数字化控制和 Z 变换。

经典控制理论

为了避免开环控制器产生的问题，控制理论中引入了反馈。闭环控制器通过反馈来控制动态系统的状态或输出。反馈的名称来源于系统中信号的传输路径：过程输入使过程产生了输出，输出由传感器测量出并经控制器处理，结果被送到输入端，组成了闭环。

闭环控制器与开环相比，有如下一些优点：

- 抗干扰性。
- 当模型结构与实际不完全匹配以及模型参数不准确导致模型不确定时，也能保证控制效果。
- 使不稳定过程变的稳定。
- 降低了对参数变化的敏感度。
- 改善跟踪参考输入的效果。

闭环控制与开环控制在一些系统中同时使用。在这些系统中，开环控制被称为前馈，致力于进一步改善系统跟踪参考输入的能力。

PID 控制器就是一种普遍使用在闭环系统中的控制器。

闭环传递函数

系统输出 $y(t)$通过传感器 F 反馈到参考输入值 $r(t)$，然后控制器 C 根据参考值与系统输出的偏差 e 来改变控制系统 P 的输入 u（图 5.1），这种类型的控制器称为闭环或反馈控制器。

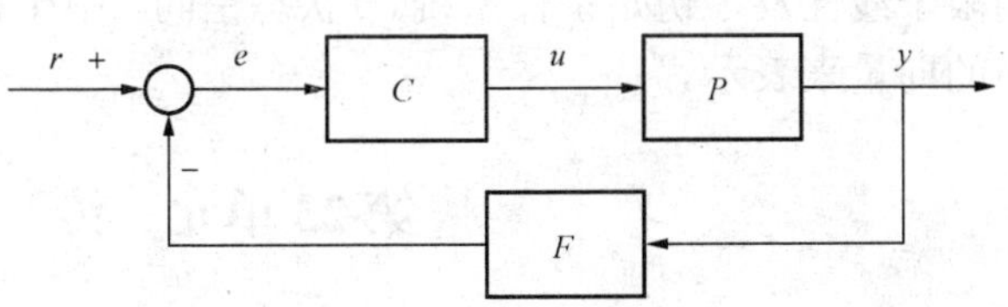

图 5.1 闭环控制系统

该系统被称为单输入单输出控制系统，有多个输入/输出的即多输入多输出系统也很普遍。在那样的控制系统中，用向量代替简单的标量来表示变量，对一些离散参数系统，向量可以是无限维。

如果我们假定控制器 C，对象 P，传感器 F 均为线性和时不变量，上述系统可利用针对变量的拉普拉斯变换来分析，现给出如下关系：

$$Y(s)=P(s)U(s)$$
$$U(s)=C(s)E(s)$$
$$E(s)=R(s)-F(s)Y(s)$$

用 $R(s)$表示 $Y(s)$：

$$Y(s)=\left[\frac{P(s)C(s)}{1+F(s)P(s)C(s)}\right]R(s)=H(s)R(s)$$

式子 $H(s)=\dfrac{P(s)C(s)}{1+F(s)P(s)C(s)}$ 被称为系统闭环传递函数，分子是从 r 到 y 的前向增益，分母是 1 加上反馈环的增益，所以称为闭环增益。如果 $|P(s)C(s)|>>1$，即每个 s 因子的系数比较大，并且如果 $|F(s)|=1$，那么 $Y(s)$近似与 $R(s)$相等，这就意味着只要设定参考值就可以控制输出值。

PID 控制器

PID 控制器可能是使用最广泛和最简单的反馈控制器。PID 表示比例—积分—微分，表示三个环节对误差信号的作用，产生控制信号。如果 $u(t)$是传送给系统的控制信号，$y(t)$是测量得到的系统输出，$r(t)$是理想的输出，跟踪误差 $e(t)=r(t)-y(t)$，PID 控制器的一般表达式为

$$u(t)=K_{\mathrm{P}}e(t)+K_{\mathrm{I}}\int e(t)\mathrm{d}t+K_{\mathrm{D}}\frac{\mathrm{d}}{\mathrm{d}t}e(t)$$

理想的闭环系统动态过程是通过调整三个参数 K_{P}、K_{I} 和 K_{D} 来获得，常常通过反复的"微调"，并没有依据对象模型的具体方法。比例环节保证了系统的稳定性，积分环节可以克服阶跃干扰的影响，微分环节克服了系统响应超调过高的影响。众所周知，PID 控制器能够构建成一流的控制系统，然而，对一些更加复杂的系统，如多输入多输出系统，它们还不适用。

现代控制理论

与经典控制理论中的频域分析法相比，现代控制理论采用时域状态空间来表示系统。输入、输出和状态变量用一阶微分方程联立，用它们来表示系统实际的数学模型。为了抽象地表示输入、输出及状态，用向量来表示变量，微分和差分方程写成矩阵形式。状态空间表示法提供了一个方便和紧凑的方法来对多输入和多输出系统进行建模和分析。已知输入和输出，我们可以不必用 Laplace 变换来表征系统的信息。不同于频域分析法，状态空间表示法并不局限于线性及零初始条件系统。"状态空间"中坐标轴表示状态变量。系统的状态可通过空间中的向量来表示。

第 23 单元　传　递　函　数

概述

传递函数是描述系统输入和输出在空间或时间频率方面关系的数学表达式。例如对于光学成像设备，传递函数是表示点扩散函数的傅里叶变换，也即是在视觉范围内某个点产生的强度分布。

解释

传递函数通常用来分析单输入单输出电子滤波器，例如，其主要应用在信号处理、通信理论和控制理论中。此术语往往是专门应用于线性时不变系统，本文同样也是如此。大多数实时系统具有非线性输入/输出的特点，但许多系统在标定参数范围内运行时，其特性近似线性的，这时 LTI 系统理论是可以运用到输入/输出的特性分析中。

用最简单的形式表示时间上连续的信号，输入 $x(t)$和输出 $y(t)$，其传递函数是输入和输出拉普拉斯变换 $X(s)$、$Y(s)$的线性映射：

$$Y(s)=H(s)X(s)$$

或者

$$H(s)=\frac{Y(s)}{X(s)}=\frac{L\{y(t)\}}{L\{x(t)\}}$$

其中，$H(s)$表示线性时不变系统的传递函数。

在离散系统中，函数类似地写成 $H(z)=\frac{Y(z)}{X(z)}$，通常表示脉冲传递函数。

由微分方程直接推导

考虑一恒系数的非齐次线性微分方程：

$$L[u]=\frac{\mathrm{d}^n u}{\mathrm{d}t^n}+a_1\frac{\mathrm{d}^{n-1}u}{\mathrm{d}t^{n-1}}+\cdots+a_{n-1}\frac{\mathrm{d}^n u}{\mathrm{d}t^n}+a_n\frac{\mathrm{d}^n u}{\mathrm{d}t^n}=r(t)$$

当 u 和 r 是关于 t 的平滑函数，L 是定义在相关函数范围中的算子，通过其将 u 变换成 r。使用该类型方程，通过强迫函数 r 可以限制输出函数 u。写成算式 $F[r]=u$ 形式的传递函数是 L 的右逆元，因为 $L[F[r]]=r$。

齐次方程 $L[u]=0$ 可以通过令 $\mathrm{u}=\mathrm{e}^{\lambda t}$ 解出。通过置换得到特征多项式

$$p_L(\lambda)=\lambda^n+a_1\lambda^{n-1}+\cdots+a_{n-1}\lambda^n+a_n$$

如果输入函数 r 同样可以表示成 $r(t)=\mathrm{e}^{st}$ 的形式，那么可以很容易解出该非齐次方程。在这种情况下，通过令 $u=H(s)\mathrm{e}^{st}$，则当且仅当 $H(s)=\frac{1}{p_L(s)}, p_L(s)\neq 0$ 时有 $L[H(s)\mathrm{e}^{st}]=\mathrm{e}^{st}$。

将其看成传递函数的定义需要仔细区分复数与实数之间的区别，传统上 abs$H(s)$表示增益，而–arctan $H(s)$表示相位滞后值。

信号处理

对于某一线性时不变系统，令 $x(t)$表示输入，$y(t)$表示输出，$x(t)$、$y(t)$的拉普拉斯变换为

$$X(s)=L\{x(t)\}=\int_{-\infty}^{\infty}x(t)\mathrm{e}^{-st}\mathrm{d}t$$

$$Y(s)=L\{y(t)\}=\int_{-\infty}^{\infty}y(t)\mathrm{e}^{-st}\mathrm{d}t$$

系统输出通过输入和传递函数 $H(s)$相乘得出

$$Y(s)=H(s)X(s)$$

传递函数因此为

$$H(s)=\frac{Y(s)}{X(s)}$$

特别是，如果一个复杂的含有正弦分量的复杂谐波信号，其振幅为$|X|$，角频率为ω，相位为 arg (X)，有

$$x(t)=Xe^{j\omega t}=|X|e^{j(\omega t+\arg X)}$$

其中 $X=|X|e^{j\arg X}$ 是线性时不变系统的输入，那么与其相对应的输出部分是 $y(t)=Ye^{j\omega t}=|Y|e^{j(\omega t+\arg Y)}$，即 $Y=|Y|e^{j\arg Y}$。

注意到线性非时变系统中，输入频率ω不变，改变的仅仅是正弦曲线的幅值和相角。频率响应 $H(j\omega)$表示对应每个频率ω增益方面的变化。

$$G(\omega)=\frac{|Y|}{|X|}=|H(j\omega)|$$

相角变化

$$\phi(\omega)=\arg Y-\arg X=\arg[H(j\omega)x]$$

相位延迟为

$$T_{\phi}(\omega)=-\frac{\phi(\omega)}{\omega}$$

群延迟通过计算角频率ω对应的相位移的导数得到。

$$T_{g}(\omega)=-\frac{d\phi(\omega)}{d\omega}$$

也可以通过傅里叶变换来表示传递函数，傅里叶变换是 $s=j\omega$时的双边拉普拉斯变换的一个特例。

常用传递函数系列

当可以用一个或另一个传递函数描述线性非时变系统时，就存在着某种被普遍使用的特殊函数“系列”，通过使用一些典型无限脉冲响应滤波器来实现这些特殊传递函数。

控制工程

在控制工程和控制理论中，传递函数起源于拉普拉氏变换。

经典控制工程中，传递函数是主要的使用工具。然而，已经证明其很难广泛应用于多输入多输出系统的分析中，对于多输入多输出系统，其很大程度上被状态空间法取代。尽管如此，任意线性系统均可求出转移矩阵，为了分析其动态及其它特性，转移矩阵中每一个元素都表示某个输入变量和输出变量的传递函数。

第 24 单元 波 德 图

波德图，以 Hendrik Wade Bode 的名字命名，通常是波德幅值图和相位图的组合。

波德幅值图是不同频率对应的对数幅值图，在对数—频率坐标轴上表示，表示线性非时变系统的传递函数或频率响应。

波德图的幅值轴的大小通常用分贝表示，即是幅值增益对数的 20 倍。通过幅值增益取对数，波德图将幅值相乘变成一个简单的距离相加，因为

$$\log ab = \log a + \log b$$

波德相位图是表示不同频率所对应相位的图，同样绘制在一张对数—频率坐标轴上，通常与幅值图协同使用，用来估计某一频率所对应的相位移。例如某一信号 $A\sin(\omega t)$的幅值变小，那么其相位也相应发生变化。如果幅值缩小了 x 倍而相角滞后Φ，则系统输出信号为$(A/x)\sin(t\omega-\Phi)$，相位移一般是关于频率的函数。

相位可以将图形上的对应值直接相加，事实上，如果将相位看成是复数增益中复对数的虚部，那么可以直接经过数学计算得出。

幅值和相位波德图的变化常相互影响——系统幅值响应的变化可能会改变相位特性，反之亦然。对于最小相位系统，利用 Hilbert 变换，相位和幅值特性可相互转换。

如果传递函数是含有实数极点和零点的有理函数，那么波德图可以被近似为一条直线。这种渐近逼近方法被称为直线波特图或未修正波特图，通过遵循一些简单规则，这种图可以手动绘出，因此该方法是有效的。一些简单图甚至不需要绘制就可以直接预测出。

该近似法可以对每一个截止频率对应的值进行进一步修正，得到的图被称为波德修正图。

手工绘制波德图法则

波德图绘制的前提是可以把函数的对数形式 $f(x) = A\prod(x+c_n)^{a_n}$ 看成是其极点和零点对数之和：$\log f(x) = \log A + \sum a_n \log(x+c_n)$ 。

绘制相位图就是利用该思想，绘制幅值图间接利用该思想，但是每个极点或零点对应幅值的对数总是始于零，只是产生一个渐进的变化，因此该方法可以简化。

直线波德幅值图

通过使用公式 $20\log_{10}X$ 计算出幅值分贝值。传递函数的形式为

$$H(s) = A\prod\frac{(s+x_n)^{a_n}}{(s+y_n)^{b_n}}$$

式中，x_n 和 y_n 为常值；$s=\mathrm{j}\omega$；a_n，$b_n>0$；H 为传递函数。

- 在$\omega=x_n$ 对应的每个 s 值处，直线斜率增加 $20a_n$ dB/dec（$20a_n$ 分贝每十倍频程）；
- 在$\omega=y_n$ 对应的每个 s 值处，直线斜率减小 $20b_n$ dB/dec（$20b_n$ 分贝每十倍频程）；
- 波德图上的初值取决于取值范围。通过将频率ω的初值代到函数中，计算得到 $H(\mathrm{j}\omega)$，从而确定初始点。

- 初始值对应的函数斜率取决于小于初值的零极点数目和阶次，斜率可以根据第 1、2 两条规则确定。

许多情况下，不能简化的 2 次多项式 ax^2+bx+c 被近似为 $\left(\sqrt{a}x+\sqrt{c}\right)^2$。

注意到当ω与某一 x_n 或 y_n 相等时，零点和极点就产生了。这是因为所涉及的函数是计算 $H(\mathrm{j}\omega)$，因为它为一复函数$|H(\mathrm{j}\omega)|=\sqrt{H \bullet H^*}$，因此在任何存在零点或极点的位置，该点都与关系式（s+x_n）有关，对应的幅值大小为$\sqrt{(x_n+\mathrm{j}\omega)\bullet(x_n-\mathrm{j}\omega)}=\sqrt{x_n^2+\omega^2}$。

修正幅值图

修正直线幅值图：

- 在每个零点处，幅值提高 $3a_n$ 分贝。
- 在每个极点处，幅值减少 $3b_n$ 分贝。
- 用一条平滑的曲线连接这些点，并把直线作为渐进线。

我们注意到该修正方法并不包含如何处理 x_n 和 y_n 值比较复杂的情况。对于那些不能简化的多项式，最好的办法是计算出传递函数在极点和零点与该多项式相对应的幅值，并且在渐进线的上方或下方绘出极点或零点对应的实际幅值。

直线相位图

对于如上述形式一样的传递函数

$$H(s)=A\prod\frac{(s+x_n)^{a_n}}{(s+y_n)^{b_n}}$$

绘制图形的主要思想是，先单独绘出每个极点和零点对应的图，然后把它们相加。准确的相位图通过计算$-\arctan(\mathrm{Im}[H(s)]/\mathrm{Re}[H(s)])$得到。

对于每个极点和零点，绘制相位图规则：

- 如果 A 为正数，初始角度为 0°；
- 如果 A 为负数，初始角度为 180°；
- 在每个$\omega=x_n$处，斜率增加 $45a_n$ dB/dec，起始点为$\omega=x_n$的十分之一；
- 在每个$\omega=y_n$处，斜率减小 $45a_n$ dB/dec，起始点为$\omega=y_n$的十分之一；
- “不稳定”的极点和零点特性相反；
- 当相位变化 $90a_n$ 度或者 $90b_n$ 度时，线段的斜率又变为 0；
- 当绘制出每个零点或极点的线段后，将这些线段组合在一起，得到最终的相位图，也就是说，最终的相位图是先前每条相位图的叠加。

幅值图

上述传递函数的幅值通过增益表达式 A_v 计算得到：

$$A_v\mathrm{dB}=20\log|H(\mathrm{j}\omega)|=20\log\frac{1}{\left|1+\mathrm{j}\dfrac{\omega}{\omega_c}\right|}=-20\log\left|1+\mathrm{j}\frac{\omega}{\omega_c}\right|=-10\log\left[1+\frac{\omega^2}{\omega_c^2}\right]$$

当在对数坐标系中描绘的不同输入频率ω对应的幅值曲线可以被近似成两条直线，它构成了传递函数的渐进幅值波特图。

- 对于小于ω_c的角频率，幅值图是一水平直线，对应的幅值为 0 分贝，因为在低频区，$\dfrac{\omega}{\omega_c}$很小，可以被忽略，使得幅值分贝值近似为 0。
- 对于大于ω_c的角频率，幅值图是斜率为-20dB/dec 的直线，因为在高频区，$\dfrac{\omega}{\omega_c}$很大，分贝增益的表达式可以被简化为$-20\log\dfrac{\omega}{\omega_c}$，其是一条斜率为-20dB/dec 的直线。

这两条直线在转折频率处相交。可以看出，远低于转角频率时，图形没有衰减，与单位穿带增益相一致，也就是滤波器的输出等于输入；而大于转角频率时，产生衰减，频率越高，衰减越多。

相位图

相位图的获取是通过$\varphi = -\arctan\dfrac{\omega}{\omega_c}$公式绘制所给传递函数对应不同$\omega$的相角而得到，其中$\omega$和$\omega_c$分别指输入和转折频率。如果输入频率比转折频率低得多，$\dfrac{\omega}{\omega_c}$的比值很小，因此相角接近与零。随着比值的增大，相角的绝对值增大，当$\omega=\omega_c$时，相角为-45°。随着比值增大到输入频率比转折频率大的多，相角值无限接近于-90°。相位图的频率坐标成对数比例的。

标准图

幅值和相位图的水平频率轴可以用标准化的频率比值$\dfrac{\omega}{\omega_c}$来替代。在这种情况下得到是标准化的图，因为所有的输入频率用转折频率ω_c的倍数来表示，频率单位因此不再使用。

第 25 单元　过 程 控 制 系 统

过程控制系统

自动过程控制系统是指将被控量为温度、压力、流量、成分等类型的过程变量保持在需要的运行值的系统。实际过程是动态的。变化总是会出现，此时如果不采取相应的措施，那些与安全、产品质量和生产率有关的重要变量就不能满足设计要求。

为了说明问题，让我们来看一下热交换器。流体在这个过程中被过热蒸汽加热，如图 5.2 所示。

这一装置的主要目的是将流体由入口温度 $T_i(t)$加热到某一期望的出口温度 $T(t)$，如前所述，加热介质是过热蒸汽。

只要周围没有热损耗，过程流体获得的热量就等于蒸汽释放的热量，即热交换器和管道间的隔热性很好。

在这个过程中，很多变量会发生变化，继而导致出口温度偏离期望值。如果出现这种情况，就该采取一些措施来校正偏差，其目的是保持出口温度为期望值。

实现该目的的一种方法是首先测量 $T(t)$，然后与期望值相比较，由比较结果决定如何校正偏差。蒸汽的流量可用于校正偏差。就是说，如果温度高于期望值，就关小蒸汽阀来减小进入换热器的蒸汽流量；若温度低于期望值，就开大蒸汽阀，以增加进入换热器的蒸汽流量。所有这些操作都可由操作员手工实现，操作很简单，不会出现什么问题。但是，由于多数过程对象都有很多变量需要保持为某一期望值，就需要许多的操作员来进行校正。因此，我们想自动完成这种控制。就是说，我们想利用无需操作人员介入就可以控制变量的设备。这就是所谓自动化的过程控制。

为达到上述目标，就需要设计并实现一个系统。图 5.3 所示为一个可行的控制系统及其基本构件。首先要做的是测量过程流体的出口温度，这一任务由传感器（热电偶、热电阻等）完成。将传感器连接到变送器上，由变送器将传感器的输出信号转换为足够大的信号传送给控制器。控制器接收与温度相关的信号并与期望值比较。根据比较的结果，控制器确定保持温度为期望值的控制作用。基于这一结果，控制器再发信号给执行机构来控制蒸汽流量。

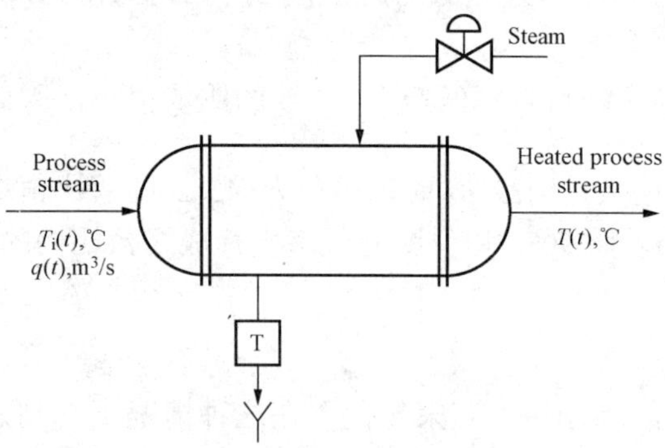

图 5.2　热交换器

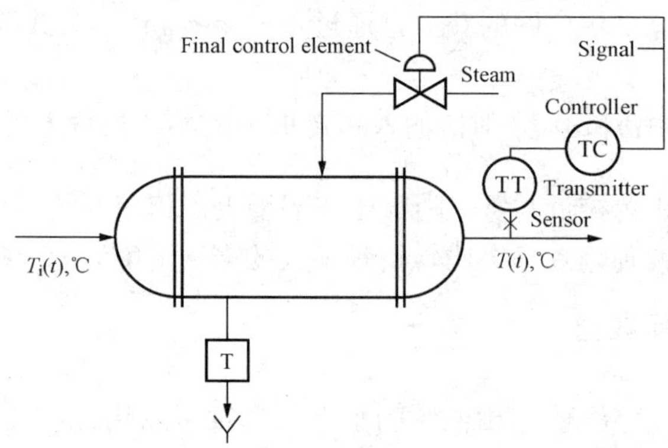

图 5.3　热交换器闭环控制

下面介绍控制系统中的 4 种基本元件，分别是：

（1）传感器，也称为一次元件。

（2）变送器，也称二次元件。

（3）调节器，控制系统的“大脑”。

（4）执行机构，通常是一个控制阀，但并不全是。其他常用的执行机构有变速泵、传送装置和电动机。

这些元件的重要性在于它们执行每个控制系统中都必不可少的三个基本操作，即

（1）测量：被控量的测量通常由传感器和变送器共同完成。

（2）决策：根据测量结果，为了维持输出为期望值，控制器必须决定如何操作。

（3）操作：根据控制器的处理，系统必须执行某种操作，这通常由执行机构来完成。

如上所述，每个控制系统都有 M、D 和 A 这 3 种操作。有些系统的决策任务简单，而有些很复杂。设计控制系统的工程师必须确保所采取的操作能影响被控变量，也就是说，该操作要影响测量值。否则，系统会变得不可控的，还会带来许多危害。

自动过程控制的重要术语

很有必要定义自动过程控制领域的一些术语。第一个是被控变量。它是指必须维持或控制在某一期望值的变量。在前面的例子中，过程出口温度 $T(t)$即为被控变量。第二个是设定值，被控变量的期望值。控制变量是用于将被控变量保持在设定值的变量。在上例中，蒸汽流量是控制量。最后，任何使被控变量偏离设定值的变量称为干扰或扰动。多数过程中都存在各种不同的扰动。在图 5.2 所示的换热器中，可能的扰动有入口温度 $T_i(t)$、入口流量 $q(t)$、蒸汽质量、环境条件、流体的成分和结垢等。在过程工业中，自动化的过程控制通常需要扰动的存在，明确这一点很重要。如果没有扰动，设计运行条件不变，那就没有必要不停地对过程进行“调节”。

重要的术语还有下面这些。开环是指被控过程与控制器分离的情况，即控制器并不采取任何操作将被控变量维持在设定值。开环控制中存在的另一种情况是，控制器产生的动作对检测没有影响。在控制系统的设计中，这是主要的缺点。闭环控制是指控制器被连在过程中，被控变量与设定值比较后产生校正作用。

根据这些定义的概念，自动过程控制系统的任务可以阐述如下：一个自动过程控制系统的任务是在出现扰动时利用控制量将被控量维持在设定值。

调节和伺服控制

在一些过程中，被控量由于受到干扰而偏离一个固定的设定值。调节控制是指设计系统来补偿扰动。在其他一些情况下，最主要的干扰是设定值本身，即设定值随时间而变化，被控变量就必须随设定值而变化。伺服控制就是为此目的而设计的控制系统。

在工业过程中，调节控制比伺服控制更普遍，但其基本设计方法实际上一样。因此，自动过程控制中的许多原理对两者都适用。

过程控制需要的背景知识

为了很好地实现自动过程控制，工程师首先必须掌握工艺过程的原理。在研究过程自动控制时，掌握过程的动态特性也很重要。因此，建立描述不同过程的方程组也很必要，也就是所谓的建模。要做到这一点，就需要掌握前面介绍的基本原理和列微分方程的数学知识。在过程控制中，拉氏变换很有用，它可以大大简化微分方程的求解及过程与控制系统的动态分析。

过程控制研究和实践的另一重要工具是计算机仿真。许多为描述过程而建立的方程实际上是非线性的，因此，解决问题最精确的方法就是数值方法，即用计算机求解。过程模型的计算机求解就称为仿真。

第 26 单元　集 散 控 制 系 统

集散控制系统属于控制系统，通常是制造系统、过程或者其他任何一种类型的动态系统。在这些系统中，控制器并不处于中央位置，而是分散在系统的各个部分，每个元件的子系统由一个或多个控制器控制。整个控制器系统通过网络相连来通信和监测。

集散控制系统是一个非常广泛的，应用于各种行业的术语，用于监测和控制分布式的设备。

- 输电网和发电厂；
- 环境控制系统；
- 交通信号；
- 水管理系统；
- 油脂精炼厂；
- 化工厂；
- 药品制造；
- 传感器网络。

原理

集散控制系统通常使用用户定制设计的处理器作为控制器，同时使用专用的互联和通信协议。输入和输出模块是集散控制系统的组成部分。处理器接受来之输入模块的信息，并发送信息至输出模块。输入模块接受现场中输入设备的信息，并向现场中输出设备发送指令。计算机总线或电气总线通过多路复用器/多路信号分离器连接处理器和模块，总线同样通过中央处理器连接着多个分布式的控制器，最终到达人机交换界面或控制台。

集散控制系统中的元件可直接连接到物理设备，如交换机、泵和阀，或者可通过一个中间系统，如SCADA系统来运行。

应用

集散控制系统属于专用系统，用来控制连续或间歇型的生产过程，如石油炼制、石油化工、发电总厂、制药、食品及饮料制造、水泥生产、炼钢、造纸。集散控制系统与传感器和执行器相连，使用定值控制来控制送给对象的物质流量。最常见的例子是定值控制环，其由压力传感器、控制器和控制阀组成。压力或流量测量值通常通过信号调节输入/输出装置传送给控制器。当测量变量达到某个值后，控制器打开或关闭阀或驱动装置，直到液体流量达到了预期的设定值。大型炼油厂有成千上万个输入/输出点，它们使用的是大型集散控制系统。然而，控制过程并不仅仅局限于流经管道的流体，还可以包括像造纸机及其相关的变速驱动器和电动机控制中心、水泥窑、采矿作业、矿石加工设施以及许多其他过程。

一个典型的集散控制系统由功能和/或地理位置上处于分布式的数字控制器组成，能够通过一个操作台控制256个或更多的调节控制回路。输入/输出装置位于控制器内部或离现场网络很远，现在的控制器具有强大的计算能力，除了比例，积分和微分（PID控制器）控制，通常可以执行的逻辑和顺序控制。

集散控制系统可以使用一个或多个工作站，它们在工作站进行配置，或通过一台离线电脑进行。通过某一控制网络来完成局域通信，其信息传输是通过双绞线，同轴电缆或光纤电缆进行。系统中可能使用服务器和/或应用处理器来进行额外的计算，数据收集及报表处理。

历史

从20世纪60年代开始，工业过程控制中开始使用早期的小型机。集散控制系统于1975

年提出。Honeywell 和日本 Yokogawa 电气工程公司在大致相同的时间各自设计出了自己独立生产的 TDC2000 和 CENTUM 集散控制系统，总部设在美国的 Bristol 公司于 1975 年也设计出了它们自己的 UCS3000 万用控制器。1980 年，Bailey（现在是 ABB 公司的一部分）设计出了 NETWORK90 系统。同样在 1980 年，Fischer&Porter 公司（现在也是 ABB 公司的一部分）设计出了 DCI-4000（DCI 表示分布式控制仪表）。

集散控制系统的产生很大程度上归结于过程控制系统中微型机实用性的增强及微处理器数量的增加。以直接数字控制（DDC）和设定点控制的形式，计算机被应用到过程自动化中已经有一段时间。在 20 世纪 70 年代早期，Taylor 仪器公司（现在是 ABB 一部分）开发出了 1010 系统，Foxboro 公司开发出了 FOX1 系统，Bailey 公司开发出了 1055 系统。所有这些系统都属于通过微型计算机实施，并与专有的输入/输出硬件相连的 DDC 应用系统。复杂的连续和批处理控制就通过该方式实施。更加保守的方法是定值控制，其通过计算机监视模拟过程控制器簇。基于 CRT 显示器的工作站通过文本及实际的特征曲线来达到过程的可视性。

控制功能块位于集散控制系统模型的中央。功能块从早期更为原始的“表驱动”软件中的直流数字控制概念开始演变。作为第一个体现面向对象的软件，功能块被自包含在源代码的“块”中，竭力仿效模拟硬件控制部件，执行过程控制中必不可少的任务，如执行 PID 控制算法。功能块继续作为集散控制系统供应商的主要方法，并得到其关键技术的支持，如当今的基金会现场总线。

分布式控制器、工作站和其他运算元件间的数字通信是集散控制系统的主要优点之一。注意力被适时地集中到能够提供重要沟通渠道的网络中，对于过程应用系统，其不得不包含了如可预测性及冗余等特殊功能。结果，许多供应商遵循了 IEEE 802.4 网络标准。当信息技术进入过程自动化领域后，该决定使得变迁浪潮具有必要性，IEEE 802.3 而并非 IEEE 802.4 协议在局域网控制中占据着优势。

20 世纪 80 年代的以网络为中心时期

集散控制系统在过程控制中为对象带来了分布式的智能性，并把计算机和微处理器应用其中，但仍没有提供对统一对象资源需求所必要的延伸性和开放性。很多情况下，集散控制系统仅仅是具备同样功能的模拟控制器的数字式替代者和人造显示板。普渡企业参考模型体现了这一点，其用来定义生产经营管理的关系，后来普渡企业参考模型成为 ISA95 标准行为的基础。

20 世纪 80 年代，使用者不再仅仅把集散控制系统看成是基本过程控制。直接数字控制一个很早的例子是由澳洲 Midac 公司在 1981～1982 年通过使用由其本国设计的 R-Tec 硬件而完成。该系统安装在墨尔本大学，使用串行通信网络，从校舍连接回到控制室“前端”。每个远程单元运行 2 个 Z80 微处理器，而前端通过页面公用存储器共同分担任务，以并行处理结构同时运行 11 个，其可以运行多达 20 000 个共同发生的事件。

我们相信如果开放性可以实现，企业中更多的数据可以共享的话，那么可以实现更具成就的事情。增加集散控制系统开放性的第一次尝试导致了今天占主导地位的 UNIX 操作系统的出现。美国国防部为获得开放性而开发出 UNIX 系统及其伴侣网络技术 TCP/IP，其正是过程工业正试图解决的问题。

于是，供应商也开始把基于以太网的网络应用到它们的私有网络协议层中，其并没有完全采用 TCP/IP 标准，但是通过使用以太网，成功运行了第一个对象管理和全局数据存取技术例子。20 世纪 80 年代也见证了第一台可编程控制器集成到集散控制系统基础结构中。研究广义对象的史学家也开始充分延伸自动控制系统的涉及范围。第一个采用 UNIX 和以太网网络技术的集散控制系统供应商是 Foxboro，其在 1987 年引入了 I/A 串行系统。

20 世纪 90 年代以应用为中心时期

在 20 世纪 90 年代商业现成部件和 IT 标准的逐渐被接纳给 20 世纪 80 年代对开放性的追求提供了动力。在那段时间最大的转变是从 UNIX 操作系统向 Windows 系统的转变。虽然在实时操作系统领域内，UNIX 或私有的操作系统中的实时商业系统仍然占据主导地位，但是，实时控制中所有事物都已经向 Windows 系统转变。

微软在台式机和服务器方面的涌入导致了如过程控制技术中对象链接和嵌入技术的发展，其是目前事实上使用的工业连接标准。互联网技术也开始在自动化和集散控制系统领域中占据一席之地，大多数集散控制系统的人机界面支持互联网连接。20 世纪 90 年代因为“现场总线竞争”而闻名，因为各个竞争对手相互竞争去定义国际电工委员会的现场总线标准，其用仪器仪表间的数字通信代替 4～20mA 的模拟通信。第一台现场总线装置产生在 20 世纪 90 年代。到 20 世纪 90 年末，该技术的发展开始出现重大势头，市场将基金会现场总线和 Profibus PA 总线应用到过程自动化中。一些供应商从头开始组建新系统来最大化现场总线的功能，从底层向上实现了功能最大化，如 ABB 公司 800xA 系统，艾默生过程处理公司的 DeltaV 控制系统，西门子公司的 SimaticPCS7。

然而，商业现成部件的影响最为突出的是硬件层。多年来，集散控制系统供应商的主要业务已经变成了提供大量的硬件，特别是输入/输出接口和控制器。最初的扩散集散控制系装置需要安装许多硬件，其中大部分是由集散控制系统供应商自下而上生产制造。不过，由如英特尔和摩托罗拉制造商生产的标准计算机部件使得集散控制系统供应商继续生产自己的元件，工作站和网络硬件的成本变得高昂。

随着供应商开始向商用组件过渡，他们还发现，硬件市场萎缩很快。商业现成部件不仅降低了供应商的生产成本，而且还不断为终端用户降低价格，他们也正越来越强烈地提出哪些硬件成本过高。以前在可编程控制器业务方面实力雄厚的供应商，如罗克韦尔自动化公司，施耐德公司和西门子公司，能够充分利用他们在制造控制硬件领域方面的专长，通过提供有效的产品进入到了集散控制系统市场。传统的集散控制系统供应商引进了基于最新通信技术和国际电工委员会标准的新一代集散控制系统系统，这导致了一种趋势的形成，即将传统概念/功能的可编程控制器和集散控制系统相结合成为所有问题的一个解决方案，命名为“过程自动化系统/控制器”。

附录 1　电气专业课程中英文对照

电工电子技术基础	Electrical Technology & Electrical Engineering
电工基础理论	Fundamental Theory of Electrical Engineering
电工技术基础	Fundamentals of Electrotechnics
电工实习	Electrical Engineering Practice
电工学	Electrical Engineering
电路理论	Theory of Circuit
电路理论基础	Fundamental Theory of Circuit
电路理论实验	Experiments in Theory of Circuit
电子技术课程设计	Course Exercise in Electronic Technology
模拟电子技术	Analog Electronics Technique
模拟电子线路	Analog Electrical Circuitry
数字电子技术	Digital Electronic Technique
数字电子线路	Digital Electrical Circuitry
工业电子学	Industry Electronics
电子辅助设计	EDA Electronic Design Automatic
工程制图	Graphing of Engineering
金工实习	Machinery Practice
电机学	Electrical Motor
电力电子学	Power Electronics
电机学及控制电机	Electrical Machinery Control & Technology
电机与拖动	Electrical Machinery & Towage
传感器与检测技术	Sensors & Testing Technology
传感器原理	Fundamentals of Sensors
自动检测技术与仪表	Automatic Measurement Technique & Meter
电子测试技术	Electronic Testing Technology
单片机原理	Fundamentals of Mono-Chip Computers
单片机原理及应用	Fundamentals of Mono-Chip Computers & Applications
电气控制技术	Electrical Control Technology
电气控制与 PLC 应用	Electrical Control and Application of PLC
机床电气控制	Electrical Control of Machinery Tools
工厂供电	Factory Electricity Supply
楼宇自动化	Building Automation
综合布线技术	Structured Cabling Technology
计算机控制系统	Computer Control System
现场总线与工业以太网	Fieldbus & Industrial Ethernet

机电一体化	Mechanical & Electrical Integration
自动控制理论	Theory of Automatic Control
自动控制系统	Automatic Control System
自动控制原理	Principle of Automatic Control
过程控制	Process Control
组态控制技术	Industry Configuration Technology
微机原理及接口技术	Principle & Interface Technique of Micro-computer
微机原理及应用	Principle & Application of Microcomputer
机器人技术基础	Fundamentals of Robot Techniques
机器人控制技术	Robot Control Technology
专业外语	Specialized English
毕业实习	Graduation Practice
毕业设计	Graduation Dissertation

附录2　论文英文摘要的书写

英文摘要是对所写文章主要内容的精炼概括。通常要求的论文摘要的字数不等，一般为200～500字。而国际刊物要求所刊登的论文摘要的字数通常是100～200字。摘要的位置一般放在一篇文章的最前面，内容上涵盖全文，并直接点明全旨。语言上要求尽量简练。摘要通常多采用第三人称撰写。摘要通常有标题、内容、关键字组成。现在我们来看一下各部分的书写格式。

一、标题（Title）

英文题名应以短语为主要形式，尤以名词短语最常见，即题名基本上由1个或几个名词加上其前置和（或）后置定语构成。短语型题名要确定好中心词，再进行前后修饰。各个词的顺序很重要，词序不当会导致表达不准。英文题名的大小写可以采用以下实词首字母大写，虚词小写。

二、摘要（Abstract）

以“Abstract”开头，接着由论文研究的问题或目的、过程和方法、结果三部分组成。

（1）说明研究的问题或目的，通常用一般现在时或一般过去时。常用句型有：

1）This paper/article describes/reports/presents/discusses…　本文叙述/报告/介绍/讨论……

2）In this paper, we/the authors present…　本文介绍……

3）A study of…is reported　本文报告……的研究

4）In this paper…is (are) presented.　本文介绍……

（2）说明方法和结果，一般用一般过去时、第三人称的被动语态表达。常用句型有：

1）Using… (technique), we studied…　我们用……（技术）研究了……

2）…was (were) measured using…　（我们）用……测定了……

3）…was (were) analyzed (reviewed)　by…（我们）用……分析（回顾）了……

4）The results showed (demonstrated)　that…　结果表明……

5）It was found/observed that…　（我们）发现/观察……

6）…demonstrated a significant improvement in…　……方面呈明显改善

（3）结论通常用一般现在时、被动语态表达，也可用主动语态表达。常用句型有：

1）These results suggest that…　结果提示……

2）These findings indicate that…　这些发现表明……

3）the data (study) show/ demonstrate/illustrate that…　数据（研究）表明/证明/说明……

4）We conclude/ suggest/ believe that…　我们的结论是/建议/认为……

三、关键字（Keywords）

科技论文的关键词应从其题名、层次标题和正文中选出，应能反映论文的主题概念。

英文摘要中列出关键词是为了满足国内外情报检索机构编制索引和二次文献及便于读者选读，所以关键词的选择须满足下列原则：

（1）能代表论文主要内容；

（2）每篇论文应选关键词3～8个，以保证论文的检出率；

（3）关键词应选用主题词，以便于检索机构的检索；

（4）英文摘要中的关键词与中文关键词应保持意思和顺序的一致性。

四、范例

Variational Bayesian Blind Deconvolution Using a Total Variation Prior

Abstract: In this paper, we present novel algorithms for total variation (TV) based blind deconvolution and parameter estimation utilizing a variational framework. Using a hierarchical Bayesian model, the unknown image, blur, and hyperparameters for the image, blur, and noise priors are estimated simultaneously. A variational inference approach is utilized so that approximations of the posterior distributions of the unknowns are obtained, thus providing a measure of the uncertainty of the estimates. Experimental results demonstrate that the proposed approaches provide higher restoration performance than non-TV-based methods without any assumptions about the unknown hyperparameters.

Keywords: total variation　blind deconvolution　variational framework　Bayesian model

参 考 文 献

［1］http://en.wikipedia.org/wiki/Main_Page
［2］http://www.siliconfareast.com/counters.htm
［3］http://www.siliconfareast.com/logicgates.htm
［4］http://www.solarbotics.net/bftgu/starting_elect_ic.html
［5］陈雪丽．电气工程专业英语［M］．北京：机械工业出版社，2006.
［6］李久胜，马洪飞.电气自动化专业英语［M］．哈尔滨：哈尔滨工业大学出版社，2006.
［7］http://en.wikipedia.org
［8］http://www.plcs.net/contents.shtml
［9］http://www.mikroe.com/en/books/8051book/
［10］http://www.phys.unsw.edu.au/hsc/hsc/electric_motors.html
［11］http://automationnotebook.com/2005_Issue_5/fyi_issue5_2005.html
［12］http://en.wikipedia.org/wiki/Variable-frequency_drive#VFD_system_description
［13］http://www.ikalogic.com/tut_closed_loop_spd_ctrl.php#3